HOUSE OF RAIN

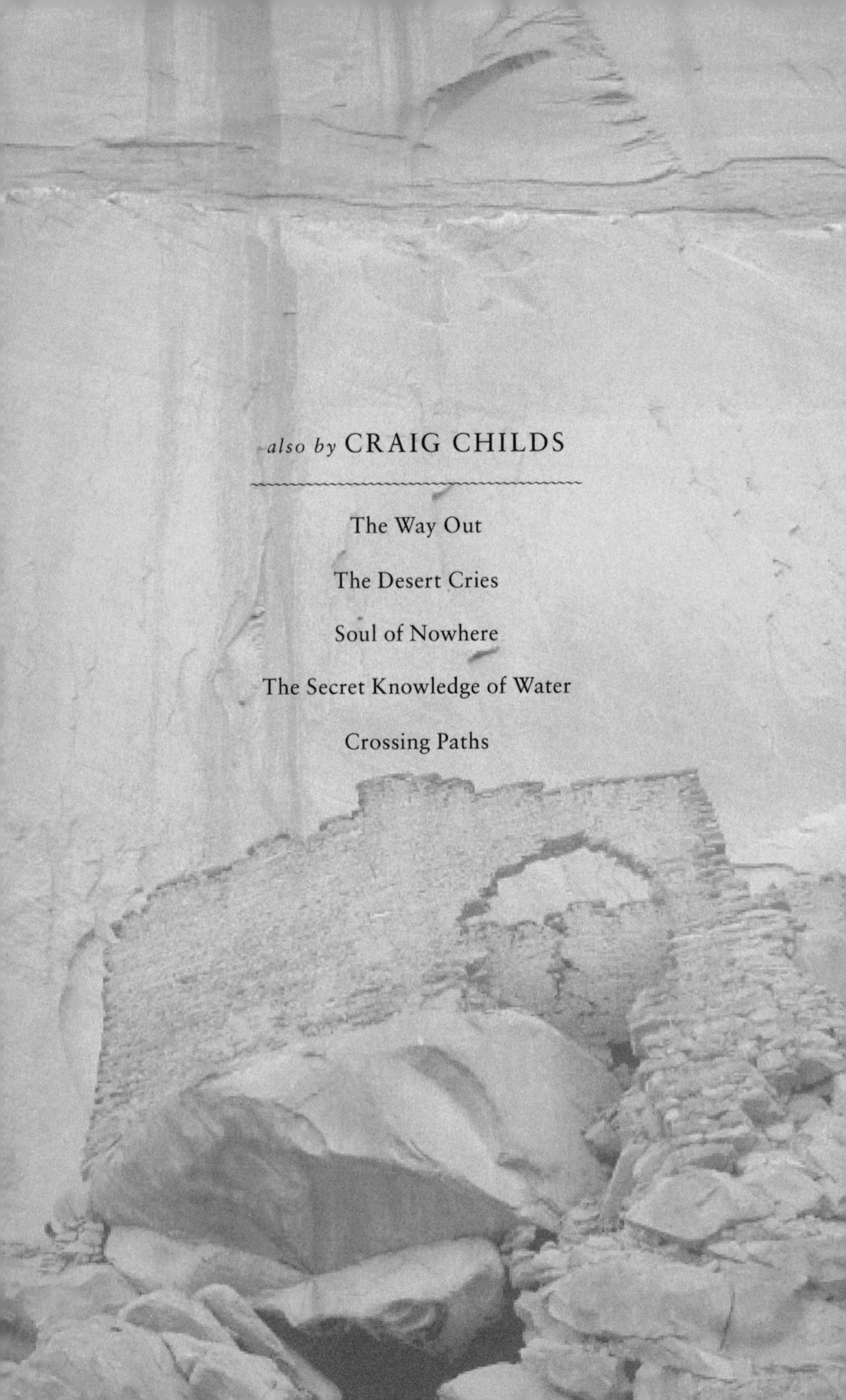

also by CRAIG CHILDS

The Way Out

The Desert Cries

Soul of Nowhere

The Secret Knowledge of Water

Crossing Paths

HOUSE OF RAIN

TRACKING
A VANISHED CIVILIZATION
ACROSS
THE AMERICAN SOUTHWEST

CRAIG CHILDS

LITTLE, BROWN AND COMPANY
NEW YORK BOSTON LONDON

FIRST EDITION: February 2007

Little, Brown and Company
Hachette Book Group USA
237 Park Avenue, New York, NY 10017
Visit our Web site at HachetteBookGroupUSA.com

Library of Congress Cataloging-in-Publication Data

Childs, Craig.
House of rain : tracking a vanished civilization across the American Southwest / Craig Childs.—1st ed.
p. cm.
ISBN 978-0-316-60817-6
1. Chaco culture—Four Corners Region. 2. Chaco Culture National Historical Park (N.M.). 3. Four Corners Region—Description and travel. 4. Four Corners Region—Antiquities. I. Title.
E99.C37C35 2006
978.9'8201—dc22 2006019112

10 9 8 7 6 5 4 3

Q-MART
Book design by Fearn Cutler de Vicq

Printed in the United States of America

For Regan

Movement, clouds, wind, and rain are one.
Movement must be emulated by the people.
—Tessie Naranjo

The secret to a long life is knowing
when it's time to go.
—Michelle Shocked

Contents

PART SEVEN: SOUTHEAST ARIZONA

PART EIGHT: NORTHERN MEXICO

Acknowledgments

I would not have been able to get my bearings in Southwest prehistory without the assistance of Mark Varien, Steve Lekson, Barbara Mills, and Jeff Dean. Thank you for generously sharing conversations, letters, and time. Archaeologists and scholars throughout the Southwest proved most willing and thoughtful during my research, opening themselves to my inquiries and freely sharing their expertise. I am most grateful to Wolcott Toll, David Wilcox, Gwinn Vivian, Kim Malville, Rich Friedman, John Stein, Tom Windes, Dean Wilson, Kathy Roler Durand, Wendy Bustard, Gary Brown, Larry Baker, Paul Reed, Ron Sutcliffe, Scott Ortman, Donna Glowacki, Susan Ryan, Joel Brisbin, Kate Niles, Larry Nordby, Carla Van West, Dave Breternitz, Eric Hansen, Hugh Robinson, Catherine Cameron, Winston Hurst, Joe Pachak, Jonathan Till, Owen Severence, Nieves Zedeño, Kelley Hays-Gilpin, Bruce Anderson, Mike Yeatts, T. J. Ferguson, Sarah Herr, Karen Adams, A. J. Vonarx, Richard Lange, Charles Adams, Daniela Triadan, Chuck Riggs, Stephanie Whittlesey, Jeff Reid, Patty Crown, Mike Jacobs, Tammy Stone, Lex Lindsay, Jeff Clark, Patrick Lyons, Anna Neuzil, Bill Hartmann, Paul Fish, Ryan Howell, Todd and Chris VanPool, and Beth Bagwell. None of these people are responsible for the final content of this book, which is a synthesis of many different viewpoints.

For access to archaeological collections, I am indebted to the Peabody Museum of Archaeology and Ethnology at Harvard University, the Edge of the Cedars Museum in Blanding, Utah, the American

Museum of Natural History in New York, the Arizona State Museum at the University of Arizona, the Chaco Culture National Historical Park Museum Collection at the University of New Mexico, the Crow Canyon Archaeological Center outside Cortez, Colorado, the University of Colorado Museum, and the collection at Mesa Verde National Park.

It is difficult to adequately thank various native people who permitted my curiosity and in return offered gentle, critical input. Respecting their confidentiality, I will not name them, and so I offer private words of appreciation.

To many libraries my debt is profound. In particular, I am grateful to Marci Myers and her assistants at the Hayden Library at Arizona State University, as well as the Special Collections staff at the Cline Library at Northern Arizona University. Thank you also to the staff of two small public libraries in Crawford and Paonia, Colorado, for keeping me well supplied.

I owe much to my editors at Little, Brown, both my mainstay, Terry Adams, and my copyeditor, Barbara Jatkola. For their editorial input, thank you also to Dawn Reeder, Bob Koehler, and Azucena Alejandre. I am grateful to my agent, Kathy Anderson, for, among many things, walking to the edge of a cliff with me and looking into the desert below, though your face was red from the heat and your heart was beating very fast.

To my young son, Jasper, thank you for accompanying me into windy, hot, cold, dusty places, and doing so with delight, for the most part. Finally, I cannot offer enough thanks to my wife, Regan Choi, for your discerning reads, your inscrutability, and above all, your fearlessness.

HOUSE OF RAIN

Prologue

The inspiration for this book came from a discovery. It was an ancient relic I found near a river flowing through the butte-studded desert of the Colorado Plateau. I paddled alone in a canoe for days into a deepening red gorge, cliffs passing slowly against each other, tributary canyons opening and closing as I traveled downstream into the wilderness. On those days I frequently tied my canoe to shore and walked into the surrounding country. I skirted rock shelves and found my way to the tops of cliffs facing stark landforms in the distance, a desolate territory of wind-sculpted stone and brittle scrub.

As I walked, I carefully studied the passing ground for broken artifacts left by the Anasazi, a people once balanced on the imaginary tightrope stretched between B.C. and A.D. They were desert hunters and dryland farmers. Every day or two I came upon their rock art carved into cliffs and boulders—eerie, enigmatic symbols lining hallway canyons. I found miscellaneous human endeavors all about—hard snubs of pre-Columbian corncobs stored in a cave, a polished grinding stone facedown in the sand.

I hesitate using the term *pre-Columbian,* defining the chronicles of ancient America by the arbitrary date of Christopher Columbus's first visit in 1492. *Prehistoric* is just as troublesome, suggesting a time before history that passed pure and unnoticed. Yet these words, however insufficient, give an ample impression of antiquity, telling of a time long before the age of steel in America and before the domestic horse, an era predating Columbus prior to most notions of history.

Time seems very thin in this landscape, as if one could reach across a thousand years merely by crouching over a lost knife blade made of crystal-shot jasper, feeling its edge still sharp enough to draw blood. The desert is a reliquary, its dryness and gradual pace preserving most of what people deposited on their way through. When the Anasazi walked away from this region some seven hundred years ago, they left it like a made house, everything in its place.

Late on the seventh day of my trip, I nosed my canoe into a nest of boulders toppled from above. I climbed to the bow, its line in my hand, and stepped out to tie up. River water purled around the boulders with a gentle, talkative sound. Even in shade at the bottom of the gorge, the air was hot, rocks having been bathed all day in summer sun, now doling out the radiation in force. I left the canoe and went on foot, carrying what I needed—a bottle of water, a pocketed bag of nuts, knife, pen, and paper. I climbed into a net of fallen cliff slabs that revealed a slight break in the gorge. There was no trail, no sign that anyone had ever been here, until I stubbed something up with my boot tip. I knelt and dusted out a piece of broken pottery. The sherd was gray as an oyster shell, its surface neatly pinched into a simple, repetitive design: remains of a broken cookware vessel dating to around the eleventh century A.D. I set it back and came to all fours, lowered my head, and blew across the ground. The pointed teeth of other pieces started to show. I dusted them out with two fingers, revealing the broken ring of a corrugated jar.

After studying this artifact for a moment, I dusted it back over. When I stood, my eyes were sharper than they had been. If there are broken vessels, I thought, there will be other things.

I began discerning shapes around me. Fifteen feet away was a slumped masonry wall, nearly all of it buried by wind and dust. Next to it a slight depression no more than ten feet across sank into the earth—the pit of a circular room—and around it I saw the glint of several sherds from other pots. This had been a prehistoric household, three or four abutting quarters and storage rooms. Not far away was a bit of flatness in the terrain where rainwater runs off the cliff, likely a plot once used for growing amaranth, pumpkins, and corn. All the puzzle pieces I could see I put back together, reconstructing a home for ten Anasazi, twelve perhaps, an extended family. They cooked with gray pots and lived in circular pit-houses.

After several hundred years of no one living here, the site had turned to rubble. Wood-and-mortar roofs had deteriorated and crashed in; doorways had fallen apart. I walked through these ghostly vestiges, things a person could pass right over and never notice. I glanced up to consider the cliff overhead, and there it was.

At first I saw only a high stack of rocks, obviously set by someone's hand into a crack. As I looked closer, I began to see the concealed outline of a tidy masonry structure that had been tucked behind a leaning flake of cliff. No bigger than a piano bench, it was a small Anasazi storeroom, a chamber known as a granary. Not necessarily for storing grain, it was just as likely a pantry for tools or special items set aside for the future.

I immediately started for it, climbing hand over hand up the cliff base, feeling an anxious press of revelation as I ascended ledges and cracks. My breath tasted hot with discovery. I had found a secret. In past travels I had seen many granaries belonging to the Anasazi, but they had all been broken open, emptied by archaeologists, by pothunters, by erosion, or even, perhaps, by the residents themselves returning many centuries later. This one had been built so that no stranger would see it, like an attic accessed through a hidden door. I entered a gap behind a shadowed rock flake, and there I knelt before the structure. It was rectangular, like a cupboard. I touched its face with probing, diagnostic fingers, measuring it with my eyes—three feet tall, two feet wide, and three feet deep.

I got up on my haunches and lightly dusted off the granary's flat roof, which was undamaged. I licked my lips, feeling their dry chap. For some thousand years not a single breeze had entered the space within this chamber, no inkling of light. Residents living below had cached something that to this day had remained untouched. My imagination raced. What tightly woven baskets were here? What painted ceramics, what woven textiles, what stockpile of cobalt blue and honey-colored seed corn left many centuries before the boom of Spanish rifles?

With a finger I traced through dust and fallen rock debris on the granary's roof, where I outlined a rectangular hatch: the way in. I blew off dust, revealing a piece of flagstone mortared into place, used to seal the granary shut.

This was no casual find. I had been looking for this for a long time, traveling untrailed desert for most of my adult life, poking into canyons and caves hoping to find intact signs of people here long before me. Their presence gave context to my brief life, to my civilization. They were the ticking sound of the clock on the mantel letting me know that time is truly passing, whole societies rising and falling to a believable rhythm. I had encountered their towering cliff dwellings like secluded castles and found their skulls eroded from the ground, eye sockets cleaned out by the wind. But never had I come upon a closed granary, a chamber untouched.

I laid my hands on the smooth hatch stone, and then I knocked lightly, causing a hollow drumming within. I put my ear against the entry as if cracking a safe.

I could split the seal with my knife blade, I thought. I would get my fingers under the stone and pry it out. I would see whatever was most valuable to these people. I was certain that upon opening this small reserve, I would understand what it meant to live in the era of the Anasazi, finding what was placed to ensure their future. I envisioned polished wooden knife handles, perhaps a filled, red seed jar with a tiny mouth, or woven pouches made of dogbane, each containing a different-colored artist's pigment painstakingly gathered from a mineral or plant. There would be ceremonial artifacts celebrating a clan's lineage, or precious tools and seeds stashed to ensure a viable crop upon their return.

These people planned on coming back, but they were never seen here again. As the story goes, the Anasazi simply vanished one day. Farming implements were left in the fields; ceramic vessels remained neatly stowed in their quarters; ladles rested in bowls as if people had been swept from the land by an ill and sudden wind. The disappearance of the Anasazi has been hailed as the great mystery of archaeology.

But I had been speaking for years with archaeologists who worked in the Southwest, and they told me the mystery was an oversimplified and outdated notion. After what they had seen in the field, none believed that the Anasazi had simply vanished. Inviting me into their studies and into the trenches of their excavations, they explained that there was not enough paper to publish all that they had found out about these people. There were not enough occasions to speak to the public of their countless conjectures. They had to keep to their discipline, digging deeper like eager animals, moles tunneling through the dark soil of time. *But since you come asking about these ancestors,* they told me, *here, take these in your hands, as much as you can carry, and go.* They glowed with excitement as they handed over hard-earned data, or they became deadly serious, or they simply gave me a name or two—Chacra Mesa, Peñasco Blanco—and sent me out the door, back to where I followed their clues and inquiries across the ground.

Over time I began discerning trails of Anasazi movement in the wilderness, the directions from which they came, an almost biblical journey of an entire culture across centuries and limitless miles. There is far more to the Anasazi than what lies in the modern American mythos, bucolic museum dioramas of men in loincloths and women's breasts bare in the sun. The land holds a far more complex and human story, evidence of migrations, upheavals, wars, and great alliances; lives of astronomers, weavers, merchants, and pilgrims.

Sunlight receded, and a field of stars overtook the sky as I sat on a rock shelf over the granary, the dark gorge gaping below. Summer heat was still rising out of the rock. My head rested on my knees, arms drawn around my legs.

I would be so careful with this if I entered it. I said this out loud. Going through someone else's treasure, I would be cautious with my fingers, my words, my thoughts. When the first stir of air entered this masonry chest, I would not even breathe.

But the granary was not mine to open. It was left by other people, a stockpile waiting for their return. As I understand more of the Anasazi, it is hard to say that they ever truly vanished. The farther I track them, the more it seems they are right in front of me, until I can nearly feel the body heat left in their footsteps. It is not unthinkable that a person might someday return to this granary, maybe a century from now, or a millennium, relieved to find an intact sign of ancestry deep in this river gorge.

I climbed down to the granary and laid my hands on its door stone, feeling the grit of blown sand, the hardness of rock. I did not want to move from here, a person to be found in a thousand years, a statue kneeling at the brink of decision. I withdrew and climbed back to the ground, leaving the granary sealed as I started back toward my canoe, the obsidian night closing around me. At the river I untied the canoe's bowline, stepped in, and swept the paddle into the water, setting a wake across a mirror of stars.

To this day my imagination has remained within the dark granary I never opened, my hands still laid upon its smooth door stone. I ache to know what is inside. Instead of breaking the seal and unpacking its belongings, I wrote this book, setting out to find who the Anasazi were and what became of them. I traveled deeper into the land than ever before, hunting through villages where no one lives, looking for ancient walkways across the Southwest. I searched the history of these people to give this granary context, to return it to a place in time when a civilization danced across this desert like rain.

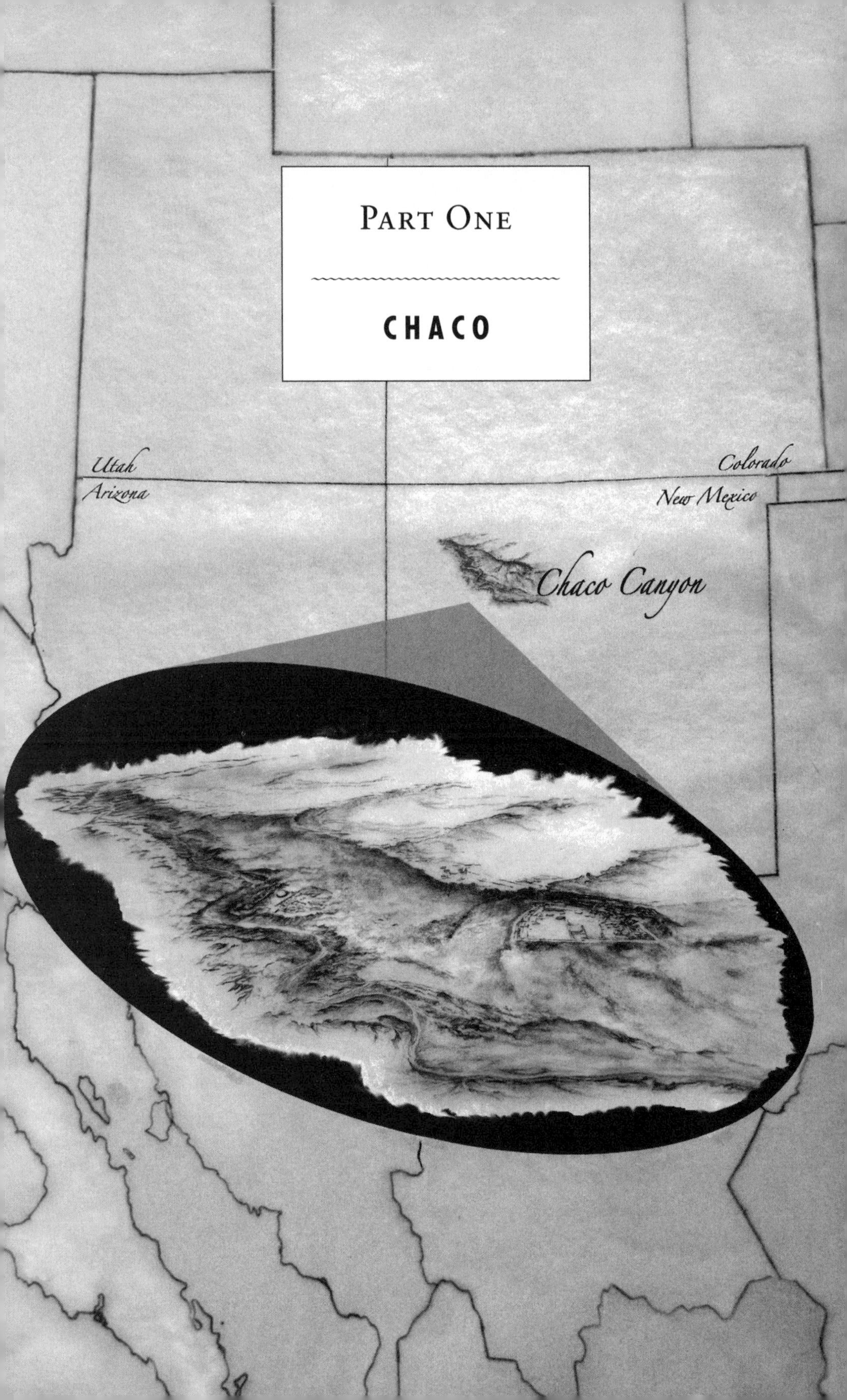

Part One
CHACO
Utah
Arizona
Colorado
New Mexico
Chaco Canyon

The Flood

CHACO CANYON

It happened quickly, as if a diviner's staff had struck the ground. Water flashed onto the dry earth. Its dark and wringing hands plunged over cactus and sage, welling around the trunks of sparse cottonwood trees. The desert groaned as its thousand parched mouths opened to an empty summer sky.

Two of us looked down at this flash flood from atop a safe, high bank. Below us water funneled into Chaco Canyon, passing through a set of mustard-colored cliffs in the barrens of northwest New Mexico. The water smelled as ripe as garbage. It was incense to me, a lurid scent that I have encountered only select times in my life, brief hours of the desert erupting into sudden and monstrous floods, where everything living and dead is channeled into a single slot. It smelled like creation itself.

The flood thundered past buff-colored boulders that had fallen from the cliffs into beds of withered greasewood and cracked clay soil. My companion, a man named Adam, had never been to this part of the desert. Standing above the flood, he glanced at me, astonished. It seemed there should not be water out here, ever. I told Adam that we were very lucky. You can wait years and not see something like this. Or you can walk out on rattleboard roads that no one has driven in years, and where you expect yet another dry wash, you find a bestial river heaving with broken trees.

Adam stood with his arms draped at his sides. His face was red from the heat. A tall man, Adam has a graceful manner, his hair long and dark. He studied the water, which was actually more mud than water, and then looked up at the sky. There was not a single cloud, no possible source for this flood as far as he could see. The blue overhead was bereft of any moisture.

One small cloud had passed while we were out walking earlier in the day. It had dragged a quarter acre of shade across the desert, and we had set off chasing it, sprinting to catch up so we could get under its shade. Before we got there, the cloud lifted its skirt and sailed off, evaporating into nothing. We were left empty-handed, my oiled hat brim wilted in the sun.

Most people think this must have been better country to live in some thousand years ago, back when an indigenous civilization of hunters and corn growers assembled in a geographic province known as the Colorado Plateau. The climate is no different now than it was then, however, just as dry at times and wet at others, and prone to the same scales of flooding. Rainfall has always been unpredictable in this desert. Farming seasons expand and contract like an accordion, leaving only slim margins for planting and growing.

The Colorado Plateau is the very edge of where one can even partly subsist on agriculture. It is a 150,000-square-mile blister of land that rises across the dry confluence of Arizona, Utah, Colorado, and New Mexico. Its surface is incised with countless canyons and wrinkled into isolated mesas and mountain ranges that stand suddenly from the desert floor up to 13,000 feet in elevation. The combination of irregular topography and infrequent rainfall gave rise to the Anasazi, an indigenous people who knew how to move. Small family groups and clans readily skirted around climate changes, transferring their settlements to high, wetter mesas or down to the sunbaked lowlands whenever the need arose.

In the late centuries B.C. and the early centuries A.D., the Anasazi lived in small villages of semi-subterranean pit-houses made of earth and wood, clusters of tiny domes the color of local soils. They occupied any one settlement for no more than ten to twenty years before moving on. Rarely would a person have been born, grown old, and died in the same place. For more than ten thousand years, the Anasazi and their ancestors walked the climatic tightropes of the Colorado Plateau, chasing the rain, leaving their camps and settlements behind. Sporadic farming began some four thousand years ago as corn and other subsidiary crops slowly made their way up from southern Mexico. But even with the onset of agriculture, the Anasazi remained a wayfaring people. Farming came to a head about a thousand years ago, and the Anasazi rose with it, reaching the civilized heights of imposing public architecture and industrial farming. Though still in motion, they began to settle in places for longer periods of time, making their homes sturdier, more permanent. Populations rapidly increased. Architecture flourished. Then suddenly they were gone.

. . .

I glanced upstream, where the scalp of a thunderstorm barely peeked over the eastern horizon. The flood had come from there, maybe thirty miles away, and had picked up everything it could carry along its way. It hissed with sand and mud, hauling across its back bobbing clods of horseshit. A car tire rose to the surface and then sank like a drowning ogre. Countless tiny moons of juniper berries nodded up and down alongside aluminum cans with their identities sanded off. We had to cross to get where we were going.

Could you swim it? I wondered. I knew better. I had once made an academic study out of flash floods in the desert, adding my own arcane contributions to the fields of hydrology and geomorphology. I knew very well how nasty floods can be, full of chaotic undertows and unexpected obstacles that may or may not break the surface at any moment. But I felt pulled toward the water.

We were heading for an archaeological site on the opposite side of this shadeless canyon about five miles downstream. The flood was going in our direction.

I carefully studied the water, my eyes tracking its fleeing surface puckered with whirlpools. There was a specific grit to the sediment and softness to the bedrock that spoke of how water travels in this region. The way shoreline plants were arranged in tiers and the scales of the terraced banks told what it might be like to hitch a ride downstream. I concluded that we had a good chance of surviving as long as we encountered no boulders along the way, no unanticipated waterfalls. Sometimes floods sing with catastrophe, but this one seemed safe.

Without looking at Adam, I said, "Let's swim it."

Adam did not look at me either. He nodded slowly, watching as chunks of shoreline crashed in, sucked immediately beneath the muddy froth.

He smiled wryly, unable to take his eyes off the water, and asked, "So this is what you do in the desert?"

"Only when you get lucky," I said.

. . .

Much of northwest New Mexico is a landscape of oblivion, an arid sink bowing into the Colorado Plateau. Ochre- and straw-colored washes loop in and out for hundreds of miles, many seeing running water for no more than a day or two each year. In some places dusty sagebrush steppes extend as far as the eye can see, and in others scabs of badlands lie naked under the sun, completely devoid of vegetation. Occasional black monoliths are visible in the distance, wind-struck jags of rock standing several hundred feet tall like lost chess pieces. Chaco Canyon lies here, in a basin a hundred miles across.

Of the deserts I know, this barren quarter of the Colorado Plateau is the most unfortunate. During freeze-dried winters, the snow blusters about like dust, and temperatures can drop to twenty below zero. Summers leave every stone hot to the touch. Looking for remains of ancient cultures, one might expect only sparse ruins, if any, ramadas of scavenged wood and impoverished households where residents tied reed mats across doorways to keep out the incessant wind. But the Anasazi left much more in their wake. Reaching a feverish peak in the eleventh century A.D., they built scores of masonry buildings, their floor plans as sizable and geometrically abstruse as crop circles. Thousands of chambers, with ceilings weighing up to ninety tons each, were constructed in Chaco Canyon. To support these structures, 250,000 trees were felled in mountains fifty miles away and hauled across the desert. The timbers were not dragged. They were hoisted and carried in procession to this canyon.

At the time, much larger population centers arose elsewhere in the Americas. The Mound Builder culture erected earthen pyramids with ramps and flattened tops along the Mississippi River. In what is now Illinois, the ancient city of Cahokia reached a population of 15,000, while in southern Mexico the stone temples of Chichén Itzá broke the jungle skyline with monolithic stone facades. The gridded avenues and pyramids of Teotihuacán near modern-day Mexico City hosted about 150,000 people, while 350,000 lived in an urban center at the south end of Lake Titicaca in Bolivia.*

Chaco, on the other hand, had a relatively small year-round population. Estimates range between a couple of thousand residents and only a few hundred. In the larger cultural picture of North, South, and Central America, Chaco was a relatively minor place. In the sparsely populated Southwest, however, it was the preeminent center, a shining anomaly of broad, clean streets, or processionals, and ceremonial buildings that once stood like cathedrals in the desert.

A traveler in the eleventh century would have approached Chaco Canyon along one of many scrupulously engineered roads. Where roads entered the canyon, stairways had been carved straight into the bedrock walls to get from the surrounding desert down to the canyon floor. There one would have found an oasis of curve-walled temples and blocky residential compounds. Housing was built on the south side of the canyon. On the north side stood public buildings two or three times the square footage of the White House in Washington D.C. Nothing like these buildings existed anywhere else in the Southwest.

These stately structures, now called *great houses,* were not residences per se. More likely they were monuments, temples, or palaces. Many of them had as few as ten residents for every fifty rooms, and most of the rooms, by the nature of the artifacts found in them, seem to have been used for religious or ceremonial purposes. Deep inside catacomb-like chambers within one great house, excavators have found the most highly decorated burials in the Southwest. Two

*On the other side of the planet and completely unaware of the Americas, medieval Europe was witnessing the construction of its first large cathedrals, and London reached a population of 10,000.

Ruins of a triple-walled structure at an eleventh-century Chaco Canyon great house. REGAN CHOI

richly dressed skeletons were discovered lying on a bed of fifty-six thousand pieces of turquoise, surrounded by fine ceramic vessels, and covered by a sheet of ivory-colored shells imported from the ocean six hundred miles away.

Great-house stonework was painstakingly created, as evidenced by straight corners and geometrically perfect circles, which were then washed with a glaze of plaster, resulting in an arresting, lofty appearance. These buildings would have looked like multistory thrones set along the promenade of Chaco Canyon.

During certain times of the year—perhaps on the winter and summer solstices, or at the beginning of lunar cycles—people traveled great distances to reach Chaco. Based on skeletal remains, these people were physically distinct from one another, and based on languages descended from that time, they probably spoke a variety of disparate tongues. People from different regions would have been recognizable by their manner, their facial features, and the weaving patterns of their robes, sandals, and skirts. Perhaps these visitors came to Chaco for religious reasons, attending festivals, partaking in celebratory feasts during years of plentiful crops, or offering their labor to help construct great houses.

In the middle of the eleventh century, the stonework alone at each great house required hundreds of thousands of man-hours. Masons broke rocks into thin, workable tablets, laborers hauled baskets of wet mortar, and woodworkers stripped timbers and evened off their ends with stone axes before setting them into place. Parts of older great houses were demolished to make way for expansions, and thousands of tons of rubble went into the new foundations. At the same time, adjacent land was cleared for future construction.

Most of this activity took place in an area of about three square miles, known today as Downtown Chaco, a term coined by archaeologist Steve Lekson. It contains a couple of dozen residential compounds facing half as many great houses, as well as tidy processionals leading toward the center. Ten miles in all directions lies a looser halo of ten more great houses and numerous contiguous living quarters. Chaco, or at least parts of Chaco, keeps going from there. Ancient roads radiate from the canyon outward to meet satellite great houses scattered across the desert. The place was built like a web, drawing people and their artifacts to the center, Chaco Canyon.

Whether people living elsewhere on the Colorado Plateau were directly involved with eleventh-century Chaco or not, they could not help being deeply affected by it. Year after year more travelers came from the hinterlands. They left tracks of broken pottery along the way—countless ceramic water pitchers and painted ollas dropped and shattered across the desert. The roads they stamped into the ground can be seen to this day from space. Chaco became the cultural center of the Colorado Plateau, and thus it is the appropriate place to begin the story of the Anasazi.

. . .

On the clear summer day when Adam and I visited, a mass of mud and water shouldered through Chaco Canyon, taking no notice of the toppled great houses standing on the dry banks above. The flood had its own business more pressing and ancient than human civilization, proud heaves of water undercutting the banks and dragging away dead and dying cottonwood trees. The floodwater ran down a wash in the middle of the canyon where we walked with accelerated hearts. We felt the anxious intoxication I imagine skydivers feel the moment before they jump. Quickly now, who knew how long the high water might last? It could drain out from under us in half an hour.

The canyon floor was about half a mile wide, leaving plenty of room for us to get away from the flood, which ran less than a hundred feet across. We headed right for it, walking through greasewood and saltbush until we found a place where we could get into the water. We had gone back to my truck and picked up a watertight ammunition box that Adam now carried. It was army surplus, about the size of a lunch pail. Adam knelt and popped it open. We stripped off our clothes and stuffed them inside, along with a pen, a journal, and a bottle of drinking water. We left on only our boots to protect our feet from whatever lay on the floor of this flood.

The sun burned our bare shoulders as we slogged through soaked clay to the flood's slipstream edge. I nervously rubbed my hands on my thighs, glancing along the corridor of the canyon. Certainly, the Anasazi had done the same, I thought. A thousand years ago someone taking a message from one compound to another must have hopped into a flood to speed the journey—or just taken an afternoon dip in the cold water, joyous over its startling appearance in this landscape where water is the rarest commodity. Maybe people used to flock to these infrequent floods, running with baskets and pots to gather mud, which they could use to make mortar or farming soil. Indeed, earthen and stone-lined canals, where water would have been diverted from the main wash toward nearby storage areas, have been detected all around Chaco. Buildings went up in fits and starts, perhaps matching sporadic flood cycles as millions of gallons of mud were suddenly available for construction. These floods also brought down precious water to be distilled for drinking. An event like this would have been a wonder and the cause for celebration.

Adam and I continued along sloppy mud banks and through cold lagoons where the flood swelled into the surrounding desert. The water had the chill of freshly melted hail. Parts of trees spun downstream in the froth. We waded in up to our thighs, and the current began to pull on us. Just before it swept us off our feet, we dove forward. Like busted rams of cottonwood trees, we were carried off.

. . .

Several million tons of sediment depart from the Southwest every day, carried in warm, muddy rivers toward the nearest sea. The entire landscape is falling apart, too dry to hold on to its soil, too weathered to remain solid. In 1941 a 300,000-ton slab of canyon wall toppled into the back of the largest of Chaco's ruins, crushing numerous rooms and throwing boulders into ceremonial chambers, where they remain today like rough-edged meteorites. What you see in the Southwest is temporary, everything caught in motion.

When archaeological crews began digging in the ruins of Chaco Canyon in the late nineteenth and early twentieth centuries, they dumped unsalvageable rubble into the wash for flash floods to carry off. From one excavation alone, led by the National Geographic Society in the 1920s, more than 100,000 tons of archaeological debris—splintered ceiling timbers and unseated wall stones—were hauled out in ore carts and fed to the wash, as if the workers themselves were agents of erosion. Everything else was packed into crates and shipped in boxcars to distant museums and private collections. A startling wealth of artifacts left Chaco Canyon during those excavations: colorful flutes and planks of richly painted wood that once hung in rooms like banners; beautifully decorated bowls and jars found stacked nearly to the ceilings of these rooms; masses of bear paws and mountain lion claws and bird wings uncovered in ceremonial contexts.

When researchers looked closely at the hundreds of thousands of relics excavated from Chaco, they realized that very few had originated in the canyon itself. Surprisingly, nearly everything turned out to be imported. Forged copper bells had come from Mexico, amber-colored ceramics from northern Arizona and southern Utah. Even the corn found here had been brought in, its kernels revealing isotope signatures of soil from farming plots at least forty miles away. At its eleventh-century peak, this canyon was a destination for pilgrims and traders from across the Southwest and beyond. They arrived with baskets full of rare stones, jewelry, crystal-tempered pottery, and exotic tropical birds, all of which they deposited in Chaco's great houses.

Wolcott Toll, an archaeologist working extensively with pottery here, explained that knowing that so much material came into Chaco when nothing appears to have gone out in exchange drives people crazy. "They believe that in order to give something tangible, you've got to get something tangible in return and take it home with you," Toll said to me. "Maybe nothing was going out. Maybe people were bringing stuff here and leaving it for no other reason than to establish their link to a very important place."

Toll believes that people were gathering from dispersed regions for special events, something required by this landscape for cultural survival. He explained that in the face of vast distances and hit-or-miss precipitation, people had to be flexible in their location, leadership, and group constitution. They picked a central meeting place—Chaco Canyon—and flocked to it to claim their place in the world. Toll found evidence of eighty thousand ceramic vessels intentionally smashed at one site. He saw this as a ritual act. It was like casting champagne glasses into a fireplace, an exploit of stunning abundance and celebration in this crumbling, bare-bones land.

Swimming a flash flood through Chaco Canyon, I began to understand in a visceral way the passage of material in and out of this place. All taste and touch and sight, my reactions unplanned, I pushed off against a tangle of tree roots and swam hard to avoid a broad trunk spinning wildly in front of me. Boils of debris rushed to the surface and disappeared just as quickly. The water felt like fists pummeling my body. As best I could, I floated with my boot tips sticking up, heading downstream, and my arms waving to keep myself straight. I glanced over at Adam, who was half grinning in astonishment as the land sped past.

I tried to laugh aloud, but the cold water wrapped around my throat, and I could not let out anything but a gasp. I shot a broad, exhilarated smile—all teeth and muddy beard—back to him. It was a secret smile, one thief to another. We had stolen our way into a place where people should not go. We were now subordinate to the whims of the elements, and it felt beautifully insane, like riding a hurricane.

I swam hard to keep near the center of the stream, out of range of snagged cottonwood trees that grew along the banks. Adam had one arm draped over a floating tree trunk and clutched the floating ammo box with his other hand. Supported by the two, he made a raft of himself, a stable vessel that bucked through eddies and waves.

I needed something, too. Up ahead was a spinning backwater of debris, and I swam into it, splashing juniper berries out of my path. The water here was slow, and I could feel deep turnings below me, my feet touching drowned cottonwood branches. I found a half-sunken, rusty Coleman ice chest and grabbed its handle. Its lid was torn off, and bullet holes were punched through one side. I swam out of the eddy, using the chest as a buoyant shield, swinging it out into the current, where it picked up speed and dragged me along.

As long as we kept our wits about us, feet dancing off submerged debris, we would make it just fine. Nothing but heads and boot tips floating with the rest of the wreckage, we were small in the water's hands. Pieces of trees heaved around us, broken branches and roots. We glided past them, following the laws of debris, spinning into knotted eddies and being spit back out. The ice chest helped keep me comfortably afloat.

When we caught glimpses of each other, we flashed signals with our faces, checking in.

We still good?

Still good.

I could feel minor shifts in the flood's composition. Snakes of sediment were coiling around my body, tongues sharp and cold darting against my skin. It was too cold. Adam and I shouted across to each other. We needed to get out, just long enough to warm up. We swam to a shallow overflow, where we paddled over cacti and woody spikes of saltbush that bit at our chilled, pink skin. I dragged the ice chest behind me to a bank of dry sand.

We sat in the hot sand, scooping it up and pouring it over our scratched bodies, washing it down our chests, burying our thighs and the tops of our feet. It must have been 130 degrees, baked by the sun. When our bones no longer stung from the cold, we dove back in, slipping around trees like lustrous eels. We repeated this process every five or ten minutes, crawling out to bathe in the sand, then pushing back into the flood.

As we rounded a corner, an ample ruin appeared above us, its walls slowly eroding at the base of a hot cliff. The building maintained the best of its stature, three stories of cleanly cut stones, the fastidious trademark masonry of Chaco. Cacti grew up through rows of opened rooms. The ruin was almost blinding in the sun, like the whitewashed plaster of a Middle Eastern village.

During the past century, archaeologists excavated painted jars as big as watermelons from the site. I had seen them in storage at a federal artifact repository, the vessels set shoulder to shoulder on metal shelves, their glossy white exteriors painted with black geometric designs. In the repository I also saw drawers packed with cut turquoise and argillite, along with finely made trinkets of wood, stone, shell, and bone. As I passed beneath this ruin, I had only a few seconds to recall its many excavated objects, necklaces and small, carved bird effigies, a wealth of civilized artifacts once ushered into this canyon.

A gateway of high sandstone bluffs appeared ahead, and at the top of one was a crown of ruins. This was our destination. The place looked large even from a couple of miles away. It was one of the first great houses constructed at Chaco, placed high enough that it would have been visible from all around. Looking up from the flood, I thought that this may have been one reason so many travelers had come here. People approaching Chaco Canyon in the eleventh century would have spotted this great citadel from afar, a masonry behemoth unlike anything they had ever seen before.

My throat strangled by the cold water, I kept my eyes firmly on the ruins ahead. Eventually, we were close enough to them that we had to start looking for a way out. Paddling and kicking fiercely toward shore, I let go of the ice chest, giving it back to the flood. We clawed through blade-sharp willows that snapped at our cold skin until we reached exposed ground and sank our fingers into the slick clay. We crawled out of the flood on hands and knees, then stood.

Mud draped off our shoulders and wormed down our legs. I turned and watched the ice chest vanish into dark waves.

Like creatures from a bog, we walked dripping and draining into the desert, moving up along tiers of sandstone, where the dead heat of summer radiated up from the ground and overtook us. The mud turned to dust as we climbed toward the top of the bluff, our boots sloshing. The sun began burning the scrapes in our skin. Adam stopped and opened the ammunition box. The sun was too strong; we needed clothes. As we slipped on shirts and pulled down sleeves to protect our forearms, we glanced at the flood behind us. It was nearly out of sight in the canyon below, a distant rumble like continuous thunder.

Not far ahead stood the ruins we sought, a tabernacle of fallen walls at the highest point of land, doors and hallways split wide open by erosion. The site is an oval with two hundred ground-floor rooms buried in the debris of the second, third, and fourth stories, which once surrounded a central mass of circular communal chambers known as kivas. No room stood wholly intact. The place looked as though it had been bombed. Tight whirlwinds scoured the ground, sweeping through gaping walls with quick, hot twists of dust.

Even though Chaco Canyon is one of the most heavily scrutinized archaeological centers in North America, many of its sites have never been excavated, their buried chambers still loaded with artifacts. This bluff-top great house had undergone only cursory explorations over the past century. I had heard that a tremendous amount of imported turquoise had been found just near the surface. But there had been no concerted excavation here. If archaeologists had the funding and political backing to break into this place, no doubt they would make discoveries that would revamp our thinking about Chaco, but up to now it has been left mostly alone.

Even with the astonishing amount of cultural material already excavated, Chaco remains one of the most enigmatic sites in American archaeology. There is so much data, so much evidence of religious and political complexity, so many far-flung associations and ethnicities, that just about any story makes sense in this desert canyon.

First is the argument over "foreign" influence versus spontaneous "local" development. Some say that Chaco was obviously an extension of empires existing at the time in Mesoamerica. Perhaps it was a miniature Tenochtitlán, with its own dusty temples lined up along the broad avenue of Chaco Wash. An expedition of Mesoamerican voyagers may have walked a thousand miles or more and planted themselves here, calling on awestruck natives to pay homage and build great houses. Others argue that Chaco was a purely indigenous creation, the quintessential work of people living in isolation on the Colorado Plateau. Those who rebuff any Mesoamerican influence insist that there were no Maya or Aztecs here and that Chaco was its own homegrown community.

Next comes the argument over function. The evidence gathered from a century of digging and mapping can support nearly any speculation thrown at Chaco Canyon: religious center, military center, government center, economic center, ceremonial center—the list is extensive. The place is thought by some to have been a colony of churches, its numerous great houses exhibiting certain recurring features thought to be religious. The repetition of specific architectural designs could also be interpreted as a form imposed by a ruling elite, the abundant goods as tithing. The outrageously copious artifacts found inside these great houses look like ritual paraphernalia: feathers and bones representing nearly every bird species found within a thousand-mile radius; a large number of wooden staffs like shepherds' crooks, their handles inlaid with fine stones; and many rooms filled with precious, expertly crafted mementos, many of which were found positioned as if on altars.

Other people take this abundance to mean that Chaco was a commercial center, a pre-Columbian shopping mall built to redistribute goods in the Southwest's notoriously unstable environment. In that sense the buildings are seen as storehouses, with some rooms stacked nearly to the ceiling with intricately painted vessels that were hardly ever used. Alternatively, the way these stacked vessels are frequently gathered around burial rooms has led some people to believe that they were offerings to the dead and that great houses were monumental tombs.

Whether this was a place of economic tribute, religious oblations, or offerings to ancestors, Chaco reached its peak in the eleventh century A.D. as the hub of an immense, pan-Southwest pilgrimage. Episodic layers of trash were left by thousands of people who seem to have arrived in waves and stayed for only a short time. When archaeologists pick apart their garbage, they find the remains of feasts and construction events that would have filled the canyon with noise.

In this vein I have heard Chaco called an ancient Las Vegas, an isolated strip of grandiose architecture in an ill-watered desert where people came from all directions to participate in flashy ceremonies and where they left all their wealth before heading home.

Finally, there is the argument over culture, over who or what these people called Anasazi might have been. In one school of thought, they were dispersed bands of primitive farmers and hunters, cliff and rock dwellers living without benefit of the wheel or any appreciable amount of forged metal. The stones used for constructing great houses were cut by using other stones, harder rock against softer.

At the same time, many envision a much more complex culture on the prehistoric Colorado Plateau, one comparable to Neolithic peoples such as the builders of Stonehenge in England or those who erected pueblo-like townships in Turkey in the sixth century B.C. They see astronomers here, priests, master masons, and warriors dressed in finely woven textiles and brilliantly feathered robes. They imagine a powerful and rigidly structured civilization.

Despite all the theories to have passed through Chaco Canyon, one thing is certain: something colossal happened here, an astounding feat of organization for a seminomadic people who had never before built anything near this scale.

. . .

Before entering the ruined great house, Adam and I stopped to gather our thoughts. My mind was still occupied by the flood, my body poised for sudden movements, whether it be fending off tree trunks or swimming with a quick burst out of a whirlpool. Time took on a different quality atop this bluff, which had seen centuries of slow decay. I bent down and unlaced my boots, pulled them off, and slipped off my wet socks. I let my bare feet feel the ground, aware of every pebble and stick. It felt better to walk this way—more slowly, more attentively than boots allowed. I tied the laces together and slung the boots over my shoulder as I walked into the ruins.

Walls and parts of walls stood here and there. Thousands of sandstone tiles lay scattered across the ground. Ceiling timbers as big as ship masts stuck out of the ground where rooms had buckled and caved in. I traced the shapes of these rooms with my bare feet, stepping lightly around fallen walls still intact as they lay facedown where they had fallen over. Some of the rooms were big enough to have held twenty or thirty people; others were as small as closets.

No one is sure what these great houses were used for, but to say that they were only one thing or another is to misunderstand the Anasazi. This compound may have been a church in one generation and a gambling domain in another. Fine layers of archaeological research have revealed elusive cycles of rise and fall among these people and their architecture. Centuries and decades of expansions and contractions give an impression of great houses in a constant state of cultural movement, during which nearly all the kivas were torn down at one time or another and then rebuilt, an impressive feat considering that some were as big as ballrooms. It is as if the people who lived here mirrored the landscape and the environment surrounding them: swift to change, as suddenly grandiose as they were ordinary, gathering around great houses at one moment and nowhere to be seen at another.

Archaeologist David Wilcox once explained to me, "We see these places, and we think of them as static, as doorways and walls that are solid. But they weren't. They were spaces meant to serve purposes, and those purposes were fluid, changing by generations, or yearly, or even daily."

Adam and I each found our own pace, separating as we passed through the ruins. Near the peak of the ruins, I came to a single wall still standing. In it was an open doorway, a shimmering blue portal looking out at nothing but sky.

Flood silt, now dried, fell off me in a wind that came through the open door. My skin was scratched raw in places. In my flesh I felt the weight of water, the flood absorbed into calluses and fingertips. My beard still had some dampness, almost cool in the wind as I scanned the horizon. In one direction I could see blanched contours of other great houses down in the wide chute of Chaco Canyon. In the opposite direction apricot-colored washes coiled in and out of one another. To the north were a few flecks of clouds, puffs of moisture blooming where heat radiated off the ground and pierced cooler layers of atmosphere. I kept an eye on these clouds, thinking maybe one would take hold and swell into a thunderhead, give someone a bit of shade somewhere, maybe a taste of rain. Each one expelled its energy quickly, evaporating as fast as it had appeared.

I stood before the empty doorway thinking this site must have been a crucial location a thousand years ago, a great beacon standing over the desert. I turned away and walked down into a field of kivas one level below, their roofs caved in and covered with bedded dust. More kivas have been found in this great house than at any other Chaco site. Their numerous round mouths opened around me, gaping at the sky, their edges rimmed in dry, feathery ricegrass.

In the sixth century A.D., a single, ceremonial kiva was built on this bluff, the earliest construction of its order overlooking Chaco Canyon. In its day that kiva was one of the larger buildings in the Southwest, a monument standing high above early Anasazi villages that had already been erected along the wash below. Within a hundred years the climate shifted slightly, and these kiva builders easily moved on, appearing to have migrated mostly to what is now Colorado, where masonry architecture and floor plans of early great houses began to appear in the eighth century. In the meantime, the high kiva fell into disrepair. A century or so later, arriving with the rains, people built an even larger kiva. They, too, left. After them came others, and then others, until by the eleventh century this bluff was topped with a proud great house, its interior crowded with kivas.

I could detect a faint rhythm among these generations of ruined kivas. It had a gentle, carrying sound—populations washing in and out of Chaco Canyon like tides, like weather. Century by century, Chaco grew until it reached an exponential climax, the canyon crowded with great houses. In this dusty corner of North America, civilization had begun.

I crossed to the edge of the great house and from here I could see the flood far below. My toes dug into dust and broken rocks as I watched the flood rush across the desert. Adam came walking languidly through the ruins. He stopped beside me and looked out at the flood, bright mirrors of water disappearing into the distance.

"This is the place I would have been," he said, appreciating the vista. "Right here."

I silently agreed. This was why we had come. It had always been the place to be.

Alignment

FAJADA BUTTE AND CASA RINCONADA

I woke to sand in my sleeping bag, gritty as I turned over from my side to my back. Looking up at the last stars of morning, with a bare arm slung across my chest, I felt the faint coolness of open air. My sleeping bag was old, a summer bag thin as a ratty blanket. Anything heavier would have been too warm on a midsummer night in Chaco. I crawled out and dressed. A thin blue line of mesas shivered in the east. I pulled out a sooted pot and heated some tea over my small stove. The blue flame flickered, no louder than a whisper, as I crouched watching a drape of ultramarine and pink rise from the eastern horizon. There were no clouds; the sky was crisp and arid.

A picnic table and a bathroom were nearby, all the conveniences of a National Park Service campground. A little more than fifty square miles of Chaco Canyon is overseen by the Park Service and listed by the United Nations as a World Heritage site, making it one of the world's irreplaceable treasures, its archaeological sites to be preserved at all costs. During the day armed, uniformed rangers stroll pleasantly around the grounds, answering visitors' questions with judicious courtesy. Some of them have spent their careers in the desert, and some are just passing through, on their way to Yellowstone or the redwoods. At night they lock the gates and return to their small settlement of white wood-frame houses, the only permanent dwellings allowed in the canyon.

Not far from rangers' housing is the campground where Adam and I had spent the night. We were Chaco's itinerants, staying for five nights before moving on. A numbered post stood in front of our square campsite, and on it was a metal clip holding a receipt saying that we had paid to be here. Adam was still asleep in his bag. I walked tea over to him: Earl Grey, double bergamot, the taste of turpentine. I nudged him, and he came to life with a sputter of words.

"Here's your tea," I said. "We need to get going."

He sat up straight, and the rest of his bag fell into his lap. "All right," he said, wiping strands of long dark hair out of his face as he glanced east at the horizon. "Yeah, all right." He reached for the cup.

After tea we got in my truck and drove out of a gravel parking lot, keeping the headlights off. I could not really see the road, but I did not turn the headlights on as we left the campground, following a black corridor of crackled asphalt. The lights would have been blinding in this sleepy blue dawn. Better just to feel our way along at seven miles per hour.

The inside of my truck was in wretched condition. Cough drops and loose change occupied the beverage holder. The clock showed some obscure time having nothing to do with any other clock in the world. Points of books poked at our sides, and the floorboards and bench seat were cluttered with disheveled papers and folders wrinkled and water stained. The cab smelled of motor oil and rancid nuts. The passenger's seat belt was inaccessible. This was my library, my den.

The road began to appear outside the windshield. Park signs became visible, black obelisks of regulations and friendly information about Chaco Canyon. After a few miles we rolled to a stop in front of a locked gate, turned off the engine, and got out. We leaned against the hood watching morning come on.

A landmark stood alone before us, Fajada Butte. It looked like a telescope observatory with a slightly round head standing in clear view of the sky, evenly distanced from the surrounding cliffs. As would be expected from any observatory, Fajada Butte's stone faces are marked with ancient symbols carved into bare sandstone. A number of these insignias are oriented toward the sky, pointing directly at the sunrise during certain key months or inscribed by the full moon at the beginning of every lunar standstill cycle. They each have a specific purpose.

The more closely I have looked at Chaco's craftsmanship—its rock art and its architecture—the more I have thought it to be the work of mathematicians and astronomers. Windows and doorways were built like compass arrows, and each great house lies on an axis pointing to particular celestial events, as if the people who came here carefully calibrated themselves with the seasons.

We leaned on the truck hood, watching a pink glaze creep across Fajada Butte's top. The sun would be rising in an hour or so, impaling everything it touched. It was June, and that sun would soon be hot enough to bake any trace of moisture right out of the ground.

A park ranger had told me that when he moved to Chaco, sunrises became his specialty. It became a pastime of his, like morning prayer, to go to particular spots where, at certain times of the year, he knew the sunrise would be dramatically framed by shapes on the horizon. He kept track of the first shoestrings of light slipping through arches and boulder gaps, tracing them to where, for a moment, they touched a pointed rock tip or a hole in a cliff wall. He said that this pursuit felt natural in this particular land, with the sky so huge overhead and the horizon picketed with cliffs and buttes. You can't help looking for the peculiar way the sun rises from one day to the next.

Apparently, the same sort of behavior was going on a thousand years ago. At least eleven great houses appear to have been designed to be architectural calendars, letting the sun or moon cast its light through their rooms, windows, and doors in a premeditated fashion. Some are oriented toward the 18.6-year lunar standstill cycle, others toward the spring and fall equinoxes.* When the sun reaches its daily apex, the center wall of the largest great house casts no shadow

---

*This form of celestial orientation is common throughout the world. In the second millennium B.C., the henge builders of northern latitudes aligned their megaliths and shrines with myriad points in the sky and on the horizon. In Japan a thousand years later, the vast stone sundial of Nonakadō was built, and in the second century B.C., aligned megalithic tombs were constructed at Brahmagiri in southern India. The Americas were not far behind. Beginning in Peru in the last few thousand years B.C. and continuing all the way up to eleventh-century Chaco, such celestial alignments were common in the Americas.

at all, regardless of the day of the year. Whatever is known or not known about the people who built here, it is at least certain that they were gripped by a profound order, imbued with an enduring sense of time and procession. Perhaps this is inevitable for anyone living beneath the sky. The sun rolls through a perpetual cycle, winter returning to winter returning to winter, and lunar rhythms span the heavens as if following a mathematical algorithm. It is only a matter of time before people on the ground, especially those without electric lights, notice all these things. Nearly every civilization has observed the odd syncopation of eclipses, recognizing that the moon and the sun are disks of exactly the same size and that the planets occasionally turn against the heavenly drift, every certain number of years or months pushing back through the stars. The period we now live in, the twenty-first century, is perhaps the only time in human history when common people have held so little knowledge of the sky.

As if trying to cobble some of this knowledge together, Adam and I had come this morning of June 21, the summer solstice, to see the sunrise. We were here at the turning of the annual tide—the longest day of the year, when the sun rises at its northernmost point in the sky, reaching the farthest swing of its pendulum. The sun has nowhere to go from here but south, swinging back toward winter.

The morning was absolutely silent, not a stir of a breeze as Fajada Butte's flanks began to glow. A second vehicle arrived and parked behind us. The driver turned off the engine but did not get out. And then a third car arrived. Car after car began to appear, stopping one behind the other, until about forty of them made a long train along the broad floor of Chaco Canyon. People were gathering this morning to pay attention to time in a way that is steadily being forgotten.

. . .

Of course the ancient calendars of Chaco could be nothing more than a coincidence of neatly done architecture. Most American towns and cities, for example, are laid out on north-south grids, imbuing our daily backyards and sidewalks with apparent cosmological significance. I imagine that if we started looking, we could find beams of light breaking between fence posts on the solstice, illuminating bird feeders and water spigots, and moonrises that chart their way across windowsills with extraordinary accuracy. Some people argue that this is the case with Chaco. I once visited a pair of researchers who were convinced otherwise.

In 2000 John Stein and Rich Friedman were charged with the task of remapping Chaco Canyon, building upon plane-table maps made in the 1970s. Using more recent technology and a new set of questions, they discovered a rigid and fundamental order in all levels of the structures at Chaco, a master plan of alignments that had never before been recognized. They worked in an office cluttered nearly to the ceiling with folders and scrolls of maps, a back room of the sheriff's department in Gallup, New Mexico. Most people working at the department were unaware that these men were even there, that in the back of their building the cultural apparatus of an entire civilization was being pieced back together.

Friedman sat before a bank of computer screens that rose from stacks of books and rolled-up maps. His hands moved from one keyboard to the next as images flashed onto the screens, one map and then another, some made into three-dimensional re-creations of archaeological sites, others flat-plan views showing lines of ancient roads and great-house walls projected through each other like neural synapses. Hoisted on my hip was my baby son, Jasper, who sputtered and squeaked at these maps. To my side stood my wife, Regan, complimenting Friedman from over his shoulder, appreciative of the many layers of data that he had made so visually attractive.

Stein stood back and interpreted what we were seeing. He explained that in the most recent remapping they had found hills in Chaco Canyon where there should not naturally be hills, places that must have been built by humans, so weathered now that hardly anything remains of them but heaps of earth. He said that ramps are barely visible on some of these hills, and some have steps leading toward their tops. They discovered that these hills were lined up with the great houses, which in turn were lined up with various heavenly features. Previously, the hills had been dismissed as indecipherable, left off the archaeological maps because no one knew what to call them. Now that Stein could see them clearly, he thought of them as small pyramids, human-made mounds capped by thin masonry veneers. Not living quarters, not structures with rooms or roofs, they may have been places just to stand and look, viewing platforms from where you could see your exact location in this cultural and earthen labyrinth of Chaco.

"Nothing is out of place here, nothing arbitrary," said Friedman, shoulders hunched over one of the keyboards, face turned up to the computer glow. "The way we can see it now, everything has some sort of relationship to something else."

The internal structures of buildings seemed to incorporate geometries of a much larger composition. Stein explained that if the scale of one's perspective is limited to one building, there may be no apparent meaning in certain angles, alignments, or positions of architectural elements. But if you put it all together on a map, if you extend the lines of interior rooms and walls and the pivots of kivas out for miles in all directions, you see that they match up with lines extending out of other buildings, as if they were all formed by a single idea.

Stein and Friedman were genuinely excited about their work, voices charging ahead of them as they unraveled the many details they had brought to light. From reading their reports I knew they had a peculiar eye for detail. By profession, Friedman is a geologist, which gives him an edge on seeing how these sites fit into the land. Stein is a longtime Southwest archaeologist. He coauthored the maps of Chaco from the 1970s, having been present during an era when teams of fieldworkers, drunk on discovery, went driving and walking over every hill and dale in northwest New Mexico. These teams mapped whatever prehistoric roads were big enough to see, measured every mound of a great house moldering away in the desert.

Stein had wanted to go back to Chaco ever since. He was confident that if he looked more closely, he would find something different. He and Friedman walked the land again and in their office sorted through black-and-white photographs taken for a soil survey in the 1930s. They also looked at recent multispectral imagery acquired by satellites, showing shapes on the ground that can no longer be detected by the naked eye. Up from the bare earth rose a network of human-made contours and patterns. Friedman and Stein saw an incredible amount of earth that had been moved and formed, mesas sculpted into courts and ramps and platforms. They were now performing the tricky work of mapping how the people of a lost civilization might have once seen their universe, the concrete layout of their capital.

Staring at these computerized maps, Stein said, "Chaco is the center of a web, a half-created and half-natural landscape where everything seems to line up. You have strands radiating out from Chaco all over. And there are nodes, various outlying centers that are focuses within the web, and I think they're all intentionally interlaced with each other. There are certain places where at times of the day when the light is right, you can go out and see the landscape is literally made of lines radiating everywhere."

Friedman said over his shoulder, "It's a ritual landscape."

What Friedman meant was that people had tied themselves to points on the horizon and points in the sky. They incorporated their lives into the entire surrounding landscape in an institutional fashion—a ritual landscape. Seeing image after image of perfectly proportioned sites on the computer screens, symmetries stretched over miles, I envisioned a fundamentalist nation of Anasazi, a single ideology rising into a civilization of arid monuments.

"Could it be possible that you're just making all this up, seeing things that aren't there?" I asked.

Stein shook his head quickly. "I'm confident we're not doing that. We have enough empirical pieces to the puzzle to know this is real. It's not like an artifact you can pick up and take back to the lab, but it's there. It's real."

Friedman made a couple of keystrokes and called up dissected images of one of the maps to show how he had constructed each layer of data. He had made sure to cover his tracks with abundant research. There was no lack of data to support his conclusions.

I handed Jasper over to Regan, who soothed him into a trance.

Stein said to Friedman, "Play that sunrise video."

While Friedman worked the keyboard, Stein looked at my family and me and said, "This will blow your minds."

While his program loaded, Friedman explained that Navajo students had filmed the sunrise on the winter solstice, looking straight along a processional, a road carved into the ground about a thousand years ago, barely visible anymore. At first I could not see anything on the screen. Then I saw a few streaks of light and recognized the dark silhouette of a landmark, a square-faced butte. It was beginning to show in the dawn light, the movie playing several times faster than the customary length of a sunrise. It was a live filming, unlike the digital imagery Friedman had shown until now. We all stared as if commanded, unable to withdraw. Even Jasper stared unmoving at this accelerated dawn.

As the sun came up over the horizon, it lifted at a steep angle toward the butte, and then the light spread. Seeing the sun roll up the butte at such a speed was oddly nauseating, the world spinning too fast for my eyes. It finally mounted the butte, its bright circle cut right in half. At that moment the shadow of the butte fired across the land, falling straight along the prehistoric causeway as if the sun's path and that of the causeway had become a single entity. There could be little doubt that this was intentionally orchestrated, an event to be seen only on December 21, when the sun reaches its southernmost point on the horizon.

As the movie ended, Stein and Friedman both simply shrugged.

I thought that the average person living around Chaco in the eleventh century might have been unaware of the cultural significance attached to such an alignment, leaving that to the masons and priests. Like those of us with cosmologically oriented sidewalks and backyards, our capitol buildings aimed in the cardinal directions, some people might notice the strict arrays spreading all around, but only in passing. The alignments sink into our subconscious, a knowledge of arrangement quietly cradling us at every moment, speaking to a deeper, almost religious order underlying our own civilization.

Stein said, "I think Chaco itself is a mnemonic for the Anasazi cosmos, an extension of it."

When it was time for us to leave, the sheriff and his deputies had already gone home for the day. The hallways were silent. With handshakes and waves, and a stolen pinch of Jasper's cheek, Stein and Friedman shuffled me and my family out a back door and into the parking lot near the Dumpsters. The two of them stayed inside, heading back down the hallway as the unmarked door closed behind them, and prepared for another evening of work, eureka flashes arcing out their windows.

. . .

As Adam and I waited in the line of cars, Fajada Butte glowed brighter by the moment. A Park Service vehicle made its way to the front, an official white pickup. A Navajo woman got out, fully dressed in forest green Park Service attire—the new ceremonial dress at Chaco. Her black hair, braided down her back, was streaked with silver. She unlocked the gate. The line of cars began to move, a procession of coal-fire taillights. Like proud baton twirlers, Adam and I led the thirty-mile-per-hour parade along a brightening road, where rubble mounds and walls of great houses rose around us.

The parking lot at the other end was a madhouse—no possible way to get that many vehicles in there. The Park Service had rangers and volunteers out waving their arms as if directing airplanes to their terminals, sending all the vehicles—RVs, a school bus, unmarked government cars, and numerous private cars and trucks—into long lines along the road.

We had come from around the world to an oversize kiva called Casa Rinconada. Here, at sunrise, the first light to enter a certain window in a masonry sidewall would cast an orange rectangle onto the opposite wall. This rectangle of light would sit perfectly inside a rectangular niche, then drift slowly, changing shape slightly over several minutes, until it fit exactly into another nearby niche. Everyone's calendars and watches could be synchronized.

Casa Rinconada is larger than most kivas. In the nomenclature of Southwest archaeology, it is called a *great kiva,* a perfect circle sixty feet across. Regardless of its size, it has the same features as nearly all kivas on the Colorado Plateau from New Mexico to Nevada, the geographic extent of the Anasazi. In addition to size, there are a few regional variations on the theme of the circular kiva, such as those with floor plans shaped like a D and a rectangular form that became popular in later years. But apart from their different shapes and sizes, all prehistoric kivas share distinct characteristics. They are

View into an excavated great kiva directly across the wash from Casa Rinconada. REGAN CHOI

generally subterranean (or at least blocked deeply into a masonry superstructure), have encircling interior benches, and have uniformly articulated ventilation systems. The one thing found in every kiva floor—uniformly just off the center—is a *sipapu,* a small hole said to be a passage from the underworld to this world.

Standing inside Casa Rinconada a thousand years ago would have been like being in a dark, underground sphere, an echo chamber sealed with smoothly plastered walls. Its ceiling would have consisted of timbers corbeled into each other to form a dome held up by four pillars, each a massive pine tree weighing a ton. The only light inside would have been from a fire, or from shafts of sunlight coming through narrow apertures set high along the walls.

Now this kiva was open to the sky, its roof having long ago collapsed and been cleared away by twentieth-century excavators. About sixty of us moved slowly up the trail toward the kiva, a human-made hill lifted high enough to catch first light. The sun was still half an hour from coming up. Adam and I reached the top of the site and looked over a chest-high wall. Below we could plainly see the round floor that had once been kept in darkness. Now it was filling with blond morning light. The floor contained an orderly puzzle of cleanly cut stone furnishings: platforms, boxes, and solid, round pieces of masonry standing like altars, all of which had been unearthed by excavators and reinforced by modern masons. No one was allowed in there: park rules.

What once occurred in such a place is unknown, but there is speculation. Artifacts found in great kivas are mostly ritual in nature, floors bristling with beads and shells with very little sign of domestic activity. The original builders had drilled holes in the ends of certain load-bearing timbers, placed handfuls of polished turquoise inside, and capped the holes with a bit of putty. Caches of artifacts were hidden in the walls, including hundreds of bear paws and mountain lion claws. From all this, it is widely believed that great kivas were the ceremonial mainstays of the Anasazi. Perhaps dancers' feet pounded the floor as priests descended in radiant macaw feather robes. Any story could be imagined this morning in the brightening desert.

We moved around the circle of Casa Rinconada like pilgrims. The stonework was finely finished, as is to be expected in a kiva, smooth and curved like the ground glass of a telescope lens. Two ample T-shaped passages, grand keyholes forming a cardinal axis across the kiva from due north to due south, stood opposite each other. People paused and looked inside, as if peering into a cauldron.

The American Indians approaching Casa Rinconada this morning had faces the color of rose tea in the increasing light. Most were from a New Mexico pueblo, returning on this auspicious morning to a place where some of their ancestors may have stood a thousand years ago. Elder Anglos walked up the path, retired couples who had discovered a love for archaeoastronomy. Along with them arrived four Zen nuns, as well as a group of researchers from the National Aeronautics and Space Administration, students of the sky who thought perhaps the Anasazi had asked similar questions of the cosmos.

Before the sun breached the horizon, a middle-aged Pueblo man began to sing. Wearing a notable amount of turquoise, he stood along the kiva's east-west axis offering a traditional morning solo, intoning words of the Tewa language, studded with light consonants and sudden stops. The crowd listened to his song, not saying a word.

The man finished as the eastern horizon brightened intensely. The crowd began to collect along the kiva's eastern arc, facing west. The first light would cast its geometric show against the far wall, which we watched like a blank movie screen.

Astronomical alignments were about to be struck all around Chaco, various niches and gaps in the great houses and their kivas. These alignments are often thought to have been instructional, marking the day on which one is to plant crops or the day of harvest. This explanation is painfully simplistic, though, as if planting or harvesting was on a fixed annual schedule and had nothing to do with the wild fluctuations of frost and drought that come every year. I imagine that instead of rudimentary to-do calendars, these astronomical features had been made by the Anasazi to observe the manifold patterns visible from here, confirming the peerless order of the world, cycles on which to hang annual ceremonies. Like the park ranger who stands for almost every sunrise, and like all of us who had come to Casa Rinconada to see this morning's event, many great-house builders had probably positioned themselves in the right place at the right time so that signs from the sky would shower down on them.

. . .

The eleventh-century apex of Chaco happened during a striking convocation of omens both on earth and in the heavens. First came a dramatic supernova in A.D. 1054 at the same time the great houses reached their full height. According to detailed Chinese accounts from that period, the supernova was as bright as the full moon for almost a month, visible in the middle of the day. At night it bathed the earth in a ghostly ruby-colored light. It was positioned in a busy cluster of constellations, off Orion's shoulder, a very prominent place in the sky. Over the next six years this light slowly faded, until it was replaced by another startling event—the eruption of a volcano in northern Arizona. A volcanic eruption was relatively unheard-of in the time frame of human generations in the Southwest, and it buried eight hundred square miles of land in glowing cinders. Numerous

Anasazi villages were enveloped in lava, and ash blanketed Chaco 180 miles to the northwest. Two years after this event, Halley's comet came trailing its white tail through the sky, and ten years after that the sun became visibly blemished with black spots as had never been seen before (or since).

Whatever preconceptions we have developed about the Anasazi, it would have been unlikely that they ignored the profundity of these various and remarkable occurrences. When the supernova first appeared, at an early July dawn, it was nearly touching the horn of the rising crescent moon. This iconic pairing was then painted and pecked into rock faces all over the Colorado Plateau, including a prominent pictograph in Chaco depicting a starburst, a crescent moon, and an upraised hand. Following the volcanic eruption, people took ears of corn and pressed them into the cooling lava, forever preserving impressions of plump kernels in black stone. Perhaps these incidents were the very events that spurred people to root themselves in orderliness, locking down their great-house walls and kivas to match the more dependable cycles of the heavens. Whether perceived as ill omens or hopeful signs, these dramatic episodes would have been strong markers in the lives of people a thousand years ago. Some must have thought it was a momentous time, one fitting for the bold rise of Chaco.

No one moved as we huddled at the eastern arc of Casa Rinconada this morning. All eyes peered to the west. Suddenly, the sky split open, and a meteorite slivered the blue horizon, its metallic green streak bright even in the morning glow. A full second of arcing, electric light marked the whole western sky. Voices of alarm rose from the crowd. Everyone had seen it, a coincidence of position. The meteorite fell beyond the horizon, striking the desert somewhere out past Standing Rock.

As this vein of light faded, many people gasped. Some laughed almost uncomfortably. I heard the word *omen* spoken under someone's breath. The Tewa-speaking man who had sung the morning song said nothing. He had already turned to face the east. I turned also and saw a pinprick of orange light break the horizon.

John Stein once told me that he had spoken to Native Americans who possessed religious authority. From these conversations he had come to believe that Chaco's architecture was more than a mere reflection of the heavenly cosmos. Instead, it was a continuation of it, a perspective from outside the cosmos looking in, a god's-eye view. There would be no coincidences seen from Chaco, only omens.

The sun's light was channeled through a portal of Casa Rinconada. A square of sunlight landed on the opposite wall in a niche just its size. I looked east, straight into the light, and saw great houses illuminated in the distance, miles of stonework ruins positioned to mirror and regard the turning sky. Across the canyon stood the behemoth of Pueblo Bonito, looking like a ship stranded in the desert, its five-story hull open, wooden ribs sticking out of the masonry. I lifted my hand to shade my face. The summer sun began scalding the bare landscape, shrinking every shadow back into itself, turning this place from an immortal calendar back into a searing desert.

Identity

PUEBLO BONITO

The east side of Pueblo Bonito is the first to be touched by morning light. Long before the sun even rises, a gentle maroon washes one side of the great house. Then a faint breeze begins moving through the interior hallways and rooms, and the old great house seems to breathe.

The first time I noticed this breeze was on an early September morning. I was here with Adam again. He had already gone deep inside the great house while I milled around some of its outermost rooms. I stopped in the thin, aqueous light and lifted my hand in front of a doorway built in the shape of a T, much like the north-south axis entrances to Casa Rinconada. I felt air passing through the doorway and between my fingers, and I thought it odd, because the air outside was absolutely still. At this coolest time of the day, the masonry walls of Pueblo Bonito still held some of the previous day's heat, enough to set up a temperature gradient and spur a subtle breeze. Back in the eleventh century, this would no doubt have been a welcome time of day, the doldrums within Pueblo Bonito stirred as cooler outside air pushed through apertures and ventilator shafts.

Pueblo Bonito is the largest of all great houses. It is built like a hive, with seven hundred rooms and about thirty kivas molded into a single, half-moon-shaped floor plan as large as the ground floor of the Sears Tower in Chicago. Most of its ceilings caved in long ago, filling the lower stories with rubble that was eventually sorted by excavators in the late nineteenth and early twentieth centuries. This site was cleared down to its bones, its every artifact carted away. The end result is a great house swept clean, empty as a cardboard box.

What business did seminomadic desert farmers have building a place like this? Chaco has all the markers of a sacred Neolithic site. Its great houses are similar to the Tarxien temples of Malta from 3000 B.C., and its stonework resembles that of five-thousand-year-old burial monuments in the Orkney Islands. The Neolithic is a formative stage that nearly every civilization has gone through, a tipping point when wild plant gathering mixed with domestic agriculture and domestic animals (such as turkeys and dogs avidly looked after by the Anasazi). Stone tools were refined to an art form, and signs of early metallurgy began to appear, usually starting with copper. During this period, hunting-and-gathering families joined into networks of farming villages and arenas of political power. As part of Neolithic development, enormous stone and wood architecture often showed up, as if people were experimenting with their newfound ability to pool labor and lift their imaginations off the ground.

The Neolithic era did not happen all at once around the world. It occurred at different times for different people, a sort of cultural protocol: China as far back as 12,000 B.C., the Greek fortifications of Sesklo around 6500 B.C., the rise of the Mound Builders in the Mississippi River Valley in 2500 B.C. Chaco in the eleventh century A.D. fits perfectly into this progression.

As I walked around Pueblo Bonito, stonework two or three stories high rose around me, clean as library shelves, hundreds of thousands of bookbinding stones all set perfectly flush against one another. I followed a faint breeze into one doorway and then the next, ducking my head and pulling in my shoulders as I went. Hallways stretched around me, long passages of repeated, symmetrical doorways. Although I prefer ruins left in a more relaxed, unexcavated state, it was a blessing to be able to walk through this compound and peer down avenues of rooms, their masonry escalating in the slowly turning light.

I entered one of the easternmost rooms and found Adam sitting on the tourist-beaten floor. He was the only other person in the great house this morning. His mug of Earl Grey rested in front of him.

Adam and I had made a habit of coming to Chaco together, driving from western Colorado, where we both lived. There was no particular chore we had to accomplish here. We simply enjoyed each other's company in this setting of crumbled Neolithic monuments.

Adam looked up at me. He had been waiting, knowing I would come to this room where the morning light show begins.

I sat near him on the packed dirt, opened a journal across one knee, and began to write. We saw different details each time we came—the air changing slightly from one month to the next, the light arriving differently.

After several minutes Adam said softly, "There."

I looked up from my journal.

A pair of lights appeared on the east-facing wall across from us, the golden eyes of morning gradually opening through masonry windows behind us. Then another light below that. And another. The ancient grandfather clock of Pueblo Bonito was still working. Its weights and pulleys spun into action as the wall before us became a field of bright nicks and rectangles cast two stories over our heads.

Almost every day Adam and I spent at Chaco began in this room. The sunrise kept repeating itself for us, but not in the same way. Midwinter sunrise comes with a different sequence of light creeping through empty beam sockets and windows skimmed with snow. High summer light arrives like bold white flags unfurling through the halls. September is methodical, one tidy patch of light after the next.

"They're a little to the right," Adam said.

I pointed my pen at the wall. "About half an inch," I agreed, noticing how the patterns changed day by day. The sun was moving through the seasons, and we could actually see the daily evidence. Witnessing this shift from one day to the next produced a heartening sensation. The universe was still turning; this much we knew.

We had memorized the order of pear-colored lights, which one would appear first, which would come last. After the final light appeared above us, we got up off the dirt floor and passed through a nearby doorway, leaving our daypacks and Adam's mug of tea on the floor. As we entered another room, the sunrise started again, and we stood back to watch. We went on like this from room to room, hustling through doorways as if passing through bulkheads deep inside a ship. We followed beams and daggers of light into farther chambers. In these roofless catacombs a single bead of light landed in a black stone box, and I touched it with my finger, a ritual of passing.

. . .

Every turn through these corridors led to an empty vault, where sunlight sliced across the vacant floor. What I was seeing was whatever early archaeologists and the National Park Service had decided to leave behind. Truth is, there is no *one* Pueblo Bonito, no *one* way to see the place. In the past, every century, every decade in fact, brought change, as this great house was extended, remodeled, partially torn down, built up, burned, cleaned, painted, and repainted. Chaco began to fade in the twelfth century as the last residents flooded into the shelter of great houses, where they subdivided big rooms into smaller domestic chambers, built hearths inside, and filled unused kivas with trash and feces. Even after that, after Chaco was supposedly abandoned, there was a revival in the thirteenth century, when people with belongings that originated in Colorado came in and fixed up the place, giving Pueblo Bonito's central kiva a clean whitewash before moving on again. The next resurgence of activity was in the nineteenth century, when, at the behest of Anglo archaeologists, Zuni and Navajo workers cleaned out Pueblo Bonito for public display.

As I walked through the morning's procession of light, my journal held open with a thumb, I recalled decades of excavation notes taken here, boxes of black-and-white photographs from early digs now stored in reliquaries around the country. Looking for the artifacts removed from Pueblo Bonito, I had wandered the long halls of the American Museum of Natural History in New York, its treasures sealed in seemingly never-ending rows of gray metal cabinets. In the Peabody Museum at Harvard, I found three stories of ceramics. In a small federal repository in Albuquerque, I went through thousands of beads in plastic cases, and painted seed jars crowded on metal shelves. In these modern storehouses I packed my journal with annotations, telling which of Pueblo Bonito's rooms contained which artifacts. This morning I put the pieces back, restocking these rooms from my imagination. I filled spaces with thousands of nested bowls, their severe geometric designs flowing from one to the next. Exotic birds went back into their burials under the floors, along with a necklace made of two thousand flawlessly graduated turquoise disks, with jet-black finger rings and painted flutes. I fit ceiling beams back into position, first setting turquoise into their sockets, then hanging feathered sashes from their heights.

One room had been a dark aviary for scarlet macaws imported from southern Mexico, the floor covered with a gray slag of bird droppings. (The macaw bones were found deformed in a way that suggests the birds had been kept away from sunlight for most of their lives.) Another room housed golden eagles—great, darkly mantled birds that would have stared with molten eyes as I entered their chamber through a narrow doorway.

Some rooms I kept empty in my mind, exactly as they were found when excavators reached them more than a century ago. Crews discovered a surprising lack of refuse—frayed strings, potsherds, charcoal, or combed human hair—that one would expect on the floors of habitation sites. They unearthed only enough kitchen hearths from the eleventh-century component to account for seventy people living in these seven hundred rooms. Some researchers have concluded that Pueblo Bonito had only enough residents to sweep the floors (at the same time, respected Chaco scholars such as Gwinn Vivian and Chip Wills think Chaco great houses were more domestic). The rest of the rooms seem to have been left for the storage of ritual paraphernalia, for offerings, and for a small number of opulent burials. Rather than being domestic, many researchers believe, the great houses of Chaco functioned more like temples, to which people made pilgrimages.

Pueblo Bonito was built around cores of burials that even by the eleventh century would have seemed ancient. These burials have been one of the enigmas of Chaco Canyon. There are not enough dead to account for the numbers that must have passed through and lived here at one time or another. Only 650 skeletons have been found in the canyon.* At Pueblo Bonito, where 131 individuals were buried, two primary tombs were excavated, revealing skeletons stacked like cordwood.

I took all the skeletons I could remember and buried them once again, draping jewelry over their rib cages, bracelets around their wrists. In a tomb consisting mostly of women and girls, I restored two young women exactly as excavators had found them: side by side, so that they were nearly holding hands, both buried at the same time on a single reed mat, their bodies draped with jewelry and covered with a turkey feather blanket.

As I walked, I added a haze of incense drifting through the rooms as if through the dinge of a high Tibetan monastery. I heard the blare of shell trumpets during festivals, ceremonies, and feast. During years of good rains and robust harvests, travelers would have come by the thousands, their baskets loaded with corn and with beautifully rendered trinkets, the finest of their wares brought from home to leave here. Feathered dancers would have made a sound like sea waves crashing against the shore, their feet pounding, their kilts and ankles loud with shell tinklers. I rehung painted wooden banners from the ceilings, their designs multicolored and involved like coats of arms. Colorful pageants may have been held in these great houses, much like those of the indigenous people of Bhutan, south of the Himalayas, where looming monasteries still function as the spiritual, political, and geographical centers for surrounding villages.

The skeletons found here reveal a cross section of the Anasazi world. The bones carry genetic signatures that identify the various people's origins. The two innermost tombs of Pueblo Bonito may

*The burials at Chaco seem to be divided into hierarchical tiers. Those living in small sites tended to be buried in exterior trash middens—which appear to have been treated very differently and with more veneration than modern American landfills. These small-site burials were often accompanied by common types of ceramic vessels and other everyday artifacts. By contrast, burials in great houses had far greater personal ornamentation, and the accompanying artifacts were of high quality, including many decorated vessels. Even among these great-house burials, some groups appear to have been much wealthier than others.

have contained two separate ethnic groups with genetic ties to different parts of the Colorado Plateau. This great house was designed like a map, with each region separated from the next by thick walls and inward-facing doorways leading to their associated burials. Some people who were physically taller than others were buried near others who were shorter and more heavyset; some with high, peaked foreheads were buried close to others with more rounded faces. Many different people—from deserts and highlands, from the San Juan River and the Rio Grande—came together here to build this unsurpassed nexus.

. . .

I walked into a narrow passage, slipped through doorways, and emerged into an open arena where kivas surrounded me. The sky turned from morning pink to an expansive blue over my head. Light was just entering a bank of rooms along the northern arc of Pueblo Bonito. I crouched and peered down an aisle of T-shaped doorways leading to one of the tombs. I was just starting to put its skeletons away when I heard a car door slam in the distance. Then came voices. I stepped into the light, taking in a last breath of solitude. The tourists were coming. The day had begun.

Gradually, the sun canted over Pueblo Bonito's eroded walls. The breeze inside turned hot. By noon the place was as busy as an anthill. Children ran through doorways, and older men shuffled from one signpost to the next, reading out loud from park brochures. Adam and I crouched in what shade remained. Along with the regular wash of Americans, contingents from Korea and Switzerland arrived, as well as a family from India, the women loosely shawled in colorful fabrics.

It was baffling to watch this parade of visitors, people from everywhere coming to this hole in the desert. Native Americans passed through, Seminoles and Choctaws coming to see what earlier Native Americans had once done. A young guide led a tour, explaining, "These are what we call our clan kivas." The tour group listened as attentively as if they were viewing the Sistine Chapel. Whose clan kivas? I wondered. Even as I carefully put all the artifacts back into this great house, checking through the pages of my notes as I went, layers were being added faster than I could count. Nothing was still. The hot September wind kicked up dust devils, hissing and sputtering through open rooms, suddenly blinding the tourists, who covered their eyes, their faces pelted with sand.

I was told by archaeologists to be careful at Pueblo Bonito, maybe even to avoid the place entirely. They said that too much data has been collected at the site, too many points of fascination uncovered. A fair and succinct conclusion can never be drawn. The place makes Chaco look too heroic; the Anasazi appear more complex and majestic than they may have been. But Pueblo Bonito is here nonetheless, surrounded by its blushing sisters: the impressive great houses of Pueblo del Arroyo, Chetro Ketl, Kin Kletso, Pueblo Alto, and the circle of Casa Rinconada in plain sight across the wash.

I did not take the archaeologists' advice. I do not know how many days altogether, from sunrise to sunset, I have spent at Pueblo Bonito looking at the same rooms, the same beaten ground. I have wandered through this great house as if it were a book I could not stop reading, its every line filled with connotation.

The T-shaped doorways, for instance, stand out like bulky crucifixes. Anasazi doorways, and everyone else's for that matter, tend to be rectangular. That is the easiest way to build them. Occasionally, around the world, there are other forms, each with certain cultural significance: the peaked arches of Islamic mosques, circular moon gates in China, and trapezoidal doorways in the Incan ruins of South America. At Pueblo Bonito and its surrounding great houses, there are T-shaped doorways mixed in with all the rectangles.

The first T shapes in the Southwest were at Pueblo Bonito, and later they spread to the remainder of the Colorado Plateau. Someone brought the shape here or invented it here. (It also appeared later at the Mayan site of Palenque in southern Mexico and in a number of Incan sites in Peru.) Perhaps it began as a functional piece of architecture, allowing people to enter with loads on their backs or facilitating the movement of air into the deeper recesses of the great house. It may then have become a symbol identifying the purpose of a room, perhaps as a privileged space, a ceremonial chamber, or a passage

Classic T-shaped doorway inside Pueblo Bonito. REGAN CHOI

leading back in time to the older burials. Whatever the T shape once meant, it was a signal to me, something that I could follow.

There are other definitive signs at Pueblo Bonito, markers that once extended clear across the Colorado Plateau. I have identified seven such markers: corn as a primary food source, the importation of birds for ceremonial use, black-on-white pottery embellished with strict geometric forms, elaborate masonry construction, subterranean kivas, alignments with astronomical and geographic features, and, of course, T-shaped portals. In this business of reassembling an ancient world, I had these primary keys to work with.

Another, less tangible sign is mobility. The Anasazi were travelers, driven by the Southwest's undulating topography, pushed and pulled by the coming and going of rain. Some researchers believe that the Anasazi drove themselves out by overfarming and by depleting wood supplies that were used for cooking fires and construction, but this is too simple an explanation. If one follows trails of archaeological markers, a pattern becomes visible of people constantly coming and going, arriving and disappearing at almost regular intervals. Although there is evidence of failing resources, the majority of Anasazi populations appear to have dealt with their problems by moving rather than by perishing.

. . .

As the shadows lengthened at the end of the day, Adam and I walked casually into the plaza-like opening in the center of Pueblo Bonito, where we skirted around kivas set deep into the ground. A circular theater of ruins surrounded us, doorways and windows bright in the last light. Behind the burials that once graced Pueblo Bonito's northern perimeter rose the brassy cliffs of Chaco Canyon.

The sun fell until its last orange bead clipped out of sight. "There it goes," Adam said, marking off another day.

We were the last people here, listening to car doors slam and seeing the red flicker of taillights in the distance as tourists returned home. In the gathering twilight a ranger arrived on her rounds. She was from Alabama, wearing a gun and a radio, her hat brim stiff. Politely, she told us it was time to go. And politely, we went.

As we drove away from Pueblo Bonito and out the gated entrance, followed by the ranger, I noticed an official work truck parked there and a uniformed Navajo woman inside. I looked back and saw the woman swing the gate closed behind us and secure it with a padlock. Then, she, too, drove away, and Chaco again belonged to no one, the moon tumbling unhindered through crumbling buildings.

Part Two

THE ROAD NORTH

Looking North

PUEBLO ALTO

I once saw a pair of Anasazi sandals so beautifully made that I right away thought of striding across the land in them, each step proud. They were loom-woven out of white dogbane, their thread count so fine I could hardly detect any weave at all. The curator who lifted them from a drawer in a museum did not offer them to me. They were too precious, the prize of the museum's holdings. She turned them slowly in her cotton gloves, close to her chest, as if she, too, wished to put them on and begin a journey. They had never been worn, not a nick of use showing on their edges, not even the trouble of sand or dirt. They were at least a thousand years old.

Walking people, travelers, those who lived on the Colorado Plateau in the early centuries A.D. are well known for their sandals. You find pieces of discarded sandals chewed and gathered in wood rat nests. Many rock art panels have images of sandal prints walking straight up the cliffs. There are sandals made of disks that cover just the balls of the feet for running, and more traditional sandals with which to walk cross-country.

The curator turned this fine pair so that their soles faced me. There I saw a delicate, woven pattern. It was a geometric image raised slightly along both soles in order to leave a message on the ground wherever the wearer walked, like stamping a seal into hot wax. I moved closer, peering at these raised designs of zigzags and square-edged spirals, imagining all the other sandals of the era with their own woven patterns, individual insignias stamped in the sand

and dust of the Colorado Plateau. People left tracks, and in these tracks they placed their identities. I pictured a person a thousand years ago dropping down to one knee and reading a print on the ground to determine who exactly had passed through.

These people were travelers from the start. Well before Chaco they had a history of burning their pit-houses in rituals of departure, then moving en masse to some other place. They were road builders, itinerants in a home landscape, and when I saw the stamp of these sandals, I immediately knew they had been leaving premeditated communiqués all across the desert, messages trailing out wherever they went.

I thought of these perfect white sandals as I began a foot journey north from Chaco Canyon into the open desert beyond. I had set water caches along a due north-south line known as the Great North Road that begins at Pueblo Alto. I had driven out on wandering dirt roads and buried gallon jugs in the sand, marking them with broken sticks so that I could find them again. These caches followed a series of great houses extending from Chaco toward the San Juan River well beyond the horizon, as well as a prehistoric road aiming straight north.

I started walking at Pueblo Bonito, carrying a week or two of supplies on my back. Late on that hot September day, I climbed out of Chaco Canyon to the highest point around, a handmade hill. I walked to the top of this rise and found myself surrounded by the weathered remains of the first great house built on this ancient road. It was the twelfth-century enclave of Pueblo Alto, most of it buried by wind and dust. Its last walls stood no more than half an inch above the surface, just enough so that I could see the compact insignia of a floor plan. With its vestiges of kivas and room blocks, the place looked like the impression made by a Japanese kanji carved onto a wooden chop and pressed firmly onto the dry parchment of northwest New Mexico.

Pueblo Alto's floor plan contains basic formalities that one would expect around Chaco: an ideogram of rectangular rooms and circular kivas bound by an arcing exterior wall on a point of land with the best possible vantage. It is unmistakably Anasazi. The sky around it is huge, every horizon brought to bear, making the ruin even more remarkable. I stood motionless at the tip of this great house, the low, angling sun still hot with summer.

I have long had a love for setting out on journeys, balanced at the starting line, every decision waiting to cast me into the future. I grew up in motion. I have never lived outside the Southwest, yet in my childhood I rarely had the same home or lived in the same state for more than a year or two at a time. Well before adulthood I believed that all was right with the world only when I was standing at the brink of every possibility, a voyage not yet taken unraveling before me.

As I stood at Pueblo Alto, I could see, about a mile in the foreground, a dry wash winding in and out of itself like a snake gliding across the sand. Beyond it was nothing, a country of arid, rolling steppes. Oblivion. If I had come nine hundred years earlier, I would have been presented with deeply cut lines radiating out from Pueblo Alto, roads built to the far corners of the world. The Great North Road was only one avenue leading to and from this place, part of a network of thoroughfares that required more labor to build than even the great houses. Workers transported unknown tons of earth, cutting and filling to keep roads straight regardless of the topography they passed through. Where it would have been far more efficient to jog around some butte or lone cliff, the roads aimed straight ahead, incorporating costly ramps or carved stairs directly up to the top.

The word *roads* is probably a misnomer. Although many are wide enough to handle multiple lanes of car traffic and they are outlined into the distance by curbs of rock and broken pottery, they seem too large for mere transportation. Instead they were likely formal processions, long public spaces akin to the National Mall in Washington, D.C. There is still healthy debate over how many ancient roads existed around Chaco. More than one hundred miles of roads have been soundly documented, and nearly three hundred miles of partial roads can still be seen. Some researchers believe that the roads continue for a thousand miles, going this way and that.

Most roads around Chaco dwindle into nothing the farther one walks from a great house, and then they reappear along the same straight line, becoming visible again as they reach the next great house. Then they dwindle again, all the while keeping their flawless bearings. One segment points straight to another from twenty, thirty, forty miles away, as if the two were linked by surveyors. In the late eleventh and early twelfth centuries, these roads were lengthened and formal monuments were built along them all the way into what is now Colorado, Utah, and Arizona. A cultural unity was spreading from Chaco outward as great houses cropped up like missions. There was a smell of empire in the air.

I was standing at the start of the Great North Road. This was one of the longest, most complete roads in the Anasazi world, stretching more than fifty miles from Pueblo Alto toward the distant San Juan River. Silent now, save for the snap of the hot late-summer wind, the Great North Road was practically invisible beneath the enormous sky. I felt like a straggler arriving nine centuries too late. I was ready, nonetheless, standing on the brink of a voyage, the walls of an upstart empire fallen around my feet.

. . .

But it was not yet time to leave. I had to wait until the right hour. Only when the stars came out would I be certain of the path ahead. I paced along Pueblo Alto's crumbled northern face, stepping over fields of rubble and walls, waiting as the sun left the sky, its spangles and streaks of light catching in high cirrus clouds. A young crescent moon lay low in the southwest, grazing the distant black rumple of the Chuska Mountains. In the drifting coolness, darkness lifted out of the east, and suddenly I saw it there, a pinprick of a star. It was the one star I was looking for, Polaris, dependable and due north in the sky.

The doubtless finger of this star pointed through windows and hallways all across this region, where buildings were aligned with the sky's axis. It emerged, as it did every night, in the center of a prominent T-shaped portal at Casa Rinconada. The star's light pointed out a line that led to my water caches, the course of the Great North Road. I gathered my gear and followed the star into the night.

Visibility

THE GREAT NORTH ROAD

I walked under the sun, middle of the day, early September. The Great North Road was nowhere to be seen, just colorful rows of brittle clay badlands stretching around me. I traveled across filigree cracks as a bluish dust rose and fell behind me.

The only way I knew the road was here was by the arrow on my compass. While my senses drifted out among dry arroyos and rambling horizons, I kept the red arrow pointing straight ahead, trying to stay with it.

The compass led to a weathered coyote den that looked like a sad, toothless mouth in the ground. I got down on my hands and knees and nosed into its wilted entrance, the soil cracked and hot under my hands. In the den's entrance, spiderwebs hung heavy with tiny pendants of fallen clay. It was the only shade I had seen in hours, not big enough even to get my head into. Nobody was home.

I got up and walked on, past pillars of purple and green clay. I finally found a hole eroded from the ground, something large enough for me to fit into. It was a sinkhole, and I crawled straight down into it, reaching a cave where I shrugged off my gear. I pulled off my hat and relaxed in the shade. A spear of daylight entered above me, deflected by the walls of this pit so that it never touched me. I set out my carefully rationed bottles of water. Every move I made smelled of dust. I took out my notes—a handful of papers—and some satellite images and aerial photographs.

I spread these images across my lap and looked for the road I was supposed to be following. At times four, even six, roads paralleled one another through here, corridors built nearly two hundred feet wide when added all together. This processional was visible from the sky, from space, but from the ground everything just blended together, stripped by a thousand years of erosion. I knew I was in the right place, though. Along the way I had found sherds from ceramic vessels, objects left in the same years that European Crusaders were first sacking Jerusalem on the other side of the world. The age of the pottery and its path from south to north told me what I needed to know: I was following an ancient line.

I once traveled one of these pre-Columbian roads with an archaeologist. In the cool of the evening, while we were sitting at our meager camp, he told me that he thought the roads were actually monuments. Camped not far from a ruined, half-buried great house, I listened to the relaxed tempo of his voice as he talked about the meaning of the word *monument,* its root being *monere,* to remind. These roads, he believed, were built ceremonially, features to be remembered down through the years, connecting old settlements to new ones. He said the word *monument* made him think of a mountain, *mon,* and the mind, *ment.*

"Mountains of the mind," he said. "I think that is what these roads were."

The terrain of northwest New Mexico is mostly flat and unbroken. People may have built roads to give the place some definition, rendering it on a human scale. They inscribed their minds onto the land.

The most abundant resource in this desert is visibility. To set a corridor from one horizon to the next would have been an act of cultural magnificence. Perhaps the Great North Road had been used for moving goods from one place to another, but it did not need to be thirty or forty feet wide to accomplish a purely economic goal, and certainly it did not need to run four or six roads abreast as it does in places. Something else was going on, something beyond simple function.

Gwinn Vivian, a longtime scholar of Chaco, sees these roads as more symbolic than utilitarian. Vivian once told me, "The straightness, or at least their directness, was because they needed to be seen from great distances. That's opposed to a more winding road that might have been more efficient, but you would only be able to see it here and there. When you've got one straight damn road you can see for miles and miles, that's a psychological effect."

I felt a sharp prick on the back of my neck. I put the images down in my lap and reached behind my collar to pluck off a bloodsucking insect, a kissing bug—*Triatoma protracta,* the western conenose. It was an opportunist down in this shaded hole, waiting for animals like myself to crawl in seeking shelter. It was no larger than a shirt button. Its wiry legs struggled for purchase, and I flicked it into the dark, where it righted itself and started back for me.

I waited for its return, tipping my head back and resting in the shade. Misshapen stalactites of clay hung from the ceiling. When the bug reached me again and began climbing along my shin, I picked it up and tossed it. This went on for a long time, until I fell asleep and the bug finally got the blood that it wanted.

. . .

I walked back and forth for days across badlands and expanses stubbled with sage. Every now and then I spotted a gentle crest where the road had been dug, but I was never entirely certain of what I was seeing. It could have been the work of the wind or coincidences of soil and erosion. I knew field archaeologists who had eyes for these ancient roads and could see them clearly. I was just learning this art. With my eyes charged, anticipation at full throttle, I saw roads everywhere: channels formed by the way sage had grown along invisible water lines, clearings made by the passage of generations of jackrabbits. Abandoned fence posts lined up in rows leading beyond the horizons, marking townships and ranges. Anthills stood like miniature great houses, where ants streamed along their own processionals, carrying treasures to their queen. Meanwhile, the sky was laced with white lines of passenger jets defining routes between the larger cities of my own civilization, a daytime ceremony that at night became points of light flashing through a bed of stars. I felt as if I were walking among layers of roads, the Great North Road being one of the least apparent of them all.

. . .

Near sunset one day I headed for a cone-shaped butte and climbed its steep flank, looking for a view. It was the first place in many miles I could get high enough to see the surrounding land—a butte standing in a council of buttes, each looking as if it were on stilts, each wearing a flat cap of rock on its head. As my boots carried me up the soft clay slope, a vista spread out before me. In most of the Southwest, a rise of a couple of hundred feet is nothing, but in this sheer, open country I felt as if I were being thrown straight into the sky. At the top I found a smooth, narrow block of caprock, where I dropped my pack and turned slowly to take in the full circle of the earth. I would camp on this high point for the night.

The butte's sunset shadow extended at least a mile into the east, a cone of shade running over meager washes and a few stranded junipers. To the south I faced a half-moon balanced on its own axis, a manila pirouette low on the southern horizon. The moon was due south, I noticed. This meant that the line equally dividing the moon's dark and light sides pointed straight at Pueblo Alto, now a couple of days behind me and barely in view from here.

Some researchers believe that the Anasazi planned their settlements and monuments to line up exactly with trends in the landscape. Dennis Doxtater, an architecture professor at the University of Arizona who has studied how various cultures align themselves on the land, took a close look at the Chaco region and discovered startling configurations. He plotted on a map every prominent archaeological site in this part of northwest New Mexico, along with the summits of the highest nearby mountains, mesas, and buttes. When Doxtater drew lines between these points—even if they were over the horizon, a hundred miles out of view from each other—a pattern emerged. Lines radiating from Casa Rinconada in Chaco Canyon passed directly through a number of great houses and straight through the centers of their largest kivas to meet significant landmarks in the distance. On his map he saw flawlessly symmetrical angles and intersections that when added together made a nearly irrefutable argument: the Anasazi, Doxtater believed, had intentionally nested themselves into a georitual landscape with impressive accuracy, possibly utilizing surveyor/priests and astronomers to determine where sites should be built.

Doxtater ran a line from the great kiva of Casa Rinconada on the floor of Chaco Canyon, out the center of its northern T-shaped portal, directly over the rim through a conspicuous gateway at Pueblo Alto, and straight to this cluster of buttes almost twenty miles away. Here the line continues through a throng of ruins and a collapsed great house, setting up an impressive long-distance alignment. He concluded that these buttes must have been a crucial axis in a landscape of "spirit lines."

Pinning this idea onto a more utilitarian model, Doxtater wondered if such a precise and far-reaching knowledge of landscape might have allowed groups of people to move along preexisting lanes of travel during times of drought without causing territorial disputes. The supposedly ceremonial sites scattered along these many pre-Columbian roads may have simply been a map to follow in both times of need and times of pilgrimage. Setting out toward a different ecological niche—as would have been demanded frequently by this environment—various groups may have been free to travel along lines connecting ceremonial sites and landmarks, perhaps the same general tracks used for the previous ten thousand years.

Inventing the Anasazi world from what we now see on the ground is a flight of imagination. But at least there is no doubt that the Anasazi constructed places to peer across the earth at one another, with causeways set into the ground at incredible cost linking these sites either continuously or by directing the eye. As a novice, unable to claim the long cultural heritage of the Anasazi, even I could stand upon a butte and see this, the moon half-opened and half-closed like a clamshell above the skyline. If a georitual landscape like the one so many Southwest scholars envision is possible anywhere, that place is here.

The sun went through its final throes, polishing the sky with a bright amber light, chasing the shadow of this butte and me for miles into the east. As I turned toward my gear and unbuckled a water bottle, I noticed that cut into this caprock were the remains of a massive hearth. As I sat down at the edge of this hearth, I noticed an ashen darkness to the soil within it, the remains of ancient fires preserved by the aridity. Pieces of broken pottery lay about, signs that long ago this place was well used.

I knew that archaeological surveyors had discovered hearths on these buttes while mapping the Great North Road. It has been suggested, rather obviously, that people lit signal fires here. What other reason could there be to come to a narrow slab of caprock high on the landscape where there is not room for even the smallest habitation and light huge fires? A bonfire on this point would have been clearly visible from Pueblo Alto, as well as from a number of other high points in the area also marked with the dark soil of ancient fires. I picked up one of the potsherds at my feet. Not from a prosaic piece of gray cooking ware, it was instead from a decorated piece of black-on-white pottery, which told me that this had been a prominent place in the minds of these people—so prominent that they had brought their finer wares here.

In the past I had slept on some of the other high points visible on the horizon. I could barely glimpse a cap of rock far to the northeast, where I had once spent a night with my wife and child. A furious thunderstorm had pummeled us that night as bolts of lightning struck the ground and a stiff rain swept by. In the morning, when the storm had cleared, I had stood on that high point, where remnants of a pre-Columbian shrine were located. The storm had left the atmosphere remarkably clear, and using binoculars I had been able to see the crest of Mesa Verde in Colorado and a notch in the northernmost horizon, more than seventy miles away, where a mountainous great house had been constructed at a place called Chimney Rock. I had turned in the other direction and seen, some twenty miles in the distance, a nip on the southeastern horizon where this very butte I was currently camping on lifts along the Great North Road. Chaco is clearly visible from here, its farthest landmarks standing on tiptoes, peeking over the horizon. Fires lit on these high points could have swiftly relayed messages north, deep into the Rocky Mountains, or west over the Chuska Mountains and down the other side, where Anasazi ruins now rest in northern Arizona. Communications could have been sent across the Four Corners into the erotic sandstones of Utah or south to the headwaters of the Little Colorado River.

Positioned on a great hearth atop this butte at sunset, I imagined spectacular sky-lighting fires, with flames curling upward as the sweating fire tender stepped back and shielded his face. Such high signals may have been torches of warfare or of ceremony. Perhaps fires were lit at the winter solstice to put a call out in the searing cold of this high desert, letting communities know that they were not alone, that they were members of a nation of great houses and villages extending beyond the horizons. I envision dry brush going up like straw, flashing brightly into branches of juniper wood. Then the surrounding nightscape would have unfolded, settlements flickering to life as if fireflies had been let out into the dark.

As I sat at the edge of this lofty hearth, I brushed my fingertips through dry frills of ricegrass and a single sprig of dropseed grass. Pieces of burned pottery lay all around, stuck in rock cracks or prostrate on the hearth's floor. A fire had not been lit here for centuries.

The sky drifted into night as a stiff wind split around the head of the butte. I hunched my back against the wind, feeling the hot breath of day fading on my neck. I ate my meal—a few squares of dried ginger, a bead of honey on my tongue, fists of nuts, and an entire quart of water guzzled down into the dry recesses of my body. As the half-moon slowly capsized into the southwest, I pulled my wool serape over me to break the wind and curled my body underneath, gaps tucked closed. I kept a peephole open, the wool pulled back from my eyes so that I could see the dark stretch of earth below. I saw no sprinkles of town lights, not even a ranch's blue-star vapor light. You could see a match struck fifteen miles away out here.

I once spoke with an archaeologist named Tom Windes who had worked for more than thirty years researching Chaco. He was one of the surveyors who had first studied these roads in the 1970s. Windes told me he had spent many nights in the desert contemplating the sky, feeling the ground beneath his back.

"I'm just a city kid—what the hell do I know about the outdoors?" Windes had said. "Where I grew up, you couldn't even see the skies at night. It's a wondrous thing to me to be around Chaco at night and look at that universe and have that feeling of how you fit in. You never get that back east, never. You can't see the kind of universe that's visible here. You grow up in trees and lights, and you can't see anything. You come out here, and it's clear for a hundred miles in every direction. That's a different mind-set. Each landscape allows or inhibits perspective, and that creates the culture. Views like you get out here, these make their own people."

. . .

The day I met Windes, I walked into his office with a satchel full of papers, stopping when I saw he was busy. At the far end of a room that stretched like a narrow closet, Windes sat in his chair swiveling across the floor, the phone cord following him as he moved from desk to desk, flipping open files and maps, rolling back, tapping his pen on paper. He spoke into the phone with a quick voice, explaining exactly what was needed: a compiled analysis of tree-ring dates. He wanted it quickly, a last-minute request.

Windes glanced up and saw me at his door. His hand waved me in and gestured at a vacant chair as he continued his conversation. Just behind him was a map tacked to the wall, and I recognized the topographic lines as those of the Chaco region. Across the map's printed intervals, Windes had drawn rays of straight lines, a network of rules crossing back and forth.

Thirty years earlier, when Windes was first working as an archaeologist surveying around Chaco, he and his crew kept finding slight mounds out in the desert. These mounds were all over the place, but they hardly deserved note compared to the great houses being documented at the time. There was little architecture attached to these scattered mounds, just some low, crumbled walls that looked like foundations for structures never completed. Very few artifacts were visible on them, and the surveyors debated about what to call them in their reports, even thinking that perhaps they should not be listed at all.

Then, digging into one of these humps, Windes came upon a bowl delicately carved out of stone, its lip inset, where a lid was seated. When he uncovered the bowl, he found a handful of turquoise inside. He looked up from this nameless site, peered across the land, and suddenly realized that he was in a very important place.

These mounds that they had nearly skipped over were each situated at a specific point—not just a high point, but one in view of no fewer than two other high points. There was a pattern. Windes started exploring lines of sight and contours in the topography, sending people to stand atop sites in the dark of night and light flares so that the old relays could be seen. He found that these sites, located twenty or thirty miles apart, had been created to communicate with each other. They were signal stations.

Sitting in his office, I could barely hear a woman's voice on the other end of the phone. She was trying to write down what he said but was unable to keep up. Windes smiled and said, his voice slowing, "Okay. Relax. Don't stress about it. I'm sure you'll find everything, and I'll look for it on my desk next week."

He hung up the phone and, without even taking a breath, leaned toward me and extended his hand to shake mine. He reclined in his chair and said, "You wanted to ask me about this signal system."

Windes is a trafficker of data. He gathers sizes and numbers. Ratios. Categories. He has rain gauges set up all over the desert, checking on precipitation patterns. Potsherds he finds are carefully labeled: Gallup Black-on-White, Mesa Verde White ware, White Mountain Red ware. He records each one, keeping track of how many have been found in each place. For decades he has been drilling plugs of wood out of ceiling beams and wall posts at archaeological sites, sending his cores to a tree-ring lab to determine the years or even the seasons when the wood was cut. This gives him a fairly accurate idea of when each site was constructed.

"Yes, the signal system," I said.

"Communication system," Windes said, planting his words like a solid explanation. "That's what it is, a network for relaying information."

"Is that the map?" I asked, pointing at the wall behind his head.

He did not have to look.

"Yes, that's the map," he said, his voice jaunty with the inflections of a comedian. "The system they had is engineered, no question about it. It links everything out there. People don't talk about it much. It's always roads, roads, roads. But what about these signals? How come we don't talk about them more? We've demonstrated that they are not random, that they are clearly planned. You've got to pause to think about it. These Anasazi guys really had it together.

I mean, this is phenomenal. You could flash messages in minutes across the whole Chaco world. It even looks like a dual-route system in some places, so if one went down, you would have another line to back it up. Whatever the hell they were talking about over these distances, it must have been pretty damned important to build such an elaborate system."

As I listened to Windes, I thought that his mind must never rest. As he spoke, his hands bounced from place to place, touching a piece of paper, tapping on his knees, returning to the same piece of paper. His movements were not neurotically quick. They were merely busy, ceaseless.

He did not think that fire was necessarily a key component of this system. He had found signs of large fires at a number of sites—such as Pueblo Alto and a butte along the Great North Road—but for the most part smaller sites, which he called shrines, revealed no charcoal or ash. He thought these were mirror relay stations, perhaps using plates of knapped obsidian flashing in the sun, or even pyrite mirrors like those used in Mesoamerican signaling systems of the same era.

I asked him about the exact placement of these sites, if they were on every high point around Chaco.

"No, not at all," he said. "They're very select. I cheated and figured out the pattern by looking at USGS maps from the sixties and fifties. When they made those maps, they did the same thing people a thousand years ago did. They went out on the topography, and they looked around to find which points were going to visually connect to as many other points as possible. They climbed up, and they stuck in steel stakes and took bearings so they could make their nice maps. They were right on top of these shrines, and they never knew it. I'd find these sites right under those old USGS datum points, so I thought, Hell, I'll just look at the USGS maps and find out where their points are. I had a high degree of success, because they were looking for the same kind of thing. They were looking for range. They were interested in visual linkages."

Windes did not bother coming up with a concrete reason that such a network would have been created. Military intelligence, religious rites, tribal gossip—who can say what the system was used for? He liked the military concept best, though. It made the most sense to him—a warning system to relay the movements of enemies, scouts checking back in. Regardless of purpose, it existed. Whether it was ever used to signal information from place to place or not, this array of linkages is evidence that these people were well connected.

"We just stumbled on it," Windes said, still amazed at his good fortune thirty years later. "We almost missed it. We almost thought it was nothing. It was that narrow of a margin, and we might have never known. Funny how that kind of dumb luck just keeps happening out there."

. . .

At midmorning I came across a dirt road cutting east to west across the Great North Road. As I stepped onto its graded surface, the stiffness felt peculiar beneath my feet. A translucent skim of the Rocky Mountains was beginning to show a long way off in Colorado. I crossed the road and walked several feet beyond its shoulder, where I stopped at a dead branch of sage stuck in the ground. I had left it here days ago. I sank to my knees and started digging straight down with my bare hands, shooting sand out behind me and uncovering the round shoulder of a plastic jug. With one hand shoveled underneath and the other one up around the jug, I lifted out one gallon of water, then another. Both jugs were cool to the touch. I placed one against my forehead, enjoying the sensation. I unscrewed the caps and filled bladders that I kept in my pack. A few drops of water escaped, diamonds hitting the ground, then disappearing immediately. I was aware of their loss—minor but obvious. An unintended offering, I thought.

Among the various ruins I had come upon in the previous days—mounds and bare walls standing in the desert—I had not imagined turquoise or brightly feathered birds hidden inside them. I had thought instead of their deepest rooms storing ceramic ollas filled with water. Most of the broken pottery documented along this road came from pitchers and water jars. I envisioned these roadside outposts as well houses—sunlight never allowed to enter and slow

Highly decorated black-on-white ceramic pitcher from eleventh-century Chaco. In storage at the American Museum of Natural History. CRAIG CHILDS

evaporation through clay, the cavernous smell of moisture. Maybe pilgrims heading to Chaco kept these outposts alive, hauling extra water and leaving it here like a toll as they passed.

The presence and absence of water ruled the people of this landscape. They were an elemental people, their civilization poised on a sharp edge of nature, the environment swirling and booming around them as if they had colonized the face of the sun. No matter how illustrious the ceremonies, how colorful the processions, the priests or caretakers would have eaten sand in every meal, sweat dripping into their eyes in the middle of the day.

With a knife I diced the freshly drained water jugs and packed them into my gear. I followed the modern dirt road for a short distance. Even though it was going the wrong way, east to west, its smoothness was appealing—a little taste of easy walking, no need for a compass in my hand.

In the distance two parked trucks came into view. A couple of men, stick figures from this far away, leaned casually over the bed of one of the trucks. They must have been talking to each other. They were too far away to notice me until I got closer, and they both turned, old Navajo ranchers, heads leaning to watch my slow approach. My boots dragged a little; my shoulders were hanging. The man closest to me had working hands, gnarled knuckles bunching at the truck bed. The other wore a green shirt, scuffed leather boots, and thick glasses. He observed me as if through a telescope.

We were within at least a quarter mile of the Great North Road in one direction or another—but I was not sure which direction. I stopped in front of the men, squinting in the sun. They looked me up and down. I had a tear in one knee of my pants from crossing a barbed wire fence, my shirt was caked with salt, and I was carrying only a small pack that had seen better days. I must have looked like a battered rowboat floating far out at sea. They looked the same to me. I nodded a greeting, showing them an open hand. Slowly they nodded back.

"If I were heading due north from here, how far do you think until I hit the river?" I asked, my voice a little quicker and higher-pitched than I wanted.

"The river?" one said, as if I were delusional, as if there was no river out here, never had been.

Turning their heads to look north, they both shaded their eyes. There was no reason for them to know how far the river was from here, when dirt roads could be taken to reach a highway, and the highway followed north to the river. No one actually walks out here anymore.

The conversation was short. There was no agreement about mileage. They said it was a long way. But it was good to hear human voices, a sound other than the wind. I said goodbye and kept walking. I felt rich with the weight of fresh water on my back. I could have gotten out a map, but I had not looked at the map in days, walking back and forth on a northward line searching for ruins, for broken pottery, for bits of glassy rock left by someone knapping a tool long ago.

As I walked, I checked over my shoulder now and then. As long as I could see the two Navajo men, they stayed put, leaning over the truck bed, watching me fade across the sphere of the earth.

Decline

KUTZ CANYON

Boots tied together at their laces swayed from my right fist as I traveled barefoot through a gusting sandstorm, my ankles stinging from blowing dust. It felt good to have these hot boots off, my feet free. On my back I carried my last gallon of water northward through Kutz Canyon toward the San Juan River.

It felt like the wind was peeling me apart. A rip in my sleeve blew open like a balloon. I walked straight into the windstorm—the white zinc plain of the wash sent skyward. I passed a juniper tree uprooted by an old flood and left stranded like the rib cage of a mammoth. Other castaways lay about, tumbleweeds and dead shadscale, the wind constantly thinning their woody bones. The wash was smooth and wide, passing through a canyon made of slumped, dry clay—eerie pinnacles and misshapen gray faces of badlands.

The last sign of the Great North Road was a weathered stairway some miles back with wooden laths barely preserved, the stairway's remains eroding out of a badland slope. No one knows whether the road keeps going north. The land is too weathered to tell, divided into slender gullies too steep for walking. Airplanes have not been able to track the Great North Road through here, nor can satellites or ground surveyors find it.

I reached down and flicked a piece of pottery out of the hardpan. It was a corrugated sherd pebbled by floods and wind, edges smoothed on its tumble from somewhere upstream. Transported over the centuries, it was simply another piece of the earth, a victim of erosion.

I did not place this sherd back where I found it. I let it fall from my hand as I walked. The wind ticked it across the ground.

. . .

Early in the twelfth century, things changed in Chaco, far behind me now. A hot drought rolled through—nothing out of the ordinary, but enough to tip the balance. Maybe the priests or governors who had promised rain and gotten it for centuries suddenly couldn't deliver, still preaching at the sky, stomping their feet, but now dusty and ineffectual. Or the people's focus merely shifted, the great houses of Chaco centuries old and not glimmering like they once did—at least not enough to rivet the attention of a nomadic people passing across the country. Chaco had grown beyond its canyon and sent out many tendrils. With the right combination of drought and timing, new great houses built in better-watered territory to the north began to prosper, stealing some of Chaco's thunder.

Chaco began to fade, becoming more of a residential site than the political-religious focal point it had once been. Its temples turned into living quarters, as people spilled into the once uninhabited spaces of Pueblo Bonito and the surrounding great houses, building hearths on the floors and remodeling spacious rooms into many smaller, more efficient chambers. Large-scale maintenance of these core great houses all but ceased, and their hulls began to creak from lack of care. Some rooms were abandoned, and their roofs weakened, rickety as mineshafts. I cannot help thinking that a slow despair crept among the final residents of Chaco, sharpened by the sudden cacophony of a crashing ceiling, a row of rooms caving in during the night, followed by a chilling silence.

The exotic wealth that had flowed for so long ceased. The grip of overfarming tightened as the entire surrounding landscape was denuded of firewood that would make winter survivable. The skeletons of children buried in Chaco trash piles show severe anemia and other diseases of malnutrition in this period of decline. Violence erupted. Rooms have been found cluttered with bones bearing the marks of weapons. Burials were dug up, funerary objects disturbed, skulls kicked around like soccer balls. Some of these burials were robbed, or at least desecrated, while they were still fresh, bones still articulated with muscle and tissue, as if vendettas were being waged, clan histories destroyed in feverish acts of vandalism. I think of other times of social turbulence in recorded history, when rivers were turned into mass graves, bodies bloated downstream from the killing fields. What might be hidden in the downstream wash of Chaco, out where the floods form braids across the desert? Perhaps there lies the fate of Chaco. It was a good time to leave.

And here lies the most common misconception about Chaco—the idea that it collapsed, that the Anasazi failed. Certainly, the canyon itself was not forgotten, nor was it ever entirely abandoned. Great houses saw occasional renovation and additions; the great kivas of Pueblo Bonito were refurbished with new paint and artifacts around the beginning of the fourteenth century. Any architecture added after the mid-twelfth century was modest, a step down from what had come before, but the place did not collapse. People's attention simply moved elsewhere, putting Chaco on the back burner.

Motion up ahead startled me from my slow, steady pace. I stopped to watch a truck gradually emerge from liquid mirrors of mirages, its shape half-concealed by the gauze of the sandstorm. It was a water truck, its metal container pitted with corrosion where much of its white paint had flecked off. It was an old-model working truck crossing from one side of the canyon to the other, down along a road I imagined I would be seeing soon. I figured the truck was here to service well pads and unmanned compressor stations scattered throughout this region. In the past days of walking, I had seen crowds of pump jacks drawing natural gas from Cretaceous shales, greasy machines moving up and down like old men bending to pick pennies off a sidewalk.

A few minutes later a pickup appeared, a Day-Glo flag hoisted high over the cab marking it as a company vehicle. A head turned in the cab window, a faraway face looking at me, wondering what queer apparition was floating down the wash this afternoon. The truck did not stop or even slow to see who I might be.

I reached the road a few minutes after that. It was a gash of concrete running perpendicular to the wash, the sharpest possible angle of erosion. I stepped onto it as if onto a deck, slowed my pace, and then stopped in the middle. My toes studied the pocked surface where concrete was eaten away. The downstream side of this road was badly undercut from flash floods mining into concrete and rebar. A sturdy guardrail of pipe stood just below that, its posts gowned with water-driven debris. The pipe had been installed to catch vehicles that might be swept away in a flood, preventing them from being entombed somewhere downstream, doors sealed closed, cab filled to the roof with mud. What a feat of labor, I thought, just to get a simple road through this canyon.

The road's surface was marked with different ages of concrete, signs of patching and rebuilding. Even with that work, a crater had collapsed into one end of the road, big enough to swallow a truck, leaving just enough space to drive around it. The off-color patchwork of repairs reminded me of a pre-Columbian public water system in Chaco Canyon that had been rebuilt seven times after seven catastrophic floods. It is hard to hold your ground in this country.

That night I dropped a quick and sparse camp beneath an overpass where a four-lane highway spanned the wash, the road from Aztec, New Mexico, to Albuquerque, a hundred miles or so away. Kutz Canyon was really not a canyon by the time it met this bridge. The wash had opened up, taking in some cottonwood trees and soft, bending thickets of willows. I sat eating from my bag of nuts as vehicles streamed across the bridge overhead, gas workers returning from the fields. They had no idea I was below them tonight, a troll under the bridge.

I walked between the concrete piers in the dark, tracing its vaults with my headlamp. Stains of mud spatters went ten feet high where floods had come slapping and hissing in the past. The concrete pillars were covered with graffiti. As if touring the decorated caves of Lascaux, France, I cast my light along the spray-painted records of life here: *Dorene Norberto, Andrew Charlie married 1983; Jenny Johnson, Andrew Charlie, married 1989; Liana Mae Cisco, Andrew Charlie married 1996.*

Beware of Andrew Charlie, I thought.

After midnight the traffic ceased entirely, not a single vehicle to break the quiet. The wind had fallen off, replaced by the smell of water. I thought it might be the San Juan River, just a few miles away. But the fragrance was more like that of rain than river water. A storm was nearby. If I needed water badly enough, I wondered, could I follow this scent? How many miles would it take until I found the remnants of a storm, shallow lenses of water left in the desert?

Perhaps this was why the Anasazi had moved. They had followed the smell of water, aware of the rains slipping away year by year, retreating from them into the northern highlands. Although there are signs of turmoil at Chaco, the end was probably not as catastrophic and unexpected as many think. It was a predictable end, a routine drought leading people away. At first people may have begun to leave Chaco by rooms, and then by clans, and then by whole villages. Only itinerant households remained in what had once been the triumphant center of the Anasazi world.

. . .

A wind came through all night, sweet and cool with the smell of rain. I woke and gathered my camp beneath the bridge. The traffic had yet to begin, too early for the workers of the gas pads, only the lonely sound of a single vehicle speeding by. I could almost feel rain on my skin, a rare softness of moisture pushing from the west. The sky was still mostly clear but for a few dark, introductory clouds. A sizable storm would be here very soon.

The wash that I followed turned into a mind-boggling field of mud cracks, dry plates breaking like piecrusts beneath my feet. Not far from the overpass I came to the steamship edifices of a gas processing station, its steel bellies rumbling and hissing behind a high chain-link fence. Hazard signs were posted all over as jets of flame shot from escape valves.

Parts of northwest New Mexico are covered with natural gas fields, tens of thousands of pump jacks connected by freshly graded roads. Many of these roads lead to this refinery near the San Juan River, where in the predawn darkness sulfuric lights cast shadows across white arcs of steel. I had to stop and stare.

I stepped up, captivated, draping my fingers through the perimeter fence. Daggers of flame torched the sky, roaring as they burst upward, venting overflow gas. Such incredible industry with not a single person around to pull a lever or check a dial. I was enchanted but repulsed. What have we made of ourselves? I wondered. What hungry, bolt-hearted machine? This processing station supported the wonders of our civilization, spitting fire into the air. After these many days of walking in the desert, existing only as a creature of flesh, damp eyes panning the horizons, I stood awestruck by this apparatus.

In a disquieting way the refinery made me think of Chaco. I remembered rumors I had heard, remarks that Chaco should never have happened, that it is stained with a dark history, with sorcery that once delved too deeply into the supernatural. Some members of the modern Hopi tribe have mentioned to me that they will not visit Chaco Canyon, that an ancient incongruity dwells there. Chaco may have been like a Tibetan temple, with colorful ceremonies and festivals, but it was also like the Mayan world of the time, rife with ritualized violence and human sacrifice. The same knives known to have been used in Mesoamerica for cutting out beating human hearts have been found at Chaco.

In the end Chaco burned. Kivas were set on fire and whole rows of houses with wooden ceiling beams and thatched doors went up in flames. It was a way of leaving things behind, the mark of an intense people on their way to someplace else.

. . .

Once when I was in the field working with three archaeologists on a road network, we gathered for lunch behind the flat hillock of a nameless great kiva, taking shelter from the wind. Broken pottery centuries old was scattered across the ground beneath our packs. Each person had a particular lunch routine, repeated day after day: one man ate handfuls of nuts from a bag, the woman carved slivers of cheese with a knife, and a second man, older than the others, unfolded the wrappings of a sandwich he had made that morning.

We had been out for days looking for undocumented Anasazi roads, taking bearings, standing lined out and shouting back and forth to each other.

The older man, one of the most knowledgeable field archaeologists in the Four Corners, was master to the younger ones. This was obvious in the seating arrangement, the younger two sitting at a polite distance but still facing the master. As he ate, he told us stories.

He talked about sites he had dug, artifacts that had come up from the ground cradled in his hands. Describing a particularly beautiful vessel he had seen, he called it ceremonial, saying it came from a special room in a ruin where priests must have handled it, priests he envisioned wearing turkey feather robes, their headdresses feathered like those of Mayan gods. As an older archaeologist, he was allowed to let his imagination wander, and we listened respectfully.

His thoughts led him to Chaco. You cannot sit with a Southwestern archaeologist for long before Chaco finds its way into the conversation. He wondered out loud if the priests of Chaco had locked themselves in their kivas and eaten nothing but corn.

"Corn pouring in from all directions," he said. "Served in beautiful black-on-white bowls. After long enough sequestered in there, they came out mad with visions."

He said he imagined Anasazi priests prophesizing in their robes, sending workers out to build fire signals and roads, aligning everything with the sun, the moon, the stars. He envisioned these priests occasionally taking out very sharp, leaf-shaped knives and sacrificing people by removing their hearts. Maybe it was all the corn they ate, he said. It drove them mad. He paused, with a wry grin, and observed the horizon. Sage folded and recoiled in the wind. I could not tell how serious he was. The others answered with reserved laughter, not quite agreement, but not disbelief.

I sat chewing on a stick of dried papaya, listening. I thought about his conjecture; it did not seem possible. Too odd, I thought. Prophets ordering the construction of an extensive road network and stellar alignments of buildings merely because they had gone crazy locked in their great houses eating too much corn? Were his comments a prankish yarn, something to get a laugh, to see how the others would respond? His voice was hard to read. He had spoken with a quarter smile on his face.

"You know the recent studies on corn, then?" I asked.

All three glanced at me, waiting.

I continued. "On the psychiatric effects of a corn-only diet?"

He nodded and went back to his sandwich. "I've heard some about it."

This was the first time I had heard a Southwest archaeologist dare mention the study, which linked the eating of corn with chemical changes in the brain. The research was spearheaded by Michele Ernandes at the University of Palermo, in Italy. Ernandes, who had been looking at connections between neurobiology and sacrificial rites in cultures around the world, found that nutrition may play a considerable role in various religious and spiritual states. It has long been known that too much corn can alter brain chemistry and lead to a variety of malnutrition diseases, the likes of which have been revealed by many Anasazi skeletons. Corn lacks two key amino acids, lysine and tryptophan. Also, though it is high in many necessary proteins, minerals, and vitamins, corn's niacin is chemically unavailable to the human body. When corn is made into a sole staple, these deficiencies alter the body's makeup, dropping serotonin levels in the brain to a state similar to chronic sleep deprivation. At its extreme this is clinically linked to obsessive-compulsive disorder, aggression, and even mystical states of ecstasy.

Ernandes's controversial research suggests that these symptoms might have played a role in mass human sacrifices and religious horrors that occurred among the Toltecs, the Mayans, and the Aztecs in late B.C. and early A.D. It was a time of unparalleled splendor in Mesoamerica, pyramids and ball courts spreading across two continents, when native corn reached its peak production. Meanwhile, tens of thousands, perhaps hundreds of thousands, of people were sacrificed every year on stone altars. High atop temples in cities that gleamed like pearl, fresh human hearts were cut out and placed in sacred vessels. This, the study suggested, might have been linked to an overindulgence in corn.

Ernandes did not leave the Southwest out of the study, mentioning a fervor that swept the Anasazi landscape. Terribly disfigured human skeletons have been found from that time, bones polished by cooking, heads severed. The authors of this study believe that corn could have been a factor, that dementia could have occurred on a cultural level.

The implications of this study are unpopular. For most Native Americans, corn is sacred and beneficial. As a food staple, it is a cultural foundation, a plant that gave birth to civilization. Calling it a drug, suggesting its effects are deleterious, is politically dangerous. People living in the Southwest actually figured out how to deal with corn's nutritional deficiencies long ago by eating beans, amaranth, or meat with every traditional meal. This makes up for the missing amino acids. Fire ash, which consists mostly of calcium hydroxide, liberates corn's niacin and is a key ingredient in Hopi piki bread. In this way corn was made safe, perhaps rendering the madness theory obsolete. Still, one can easily imagine priests who did not eat amaranth, beans, meat, or piki bread; prophets religiously indulging in nothing but corn, stewing in smoky, dark kivas, wild with visions. When a drought came and corn no longer arrived, Chaco may have turned sour, the addiction unmet.

The study on corn and madness became nothing more than a passing comment on a windy day, as we leaned against a buried kiva. No one asked the old archaeologist anything else about corn. We just waited for a pause in the wind so that we could pack up and keep moving.

. . .

It smelled like rain as I walked the last mile to the San Juan River. I left the refinery behind, its flames shooting upward as if from the mouth of a circus fire-eater. Now I felt drunk on the smell of water. A storm was pushing in from the west, rain not far away.

Dawn was coming on, its light crossing beneath bellies of clouds as I pushed through tamarisk trees and whips of young willows. Cottonwood trees lifted over my head, sturdy trunks holding up a green planetarium canopy. A damp wind clapped through thousands of heart-shaped leaves, making the sound of moving water, the sound of a river.

Crossing to the Other Side

THE TOTAH

A smooth pan of water, the San Juan River moved steadily in the dawn light. I pushed through vegetation until the water was right at my feet, its edges rippling around tree branches caught in the current.

After walking across the desert, I thought this river seemed impossible, as if it were a smuggling operation transporting a few million gallons of water past me every minute, its surface turning in gentle coils. The air was humid, both from the river and from a tropical storm blown inland and running aground on the Colorado Plateau. There was going to be a good rain. No wishing this time. I looked for a place to cross the river, my hands sliding through tamarisk branches, feeling salty drops of moisture.

The Navajo call this place Totah, a word describing the union of many rivers. The Piedra, Animas, and La Plata all flow down from the Rocky Mountains to the north and join the San Juan River within several miles of one another. These are wildly moody rivers, lifting to torrents as quickly as they fall back to persecuted little creeks. With a big storm coming, today would be their day to run wild.

I stripped to my boxer shorts and waded out through the delta of the wash formed below Kutz Canyon, slogging into thigh-deep mud. Cold water burped up from beneath my feet. I stopped out in the middle, the current sweeping gently around my thighs. Turning so that I could peer along the river's softly spoken corridor, I looked downstream, reminded that my family had once lived about ten miles from here along the riverbank.

I was conceived beside this river. At least that is what I have been told. I first flashed to life in a town built on the bankside ruins of the Anasazi. I figured that somewhere in my body's memory, back in the primeval strike of awareness when sperm and egg tapped each other's shoulders, I carry this water inside me, the first water to prop up my budding cells. Remembering where I had come from, I looked downstream, watching the water go.

I kept moving. Lightning bolted into the sky, then the air thrummed with thunder. The arms of this storm were converging, violet walls caving in from all sides. Desert gullies would run yellow today, and the Animas River would look like chocolate milk. Kutz Canyon would flood behind me, the color of chalk and chicken broth. Colors would churn into the San Juan, creating a luminous brown. Not yet, though. I walked facing upstream as the river curled around my legs. My feet sorted through cobbles, choosing the path of the smaller ones, the lesser currents.

I climbed onto a braided island of tall grass and jogged through halls of cottonwood trees, my legs red in the coolness, salted by the scratch of brush. As thunder dove through the trees, small birds let go of their branches and flitted away. Mourning doves darted ahead of me, wings whistling, and I heard spotted towhees flipping through dry leaves in the underbrush, picking up their last morsels before the rain.

Through days of crossing the open desert, I had seen only ravens in the distance, a few sage sparrows darting about, and once a spiral of vultures rising elegantly on a thermal. Nothing even remotely like the abundance of birds on this island. The riverine forest was filled with the chatter of birds situating themselves for the storm. A bald eagle rose from its dead snag, dark wings opening as it flew, and I slowed my pace, turning to watch it go.

. . .

The evidence of captive birds and feathered artifacts in the Southwest has always been taken as a sign of colorful rituals where priests were robed in feathers, dancers looked almost like birds, and feathered artifacts hung from the rafters. It has also been widely believed that with the decline of Chaco, such ceremonies waned. After Chaco fell into decay, there was never a place on the Colorado Plateau with so much concentrated religious wealth. The traffic in exotic items and turquoise that had reached a busy pace around the rise of Chaco slowed substantially in the twelfth century, and it only follows that the use of birds in ceremonies dropped off as well. As it turns out, however, this was not the case. A researcher named Kathy Roler Durand recently discovered that the use of birds and their feathers increased after Chaco lost its central power, an indication that the Anasazi structure was not necessarily weakened by Chaco's decline.

When I spoke with Durand, I was interrupting her work with bird bones excavated from various sites around New Mexico. In her office she had the entire collection of bird remains from Salmon Ruins—my destination the morning of the coming rain. She was picking through these bones to determine each species—songbirds and raptors, entire complements of waterfowl—all identified from bones and skeletons that had been unearthed. She had found from Salmon Ruins a macaw and a turkey buried together, to her a very curious and auspicious arrangement. Turkeys are known to have been used in Mesoamerica as substitutes for human sacrifices, and macaws signify a connection with the tropical regions where such sacrifices were common. It seems that everywhere Durand found the remains of birds, she also found evidence of ritual life.

Among the birds Durand was cataloging, she began noticing a surprising majority from excavated levels postdating the fall of Chaco. In the period she thought would be absent of birds, she was actually finding a florescence of them.

"Supposedly after Chaco had completely declined, I'm finding that the use of birds just explodes," Durand said. "There are so many different species of birds after Chaco's heyday, just an amazing array, that you know they were not used simply for food. I think they were using the feathers for ceremonies, like the Zuni today who use—what is it—fifty-six different species? So it seems that the use of great houses as ceremonial centers is actually increasing dramatically in the post-Chaco period."

Durand told me this just as she was making the discovery, her voice hopping along on the excitement. Perhaps the construction of great houses in outlying regions had lessened the need for long-distance pilgrimages as people began having their own temples at home. Instead of holding their ceremonies at Chaco, now they could focus on local rituals, actually beefing up their own religious lives.

Durand saw in the Anasazi world a cultural shift accompanying the fall of Chaco, a trend away from impressive wealth toward an even more dedicated form of worship. For her, birds are a key indicator of this shift. Birds began showing up in voluminous numbers in even small houses where prior to the twelfth century she had seen limited samples of avian remains.

Chaco had, indeed, fallen apart. Many great houses had been looted, entire blocks of kivas turned into trash receptacles or burned. Certain precincts had been left to deteriorate as violence became more common. But this may have been only the consequence of a cultural transformation, a reshuffling of priorities. At the same time, smaller, compact great houses were being built not far from the older ones: tight little boxes with a few kivas, their floor plans looking like computer chips rather than the expansive motherboard architecture of Pueblo Bonito, Chetro Ketl, and Pueblo Alto.

"I think more of the focus was on rituals," Durand said. "You see, people left Chaco, but some stayed. I think the people staying had ritual knowledge, and they were parlaying that into nice situations for themselves in the post-Chacoan period. If you look at the modern pueblos, ritual knowledge is wealth. That's where all these birds would have come into play. They were wealth, religious currency."

. . .

High-pitched bird warnings flashed ahead of me through trembling cottonwood leaves. I listened across the island to the coded rhythm of a woodpecker, its hollow drum work echoing back in the forest. As I jogged along, the island soon gave way to the river, and there I reached a cutbank. On the opposite side, exactly where I needed to cross, was a row of large, modern houses built back into the trees.

Picture windows peered across the water from out of deep green forests. I could see motion in some of the houses, people preparing for their day, the upper class of Bloomfield, New Mexico: gas industry employees, agribusiness owners, and government workers sipping their morning coffee.

Damn, I hadn't expected this. I thought I would be crossing in total seclusion, a clean walk from Chaco to Salmon Ruins. Instead I would have to charge partly naked through people's yards.

If I had given it any thought, I would have anticipated development along here. The Totah has long been a popular place to live on the Colorado Plateau. It is a broad flank of land connecting the desert to the highlands north of here, its growing season far better than that of the Chaco region. And it has water, free-flowing water coming down the local rivers. In the twelfth century, great houses were scattered about the Totah, and in between them appeared numerous hamlets and farming villages. The settlement pattern is much the same now as it was then. Preeminent ruins lie beneath the modern towns of Farmington, Shiprock, Bloomfield, and Aztec. The rural countryside is dotted with ranches and Navajo settlements. People have always lived here, and the San Juan River has long been a nucleus.

I had to get past these houses. Salmon Ruins, a late-edition great house, was just beyond, a site that marks the transition between Chaco and what happened afterward. One archaeologist working there felt as if Salmon had been erected by an advance party sent ahead from Chaco, people who did not even live in the place once it was built. Its construction appears to have purposefully coincided with the 18.6-year lunar standstill cycle, as if the work was timed down to the very year. Then Salmon remained virtually unoccupied until a later date, as if a carefully orchestrated migration were in effect.

It has long been debated who built Salmon, whether it was a contingent of Chaco masons and engineers or local people from the Totah imitating the techniques made famous at Chaco. The question is an oversimplification, though. It is like asking who is building the modern suburbs of, say, Phoenix. Is it the Phoenix residents themselves, people from outlying communities, or migrant workers from farther away following a contractor's instructions?*

I moved swiftly, reentering the water, stepping evenly over cobbles and sand waves. Currents mingled around my crotch as I headed for a thicket between two houses. On the other side I thrashed up a bank through barbed, chest-high Russian thistles that raked my cold, reddening skin. I found a clearing and sat there massaging the buzzing scratches all over my thighs and calves. I pulled on my pants and dry shoes.

Someone's dogs—big dogs—were romping at the river's edge. I could hear them. Of course they would find me, following my fresh scent out of the river. I snatched up a stick and rose to my feet just as they entered my clearing, tails wagging, slobber drooling off their tongues.

They had been out for the night, two black Labs, backyard escapees. They both smelled of skunk and sweat, their fur matted. One looked like a rottweiler mix and had a fresh gash across its head from leaping through barbed wire, blood thick as tar. I did not want to raise my voice, lest anyone out to fetch the morning paper hear me and call the Bloomfield police. I stared straight at the dogs and smiled as they panted and snorted, dangerously excited to see me, sloshing foamy saliva on my pants, whipping me with their soaked tails. I waved my stick around, thinking that the desert wilderness was a far safer place than a riverside encampment of houses guarded by dogs. I gave them my sternest, most affirming voice, whispering, "Good pups, good pups. You been out, eh? Keep down. You know how to sit? Sit...sit...down, down, girls."

---

*At a pre-Columbian site almost two hundred miles from Chaco, researchers once marveled at the presence of very accurate Chacoan masonry. Soon it was discovered that the stonework had actually been done in the early twentieth century by a stabilization crew. The crew had previously worked at Chaco, where they closely studied local masonry, and then mistakenly transferred their knowledge when they left to work elsewhere. This may anecdotally explain how styles of building once traveled around the pre-Columbian Southwest. People saw something they liked and took the technique back home, while masons moved from place to place carrying their practiced skills along with them.

Barely interested in my commands, they instead wanted to jump on me, to paw at my face, maybe nip off a bit of flesh before moving on. When one poked its muzzle into my pack, I snapped it on the nose with my stick.

"Go on," I rumbled. "Get outta here. *Git!*"

Which they did, bounding away, but only because they found me not as interesting as they had hoped. They broke pieces of wood as they went, tumbling in the grass, loping with the immeasurable wealth of their freedom. Alarms of yard dogs tripped through the surrounding neighborhood. I listened carefully to their path, mapping the barking trail, trying to decipher a clear way out of all this private property. Dogs were everywhere, erupting suddenly at one another. I closed my eyes, following the two escapees in my mind, setting a path. I ate breakfast quickly, nuts and a lemon drop. Then I shouldered my pack and followed the two black Labs, figuring they had at least broken the trail for me.

Now it was *I* setting off the alarms. An unleashed collie at one house, a small yapping troop at another. I did not look into their eyes as I slipped from one territory to the next, creeping directly beneath bedroom windows and into a ditch crowded with trash, up into someone's hedge, and then sprinting across a patch of mown grass. Lightning seared the air. Everything flashed white for an instant. As I came out along a driveway, thunder hammered the ground. No rain yet. A grove of mailboxes appeared up ahead. Public property, a neighborhood street.

As soon as I reached the mailboxes, I was free. My gait slowed, shoulders dropped. Just a man out for a morning stroll, a small pack on his shoulders. I walked past mobile homes and the warm smells of breakfast. Could I knock on a door? Ask for a sausage, an orange maybe? I had not had a cooked meal in many days.

From behind bushes and a wire fence, a stone wall came into view. I recognized the guild of its stonework. It was the order of masons who had built great houses early in the twelfth century. Salmon Ruins was stashed here, acres of ruins protected behind a feeble fence. The great house had been constructed at about the same time as Pueblo Alto. Salmon and Pueblo Alto were two anchor points, one in the south at Chaco, the other in the north in the Totah. Salmon Ruins' southern wall continued for blocks, its diminutive stones evenly laid. An involuntary smile spread across my face, a sort of laugh. After having walked across the desert, I found myself in a forested neighborhood abutting this ancient compound. I had bridged a gap with my own feet, a distance that many archaeologists consider to have been culturally formidable. It was nothing, though. It could have been done in a few days by someone walking at a faster pace, paying less attention to scraps of artifacts on the ground, more to making time.

Salmon Ruins, forty-five miles north of Chaco, has a bracket-shaped floor plan with a long back wall, two straight wings of room blocks to either side, and a kiva compound in the center. Compared to Chaco, this is a later style of great-house construction. New generations of masons and engineers cut off the majestic curves of their earlier great houses and replaced them with more efficient lines—the new planimetric fashion of the twelfth century. Here the layout of great houses looked more like graph paper than half-moons, but only the exterior shape had changed. The core was basically the same in square footage, placement of kivas and interior plazas, and layout of surrounding rooms. The new and the old great houses could be fit snugly inside each other.

The south wall of Salmon Ruins sent me to a highway where cars swarmed on their way to work, morning traffic loud and relentless. As I turned onto the asphalt shoulder, I wondered how many of these commuters had any idea that a great house was located here—a pinnacle of prehistoric architecture a stone's throw away. Eastbound vehicles streamed with rainwater, windshield wipers slapping furiously. Westbound traffic was dry. As I walked, the sky broke open. Louder than the cars came the roar of fresh, hard rain. I swung a black waterproof poncho over my head and my pack as one of the largest storms of the decade descended on the Totah.

Continuity

AZTEC

Billowing in my black rain poncho, I must have looked like the angel of death crossing the bridge over the Animas River, choked and throbbing with flood debris below. An archaeologist I knew at Salmon Ruins had given me a ride ten miles up to the town of Aztec, New Mexico, to spare me the walk in the rain. He dropped me off at a grocery store, where I bought a loaf of bread I now had tucked under my arm beneath the poncho. I watched half trees tumbling through the water below the bridge, the heft of their branches pounding against pilings, sending concussions up through my soaked boots. All across the Colorado Plateau the storm sent floods down, stories I would be hearing for years from companions of mine who were out in the weather that day. It was a day long to be remembered.

The wind swept up through my poncho, turning me into a swirling black apparition. The rain fell steadily. I tore the bread off in hunks, eating it as I went, taking small, even bites, chewing thoroughly. I had been subsisting primarily out of a light pack of nuts and honey for some time now. I tried to hold back and not devour this sweet, crusty bread too fast. Cheap bread, grocery store bread, but a feast nonetheless. Vehicles hissed by, sending up veils of water that blew a lush and cool wind into my face. Such a fertile smell had probably not visited the town of Aztec for a year or more.

When I reached the other side of the bridge, I turned onto a muddy neighborhood street that was being dug up for repairs, the construction halted on account of the storm, backhoes gathered like sleeping crabs. Had they found anything? I wondered. Down in the earth, had the teeth of a tractor bucket drawn up a skeleton or severed a broad black-on-white serving bowl? Every house was built on top of an archaeological site sealed closed by concrete foundations and streets. After Chaco this was the next-largest, most intensive concentration of people and architecture in the region. It was built not long after Salmon, the next step in a journey.

I did not avoid the mud. I strode right through it, resolved that I could not get any wetter, my pants already drenched well up toward my knees. I walked across the parking lot of Aztec Ruins National Monument, where the only vehicle was a ranger's truck. No one was visiting in the rain. Inside the front doors I pulled back my hood and tucked the bread into my other armpit as I worked a hand into my pocket. A man in a snappy uniform alerted himself, rising to the front desk, where I stopped and withdrew a few dollar bills, damp and in disarray. I had carried this cash all the way up the Great North Road knowing I would need it upon reaching Aztec. I tried to flatten the bills, ironing each one out in my hand, but they were hopeless, and I, the angel of death, began to look confused and foolish, so I just handed them over. The cash register drawer chimed open. The uniformed man knew who I was not by name, but just as a traveler from the outback. He gave me a comforting smile, smoothed the bills himself, and slid them into the cash drawer.

Inside the visitors' center was a small museum full of artifacts and an informative movie, playing for nobody, in another room. I passed these by and walked out the back doors, returning to the rain. A short distance away were the dark and drenched remains of a great house, the West Ruin of Aztec. I stopped at a pair of vacant benches that faced the body of the ruin. The site looked like stacks of opened crates, their neatly tabular style of masonry a perfect imitation of Chaco, and of Salmon Ruins. Thick wings of outer chambers guarded numerous kivas within. On adjacent grounds other great houses remained unexcavated, their prominences visible among tall, water-heavy trees. This was a tight community of ancient structures, but only one had been unearthed, this West Ruin, left out in the rain. The others were untouched, waiting to be excavated another day, or perhaps never.

Aztec's great houses mirror those of Downtown Chaco. They were designed to match Chaco down to the exact square footage, angled toward and away from one another in the same fashion as Chaco's great houses, even elevated around one another in a similar way: one representing the position of Pueblo Alto, another emulating Pueblo Bonito, another Chetro Ketl, and so on. This was an almost exact duplication. The distances between prominent kivas are nearly the same as well, the directions of lines formed by various walls repeated to within a small degree of accuracy. John Stein, who surveyed both sites, told me that Aztec reproduces Chaco one to one. "The West Ruin at Aztec is the dimension of Pueblo Bonito," he said. "All the architectural arrangements, the critical dimensions of symmetry, the proportions, the actual size, are based on the Bonito formula."

One hundred years after the peak of Chaco, Aztec was built to the codes of the same architectural paradigm. In essence it was Chaco picked up and moved fifty-five miles north along the terraces of the Animas River, where a new locus of power replaced the old one in a carefully manufactured gesture of continuity.

During the dry years of the twelfth century, communities of the Colorado Plateau could no longer afford to keep pumping Chaco full of corn, pottery, and other finely crafted wares. Times were lean and more utilitarian. A new center was needed, one closer to reliable water sources. The decampment of well-established communities around Chaco for these newly constructed ones in the north implies a decree, almost a form of far-reaching government.

The principal governor for these people was climate. Anasazi social networks responded to the Colorado Plateau's kaleidoscopic weather with impressive uniformity. Where many people see the failure of the Anasazi in the fall of Chaco, a different story is revealed in the Totah. Chaco was merely reborn during a rising drought. Formalized links of continuity were built into the system, allowing people to slip out from under environmental pressure and establish themselves elsewhere with their entire culture intact.

. . .

As I walked through the rain, I thought that in the twelfth century, people would have dreamed of water like this, a great house dark and drenched. I felt embarrassed almost, moving through musical, pattering sounds, rain guttering down off the hood of my poncho. I should be drinking it, I thought. I should be placing bowls under the eaves. A quarter of the year's precipitation was falling in a matter of hours.

A wet chill leaked through my clothes and my shirt cuffs began dripping. I needed shelter. Nearby was a restored great kiva standing round as a layer cake. It was built on the footprint of a former great kiva, surrounded by the ruins of the original great house, and its flat, circular roof was in good condition. It would be dry inside. I stooped into the kiva's doorway, moving quickly through streams coming off the roof. As I walked down wooden stairs into a dim enclosure far below, I draped my poncho over one arm to let it drip. The stairs led into an underground court, where four pillars reached some thirty feet from ground to ceiling. It was like walking into a grand ballroom.

The wooden steps were warped from tourists, creaking as I descended. The air inside was still. At the bottom I stopped on hard-packed dirt and sand and peered around the cavernous chamber, its ground as dry as a tomb. Coming in here felt familiar. I had taken similar refuge from the rain before, pushing open the big wooden doors of city churches, finding myself in rows of silent pews. I moved over to a plastered masonry bench running nearly two hundred feet around the circumference of the kiva, broken only by two sets of stairs opposite each other. I set my things down on the bench.

I was born to an era of stadiums and concert halls, and already today I had entered a grocery store larger than nearly anything the Anasazi ever built. Yet as I lowered my pack onto the bench, I was struck by the vastness of this chamber. In the twelfth century, it would have pushed the boundaries of what any human had ever built in the Southwest, large enough that nine hundred years ago it would have filled one with a feeling of awe, or bewilderment. In a landscape dominated by a bold and inescapable sky, entering this underground rotunda must truly have stirred the senses.

On this day Aztec's great kiva was vacant, and my footsteps sounded hollow as I stepped away from the bench and began pacing around the building. I tried to keep my movements conservative, as if I should not stir the stillness. A misty blue glow floated down from overhead, a faint light coming in through the smoke hole in the roof, illuminating high, whitewashed walls down to an even, horizontal line below which the walls had been painted cherry red. Additional light entered through T-shaped ports encircling the kiva, sharply cut vents leading to half-moon-shaped exterior rooms.

When this great kiva was first excavated, all that was found was the circle of its bench and a chest-high crop of walls with niches and what might have been wooden ladder rungs leading down to the floor. The masonry pillars had mostly fallen over, leaving four distinct stalks rising several feet out of the rubble. The floor plan was found intact, though, concentric rings of walls and rooms laid out like a coliseum. When the excavator who uncovered this site in the 1920s, Earl Morris, got to the bottom, he turned right around and rebuilt the entire kiva. It was his passion, perhaps the final archaeological obsession of his life. If anyone knew how to return a great kiva such as this to at least a facsimile of its original self, it was Morris. By the time he did this reconstruction in the 1930s, he had dug more sites in Anasazi country than anyone preceding him, loading museums with artifacts and becoming the first to excavate all the way to the floor of a great kiva. He knew how the walls should be painted and how the complex wooden ceiling might have been fashioned.

Gary Brown, the archaeologist who had driven me up from Salmon Ruins this morning, was a fan of Morris's. He told me that Morris had continued the reconstruction even when funding was yanked and his work crew dwindled. Morris was disturbingly brilliant, Brown said, weather-beaten and painfully passionate about archaeology. Brown told me that the great kiva had recently needed repainting and that he painstakingly re-created pigments Morris had used, matching their chemical components in order to remain true to the original effect. The story struck me as peculiar: a modern archaeologist trying to re-create a dead archaeologist's work, which itself was a re-creation of something the Anasazi had built nine hundred years earlier. Ancestor worship, I thought. Not ancestors by ethnicity but by place and architecture.

Excavators working on kivas repeatedly find the remains of previous masons and kivas directly below. These older kivas were often purposely destroyed—roofs burned, walls pulled down—and then new kivas were built on top, as if in a ritual act, or at least to signify a changing of the guard. Of the thirty-seven kivas excavated at Pueblo Bonito, at least twenty-two had received substantial renovations. Several were razed to their benches before being rebuilt. A kiva at the Chetro Ketl great house next to Pueblo Bonito drops down three stories through eight cycles of reconstruction, each kiva sitting slightly askew on top of the last. The original ceiling atop Aztec's great kiva was once supported by four massive timbers, and at some point the timbers were burned along with the entire ceiling, all of which was replaced by a new twelfth-century ceiling held up by four stone pillars, a feat of tremendous human and natural resources. Centuries after that ceiling collapsed, Morris came and rebuilt it again.

Even the pre-Columbian plaster on most kiva walls tends to be ten or twenty layers thick, each added at a different time. Murals of fantastic imagery are buried beneath one another, each painted layer as thin as gauze, barely covering the mural painted before it.* These kivas seem to be corridors through time, underworld passages kept in the same place but destroyed and rebuilt year by year, generation by generation, or even culture by culture.

If archaeologists were to unearth Morris's great kiva centuries from now, they would have a heyday, finding a 1930s reconstruction atop a twelfth-century original that itself had been built upon previous versions of itself. Just like the overpainted murals and the nested versions of kivas found all across this region, this would be a clear example of continuity. Nine hundred years after the site was abandoned, someone came and rebuilt it. Future archaeologists ex-

*Ceramic archaeologist Patty Crown has noted this same phenomenon on certain Anasazi vessels. Original designs on certain ceremonial jars were covered over and replaced by new designs or by a simple white finish to give vessels a new look. Crown found that repainted vessels were actually fired again, perhaps multiple times, to seal each alteration and give the vessels a variety of appearances over time.

Two kiva circles nestled in room blocks at twelfth-century Aztec. REGAN CHOI

cavating this great kiva might notice that the fine facing stones used for its superstructure are original, gathered from the building that preceded it. Meanwhile, the stones selected for the wall cores were imported from twelfth-century ruins along the La Plata River twenty miles away, as if this site were built to tie history together, to renew time.

. . .

I tilted my head back and looked up into the cat's-cradle shadows of the ninety-ton ceiling above me, timbers crossing back and forth in a work attesting to Morris's engineering talent. Morris had fit the crossbeams together on paper, then hoisted them into place with a Navajo crew.

The percussion of rain increased on the great kiva's roof and then let up, giving a slow rhythm to the day as I walked steady circles around the pillars, then sat for a long spell looking up through the faint shaft of light coming down the center. Thunder sounded through the walls. A shadow fluttered at one of the entrances, and the park ranger appeared in his raincoat. In the middle of shaking off his coat, he stopped, surprised to see me here. He recognized me, the angel of death who had come in from the rain a few hours earlier.

He asked if everything was good, and I told him I was doing fine, thank you.

"Would you like music?" he asked.

I looked up at him from the ground floor.

"Music?"

"Flute music."

Then he laughed knowingly, saying, "It comes with the kiva."

"Sure," I said. "Why not."

He pressed a button mounted on a post, put his coat back on, and went back out into the rain. A cascade of flute music emanated from speakers tucked among the ceiling beams. I stood still for a moment, a little surprised, recognizing immediately that the music was played not on a Native American flute, but on a traditional Japanese *shakuhachi.* I would later find out that the performer on the recording was Navajo, playing a song called "Zuni Sunrise."

This kiva was tangled in eclectic ancestry, unrelated histories passing in and out of each other, brought together by this place. What was it Einstein said, that time and space are the same entity? Does that mean that if you stand in one place and are a keen enough observer, you can see clearly through time's entire lineage?

The flute music finally came to an end. I was grateful it was over. Its tones had highlighted a few too many of the memories here, and I could barely make my way through their muffling, ironic weight. I began walking once more, hands behind my back, my pace slow and even, as if I was touring an art museum. I listened to the older rhythm overhead, one that must have been heard occasionally in the twelfth century, the sweet dance of rain falling on the roof.

Moon Watchers

CHIMNEY ROCK

I carried Jasper on my back as I walked with Regan along a mountain trail in the late-afternoon light. The trail led to a sledge of cliff, an eroded ridgeline standing at nearly eight thousand feet in southern Colorado, not far northeast of Aztec. Upon this ridge called Chimney Rock, the Anasazi had outdone themselves. Here they had erected a multistory complex like a trophy, the highest and one of the most isolated great houses. It was built in the eleventh century during the height of Chaco and has since been beaten into ruins by weather.

Yesterday's storm left the atmosphere as clean as museum glass. I could feel it in my lungs, the sharpness of a world reborn—summer shaken out, folded, and put away for another year as the brisk garments of autumn were laid across the land. A brushstroke of snow ran clear across the southern Rocky Mountains before us. A few clouds remained, stragglers caught in high, forested basins and up against timberline slopes well inside the state of Colorado. Engorged rivers slowly subsided, leaving wreckage strewn for hundreds of miles.

Regan bundled Jasper into her coat, and we approached the great house, its exposed rooms as orderly as the slots in a cash register drawer. All around us lay the pastel sky of early evening. The Piedra River snaked southward, opening a gap in the land through which I could see the barrens of northwest New Mexico, the land of Chaco and the Totah. Strolling around this great house on such a high point, I was reminded of Buddhist prayer flags and stupas erected in stiff, mountainous winds, claims of holiness and splendor soaring above the earth.

Nearly two hundred people had come this evening, their casual movements pressing against the sunset sky. They were here to watch the rising of the summer's last full moon—people carrying ticket stubs showing that they had paid their ten dollars and signed waivers freeing the Forest Service from any liability in case they stumbled off the edge of the ridge.

For various convincing reasons, this site is thought to have been a lunar observatory for the Anasazi, a place that may have been used to confirm and commemorate one aspect of the lunar cycle. When the moon reaches its northernmost point, an event that begins every 18.6 years in the lunar standstill cycle, it rises directly through a pair of massive, natural towers off the end of this ridge.* The towers stood high in fading light, two dark, knobby monoliths eroded from the far end of the ridge. These towers form the chimney of Chimney Rock, a set of imposing twins aligned so that, seen from this great house, they are almost touching, leaving a narrow vertical strip of sky between.

Walking through this nighttime verge, Regan cradled our son in a deep-blue fleece checkered with moons and stars. I stood just behind her, blocking the cool breeze. Beyond her shoulder the river valley below became a pair of parting hands revealing the desert farther into New Mexico. A fire lit at this site—perhaps the moment the moon slid like a marble into the slot between the twin towers—may have quickly relayed its light to Pueblo Alto, leapfrogging down the Great North Road from signal to signal, finally touching Pueblo Bonito on the floor of Chaco Canyon. Gazing into this southward gap, I wondered how far beyond Chaco the message might have gone, on

*During this major lunar standstill, the full moon of the winter solstice comes up between the twin towers of Chimney Rock at sunset. During the following spring equinox, the half-moon rises through the towers at midnight. Around the summer solstice, the shadowed new moon rises in the same place at sunrise. And at the autumnal equinox, the half-moon breaches the narrow gap at noon.

down the dry bends of the Rio Puerco to the ancient communities of Manuelito Canyon and farther to a great house in the Painted Desert of Arizona, perhaps all the way to the high end of the Mogollon Rim, a couple of hundred miles away, where there is a great kiva perched in a forest, a southern twin of Chimney Rock.

Tonight's moon was not going to thread the needle. It was to rise almost dead east, a prosaic location out across a far ridge and nowhere near the two towers. But for tonight a commonplace moonrise would be good enough. After this the Forest Service would close the site for the season, blocking the road for the coming of winter.

. . .

I once came to the crest of Chimney Rock on a cold Christmas night. I had a candle burning, although it was not necessary, the sky blazing with moonlight. At least the little flame warmed my face. I was taking shelter in a modern fire lookout, a wooden Forest Service building that had been constructed between the great-house ruins and the two rock towers. Windows framed the entire surrounding view, a snowbound landscape radiant under the moon. When the candle burned down, I descended to the frozen ground below the lookout. Out in the open I pulled my sleeping bag from my pack and unrolled a pad across the ground. For the rest of the night, or at least the stretch of it that I lay awake, I watched the moon sail past as satellites cruised the deep winter blue of stars.

The next morning I crawled out of a bed of frost and sat between a pair of kivas as the sun rose. I stayed on the ridge watching the sun go about its rounds, the shadow of Chimney Rock sweeping across forests like the arc of a sundial.

When the sun had nearly completed its circle on this short winter day and began riding low in the southwest, other people showed up. This was not a summer tourist crowd, but a group of twenty or so researchers in various scientific disciplines. Forest Service workers walked ahead of them, chipping ice off the trail and salting the rock steps as if casting rose petals for arriving pilgrims. An elderly ethnohistory professor came behind them, stamping her cane. Two astrophysicists, both somewhat elderly, followed her, tottering along the trail to reach the great house. Behind them came other researchers, archaeologists.

A tall man named Ron Sutcliffe had made all the delicate calculations, determining when and where the moon would rise. He had come for months of moonrises, waiting like a silent monk at three in the morning, noon, sunrise; checking and refining his computations in preparation for tonight's event—the first night in almost eighteen years that the full moon would appear between the towers.

Sutcliffe seemed a little nervous, distractedly going through the numbers in his head. A tall man with a graying beard, Sutcliffe towered over everyone else, a good stature for a sky watcher. Standing on the deck of the fire lookout, he raised his hand and announced that anyone to the right of his arm would not see the moon. You would want to be to the left at the appropriate moment, which he had figured to be 5:29 P.M. To arrive at this moment and this place, he had designed algorithms based on spherical trigonometry, all of his work done first by hand and then entered into a computer for fine-tuning. He had made a map of the heavens and then one of the ground, putting the two together, matching landscape with celestial motions. In this way he had created a calendar of both earth and sky.

As I watched Sutcliffe pace the deck, I imagined a person of much the same station a thousand years ago, also nervous as everyone lined up—macaw feathers blooming from their hair, turquoise and shells adorning their bodies. Among the crowd there may have been some well-dressed and fierce-looking people who had come all the way from southern Mexico and could not be disappointed. There must have been such a person as Sutcliffe, a moon watcher who made the final call and said that after almost two decades, the moon would rise at this moment and could be seen only if everyone stood in this particular place.

Sutcliffe considered his possible errors as he checked the horizon. Cameras on tripods lined the deck in the six-foot viewing zone he had established. These were eyes positioned to tell the story later: automatic timers, shutter speeds set slow to catch the quality of the coming moonlight. Even someone's personal camera, a little point-and-shoot, sat on the deck railing facing straight between the towers. Sutcliffe had announced earlier that this was principally a naked-eye experience. He requested that no flashes be used and that the tripods not hinder anyone's view. The event was to be experienced by living people, as it had been before. The scientists did not object. This was not, in fact, an entirely scientific undertaking. We had all come merely to see what could be seen, to place ourselves at what may once have been a sacred crossing of time and place.

Twenty warmly dressed people huddled behind the field of cameras. They were silent, focusing all their attention on a single point, a dark space in the distance.

"First light," Sutcliffe said. "There, first light."

He was pointing at a faint glow pinched between the towers—not the bare moon itself, but almost. Sutcliffe's eyes were good. He had stared at this horizon for years now, able to spot its slightest aberration.

Voices stirred. One of the astrophysicists commented that this must have been a powerful event to witness long ago. Wistfully, he said it was too bad no one worshipped this particular moonrise anymore. I wondered, Does he not see this cluster of cameras we have set up? Does he not notice that twenty of us have crowded together in a windy December chill atop this ridge just to watch a single moonrise? In my mind this was an unquestionable form of worship, but I did not say anything. It was not my place, and I did not want to miss the first fleck of light.

Sutcliffe said that it was best to remain quiet for the duration. He asked for the time.

Someone said 5:29.

He said nothing else.

Into the breach of the towers an eggshell light broke the sky. The moon rose, exactly when and where Sutcliffe had said it would, piercing the space between the towers.

. . .

When a great house was built on this crest in the eleventh century—an outpost of Chaco, predecessor of Salmon and Aztec—people lived from the river bottom clear up to the height of the crest, with

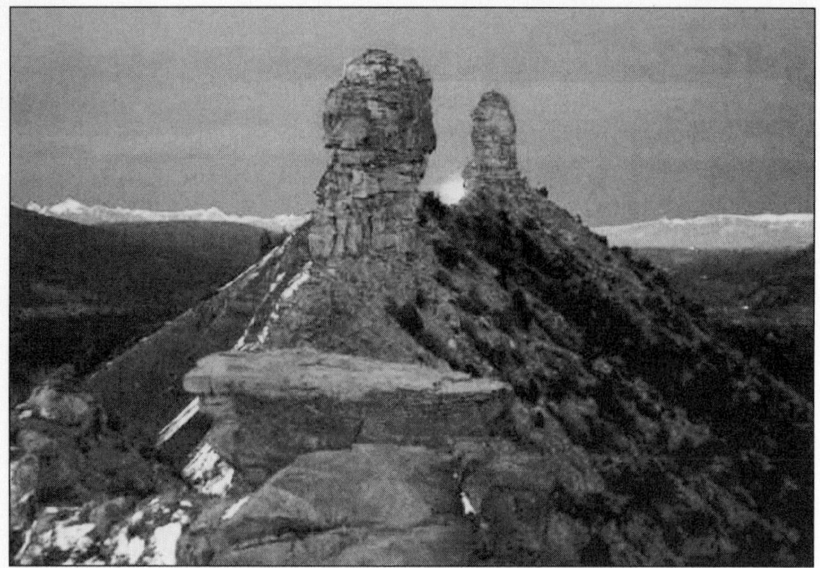

First full-moonrise between the Chimney Rock towers during a major lunar standstill, photographed December 26, 2004. CRAIG CHILDS

the more noteworthy settlements located on top. But why would people be living on this high, dry, and unprotected ridge when water, wood, and farmland lay far below? Eighty-one households, with about 360 residents, had been constructed on this exposed ridge, their ruins still visible. As one survey team wrote, "We hesitate to resort to the tired cliché of explaining the unexplainable as ritual, but in the case of Chimney Rock occupation, this explanation does have its merits."

Limited amounts of prehistoric trash and daily-use artifacts atop the ridge, coupled with massive, permanent architecture, imply a remarkably intense but brief use of Chimney Rock as a residence. The tree-ring dates acquired here suggest that short periods of occupation and construction occurred during two consecutive lunar standstill cycles, A.D. 1042 and 1060.

The Forest Service fire lookout was built some thousand years later, the wooden structure shaped like a squat pagoda, something that might easily be mistaken for a ceremonial site. Crowds gathered along the lookout deck on this autumn night as if waving goodbye from the railing of a cruise ship. I stayed below at Regan's side, Jasper content and bundled against the slight and changing wind.

Tonight's lecture was given by a Forest Service scientist named Glenn Raby, who stood at the base of the fire lookout. Just enough twilight remained for me to make out his figure. Well-spoken and animated, versed in recent research and ethnography, Raby gave an articulate description of lunar cycles and then explained that it was merely a quirk of geology that these towers happen to fix so accurately on the lunar standstill cycle. He called this a sensitive landmark, a sacred place belonging to those descended from the Anasazi—modern, indigenous clans who claim ancestry with this ruin. At Chimney Rock we should behave with attentiveness and respect, Raby said. He reminded the onlookers that scientific research is only a thin veneer; there are more ancient customs. He spoke the names of the September moon: *Yellow-Leaf Moon; All-Ripe Moon; Little Sandstone Moon.*

As he said this, I looked up at the first stars—one blue, another pink, a third a frail pinpoint of white. I held my hand on Jasper's chest. The lecture ended, and the three of us found our place over the cliff edge on the eastern side of the ridge. People sat around us on blankets. Quiet conversations floated up and fell back as we watched a mound of light pushing up in the east. Jasper lay against Regan's shoulder, and I stood beside her, feeling the crook of Jasper's body.

A fleck of white light nicked the horizon, followed by a quick shuffle of voices, fingers pointing, and then silence. The moon lifted out of the earth bright as a bomb, the perfect full circle. It pushed upward, displacing the horizon around it. Jasper woke for a moment, his eyes open to the moon from behind his mother's guarding hand.

Once the moon was free in the sky, the talking resumed, laughter over near the fire lookout. Forest Service docents announced it was time to leave; everyone must have a flashlight; please walk very carefully down the trail. Like seat belts unsnapping on a halted airplane, lights sprang on all around us. People began moving around the great house toward the narrow trail below.

A docent came to urge us along. Regan spoke almost in a whisper, leaning gently toward the woman. "He's finally asleep. We'll just come down last so it will be quieter—so he doesn't wake up."

The docent ducked her head slightly, whispering back, "Oh, yes, well, we can wait for you down lower."

"Thank you," Regan said.

The docent left.

As the last people descended, we came up behind the tail end of the crowd. Below us a procession of lights moved into the darkness—people strung out for a quarter mile, each flashlight illuminating a circle of ground along the switchback trail. Their lights stretched into a singular column of lanterns swaying along the lower ridge.

Strung all together, the people looked like worshippers, with their small white globes dangling in the blackness. As I watched them descend, I thought they looked as if they were stepping off into space, their lights trailing over the open vault of the land. I was reminded of the scale of this landscape, the vastness of horizons that once gave rise to the Anasazi. These ancient people often sought the highest points they could find, places that stretched the eye beyond its limitations. They lifted their great houses and studded distant buttes with buildings and fire signals so that they could see and be seen. In doing this, they left an unmistakable trail to follow—those lights below me, rocking gently into the sky.

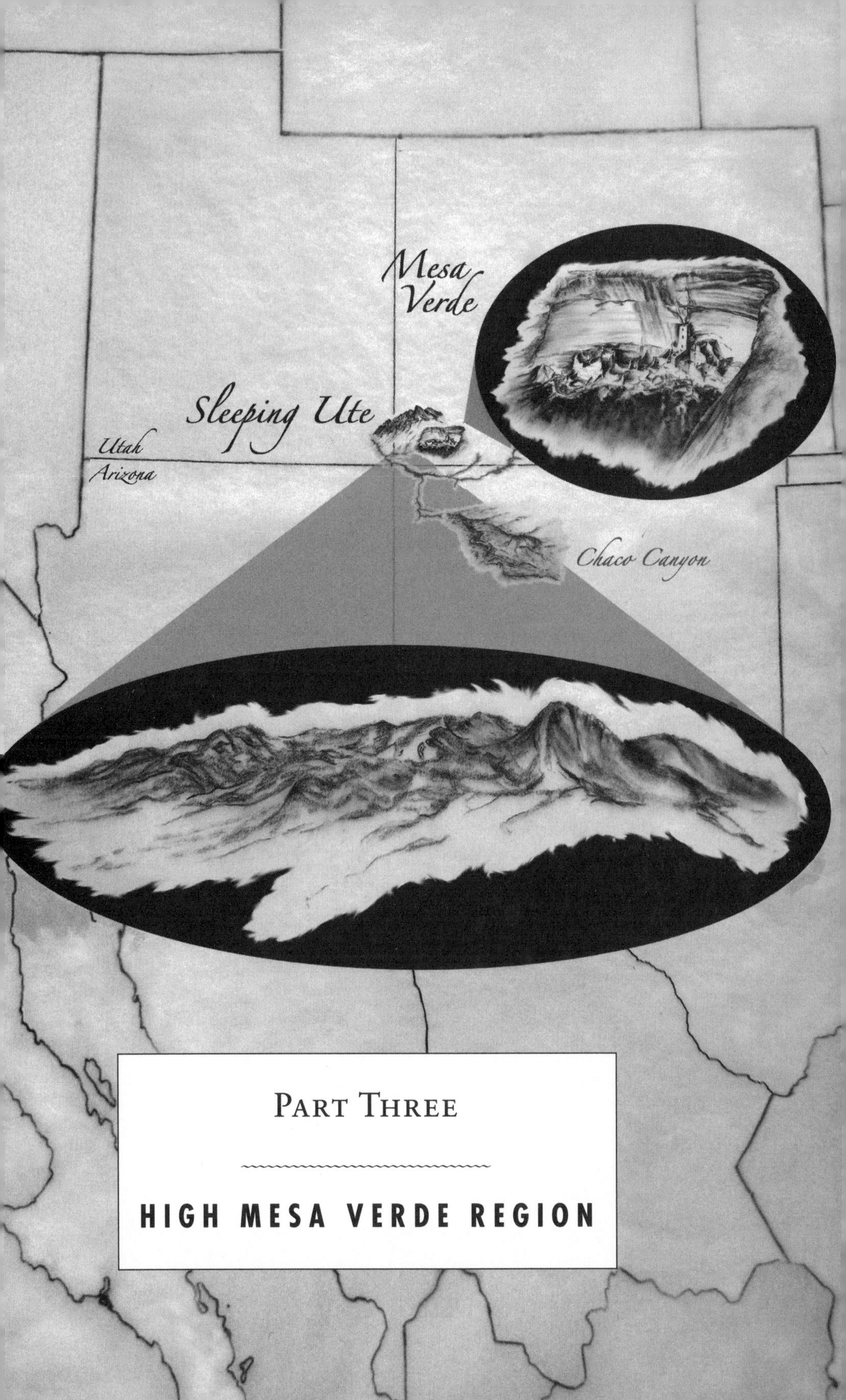

Part Three

HIGH MESA VERDE REGION

Memory

SOUTHWEST COLORADO

White beams of headlights opened the highway. A dotted centerline flashed by, counting out a steady rhythm. Mark Varien was the driver, a compulsively passionate and equally gentle archaeologist out of Colorado. Varien is in his early fifties, a man with full white hair. He kept fiddling with the radio as he spoke, although the stations were faint and he seemed not to care. It was a way of keeping on track, of reminding himself that he was still driving. As we traveled through the night, Varien told stories of migrations, his tales seesawing back and forth between New Mexico and Colorado. He rebuilt time, conjuring a thousand pueblos, monuments of data. He had spent decades digging in the ground and poring over research, looking not just at large, impressive sites but also at the more telling hamlets and villages that had once filled the spaces between. The land, he found, was absolutely covered by people, just not all at the same time.

Varien told me he once excavated a thirteenth-century kiva in the Four Corners area through which we were driving. He dug deeper and found that the kiva's foundation was built inside an older, wider pit-structure. The pit-structure had been built around A.D. 625 and was abandoned long before 1225, when the kiva was constructed inside it. Then Varien came along seven hundred years after that, next in line. The even spacing of these three separate events enchanted Varien, giving a context for him to work with—some idea of how long a site might have waited for someone to return before construction would begin again and what the site might have looked like after being abandoned for hundreds of years.

"They were coming back to the same places," Varien said, his voice calm but leading forward. "Their landscape was not just a physical one. I think they were moving within a landscape imbued with meaning. Over the centuries, people left these regions full of objects that had meaning, and the natural landscape came to be associated with stories of things that happened there. They became not just buttes and mesas, but *people* and *houses* and *burials* and *hilltop shrines*. When folks returned to a particular place long after it had been abandoned, they saw something very similar to what we are seeing now. They found a landscape still alive and inhabited, even if no one actually lived there anymore."

On this night Varien and I were returning from an archaeological site near the San Juan River in New Mexico, driving into Colorado in the early dark of winter. Intervals between oncoming vehicles had been long—a truck with a lazy left headlight ten minutes ago, a beady-eyed Jeep after that.

Varien explained how people left this part of the Colorado Plateau nearly vacant back in the tenth century, before the height of Chaco. They migrated out of southwest Colorado, many going to the Chaco region, where they perfected their masonry techniques by building great houses. They later returned to southwest Colorado during a dry spell, heading up from the south and reestablishing their claims in this higher, wetter region. He described a boomtown atmosphere as people came back—citadels rising on the high points, villages and households appearing across the countryside. Settlements more than doubled in size in a matter of a couple of decades, mushrooming into communities sometimes ringed with hundreds of kivas.

"The rate of growth for this period exceeds what you would expect from birthrates," Varien said as he drove. "People moved into the area in truly large numbers. It's one of the clearer cases of migration that I've seen."

All this happened out in the dark to either side of the highway, a region of clay gullies and saltbush that I could not see but knew well.

I had my own well-traveled memories along here, having driven this particular highway more times than I could possibly count. In the invisible world beyond the headlights, I envisioned Sleeping Ute Mountain and farther northwest the snow-headed Abajo Mountains, like blue pyramids on the horizon. Out the side window I could detect the hard, dry crest of Mesa Verde, its steep slopes decorated with countless tumbled boulders.

In my earliest memories I am driving past these landmarks, my small face in the window watching the stippled horizon of Monument Valley come into view or the threatening snows of the Rocky Mountains engulfing us as my mother drove us to the ends of my known world and back in our blue Volkswagen bug. Half of my family lived in Arizona and the other half in Colorado. I grew up burning a path between the two states.

My mother was single, and we moved as frequently as once every year or two. Why we moved so often I never learned, but it became a habit that I adored, a way of living I could not do without. My mother worked as a secretary, a waitress, a carpenter—no evident occupational need to leave one state for another so frequently. Even now when I ask her about our moves, she tells me they were each circumstantial, that she would rather have stayed put but things kept coming up, a thread of aspiration perpetually leading our small family of mother and child across the Southwest. It was as if we were looking for the center of a whirling spiral. Every time we found the center, it slowly dissolved from under us, and we left to follow it elsewhere.

Migration simply happens to some people. Maybe a restless, spring-loaded gene keeps us on the move, or an alignment of perpetual coincidences pushes us from place to place. It is the tether, though, that I find most fascinating, the return to the same regions. My mother and I traveled the same highways on our repeated moves, north to south and back again. A sort of hardwired stability developed in me as my home became an entire landscape where I lived not in a place, but along a series of lines tracing back and forth, connecting one anchor to the next.

The impulse that commands me to go is balanced by another that commands me to stay, the two working together to send me into quick but returning orbits around certain places: the Mogollon Rim of Arizona, the low desert south of there, the high desert north, and the castle perimeter of the Rocky Mountains beyond. I am constantly in motion among these landscapes, yet my life rarely ranges any farther, tethered by history and experience to the Southwest.

Tethered nomadism is something the Anasazi managed on an escalated scale, except instead of moving and returning within a person's lifetime, they did it over centuries. This pattern is reminiscent of monarch butterflies taking multiple generations to migrate away and then return to the same place, so that the one who returns to the breeding ground is several generations older than the one who left.

I watched familiar highway signs speed by, each side road leading to a wealth of places and recollections in my mind. What a treasure the Anasazi must have had, knowing this landscape not merely through individuals, but through a collective history, the experience of thousands of lives having crossed back and forth until the land beamed with their memories.

Varien had once directed me to the work of one of his colleagues, Lee Horne, who was looking at agricultural tribes still living in Middle Eastern deserts. The adaptations of preindustrial farming communities in that arid climate are much like the adaptation of the Anasazi. In the Khar o Tauran of northern Iran, there are adobe villages—some abandoned, others still in use—that closely resemble villages from the pre-Columbian Colorado Plateau. They lack the grandeur and public architecture that was commonplace among the Anasazi, but their adobe residential sites look like what one would have found in the Southwest several centuries ago.

Horne noticed the presence of far more villages and habitation sites in the Khar o Tauran than were required to accommodate the number of people. No site seemed to be permanently abandoned, as ruins were frequently returned to and rebuilt into livable conditions, either in an ad hoc fashion by itinerant families or wholesale by an incoming population. These communities expanded and contracted over the years as residents moved frequently into central regions and back out to the hinterlands in step with small-scale climate changes.

In the 1950s three-quarters of the core villages were occupied; by the 1960s nearly every village was full; and then in the 1970s most were empty. Smaller family sites beyond these villages grew and shrank inversely, absorbing the populations before funneling them back into their centers.

On the surface these sites appear to be erratic and unstable, quick to fall apart, but this is an illusion. The same Khar o Tauran villages have been in use for more than two thousand years. Agricultural life in capricious desert environments demands this combination of mobility and permanence, settlements ready to disband at any moment as rainfall recedes by an inch in a year—a matter of perhaps only one storm—and just as ready to reassemble in the same places when that inch returns. Seen from a short-term perspective, these cultures might appear to be weakly assembled, their histories constantly left in ruins. Longer observation reveals an ingenious social plan, one composed of slender strands of cultural connections stronger than any steel but very hard to see.

. . .

Varien's right hand absentmindedly drifted toward the radio again, toying with its volume, tuning in the next station as the last one faded out. He told me that the mysterious disappearance of the Anasazi is a problem of vision. If you lay a frame over the ground and look through it, you will see people living in a place, say, in the tenth century. Then they are suddenly gone from your frame. Some time later, say in the eleventh century, they appear again as if out of nowhere. And then at some point they are gone again. The problem is that you are not moving your frame to follow them. You are simply looking at them through a narrow crack in the door, astonished whenever they pass from view, saying they mysteriously disappeared.

"When they moved, it was rarely into unoccupied territory," he said. "Their migrations were formatted by a social landscape. Of course they moved to places where they could access water and croplands, but these were also places of social resources, where migrants had to negotiate where and how to live."

People began moving into Colorado between about 1060 and

1100, which must have been a powerful time to be here, when everyone was coming home to roost. It was a time when it mattered who you were and what sorts of things you could still recall about where your ancestors once lived. The people who had maintained a cohesive memory of this landscape might have been ahead of the game, able to stride to a hilltop of rubble and proclaim without any quibbling that this was where their ancestors had built hundreds of years before.

As Chaco declined, populations in southwest Colorado continued to rise steeply into the twelfth and thirteenth centuries. Designs painted around the exterior rims of Anasazi bowls from the thirteenth century contain a code that may explain how these incoming people related to one another. Prior to this, Anasazi bowls were painted only on their convex insides, while the exteriors were left a blank, glossy white. As people began crowding into southwest Colorado, however, potters started painting narrow, intricate bands around the outsides of their bowls, just below the lip. Each bowl now carried its own geometric signature, a black-on-white design that would have conveyed a message to onlookers, signs of identity. In a time when many groups were traveling, trading, and living among one another, it was necessary to express identity and perhaps origin, claiming who you were and where you were from. A picture has emerged of this complex period in Anasazi history—a convention center atmosphere of people mingling and scanning each other's name tags.

Varien said, "Remember that on the ground these people's lives were each a result of a unique history. I think they got mad at each other. They fought. They pulled up stakes and moved. Individuals were interacting with other individuals, households interacting with other households and with kin groups and with greater corporate entities."

As Varien outlined the way in which people once moved, I placed my hand on my side window, feeling the outside temperature through the glass, the cold winter night racing by. We were driving so fast that we cut open ceaseless frames of the Anasazi world. Such a strange way to move, I thought. It is no wonder that we have difficulty imagining the mechanics of Anasazi migration, that a number of researchers resist the notion that these people had the ability to move their entire cultural system from place to place like a shell game. Whole schools of archaeologists have believed that migration was not something that happened here. This widely felt resistance arose, I think, from the advent of the automobile. The land became inaccessible when asphalt highways were strung across this region. Entire pieces of the Southwest turned blank as cars were sent on long detours around mountain ranges and canyons. Walking is out of the question. The tone of this conceit can still be heard among certain scholars who speak as though places such as Chaco and southwest Colorado were so far apart that groups of people living in them were carrying on wholly separate lives, only distantly aware of each other.

It is only a couple of hundred miles, though, from Chaco to southwest Colorado, a long distance to drivers who sail along a highway that renders the surrounding land untouchable. Walking a couple of hundred miles is a different experience entirely, shorter in a way, filled with a heightened recognition as each landmark takes hours or days to reach. As you walk, over the days landmarks such as Sleeping Ute Mountain and Mesa Verde acquire personality, their faces slowly changing on the horizon. You discover that Chaco is merely a front porch to the house of southwest Colorado. This may have been the actual center of the Anasazi world.

I kept looking into the dark, my mind tricking my eyes into seeing waves of people passing through nine hundred years ago, families loaded with their most crucial belongings, caravans trekking through gaps and along washes. They marched past with domestic dogs drifting out ahead and behind to keep an eye on things, barking suddenly at the sight of other people: other processions of cousins and uncles, nobles in macaw robes exiled from Chaco, and also people who must have looked not familiar at all, the darting lope of hunters and scouts from other tribes. Everybody was coming back to Colorado.

Movement

NORTHERN SAN JUAN BASIN

The light grew thin and golden as the winter sun dropped toward the western horizon. I was trying to reach high elevation for sunset, climbing toward a 9,000-foot crest, boots and shins plunging through hard, windswept snow. The Northern San Juan Basin spread below me, the neatly contained heart of southwest Colorado. The basin is not a depression as the name suggests; rather it is a plank of land tipping ever so gradually away from the Rocky Mountains, its scattered creeks flowing south to the San Juan River like water off the back of your hand. It is a cold place in the winter, receiving far more snow than would ever be seen at Chaco. I had to hurry up this crest to catch the sun before it was gone. The wind bit sharply at my face, pushing me the other way, streaming around my body into the gulf of sky to my back.

I came bundled with as many warm layers as I could wear, and still the wind reached its chill, bare hands all the way to my flesh. My eyelashes froze, the tops and bottoms pinned to each other every time I blinked. I arrived at the top of the crest a couple of minutes before sunset and found a fire lookout there at the end of a road that no one had driven since October. The lookout radio antennas moaned in the wind with an eerie, celestial sound. I stepped up over snowdrifts and pawed against a window. I looked inside at a sheltered wood interior, maps neatly stowed as if on a ship's bridge. It was a curious mark of stillness in this gale, an optical illusion of peace.

A carnal light touched me from below, the sun now riding beneath me, just about to set along the southern tail of Sleeping Ute Mountain. I turned away from the lookout and pushed farther through the snow so that nothing blocked my view—no window, no wailing radio antennas. I came to the edge of the crest, where cliffs and ravines fell thousands of feet into the basin below. I was out on the tip of the earth.

The Northern San Juan Basin was the most populous region of the Colorado Plateau in the twelfth and thirteenth centuries, probably in the whole time frame of the Anasazi in the Four Corners. Migrants broke through the gates of surrounding regions and moved into growing, preexisting communities or built quick settlements of their own on the outskirts. An increasingly dry period had set them in motion, leaving much of the surrounding desert vacant.

From this summit the basin looked like a map spread across a table, mountains and mesas holding down its edges like paperweights. In the last direct light I could see the basin's varied terrain, nothing like the desolate country around Chaco. It has all kinds of topographic nooks and crannies, dotted with high points instead of being sunken into a brooding hole as at Chaco. This is where I would have come, too, I thought. The place had the feel of a geographic neighborhood, an intimate circle of land eighty miles across, with views looking out through gaps between exterior landmarks.

As the sun set, I could not help staring directly at it, the remaining half circle burning into my eyes, an apricot welding itself onto the earth. It dropped just beside a nut of a butte. I watched as the sun became a crescent, and then the quick closing, a final shaving of light pinched out.

What was left was a bright, painful light lingering on my retinas. I blinked it away, eyelashes frozen and snagging on each other.

. . .

An archaeologist named Donna Glowacki followed the prehistoric movement of pottery throughout this basin, tracking the origins and destinations of vessels as if she had her nose to the ground and was sniffing around the skirt of Mesa Verde, across canyon rims outlining the Great Sage Plain, and up the slope of Sleeping Ute Mountain, all

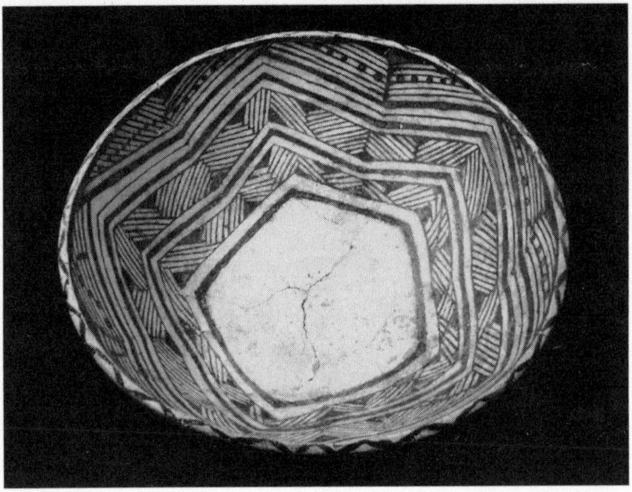

Thirteenth-century Mesa Verde Black-on-White bowl found in the Northern San Juan Basin. In storage at Crow Canyon Archaeological Center. CRAIG CHILDS

contained within the Northern San Juan Basin. She knew that to understand how people actually lived in the past, one must see the lay of the land, must grasp how it is shaped and how humans would have once fit into its folds.

A trim woman in her thirties, ivory face framed by raven hair, Glowacki had not intended to become a student of landscapes. Her interest began with ceramics. Trying to understand patterns of Anasazi movement, she took more than a thousand pottery samples from the Northern San Juan Basin and through analysis of atomic structures determined the geographic source of the clay. This told her where the vessels had likely been manufactured, different from where they finally ended up. Glowacki then drew a map showing pots starting in one place and ending in another. The movement of decorated wares most likely represented trade, while that of utilitarian vessels conveyed the uprooting of whole households. The pots had to have been transported by people, so her map became one of human travel, the patterns bold and indelible where populations had tramped paths back and forth into the ground.

"It's just the way people work," Glowacki told me once. "If you have a migration, then you have return migrations. People go somewhere, and then some of them move back, or they just come back to visit, and you get information flow that keeps turning around on itself, making pathways. All their travels across the area helped pave the way for larger, later movements. These people were constantly setting the stage for motion."

Studying this Anasazi traffic, Glowacki noticed that vessels had a tendency to move from only one place to another place, evidence of regional alliances and trade relations. She was able to see what looked like political boundaries, borders opened in one direction and closed in another, as people from Mesa Verde related more closely to people from Aztec in the south, while those on the Great Sage Plain in the middle of the Northern San Juan Basin had strong affiliations with Utah to the west. What was usually thought of as a broad wash of generic Anasazi looked to Glowacki more like a congress of individual parties traveling and trading among one another.

As Glowacki became more familiar with this landscape, she realized that patterns of movement she had defined were ruled by geography. People used the shape of the land to determine their interactions, their boundaries, and their routes. Glowacki said, "I never thought of it that way until I got out on the ground, where I had to survey these community centers and actually have a good look at this place." Mesa people lived in a different way than canyon people. Some accumulated in longtime settlements on the Great Sage Plain in the middle of the basin; others formed roving groups that traveled in and out among peripheral hills and slopes, leaving behind peripatetic villages and encampments. The surrounding landmarks struck Glowacki as signposts delineating one local district from another, as if the migrants, pouring into a processing station, looked up at the signs to see where they were supposed to go.

. . .

I watched small storms gather around Sleeping Ute Mountain. Streaks of snow spun up Mesa Verde's gray-green flanks. The behemoth, timberline range of the San Juan Mountains stood theatrically to the north, a snowy backdrop.

Like stars, lights began to appear on the land below. Bright blue and green dots came on, ranches and farmsteads revealing themselves. As they appeared, I began to see the outlines of small settlements, houses and their vapor lights forming long lines that showed the presence of farm roads. The lights increased toward the distant town of Cortez, a dish of bright jewels laid at the foot of Mesa Verde.

The Northern San Juan Basin was once the most populated region around. For every house I could see, there was an Anasazi village, or a prominent pre-Columbian town, beneath it. The settlement patterns have hardly changed, with people now living in the same places they did before, building along the same grids. The landscape still tells us where to live, where to go. I watched distant headlights creep along invisible county roads and across the strand of an east-west highway. Do they know they are tracing paths marked out centuries ago? I wondered. As they sit in their cars, following their casting headlights home, do they realize they are living in homes built atop ancient buildings, tending farms where crops were grown long before them?

I looked down into these pinpoint lights and remembered that when a new swimming pool was dug at a Cortez motel, the work revealed a block of masonry rooms in the ground below, where human bones stuck up like bent cornstalks. Some of the older residents still remember having picnics beside the weathering hulks of great houses, Sunday afternoons spent with the family digging up artifacts for mantelpieces. I know of a man living just outside Cortez who bulldozed straight into a great kiva on his property—roof beams snapping across his steel blade. He parked a collection of wrecked cars in the kiva's open circle, adding himself to the procession, the next step beyond Glowacki's map, where people move their belongings from here to there and back again.

I stood over all this movement taking the edge of the wind against my face. The temperature was dropping rapidly as the sky began to freeze. Time is moving, I thought. I could feel it. There are places in the world where no clocks or calendars are needed, landscapes where time is as palpable, as abrasive, as any of the elements, sharp as hail. The swift clouds parted for a moment, and in that instant I saw stars. I craned my neck around and watched them race by.

The Art of Leaving

GREAT SAGE PLAIN

Susan Ryan called to tell me that her excavation, a four-year obsession on the Great Sage Plain in the middle of the Northern San Juan Basin, was going to be buried. An ancient village she was carefully unearthing would soon disappear under the blade of a tractor, turned back into an unrecognizable hill of greasewood and dry grass.

Ryan, a field archaeologist, wasn't remorseful; this was part of the plan. An archaeological research group had given her four years to excavate the site and to map its labyrinth of rooms and ceremonial chambers. Then she had to bury the whole thing, making it appear as though her crew had never been there. This is simply the business of modern archaeology in the Southwest: before you leave, you clean up after yourself.

But her time was running short, and when she called, her voice was tinged with urgency. "You need to come see what we've found," Ryan said. "I've got a new map in my head. You need to come before it's buried."

When I had first visited Ryan at her site years earlier, I was struck by the way she moved, how her thin jeweler's fingers touched each object with unusual care and inquiry. Although she was only in her twenties at the time, she had been handpicked to lead this dig. She was a natural at finding barely detectable shoulders of ruined walls buried beneath windblown dust and greasewood. Ryan could map ancient dwellings and structures simply by stepping over the ground, as if she could see through the earth itself. Her superiors said that she had the potential to become a great archaeologist.

So when she called to say she had a new map, my interest was piqued. It was an emotional map, she said, woven of the countless strands of data accumulated as she watched the seasons and years tilt across the site. She was able to reconstruct centuries of Anasazi life in a very personal fashion, distilling the insights that come only from assiduous fieldwork, using her dusty hands to pursue her questions.

Ryan said that she could see clearly what had happened in this place so long ago. But she could never publish or write about this map within the confines of her profession. The knowledge she had gained was too private and instinctual.

I left right away to meet her.

. . .

The Great Sage Plain in southwest Colorado is actually not much of a plain; it is a gentle slope cut apart by numerous canyons that cannot be seen until you walk right to their edges. Above these canyons are hilltops and ridges marked with high mounds that once were villages and great houses. Ryan and her crew had opened up one of these hills, revealing a cluster of stone houses and kivas ringing an elevated center, a sort of abbreviated citadel looking out across a landscape of other small citadels.

When I arrived to see Ryan's new map, an early-season snow was blustering out of the west, shoving and bumping over a hill in a country too high to be desert, too dry and scrubby with cheatgrass to be a pasture. Dressed warmly to meet the wind, I stopped near the peak of the dig site and peered around its seamless horizon. The cape of Sleeping Ute Mountain stood in front of me. Just off my left shoulder, Mesa Verde seemed smug as a cat on a windowsill, tail curled around its body. To my right and far in the distance stood the reddish, upright slabs of Monument Valley in Arizona and Utah, and farther away in Utah were the powder blue pyramids of the Abajo Mountains. At my back, the San Juan Mountains lifted like crystals of ice.

Ryan once told me that she knew why people had built in this place: it felt like the center of the world. Of course one would build here. She was attached to the notion that people lived in places that felt good, that were visually familiar.

The excavation had revealed a compact, early-twelfth-century great house standing on a hilltop that was the center of the site. It was built just after the height of Chaco. This great house was a smaller version of the structures in the Chaco area, about 150 miles to the south, only with a northern flare, a looser treatment of the stonework and kivas done in a recognizably local style. As populations increased dramatically from the twelfth to the thirteenth centuries, this great house acted as a magnet. A larger settlement accumulated around it, new kivas and residential structures built right up against the old great house, its rooms expanded and redone over a two-hundred-year period. The same thing happened on high points all across this region, where century-old great houses became cores of residential settlements as they were overcome by waves of incoming migrants. Ancient clans reunited in this country, marking the outsides of their serving bowls with ornate symbols to tell of ancestry and alliances. These serving bowls are larger than any made before, suggesting a time of feasting, of great gatherings.

Up ahead, workers pushed wheelbarrows up a ramp, where they dumped all the previously gathered soil into a block of several rooms, burying the excavation back inside the earth. I could still see some of the exposed walls, fine masonry with horizontal courses banded like brickwork, going under with every heave of a shovel.

I found Ryan moving among the pits. She came to me with a smile, her eyes sharp and blue. Her cold, pink earlobes stuck out from under her wool cap, sporting six small earrings. We hugged like bears in our robes of winter clothes and then walked around the site slowly, side by side, as she gestured down into the trenches.

Ryan had been cautious in her four years at this site, preferring to dig only where she thought it necessary. In the last months, however, she had gone deep, straining the backs of her crew. Ryan was like an archer drawing her aim to perfection before letting the arrow fly; she waited until she had mapped the place in her head before driving down to its foundation. She found treasures down there—not necessarily the kind that glitter on museum shelves, but small, private remnants of a complex and well-orchestrated society.

I told her that I was surprised to see so much of the site exposed. I had worked here the previous summer, digging into a trench with a metal trowel and a small hand broom. The excavation had been delicate and slow, hours spent whittling around potsherds as small as pennies. Now I could see where this work had gone. Trenches that had been only two or three feet deep now dropped fifteen or twenty feet into the ground, revealing masonry walls all the way down—walls that had once stood in the open and after abandonment had been buried in roof rubble and centuries of wind-driven dust. The site turned out to be far more elaborate than Ryan had expected. Over time the Anasazi built village upon village on this high point, with an ancient great house buried in the center like a diamond.

As we walked, Ryan explained the myriad technical facets she had uncovered, the types of pottery or architecture that indicated one pre-Columbian group or another. She told me that she felt as if she could see an ancient life teeming below her feet. After so much digging, she was now aware of interactions between groups of people, how the building of one room had affected the building of another, kivas of Chaco heritage erected beside those built in a more northern Mesa Verde style. In her eyes this settlement perched high above the Great Sage Plain was a cultural menagerie.

These were people of ceremony, Ryan said—not just religious ceremonies but repeated, daily acts, similar to the way we set forks, knives, and spoons on the table and arrange our shoes at the front door. The way people left objects behind, even the way they sorted their trash, carried distinct signatures.

Ryan had found spirals carved into stones on a prominent south-facing exterior wall of the great house, like address numbers on a front door. When the great house was later expanded, the spirals were enclosed by a room and concealed under fresh plaster, implying that they were no longer needed. Her excavation disclosed fingerprints pressed into wall mortar and artifacts left in purposeful positions all around. She could see ancient hands, see the people sleeping, see them choosing how to place objects on the floor or the hearth. But there was no methodology in her profession that would allow her to express this. After the dig was buried, she would write up the quantifiable data, filling volumes, yet there was no way to express this deeper map formed in her mind.

. . .

What impresses Ryan most is how people finally left this place. Toward the end of their occupation, the population skyrocketed; people were moving in from all around. Then, late in the thirteenth century, the site was suddenly empty—and not only this site, but every site around here. This was the famous Anasazi disappearing act, the moment when these people are said to have vanished off the face of the earth. Ryan thinks that by enlarging their settlements, they might have been preparing for a mass exodus.

"Are they gathering together so that they can depart as a single, cohesive group and build their own place somewhere else? Is there safety in numbers when you're migrating?" she asked. "Is it easier to start a community down the line? Yeah, I bet it is. You need large numbers to do the different jobs, to get homes built. Maybe they all know that they are about to migrate, and so they come together to organize themselves."

As we walked, she said, "There are all these theories about violence and drought from that period. Why couldn't it be as simple as *it's time to go*? This culture is sedentary and nomadic at the same time. Maybe ecologically it makes sense, so you don't overstay your welcome. Sometimes you just up and go."

Exactly how they up and went was Ryan's most pressing question: what happens when a large and fairly stable population leaves all at once? The answer came from kivas she uncovered. Many of these circular, underground chambers were disassembled at some point, their large wooden ceiling beams pulled out and used for new construction elsewhere. This was not unusual for a place that was inhabited for a couple of centuries, but the last kivas to be used were treated differently. Almost all of them were burned, their massive wooden ceilings turned to char and crashed in.

"It used to be assumed that fires like these were catastrophic," Ryan said. "They were thought to be the result of warfare or accidents, someone cooking when a spark gets into the ceiling. That has been the explanation at least, because when you look at the floors, you find all these tools and goods left behind under a burned ceiling, as if they had to run to get out."

But it must have taken a lot of work to get ceilings like these to catch fire, and Ryan doubts that it was an accident. The next, most obvious conclusion is that invaders intentionally set the fires. The problem is that Ryan has found no evidence of violence at her site, nor at any of the other hilltop sites immediately surrounding it. In fact, the end seems to have been peaceful. When people finally migrated away, leaving the site empty, they did so in a very orderly fashion, burning their kivas behind them.

But it was more than orderly. On the floor of one of these burned kivas, Ryan came upon a large bowl inverted like a helmet, the designs painted around its exterior rim indicative of the late thirteenth century, the moment just before the site was entirely abandoned. When she lifted this bowl, she found two baskets neatly stacked beneath it. The bottom basket contained a cache of coarsely ground corn. The basket above it held a small pile of corn, ground as finely as pastry flour. This was not corn stored for eating. It looked like an offering, one set there before the ceiling collapsed in a heap of fire and embers. Around this assembly, she found ceramic ladles nested into each other, and other artifacts placed just so. The kiva floor looked like a giant altar, everything situated for the burning.

The fires could have been deliberately set as invaders approached, the way Russians burned their towns as Napoleon's army drew near, but Ryan sees these acts more as ceremonial procedures, the kind of thing you must do before intentionally leaving a place. In cultures around the world, important objects that need to be retired tend to be dealt with in one of three ways: they are buried, put underwater, or burned. This is done to take something powerful out of circulation, so it can no longer be used if it falls into the wrong hands. In the case of the Anasazi, burning was the method of choice. This pattern of what Ryan and other archaeologists call *ceremonial burning* did not appear only in the thirteenth century. During the previous wide-scale abandonment of southwest Colorado in the tenth century, the same kinds of burned structures can be found, their floors left in a ceremonial fashion. Burning dates back even further, to the early centuries A.D.—the history of the Anasazi marked with pit-structures set on fire as people departed. It seems to be a sign of impending migration.

"I'm a believer in ritual abandonment," Ryan said. "I like to think these structures had a life, that they weren't just stacks of rock. When it was time to leave, you did not just walk away. You paid your respects."

As we walked through these exposed ruins, the wind darted against our faces. Ryan looked to the west at low platinum clouds as her crew buried all that had been excavated. Her eyes were narrow against the spitting snow.

"It looks like the weather's chasing me out of here," she said.

. . .

Ryan returned to the backfilling and left me to wander around the site. My shoulders were down, my arms tight at my sides to hold my body's warmth against the wind. The site looked like layer cakes cut open. I returned to a trench that I had dug the previous summer. When I was last here, it was no deeper than a coffee table. I was surprised now to find it as deep as a pair of armoires stacked inside the ground. The person who had most recently been working the trench—a woman who told me she was starting to make a career out of this single trench—was gone, called out to work on the backfilling.

I climbed down a ladder to see what had been exposed. Snow fell like feathers to the floor, where the wind was completely blocked. A second trench opened even deeper below, and I came to my knees at its edge. I could see that the work had turned urgent—the dig narrowed to a smaller space as time ran out. The woman who had worked this trench told me that she had been expecting to reach the bottom of the settlement with every stroke of her trowel, coming upon sterile, natural soil, but instead the stonework wall kept leading

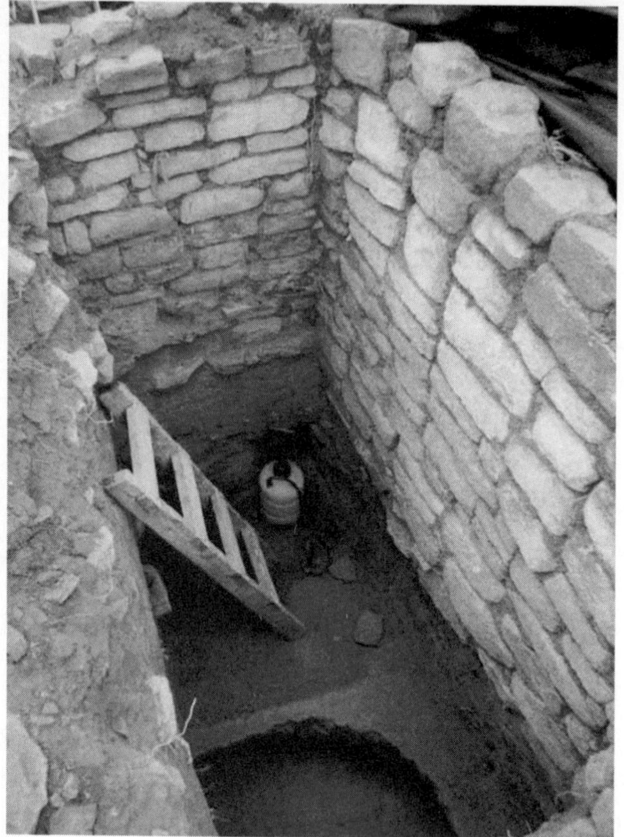

Walls excavated at Susan Ryan's dig in 2004. REGAN CHOI

her down. She had resorted to this furrow, a question mark that simply led deeper through a roof that had fallen in and through layers of refuse buried below it.

Peering into this dim second hole, I could see a third, smaller ditch inside. I had no idea the site went this far into the ground. The excavator told me that she had dug a space not quite wide enough for her hips, figuring that she was about to reach undisturbed earth. But cultural material had sent her farther down until she was suspended by her hip bones, digging the final groove with one arm extended as far as she could reach. There she had found a kiva, buried in the foundation of this settlement. I could see the slight curve of its bench and the square edge of one of its pilasters. It was an old-style kiva, the encircling frame made of earth and only its pilasters made of stone.

I went down headfirst until my shoulders were wedged in the opening, my head dangling. How many abandonments had occurred here? How many different groups had settled this place over the centuries and then left?

When I looked up, Susan Ryan was standing at the edge of the trench. Flecks of snow bounced off her jacket, falling fifteen feet down, then landing on me.

"You found the kiva," she said.

I sat back on my haunches and nodded, looking up at her.

"How old is this kiva?" I asked.

She shrugged. "It was built in the late Pueblo II period, so I would guess it's about A.D. 1060 to 1140."

And what would be found on its floor, if there were enough time to get down there? Another burned roof? An ancient rite of abandonment, artifacts left in a ritual departure? There would be no more digging in this trench, no more answers. The backfill was coming

"I have to tell you something about snakes," Ryan said, sitting cross-legged at the edge of the trench, looking into the rising wind. "Part of my map, I suppose."

I knew that from where she was sitting, she could see the range of the earth under oncoming clouds: Utah, Arizona, and New Mexico, all visible at a single glance.

"You know we always had gopher snakes here," she said. "I saw some five feet long."

I knew the ones, elegant cream-colored reptiles found in the morning under the trailer or slipping away through the greasewood in the afternoon. Ryan told me that for reasons she did not quite understand, she felt soothed every time she saw these snakes. They were good company, pliant, not poisonous. Sometimes she slipped a hand beneath their cool, pearly bellies.

"At the end of the last season, rattlesnakes started showing up," she said. "We just never saw that many rattlesnakes before, and suddenly I kept finding them."

Ryan said that she had the feeling the rattlesnakes were urging her off the site. She mentioned this to a few of her colleagues, but no one took her seriously. Such feelings, like her emotional map, are impossible to quantify and therefore unprofessional.

I told her that I knew an archaeologist who had excavated a post-Columbian Zuni site down in New Mexico, and when he had asked around, trying to figure out why the place was abandoned, people had told him that a rattlesnake had gotten inside. As simple as that. It did not seem peculiar to him that in the desert, in a building with a sheet of fabric for a door, a rattlesnake would show up. But it had made an impression on the residents, sending them packing. Maybe a rattlesnake is all a migration needs to get going, an omen that sets it off.

I said to Ryan, "I can see why you think it's time to leave. Rattlesnakes are a pretty strong message."

She nodded. "Fitting, maybe," she said. "Driven out by the buzz."

It was more than superstition, though. A couple of years back, Ryan had been digging out the bottom of another kiva site when she unearthed an eight-hundred-year-old snake skeleton. The snake was stretched out on the kiva floor, and its skull was conspicuously missing. Usually, a dead snake is found coiled in rocks, its vertebrae scattered like dice, but this one was straight as a ruler, cleanly intact but for its head. Just before the chamber had been intentionally buried in refuse and rubble, before its ceiling beams had been pulled out, a headless snake had been laid across the hardpan floor.

Shortly after finding the snake, Ryan brought a group of American Indians to the site in order to make sure they were comfortable with her work. When she approached this exposed kiva, she mentioned her curious find. One woman from a western pueblo suddenly stiffened. Without explanation, she turned and walked away, keeping her distance from the entire site. Ryan understood that the woman was carrying a private piece of knowledge, something that told her what it meant to find a headless snake on the floor of a kiva.

Ryan said to me, "It'll be good to have this place backfilled. I've noticed some decay in the walls. We've gotta get things closed up. I think we've done enough here."

Nearby, workers were backfilling a partially excavated kiva. One worker threw in ancient building stones, while another shoveled in dirt. The mix of dirt and stones was measured, so that once the room was filled, the ground above it would not sag. Future visitors would never know that anything had happened here.

Has it always been this way? I wondered. Ryan was not the first person to close this village. She was merely the next in line, a woman mindful of small acts, making sure the rooms were properly buried so that her presence, too, would fade with time. This is a new ritual of departure, a twenty-first-century abandonment.

Ryan's dig begins to answer the question of how the Anasazi left the Four Corners region, revealing actual ceremonies of departure. The question of why they left remains. Just before the area was vacated, there came a dramatic shift in settlement patterns. Many people began living as if in fear, using the land in a defensive manner. This signaled that the end was near. The foremost place to witness this change is Mesa Verde. When I climbed the ladder up from the trench, I could see the mesa towering over Ryan's dig. It looked like a castle standing in the clouds, a place to hide.

Protection

MESA VERDE

I held the pay phone receiver in the crook of my neck and tried to listen through the flapping of my notes and the roar of the winter wind skating across Mesa Verde. A woman spoke on the other end, but I heard not a word. I had come to the park visitors' center, to which the phone was attached, to make calls, turning the pay phone here into an office for the afternoon. The center was closed for the winter, the corners of the building webbed with old snow.

Switching to my left ear, I said, "Sorry, I didn't get that last thing."

"Your research project looks like it will be accepted," she said. "The park superintendent has looked at your proposal. There are just a few details."

"Good, good," I said, hunching my back to block the wind. I had turned in a proposal that would allow me to go into Mesa Verde with a park archaeologist and spend time inside a particular cliff dwelling.

I barely caught her next words. She was telling me how much it would cost. I switched the phone to my right ear, my knuckles sharp and cold. "What was that?" I said.

She repeated the figures as I scribbled them down on a piece of paper. Two hundred dollars for the permit. One hundred fifty for the application fee, so that my proposal could receive an official stamp. And fifty for every hour spent at the cliff dwelling.

"Fifty dollars an hour," I said. "That's kind of steep."

"Excuse me?"

"I said that's a lot of money. I don't know if I can come up with that kind of money."

The woman was quiet, and I imagined her glancing at the clock in a warm office where the air does not move except through ceiling ducts. I suddenly felt foolish clutching at this pay phone with a piece of paper ticking violently under my hand.

Prior to this I had gone into Mesa Verde like everyone else, instructed along by signs and rangers as if touring a crowded art museum, hands kept to myself while I gawked at the beauty of the mesa's cliff dwellings. What happened here in the thirteenth century was extraordinary. Settlements that had previously sprawled across the lush top of the mesa were left empty. People ducked into the shelter of local canyons where they constructed unparalleled villages, vaulted architecture protected in caves, neighborhoods as compact as Hong Kong tenements. Kivas looped around one another back in the shadows. These structures are all called cliff dwellings, even though some look more like churches than actual dwellings—much like Chaco's great houses, some have more ritual spaces than domestic ones.

Asphalt paths lead in front of certain dressed-up cliff dwellings where the public is allowed, and there I would come up against the Do Not Enter signs, my imagination pressing back into the shadows and black doorways. The ranger would tell us now to turn our attention elsewhere to take note of some other feature along the tour, while I would keep staring past the sign imploring me not to enter. Eventually, the crowd would move on, and I would dutifully follow. The glimpses I got inside these sites were too fleeting and abbreviated for my taste.

So I approached the park with a request. I wished to examine one of the cliff dwellings more closely, to drift through its spaces day after day. Nothing purely scientific, I said. I just wanted a closer look, room by room, if I might.

My proposal had been accepted, but in reality it had not. Fifty dollars an hour was well out of my reach.

"Well," the woman said, her voice genuine on the phone. "Feel free to give us a call if you have any further questions."

I said goodbye and hung up, staring at the numbers I had written down. Frustration welled up inside me. I collected my things and walked to a low wall intended to prevent people from falling into snow-lined canyons below. I leaned over the wall, looking down the gashes that stream through Mesa Verde's forested, stony flesh. In classic Anasazi style, this stonework visitors' center was built at one of the highest vantages, peering across an isolated piece of land, a realm of dark and spiked conifers, a secret place. I could barely see where in the distance cliffs began bowing back into caves, burrowing into a country that lay unseen within, canyons made exquisite by forces of erosion. Within these canyons were six hundred documented cliff dwellings, each waiting silently beneath the sloping deck of Mesa Verde, not a soul around.

My earliest memory of Mesa Verde, from maybe the age of eight or nine, is of a ladder. It is stretched beyond reality in my recollection, a wooden ladder rising up a cliff, testing any acrophobia that dwelt in my nervous system as I climbed rung by rung toward a mansion of stone high overhead. I do not remember what the cliff dwelling itself was like, only the earth falling away beneath me as this ladder lifted toward a place never meant to be reached by intruders like me.

Mesa Verde has always been a well-protected place. It is the hope chest of Southwest archaeology, where cliff dwellings have remained neatly sheltered for centuries, artifacts preserved inside them as if curated. Ceramic mugs have been found still dangling from wall pegs, blankets rolled and stored inside fat jars. Pre-Columbian structures in Chaco or Aztec have steadily diminished beneath the open sky, each year buried deeper by blowing sand, their walls eroding and collapsing under their own weight. Meanwhile, whatever was placed in Mesa Verde was still here when archaeologists first arrived at the end of the nineteenth century, finding relics covered with dust and a little rubble, but well guarded within these dry, hollow cliffs.

My frustration with the park's bureaucracy began to subside as I looked across the clipped tops of these canyons, thinking of the archaeological value placed here. Of course, I thought, the Park Service should not be letting in strangers like me to wander unchecked through the treasured halls of the mesa. This is, after all, hallowed ground, as guarded now as it may have been eight hundred years ago. Anasazi sentries have been replaced by armed rangers and by a backcountry bristling with motion sensors. Wilderness riffraff has been kept out, the hordes who would stain these delicate ruins with their greasy hands, who would eventually push down all the ancient walls and demand that libraries of informative signs be erected in their place. If I were given carte blanche, I would somehow be disappointed.

By its physical nature, Mesa Verde is not a public place. It is geographically private, a fortress. The mesa tilts up from the Northern San Juan Basin, with a leading edge rising thousands of feet over the greasewood barrens below. Access to the top is limited by a number of pinch points, likely places to build entrances where each person coming through can be checked. The mesa is a topographic Babylon, its gates guarded by lions and bulls, canyons and cliffs, while inside lie naturally arched passageways and hidden slabs of masonry buildings, more rooms per square mile than anywhere else in the Southwest.

In the thirteenth century, Mesa Verde stood in the middle of the most densely populated region in the Southwest, a region housing more people than live here today. The many lowland Anasazi living below Mesa Verde must have looked up often at this looming landmark—a man using a stone hoe scratching dry ground stopping to peer at Mesa Verde's abrupt edge above him. What mental pictures must he have had of a place he perhaps never visited? Graceful masonry towers set back into the shade of canyons he could not see; high, cliff-bound villages surrounded by the sounds of dripping springs and by loops of wild grapevines—a paradise, a secret garden.

I do not imagine a person would ever have ascended this huge battlement of earth without invitation, without paying a toll. I gathered my things at the closed visitors' center and walked off to find another way in.

. . .

Later that winter a blizzard coasted up and over Mesa Verde, leaving the tree trunks and the park's roadside signs decorated with streaks of snow. The storm fussed across the mesa top, but down in one of these canyons, back inside the rooms of a dwelling called Spruce Tree House, the air was still. Gray daylight turned to dust and drifted in through open windows and doorways, barely illuminating the cobwebby attics of ancient rooms.

I crouched slowly through a T-shaped doorway and entered a darkened chamber, where I reached down and touched the icy floor for balance. Walls around me were finely finished in plaster, cold as a stone castle in the middle of winter. I felt as if my moments inside this unstirred cliff dwelling were not the ones I had bargained for in my life. They were a surplus, gleaned from the invisible edges of time, everything around me suspended, unchanging.

I had found a way into Mesa Verde. Every fortress has a back door, a sentry willing to engage in conversation. I had begun talking around the park, explaining that I was tracking the Anasazi, traveling along trails of archaeological bread crumbs. Some rangers, though they wore chattering radios and were trained to shoot moving targets, revealed a heartening softness for this place. In their years of guarding archaeological sites, they had lingered after closing time, pausing before they locked the gates to listen to the silence behind them. They said that on certain nights, they would walk to watch moonlight flower across the cliff dwellings, and they were astonished by the sense of time this sight engendered, by the majestic stillness of these places.

When most of Mesa Verde was closed for the winter, a ranger asked me down to a ruined cliff dwelling called Long House, where we walked through chambers as quiet as a vacated church. She wanted me to experience the place when it was not crowded with tourists, telling me this is how she imagined it was before we got here, a pocket of ruins slowly drinking the morning light. Showing me through Long House's complicated architecture, she said that the Anasazi had made their edifices beautiful when they could have more easily built quick row houses. She thought they had been people of conspicuous elegance.

She introduced me to others, and soon researchers were unrolling maps across their desks for me, their fingers dancing excitedly to show their findings. They had unearthed the remains of impounded reservoirs with steps leading down to them, like a utopian Maxfield Parrish painting, and had found trees that had been manually straightened when they were still young so that they would grow into good construction timbers. These researchers showed me the park's locked vaults, where we looked through hoards of artifacts—bowls and ceramic mugs, necklaces of finely polished beads.

I told them that if I could have any wish, it would be to spend time inside Spruce Tree House, the second-largest cliff dwelling on the mesa. It stands right under the visitors' center and has a paved trail leading to it. I had lingered in front of it many times, my eyes straining to see into the dark, receding chambers where I was not allowed. I sensed that the site was much larger than it appeared. There were other dwellings far more remote and handsome in their robes of debris, but this was the one I wished for, Spruce Tree House swept clean and polished until it looked like a museum piece. The paperwork was signed, and I was taken down.

Doors opened around me. I passed through them, craning my neck, looking up through gaps of fallen ceilings straight above me, where wall plaster changed color from one level to the next; the walls of these rooms were banded with multihued murals. This had once been a remarkably colorful village, occupied by artisans.

I stopped in a room with a floor pitted with holes where looms had once been anchored. A room of weavers, I thought. These people were in possession of loom-woven textiles—kilts, shirts, and leggings patterned with intricate designs and interwoven with vibrantly dyed strands. Someone had etched a number of geometric designs into the stone threshold leading into this room. When I looked closer at these etchings, I noticed that they were the same designs one finds on Anasazi textiles, stairstep patterns set against each other. A weaver had sat on this threshold planning out a pattern for his loom work, scratching it into the rock.

. . .

Before the thirteenth century and before the Anasazi began building their settlements in canyons and on cliffs, their populations had grown to near the carrying capacity of the land. A few centuries of generally good weather had resulted in vigorous crop growth, which had made for more populous settlements, stimulating trade and expansion. Desert great houses had taken off and spawned replicas in faraway places. Of course, decades of hard drought had been scattered throughout, but the people were used to such affairs, mobile enough to leave places like Chaco to reach higher ground in time to plant their corn. Only now this higher ground was supporting more settlements than ever before, people of complex and disparate ancestry all gathering around the most well-watered and seasonable territories, their numbers heavy on the land.

Entire villages and towns were abandoned during a debilitating drought in the thirteenth century as people moved into defensible positions and to the last places of water. This happened not only at Mesa Verde but also all across the Colorado Plateau. Populations that had been enjoying centuries of growth and prosperity were now driven up in elevation, finally forced into the crags and sharp places in the land where they could defend their last resources. Surrounded to the south by flanks of desert and to the north by the bitter winters of the Rocky Mountains, the highland province of the Northern San Juan Basin became isolated from the rest of the Southwest, and for that matter from the rest of the Americas. Thirteenth-century aridity deepened the isolation, as trade with outside regions virtually came to a halt. Shell had previously been a crucial import for jewelry and offerings and was hardly seen again. Likewise, the importation of southern pottery styles such as White Mountain Red Ware and Tsegi Orange Ware diminished to a trickle, and the tropical bird trade ceased entirely.

The Anasazi, accustomed to sprawling communities and open skies, now lived in towers and packed cliff dwellings, breathing one another's breath, inhaling the smoke of winter fires from down the hall, listening to other people's sexual activities. They began experimenting with elaborate organizational schemes in their floor plans to keep order. Public architecture flourished across the region, and great kivas and plazas sprang up inside precarious cliff sites. Structures were built with concentric layers of rooms to regulate the movement of residents and visitors and to keep certain people away from others. The Montagues were now living just downstairs from the Capulets.

From numerous lines of ethnological and archaeological evidence, it appears that the Anasazi kept rigid systems of lineage. Namely, they were matrilineal. The named head of each Anasazi household was a female. That system was then separated into moieties, intermarrying groups that kept their own customs or at least their own neighborhoods. Many of Mesa Verde's cliff dwellings are divided into two wings thought to represent two separate moieties living in close proximity and able to marry back and forth. At Spruce Tree House pools of eligible husbands and wives were kept apart by a block of tall, spacious rooms painted more elaborately than any of the others where people would have met in organized, ritual activities perhaps akin to high school dances.

Floor plans of the Mesa Verde cliff dwellings are obviously based on social engineering, designed to regulate contact between groups of people. Even the way separate dwellings were built in relation to one another suggests larger corporate divisions and unions. Not just a concentration of hundreds of cliff dwellings jammed in here and there, Mesa Verde was a federation of settlements, different canyons and drainages having their own interrelated alliances. Cliff Palace, the largest and perhaps most impressive site on this mesa, looks like a boxed-in version of an old great house—too many kivas and too few residential rooms for it to count as a true living space. It must have been a ceremonial locale, perhaps a gathering place for all of Mesa Verde.

. . .

The first time I was shown into the back rooms of Spruce Tree House, I carried my infant son with me, his little body tucked against my hip as we ducked through doorways. The archaeologist with me said it was good to see a baby back in these chambers. He imagined a cliff dwelling once full of life, like a schoolyard, where untethered voices rang through its rooms. He said the inner rooms of Spruce Tree House had been vacant for too long.

This time through, I was here alone on a chilled winter day, writing in my journal with a crabbed hand. I walked back and forth through rooms until Spruce Tree House's floor plan was nearly as familiar as that of my own house.

I stopped over a kiva that had been built toward the back of the dwelling, as secluded as a bathhouse. Its circular enclosure dropped into the ground below, its timbered roof missing. Peels of plaster hung from the inside, revealing patches of construction stones turned a pinkish color where they had been oxidized by an intense fire. The fire had been contained, kept from escaping into the surrounding rooms, most likely set upon the residents' departure. People at Mesa Verde were doing the same thing that people at Chaco and Aztec and on the Great Sage Plain had done, igniting their holy spaces as they set off on a migration.

I imagined roils of smoke pouring out of this burning kiva, flowing through one doorway after the next, choking the upper-story rooms. I held up my hand, feeling the air where the tips of my gloves were cut off. The air was moving, almost imperceptibly. I followed it, envisioning the path of smoke eight hundred years ago as I passed from room to room. I walked into an open plaza, where I stopped before a two-story wall peppered with T-shaped entries. Smoke would have poured from them as if they were weeping.

Beside me a single T had been painted on a second-story wall, its white pigment now faded against fawn-colored plaster. There were T shapes all around me, even more than I had seen at Aztec and Chaco, a sign carried here from the desert. This was one of the bread crumbs that had led me here.

While working at Spruce Tree House in 1891, an anthropologist named Gustaf Nordenskiöld found these many precisely shaped doorways to be far more than just architectural convenience. He noted that in the ruins at Mesa Verde, the T shapes belong to the rooms that were most frequented in everyday life, fashioned to allow expedient ingress and egress, as opposed to the rectangular doorways, which could be sealed shut with stone slabs. In his mind the T shapes denoted public spaces rather than private ones, doorways that remained open, while others could be closed.

Wooden ladder leading down into a kiva in front of T-shaped doorways in Mesa Verde's Spruce Tree House. REGAN CHOI

Nordenskiöld also noticed that the T shape arrived late in the occupation of Mesa Verde, associated with sites he found to have been constructed with more care and skill than sites lacking T shapes. It was as if a specific group of people had arrived late in the game, people of the T—perhaps former residents of Chaco or Aztec taking root in Mesa Verde. Or perhaps the T indicated a sort of growing social identity, a cult or a rising religious faction.

With the T came an era of conflict. The late thirteenth century saw cultural turmoil and pockets of extreme violence across the Four Corners region. Even before substantial evidence of violence was unearthed by archaeologists in the twentieth century, Nordenskiöld believed that the Mesa Verde cliff dwellings were defensive wartime settlements. Near Spruce Tree House he noted "a number of very small, isolated rooms, situated on ledges most difficult of access." He posited that these rooms could have been defensive turrets, "archers being posted there when danger threatened, so that the enemy might have to face a volley of arrows from several points at once."

He continued, "In such a position a few men could defend themselves, even against an enemy of superior force."

When Nordenskiöld mentioned these turretlike rooms to Jesse Walter Fewkes, a prominent Four Corners archaeologist of the time, he was presented with a very different view. Fewkes believed the small structures to be shrines where offerings to the gods were deposited. At least one was built very near a spring, which must have been considered especially sacred during the Great Drought of the late thirteenth century.

The views held by these two researchers epitomize a debate, which will probably never be resolved, over whether cliff dwellings in general were urgently defensive or were simply good, safe places to live, holy places even. On the one hand, Mesa Verde's cliff dwellings were indeed built at a time of escalating hostilities in the surrounding countryside. Some of their outer walls were built far thicker than necessary, as if to fend off a frontal assault. On the other hand, very little evidence of violent death has been documented at Mesa Verde, even while archaeologists excavating the land below have uncovered sacked villages and legions of charred human remains.

Many modern archaeologists are beginning to question the warfare hypothesis at Mesa Verde, looking toward more complex social explanations for why people moved into these cliff dwellings. Perhaps they came here to get closer to water sources. Or perhaps, rather than strict battlements, the dwellings were built to hold a place in the imagination—signs of extraordinary endeavors, a loftiness surpassing everyday architecture. In this way they may have been like the high monasteries of the sixteenth-century Qing dynasty in China, where buildings supported in the cliffs with spans of timbers were reached by stairwells carved in stone.

Whatever these cliff dwellings were, they represent a transformation of settlement styles as the people of Mesa Verde left open country for sheltering canyons. T-shaped doorways appeared in great numbers at this time, their dark, sharply outlined forms standing boldly on the faces of dwellings. These may have been the first gated communities of the Southwest, people taking their prosperous lives out of view from the teeming masses in the land below, guarding themselves within the bowels of Mesa Verde. The T shape may have been their symbol, their flag, in this time of change. With one glance you would have known who they were.

. . .

I slipped through a T-shaped doorway and into a room where I found an extension ladder leaning against a wall. An archaeologist had been working here as part of an intensive architectural survey measuring every stone, every swab of plaster inside this dwelling. I stepped onto the ladder and climbed through caved-in ceilings, three stories up, where white streaks of bird droppings ran down the wall like candle wax. The ladder bowed a little, stretched to its full extension, the top padded with fabric so as not to damage the plaster against which it rested. As I remained with my hands on the top rung for a few minutes, looking over the head of Spruce Tree House, I began to hear voices. I peered across half-broken rooms to where a light snow was falling outside. Visitors were coming, the afternoon tour.

Like a mouse startled back into its hole, I climbed down the ladder. I passed quickly through one low doorway and then another. As voices rose into the sandstone cave, I skulked back into the shadows, the storyteller rhythm of the ranger nipping at my heels. I had permission to be here, but I did not want to be seen, Gollum lurking in the halls.

As the tour group gathered at the front of Spruce Tree House, I shifted back through deeper rooms. I looked over my shoulder at the tour through gaps and openings. What were they seeing here? Where did their attention lie? Some were caught in wells of curiosity, squinting into dim rooms, trying to imagine what this place was like eight hundred years ago. Others watched the snow outside, inhaling the serenity of this cold day. Still others listened with schoolroom attentiveness while the ranger told familiar stories, hands clasped behind her back.

After several minutes I noticed a young boy staring at me through a long shaft of doorways. He startled me. I did not move. I didn't think anyone could see so many layers deep into the ruin. He was not listening to the ranger as he peered straight in my direction. He does not see me, I thought. I recognized the peculiar look of hesitation, uncertainty. He thought he saw something inside the dwelling, maybe a set of eyes in the dark, framed by sequential doorways; maybe a ghost; probably nothing. I stared straight back at him, not daring to move and prove him right or wrong. I wondered what memory was being planted, what impression would remain in his mind. I wanted to whisper to him, *Yes, it is true. There are things happening back here in the dark—layers of rooms extending deeper than you can see, archaeologists sweeping and measuring, a writer hovering at his journal.*

The boy's mother said something to him, told him to listen to the ranger. The boy looked away for a moment, and I slipped out of view so that when he looked back, no one was there, a daydream gone.

· · ·

The tempo of the ranger's voice changed slightly, and I heard the shuffle of clothing, people moving another few yards down the chain to see the next archaeological feature. I darted into the open when their backs were turned. I reached a wooden ladder poking out of a floor hatch and climbed down into the ground, swiftly vanishing into the darkness below.

The day ended there. In fact, the entire world seemed to end as I descended into the ceremonial kiva, a place to wait out the tour. Passing through the cold cellar light—my hands tracing grease-worn rungs, my boots softly touching the floor as voices outside subsided into a muffle—I closed my eyes for three slow seconds to adjust to the diminished light. When I opened them, I saw dust floating in a faint shaft of halfhearted daylight.

I let go of the ladder and turned slowly inside this underground sphere. Six smoke-blackened masonry pilasters emerged from an encircling bench, giving the walls a sharp, three-dimensional appearance even in the dim light. The ceiling was made of wooden beams corbeled across each other, and they dripped with the dark syrup of rodent urine. The circular room smelled of old molasses, the familiar odor of a cave.

I walked around the back of the ladder, where I came upon a flat stone planted like a plaque in the floor. The stone was original, something used to deflect drafts of air that would have poured down the ventilator shaft behind it. Every kiva has one of these deflector stones, as customary as a welcome mat. I stepped around the stone and crouched at the ventilator shaft. The square masonry hole in the wall was the size of a shoe box, down low so I had to set a hand on the floor and drop to one knee to peer inside. I could see a shape, something that appeared to be a large feather. I had not noticed this before. I squinted through wasted spiderwebs and reached in, tentatively. I lifted out a feather, seeing that it was old, stripped by weather and rodents. Still, I could tell by its squared-off top that it had come from a turkey. I settled back on my haunches, turning the feather between my fingers. An odd thing to find in this shaft, I thought.

The Anasazi once kept pens full of domestic turkeys. Their feathers were used for blankets and robes, and they were an abundant resource for ceremonies, especially as the importation of exotic feathers dwindled in the thirteenth century. But this was no Anasazi feather I had in my hand. Turkeys still inhabit these canyons. This feather looked to be no more than a few years old. It had drifted in from the wild, a dervish.

Among the modern clans of the Hopi who are descended from the Anasazi, turkey feathers represent the scintillating underworld, their white, flat tips symbolizing water churning up from underground. Turkey feathers are planted in fields to attract rain. Some of the surviving tribes far south of here, in southern Mexico, Central America, and South America, believe that the turkey represents Tlaloc, one of the most powerful and ancient gods in the Americas, a governor of water said to live underground in the House of Rain.

In certain societies of ancient America, turkeys were killed in place of humans, their heads ritually cut off as offerings to water spirits. Even in Chaco both intact human skeletons and those of beheaded turkeys have been found in kiva floors, buried in the hollow spaces between deflector stones and ventilator shafts. Buried, as a matter of fact, in spaces nearly identical to where I was now crouched with this turkey feather in my hands.

I slowly turned the quill, wondering whether someone had intentionally placed it in the ventilator shaft. Perhaps this had happened during a private ceremony. The park allows for such things when native tribes claiming local ancestry seek permission. A person may have come with a recollection of arcane traditions, knowing the connection between turkeys and ventilator shafts, placing the feather as a way of saying that the Anasazi have not died.

I reached into the shaft and settled the feather back into its hammock of spiderwebs. It's best to leave such things where they lie.

From outside the kiva I heard the ranger's muted voice. Instead of calling these people Anasazi, she used the term *Ancestral Puebloan,* respecting the connection between these cliff dwellers and the modern Pueblo tribes still living in the Southwest. In a pleasant tempo she told a story that has been repeated through the decades: the everyday lives of these people came to a sudden and mysterious end late in the thirteenth century. No one knows why. They left only these ruins for us to consider.

The ranger did not mention that kivas were burned, either in an act of ceremonial departure or as a ravage of war. In this very kiva, late-nineteenth-century excavators found human skulls stacked inside the ventilator shaft where I had picked up the turkey feather. Air flowing down the shaft into the kiva would have passed through the nose bones and unhinged jaws of human skulls. She said nothing of this, nor of the skeletons unearthed around Mesa Verde with faces chopped out, limb bones smashed open with stone hammers. Perhaps wisely, the ranger avoided such controversial subjects, describing the Anasazi only in a pleasant, upbeat voice as she led the afternoon tour away from Spruce Tree House. I remained in the kiva, my face turned toward the winter light falling down the ladder.

Devastation

BELOW SLEEPING UTE

Playing the pedals of his pickup, Hugh crashed us through a plane of fresh snow, the truck lurching and falling back as the rear wheels fishtailed and his hands spun the steering wheel first in one direction and then the other. We were on a final pier of land northwest of Mesa Verde. The road had been swept nearly out of existence by a recent storm. All that remained was a clean surface of snow cast into elliptical drifts between plumes of juniper trees. The pickup swished for miles across this white and drifted world, Hugh's palm guiding the steering wheel. He didn't dare to slow down for fear of becoming stuck.

The crease between Hugh's dashboard and the windshield was a museum of small animal skulls, various feathers, and peculiar root burls—the kind of display I had seen in many different trucks, the treasures of peregrine adventurers. A winged knot of a vertebra swung from the rearview mirror. The cab smelled of motor oil and old paper. Two dogs plunged their black noses against the campershell glass behind us. Hugh's vehicle was the same model as my own, same year, same smell, only a different variety of objects on the dashboard.

Hugh had been doing research up at Mesa Verde, sketching hundreds of designs from thirteenth-century serving bowls. He was edgy from too much time indoors; he needed to move. When I had last gone through a storeroom of artifacts with him, he had used the tip of his pencil to point out some of the more curious ceramic designs.

But then he had looked at me and said, "You know what I really want to do is get the hell out of here."

Hugh was nearly incapable of working inside. The bowls he was researching, no matter how ornately painted, were all starting to look the same under a wash of fluorescent light. He had told me he knew of an intriguing place down in the canyons beyond the isolated rise of Mesa Verde, out where he thought the true center of thirteenth-century Anasazi life lay. A couple of years back he had surveyed an archaeological site in the bottom of Yellowjacket Canyon where a massive wall of bedrock rises, a place nearly encircled by kivas.

Now that we were out here, Hugh was not sure exactly where we were. As snow came up across the hood, he stayed crouched over the wheel so he could see out the windows, taking quick bearings off the mountainous train of Sleeping Ute to his left, the bergs of the San Juan Mountains standing in a clear, crystalline sky to his right. Straight ahead stood the snow-blue island of the Abajo Mountains in Utah.

"Far enough," Hugh said, and he swiveled the steering wheel, causing us to wash sideways against the road so that we could see Mesa Verde plainly and suddenly out the windshield.

Before momentum was lost, Hugh dropped the gearshift into reverse, which sent us kicking backward, then quickly into first, where the tires only spun. He pulled the emergency brake, and for the first time in half an hour the pickup came to a halt. We had carved a snowbound line for miles.

Hugh got out to have a look around. I did the same, breaking through the wind crust on top of the snow, sinking knee-deep. The sun fell into a long winter slant, and I wondered about how far we would be able to walk before nightfall.

Hugh called out, "How's that side?"

I crouched at the back wheels with my haunches resting on the crust. We were in over the tops of the tires.

"Deep," I said.

Hugh flipped open the camper shell, and out blew two dogs. They plummeted away, their muzzles probing the snow. Hugh crawled inside and banged around.

ı differs from what archaeological scholars say. When I pre-
ed this excavation account to a widely published archaeologist,
dismissed it as ill informed and technically misleading, saying
the surveyor's description of the site was so surreal that most
aeologists would have difficulty recognizing it. What the field-
ker described as a crime scene would have been handled far more
ically by her—aspects of dreadfulness tidied up by an academic
guage. Such a sanitized view comes not from a lack of imagina-
ı, but from an understandable reluctance on the part of estab-
ed researchers to openly discuss taboo issues. Cannibalism and
rfare among the Anasazi have hardly been popular topics, often
ng handled with reticence, grimacing, and even denial.* Native
ıericans especially regard archaeologists who have addressed such
ics as meddling and insensitive, asking why such an unpleasant
tory must be brought to light. Many archaeologists respect this
w and speak guardedly about prehistoric violence. Fieldworkers,
wever, often come back wild-eyed with tales of crushed finger
nes, terribly disarticulated skeletons, and a cannibal's shit dropped
o a storeroom, the lid closed over it.

Whatever attitude is taken, there is no getting around the evidence
at for a period of time the foot of Sleeping Ute was most certainly an
ıfortunate place to be. I stood in the snow and looked up at the
ountain, feeling a familiar sense of ghastly apprehension. There are
aces like this all over the world. In every country and from every
ge, there are mass burials, torture chambers, places of horror where
ıe most rational mind cannot help being overwhelmed.**

The great-house village Susan Ryan had excavated was not far

For alternative views, see Christy G. Turner and Jacqueline A. Turner's *Man Corn: Cannibalism and Violence in the Prehistoric American Southwest* and Ste-en A. LeBlanc's *Prehistoric Warfare in the American Southwest.*

*The study of warfare among the Anasazi has made repeated appearances n Southwest archaeology. One archaeologist has noted that whenever the Jnited States is at war, research in the Southwest leans toward the study of violence. In times of relative peace, researchers on the whole have regarded the Anasazi as a more nonviolent culture, momentarily putting aside evidence of conflict.

The closest landmark was Sleeping Ute Mou
foot-tall body soft with snow and low afternoon
tain, sacred to the Utes and strictly off-limits, had
own personal landscape like a haunted mansion.
self traveling around its flanks, glancing up and
might be hidden in its woodland slopes, in its conce
never dared to go up there.

The density of archaeological sites around the m
boggling. One survey found nineteen pit-house villag
a couple of square miles. In the final years of occup
thirteenth century, migrants were arriving and estab
villages, until the area became a ring of busy encampn

What surveyors have found at these sites has con
deal to my sense of eeriness. One crew uncovered hur
tered all over the place, as if the people had been hack
also uncovered catacombs stocked with food where t
more human skeletons—not burials, but people who
dered. One of the surveyors told me that his excavatio
a crime scene—people killed trying to get away, others
hiding places.

This fieldworker explained that he and his colleagu
a grinding stone that contained crushed human finger b
point they knew that the slaughter had gone beyond t
customary violence.

The surveyors had loosened a stone slab in the grou
a deep, teardrop-shaped storage chamber below, its ro
lined neatly with stonework. The chamber was conspicu
but for a single, bold human defecation laid right in the
of the surveyors had done his master's thesis on pre
human feces, and he identified the material immediatel
pumice white color, which indicated that the person had
bone marrow. He said, "We shaved it down to a core tha
would not be contaminated by any of us, and then it was
they found the presence of human DNA. Not only on
DNA, but DNA from four different people." Whoever left
ment had been a cannibal.

What one hears about prehistoric violence from fiel

from here, a day's walk at the most. Ryan had found her site evacuated in an orderly, seemingly peaceful manner, while nearby villages had come to bloody, appalling ends. Obviously, the Anasazi did not all share the same fate.

. . .

Hugh emerged from the camper shell with a jangling fistful of tire chains. In the other hand he carried an army surplus shovel, a sturdy German tool with a short wooden handle and a folding metal blade. He went to work right away digging out the tires with swift, pawing strokes. When enough space was cleared, we lugged the chains into place.

Hugh jumped into the cab and urged the pickup to move while I pushed from behind. The chains spit out the back end as the pickup got just enough purchase to spin in the other direction, yawing ten feet ahead. I ran behind it to push. When the pickup bogged down again, Hugh shut off the engine and stepped out. "At least it's pointing the right way now," he said.

I backtracked to haul the chains out of the snow, fingers pink and cold as the dogs romped around me. Hugh studied the snow, hands on his hips.

"The snow will harden up in the cold," he said with a shrug. "We should start walking before it gets too late."

Hugh threw on a small daypack and tightened it with a quick tug of the straps. He had the mannerisms of a climber, a person well versed in travel through difficult places.

I grabbed a satchel of warm gear, a pair of gloves, and an extra water bottle. Hugh was ready, waiting. I closed the cab door, and he gave me a quick nod before turning and running north across the snow, a swift, light-footed dance. I followed, heavier than Hugh, breaking through the crust as we set out in search of a small Anasazi fortress he had surveyed.

I followed Hugh's prints, keeping on his trail as he faded through stubs of trees, the dogs lunging this way and that. I glanced around as I ran—keeping track of where Sleeping Ute stood and where Mesa Verde broke the skyline—so I could find my way back. The easiest place I know to get lost is in the topiary madhouse of a piñon and juniper forest, branches hanging at eye level, passageways opening in every direction, trees nearly identical in shape and size. At least we had the dogs with us; they would find the way.

Padding across the crust, distributing my weight so that I would not fall through, I finally caught up with Hugh, who had stopped at the edge of a fall. The dogs were poised beside him, their tongues lapping up the cold air. A canyon dropped into the earth below. The world turned from horizontal to vertical. Rims and cliffs of more distant canyons peeked over each other's heads, erosion cutting the land apart. We stood at a drifted cornice, peering as far over the edge as we could. The topography changed so quickly from woodland to canyon that it felt aggressive, almost violent.

"This it?" I asked, using as few words as possible so Hugh would not hear that I was out of breath, so he could not tell that I was ten years older than he and that I had not been out walking enough over the past couple of months.

"Yeah," he said, looking down. "This is the canyon." He was not breathing hard at all.

The land below us was made of steep tiers and brittle bands of cliffs and boulder chutes buried in snow. At the bottom stood a horn of a stone, a natural geologic feature. It was a lone bedrock wall staggering up from the floor into the sunlight. It looked like a place for a last stand, a thumb of earth down in a hole.

"And that's the site down there?" I asked.

Hugh looked down about a thousand feet at this sturdy butte. He nodded his head. "That's the place. That's where they went."

. . .

Nightfall was on my mind. We had a few hours left, and once we started into the canyon, it would be a long way back out.

Hugh looked toward me, but not into my eyes. He was scrutinizing the horizon behind me, checking landmarks. This was the last place where any of the surrounding world could be seen. Once we were in, the canyon would have us. The sun was a brilliant marble lying low in the southwest.

Hugh said, "See you down there," and suddenly launched off the edge. His boots kicked a tuft of snow from the lip as he shot straight down. The dogs leaped behind him, snouts swimming through the snow.

I hesitated for two breaths, watching Hugh bound between obstacles and then out of my sight off another edge. I kicked off, plunging into the canyon behind him, snow packing into the cuffs of my pants, sharp kernels of ice collecting deep in my socks and boots. Half in free fall, my body spilled into Hugh's tracks.

Direct sunlight vanished on the north side of the canyon. We were no longer in a sweet-smelling juniper thicket. Down here piñon pines grew across the tops of outcrops and cliffs smelling of ice. I jumped down through piles upon piles of snow, skidding, falling, gloves soaked through and hands needled with cold. No longer was I directing my body with my mind. I ran on instinct, with my arms spread, flying in the air with knees tucked for one, two seconds, then touching ground, feet diving beneath the snow into boulders and the trunks of fallen trees.

Seven hundred, eight hundred feet down, I came breathing hard to where Hugh had stopped. The dogs stood at his side along the top of a snow-covered arc, a bedrock cliff reclining into the canyon floor below. Some places were too steep for snow to gather, falls revealing wet red sandstone as slick as ice. One of the dogs let out a whine and nervously glanced elsewhere.

Dogs are no fools, I thought.

Hugh was looking for another way, hand rubbing the back of his neck. I pulled off my gloves and snapped them out. One advantage I had over Hugh was that I had spent many years traveling in the winter canyons. He had been raised in North Carolina, not a place of snowbound cliffs in high plateau country. Now was my chance, I figured. I could get the jump on Hugh. Saying nothing, I leaped forward and skated down the tilted face of snow. Small avalanches let loose, slabs breaking from the bedrock. My knees buckled and my gloved hand scraped down behind me like a rudder as I carved a long slalom into the lower canyon.

My fingertips scraped against the rock below the snow, my boot soles cutting like brakes. Out of the corner of my eye, I saw a sudden white mass shooting past, two dogs and a man poised downward.

Damn. He is *quick.*

Maybe fifty feet from the bottom, the bedrock became too steep. I hit my ass and my shoulder blades, and snow packed up into my nostrils as I gained speed, out of control. I flailed, went upright for a quarter second, and was down again, when I suddenly hit solid ground. With a sharp spring in my knees, I stood, staggering slightly but holding my composure, showing Hugh I was still alive, no broken bones. We had reached the bottom of the canyon. My heart was thumping up in my throat.

Hugh turned to me and said, "It's right over this way."

He jogged away.

I let my breath settle, watching him go.

. . .

In the sunlight along the canyon floor, Hugh's gait remained swift as he navigated among juniper branches and wash-bottom boulders. He moved with elegance, as if guided around obstacles by a fine silver string. The dogs fanned out into the scrub forest ahead of him, slopping through the snowmelt mud. Low, snub-nosed cacti were all over the place, withered by the cold.

The day would be ending soon. Tonight the world would crackle and become still, the stars held up in a frozen sky. This canyon would not be a safe place for us, and I kept glancing up as we moved, looking for a better route up than the one we had taken down. It was a long way out of here. We were at the bottom of a deep laceration in the earth. Ahead the lone cliff we were aiming for lifted magnificently into the sun. We scrambled up its lower, south-facing ramparts, passing through barbs of broken pottery where the snow had melted.

The bottom of this upright landform was sheeted in naked bedrock like a moat, a steep, exposed ring of land that had to be crossed in order to reach a settlement up higher. I could not see the settlement Hugh was leading me toward, but the pottery that had washed down was evidence enough that people had lived in substantial numbers all around the foot of this cliff.

Bedrock softened into terraces of soil, where we slowed our pace, stepping over impressions of ancient buildings, only their foundations remaining. Working on a survey crew, Hugh had roughly mapped four clusters of masonry dwellings and twenty-seven kivas wrapped around the rock face above us. Protected sites like this cropped up all across this region in the mid-thirteenth century, more kivas than had ever been seen in the past. One site several miles away sprouted more than four hundred kivas around the rocky head of Yellowjacket Canyon. As much as this had been a time of hostilities, it was also a time of alliances and collaborations. Settlements were cementing themselves together with communal architecture. Gatherings were held, feasts prepared in large serving bowls. Year by year the average size of cooking vessels grew, suggesting that labor was being reorganized, that extended households were living and eating together. Many settlements in the area looked identical to one another, with small household pueblo units facing south, their trash middens and small domestic kivas placed out front. Larger communities were aligned the same way, blueprints repeated on multiple scales, a sign that people were integrated into a larger ideology. At the same time, new pueblos were being built that looked entirely different, D-shaped buildings with floor plans reminiscent of Chaco, leaving some researchers to imagine a last-minute attempt to build Chaco once again. These sites were constructed at the heads of canyons and at defensible cliff edges and were often surrounded by formidable masonry walls. Rather than being based on strict north-south footprints, these new pueblos were built to fit into local topography. The combination of precise south-facing pueblo communities and those built into defensive terrain suggests that people residing near one another were living by two different sets of principles, or at least were employing markedly different strategies.

As I moved among these subtle ruins and looked up at the intimidating rise of this singular cliff, I thought not so much of accords as of defense tactics. These people had backed themselves into a corner with no escape route, a place for a final stand.

Hugh led me to a gap where we could see into another nearby canyon. A tower had been built in this gap, its north half still standing and its south half having fallen into rubble. It had been erected atop a huge boulder, yet another moat to be crossed. I circled the tower, checking its vantages, and noticed it had a clear view of nearly every angle from which people could approach. Eroded out of the slope were several older potsherds, early Anasazi black-on-white from the days before Chaco. I picked up one of them and rubbed it clean with a dab of spit and my thumb. It had thin black lines of paint dating back to a previous era of violence on the Colorado Plateau—not as devastating as this thirteenth-century upheaval, but a noteworthy period of aggression and early fortification nonetheless.

I asked Hugh about the sherd, and he said that a fair amount of tenth-century Piedra Black-on-White and Deadman's Black-on-Red pottery had turned up at this site, styles telling of an earlier age. He took this to be evidence that the place had been used as a stronghold more than once. The Anasazi coming back to such defensible locations after centuries of abandonment could be likened to modern Brits moving out of Dublin and London to reoccupy the Norman castles of the Dark Ages. Taking up positions that others defended long before is a customary maneuver during ground wars. In World War II, for example, decisive battles were fought exactly where other battles had taken place during the Crusades, with the Germans backing into hilltop towns along the Gothic Line in Italy and holding ground that had been difficult to topple a thousand years earlier. The shape of the earth has long defined the strategies of men.

Seeing these older sherds in the snowmelt soil made me think that the thirteenth-century Anasazi knew what was happening at this location, that they were building once again on top of their own past. Did they experience hopelessness upon finding the remains of earlier people who had sought shelter at this cliff, or were they encouraged?

I asked Hugh what he thought about people returning to this place, about the correlations of potsherds and cycles of movement. He sat on a sun-warmed boulder, plucking tags of ice off one of his dogs.

"Who knows?" he said, his gaze roving the snowy escarpments just above us, keeping an eye on the receding day. The shadows were quickly deepening as he flicked ice away with his fingers. "It's all speculation anyway. Too much black box archaeology if you ask me. Stick your findings into a computer and arrange them until the numbers prove your point. I think hardly anybody comes out here these days. Everything they need is in storage or in the databases anymore."

Hugh stood and walked slowly away. He turned and gestured with his chin for me to come, a nick of a smile letting me know that he could not be taken seriously, that he was tired of archaeology today, that he had spent too many months sitting indoors analyzing pottery. He was down here for the snow, for the sun, for the feeling of getting his heart pumping and his muscles moving.

I followed him up to where the snow was completely melted. We stepped over former walls and through slight washes that had netted hundreds of pieces of pottery. A cold breeze began to blow from the lower reaches of the canyon, indicating a shift in the day. The copper light was coming in lower, stirring the first shadows of evening.

We reached the base of the standing cliff and crouched back into its rooms of fallen boulders, the wind blocked, our backs warm against a southern face. This cliff was a solar collector, a bolt of heat in the middle of winter. We squeezed off our soaked boots, pulled out their tongues and insoles, and draped our socks over warm stones. Steam rose from them and drifted away.

As the dogs panted and found places to rest, I asked Hugh about the lay of this island community, what he had observed when he had surveyed here. He shied away from my questions, eyes scanning the ground. "I'm not really an archaeologist," he said.

I looked at him and then looked away. I knew already from his dashboard that he was a traveler, not an archaeologist. I wanted to tell him I wasn't really a writer, but he did not need to hear that.

We sat in silence. Glowing boulders stood around us. We were sitting in the last oven of the day. The fluorescent lights of the research lab were being cooked out of Hugh's eyes. The rings of keys and locked cabinet doors, the countless mysterious derivations of pottery styles—everything fled from him into the sun, rising in thin wisps of steam.

. . .

The archaeological record from the thirteenth century around the Four Corners reads like a war crimes indictment: infants and children burned alive, skeletons marked by butchery, entire villages left with bodies unburied. Rock art depicts people bearing round decorated shields and using weapons on one another. At the time, populations were consolidated into local alliances, some settlements becoming very large and elaborate, surrounded by walls and guarded entry gates. People began using landscape in a defensive manner, turning terrain into fortifications for cliff dwellings and canyon head settlements.

Normally during a drought, Anasazi population centers would have disbanded, sending people into the hinterlands to farm in smaller, more sustainable groups. However, with increasing conflict people moved closer together for protection rather than spreading apart. They were protecting themselves, it seems, from one another. Too many communities had been established in too small an area. Burgeoning populations were competing for dwindling resources, contending with language barriers and scores of divergent heritages. The era was ripe for civil war.

A number of large settlements have been partially excavated at the foot of Sleeping Ute Mountain, and two of them—Sand Canyon Pueblo and Castle Rock Pueblo—have revealed what looks like massacres. Castle Rock was built around a sturdy mast of rock, a natural watchtower at the bottom of the mountain. Excavating only about 5 percent of this site, crews came upon the partial remains of forty-one bodies in a state of disarray. Most of the remains of a man with much of his face removed were found in one room, while his right leg—the bones still articulated—was found in another room more than three hundred feet away.

A field archaeologist from the Castle Rock excavation felt that the attack must have been well organized, telling me, "Even if they picked a time when most of the adult men were not there, you're still going to have some resistance. People are armed. Everyone is on foot, and all they have are bows and arrows, knives, and stone axes." This researcher figured that up to two hundred warriors would have been needed to bring down the settlement.

Sand Canyon Pueblo, not far north of Castle Rock, came to a similar end. A massive fortification with 420 rooms, 90 kivas, and 14 towers, the pueblo had been built around the craggy head of a canyon, where it is now buried in the oceanic green of a piñon pine forest, its ancient mounds and pits evenly blanketed in dirt and piñon needles. Heaps of fallen buildings are gathered closely together, broken up by airy plazas and a prominent half-moon-shaped structure with the remains of smaller buildings within. Although construction of this site was swift, it was built with considerable planning as to how internal neighborhoods were to interact—precincts partly closed off from one another, divisions within divisions. The pueblo was enclosed by a one-story perimeter wall that must have made for an impressive sight, daunting to any invaders. But the wall did not hold.

Excavators at Sand Canyon found a bedlam of human bones. The corpses had not been formally buried but instead were left scattered about in the pattern of a slaughter. Death had come quickly to these people, terror raining down on them.

. . .

A white ceramic bowl sat on a drape of black felt. It had been excavated from Sand Canyon Pueblo. Wearing cotton gloves, I reached out and tipped the bowl slightly, as if arranging the moon in the night sky.

Inside this vessel lay a geometric filigree of thin black lines. The center was an empty pentagon. From it black paint radiated outward, like the ripples created by a stone dropped into the water. These kaleidoscopic ripples—enlarged, crosshatched, and locked together—filled the bowl to its rim.

I was photographing vessels from Sand Canyon and Castle Rock. I took a picture of the bowl, then stepped back. From site reports I knew that it had been found not far from the skeleton of an eight-year-old. The child had been thrown onto the hearth of a kiva, left arm and leg twisted horribly backward. A lethal blow had been struck with an ax to the back of the head, and cut marks on the skull indicated scalping. Archaeologists who worked on these sites are hesitant to use any provocative language, but what they found calls up scenes of hysteria as warriors sacked the pueblo, weapons and shields clattering, mothers crying out for their children. One archaeologist told me that *hysteria* is far too sensational a term, suggesting that the attack—which she called a "warfare event" in keeping with archaeological nomenclature—may have happened at night, when the people were asleep, as if carnage wrought in darkness was somehow more peaceful, slumber rolling over into death.

Such a quiet annihilation seemed strangely plausible from where I stood eight hundred years later—vessels resting calmly around me—but I knew that it had not happened that way. Most of the recorded deathblows had come from behind, the backs of the skulls depressed or smashed in. The holes in the skulls matched the size of stone axes found in the area. People had been taken down in hand-to-hand combat; these had not been quiet deaths.

A man walked in through the open door behind me, carrying another vessel, a grapefruit-size seed jar that he held in front of him as if cupping a newborn. He was the director of this lab, keeping track of all the artifacts removed from a number of excavations in southwest Colorado. He set the seed jar on a table behind me, adding it to a growing assembly of beautiful intact vessels.

The lab director admired the jar for a moment—its small round mouth and black inward scrolls of paintings down the sides. He turned to retrieve another from the storage room.

I went on with my work, moving from one vessel to the next. So many intact vessels had come from these two sites, and fine ones, too. Susan Ryan's great-house excavation on the Great Sage Plain had not produced anywhere near this number or quality of vessels. Ryan had dug into a site that had been formally abandoned, its rooms prepared for departure like a body bathed and dressed for the grave, artifacts neatly arranged on the kiva floors before the roofs had been set on fire. The more valuable vessels had been carried away as the people had left on their migrations. The residents of Sand Canyon and Castle Rock had had no such opportunity. They had been caught unaware, leaving everything in its place.

I had handled vessels from Ryan's excavation, and they had

Seed jar found in a kiva at the Sand Canyon Pueblo. In storage at Crow Canyon Archaeological Center. CRAIG CHILDS

seemed cold, like museum pieces. These pots from below Sleeping Ute were vibrant against my cotton gloves, hot in my imagination. They represented unfinished lives, people caught and killed in the middle of their days. The seed jar that the lab director had just brought in was only half-painted, part of it seemingly unfinished, as if time had run out unexpectedly.

I picked up a bowl that had been found in a room with an unburied infant and a decapitated man. Every bone in both of the man's legs had been spirally fractured, indicating a great deal of force; his long bones had been beaten into splinters while they were still fresh. Torture, perhaps, or a brutal desecration of the dead.

As I set this bowl on the black felt, I saw shadows streaking across walls, women with knives slashing furiously at their attackers. At the same time, I sensed the daily clatter of life, the bowl set on the floor as someone turned to fetch a bundle of firewood, a baby toddling toward it with an irresistible grin, her fat little fingers latching onto the fine ceramic rim. And then a warning cry. A crash of bone. A figure in the doorway.

The context of these vessels from below Sleeping Ute belies the common notion of the Anasazi merely as peaceful farmers, naked and quarter-dressed peasants strolling barefoot through museum dioramas, their tiny brown faces agreeable and intent. This widely held concept of a purely tranquil people strips them of their authenticity, making them either woefully simplistic or divine in their serenity. In a world racked with thousands of years of wide-scale violence, where even Buddhists have gone to war, perhaps we invented the idea of the Anasazi to soothe our troubled minds. Meanwhile, there is ample evidence that these people were not at all immune from hostilities. Like the rest of us, they engaged in death.*

Next I photographed a mug excavated from the floor of a kiva. Other mugs like this had been found at Castle Rock, and material caked inside them revealed the molecular remains of myoglobin with chemical signatures found only in humans. The same material had been found inside two corrugated cooking vessels. Human muscle tissue had been cooked. Although cannibalism has been a hotly contested issue, signs of it among the Anasazi have been appearing in different forms for more than a hundred years: the same kind of butchering marks on human bones that you would find on the bones of game animals and wear marks on the bone tips consistent with bones cooked and stirred in a pot. Skulls have been found baked, cradled in a fire so the backs are burned and the faces subsequently chipped away, perhaps to get at the simmered brains.

A great deal has been made of these finds, and for some the perception of the Anasazi has shifted from passive agrarians to brutal cannibals. The evidence, however, does not wholly support this view. Signs of cannibalism appear to be very localized, in places where violence reached a peak and everyday lives gave way to a holocaust. If nothing else, cannibalism suggests that these people were more complex and some faced a more troubling end than we previously imagined. As I photographed the mug, I thought, what would we make of Auschwitz if we excavated it a thousand years from now, or the Cambodian killing fields? Wherever there are humans, there are atrocities.

---

*For a historical, visual reference to orchestrated cultural violence in the world, see Jacques Callot's 1633 woodblock print *Les Misères et les Malheurs de la Guerre,* depicting a mass hanging in France; the Japanese Momoyama screen paintings of an 1160 insurrection at Kyoto; or even brittle photographs of American Civil War battlefields.

Why did this happen among the Anasazi? Perhaps there were factions involved in Mesoamerican-style death cults borne into the Southwest on trade routes from Mexico, dangerous splinter groups able to gain power in a time of crisis and drought. There may have been people indulging in the darker sides of a religion holding cannibalism as a tenet. Or eating a person may have been an act of supreme political or military dominance, as it has shown itself to be in cultures around the world when one group utterly obliterates another, eating the hearts or livers of exceptionally potent enemies. The evidence left behind at some Anasazi sites points to ritual killings—not just people being eaten for food value, but people butchered in precise manners. Perhaps this is merely what happens in a multifaceted cultural environment that has suddenly collapsed. No doubt there were both heroes and barbarians. If this evidence of violence in the Southwest proves anything, it proves that the Anasazi were human, prone to both flaws and glories.

The lab director came through the door again, now carrying a large jar. Paint danced fancifully across the clay, a sashay of black curves. The room was full of pots, no more space on tables and shelves, so he handed the jar to me. It rested like a globe in my hands, the whole of the world.

As the director left, I stood with this vessel, looking down at its swaying patterns. The paint had been applied more quickly than on some of the others, especially the lidded jars that had been found in kivas. On this one a number of lines overshot their marks, brushstrokes laid too long, a smudge of pigment mixed with too much water. The personality of the artisan was somehow made more real than in a work that shows no defect at all. The vessel seemed to move in my grasp, singing of effort and a trembling hand, a story of the living. And yet it contained a story of annihilation. I moved pots aside and set it down, exhausted from all the death.

. . .

In the canyon light slid back like screens of silk, the world darkening, blue upon blue. Hugh and I had an hour, maybe an hour and a quarter, before evening stars would begin to show. In a canyon of ice and boulders hooded with snow, I kicked in every step to find solid ground below. My pants were frozen like iron bells from the knees down. I stopped and glanced behind me. Hugh was coming up along a trough I had cut through the snow, his steps as slow as mine.

The reclined cliff we had descended earlier was not an option, an impossible bare-handed climb on a sheet of ice. Instead we aimed for the head of a steep side canyon we figured would take us up through the forest and back to the pickup. Tumbledown boulders made the bottom of the side canyon too treacherous in the snow, so we balanced along the sidewalls, attending to contours of short cliffs and inward gullies. The dogs poked in and out of every route they could find, but I did not trust their choices. I took my own way, at my own level of comfort, passing into a ravine of fallen piñons, boot soles navigating under the snow, a gloved hand down for support.

There was no extraordinary danger of getting lost. Chances were good that we would reach the top and find the pickup. If not, we had enough gear to live through a single night—the makings of a fire, the ability to dig ourselves a snow cave—although we would probably be heavily frostbitten. This was the hard kernel of winter. It was the time of deep cold when, in the thirteenth century, the hatches would have been sealed closed, the pueblos huddled in isolation. Maybe only the scouts, the hunters, would have been out, returning at dusk, ducking into rooms in their robes and leggings. Everyone else would have remained in their chambers, perhaps gathered for warmth in the kivas. It seems significant that in these higher elevations north of Chaco, kivas became much more prevalent than in previous centuries. Communities hoarded kivas like coins. These underground chambers may have become sacred for new reasons, places for everyone to gather in winter firelight, wishing the long nights away.

In these darkest months I imagine kivas filled with the sounds of snores and blankets pulled up, a dog waking with ears perked to some movement, a family drifting down the ladder looking for a place to lie down, wrapping the children in turkey feather robes.

As I dug ice out of my boots with the crook of a finger, I thought this would have been an especially dangerous time. There could be no more devastating an attack than in the middle of winter. Where would you run in your bare feet, in the thin blanket grabbed in the last reckless moment as your pueblo burned behind you?

Every returning scout, I imagine, would have been a blessing, the stamping off of snow, a report that all was frozen and quiet in the land beyond.

I found myself at a dead end, stuck at a snow cornice over a drop. Hugh shifted direction, breaking trail up and around through pillows of brush. I backtracked and followed him. We crawled through low gaps in the trees, hands clearing branches out of the way, gloves tinkling with shards of ice.

Hugh found the way out, emerging onto an arm of smooth land. The sky opened, clear but for a thin whorl of high clouds. This night was going to be rich with stars and vacuously cold.

The snow was harder on the plain, its surface smooth and windblown through a maze of juniper trees. We padded across the snow crust, breaking through in weak places, shattering into shards at our shins. We moved with the quickest steps we could muster, looking for our prints from earlier in the day. I paused to catch my breath in this final glacial light. As I glanced through the piñons, I saw Hugh in the distance. He looked like a ghost in these halls of twilight, his movements appearing in one place and then another, a missile of a dog diving into view every now and then. Whips of wind scoured the snow, stinging my face.

It was a relief to be out of the canyon and up where I could see the full sky again. I thought of Susan Ryan's excavation, her site out in the open. It seemed meaningful that she had found no signs of violence there or at any of the nearby sites, while the canyon country below bears so much evidence of war. The old great houses and their rings of villages were not built in canyons, not piled against cliff bases. They were clearly open to attack should anyone have wished, yet they seem to have been left alone. Perhaps this is because they are much older than, say, Sand Canyon Pueblo. They may have been part of deep-rooted alliances. Many were in view of two or more nearby settlements, so that if one was invaded, the others would have been notified immediately, able to mobilize fighters at a moment's notice.

Who was attacking whom? Wandering gangs, hunter-gatherers, old enemies, warring clans? No definitive answer has been found. For a long time researchers have been looking for evidence of outsiders, people who were not Anasazi, but no outsiders have been found. The attackers, it appears, were the Anasazi themselves. The Anasazi were not merely one group of people. They were many. Even in the context of a single settlement, multiple ethnicities have been found, some groups of skeletons within a pueblo displaying more injuries—both healed and fatal—than others. In one case, a number of buried female skeletons from a distinct ethnicity were marked with healed wounds indicative of those seen in modern domestic-abuse cases. Perhaps these women were captured from another group and treated poorly. Whatever the case, there were differences among people that may have fueled conflict in times of strife.

Traveling beneath the dark throne of Sleeping Ute, we finally found our prints from earlier in the day—the crust broken open, plates thrown sideways as if an icebreaker had barged through. We fell into these old steps, plodding now.

Our trail led straight back to the pickup, its grille peppered with clods of snow. Hugh let the dogs into the camper shell—a scrabble of claws on the tailgate, fur shedding continents of ice. We got into the cab, our clothes crackled and bunched, our shoulders pressed against each other's, cushioned by our coats. Hugh started the engine. The heater roared, slowly melting the windshield, shapes clearing from the ice matching the various items on the dashboard. My beard dripped into my lap.

Hugh pushed the stick into first gear, and the tires took hold. It was cold enough now, the snow clotted and hard, that we sailed across this jetty of earth, a lone pair of headlights moving through the night.

Loneliness

NEAR HOVENWEEP

Mountain lion tracks led across banks of old snow and between boulders that had fallen midway down a canyon. The tracks were no older than an hour; round pads, round toes, claws retracted for travel. I followed them, glancing farther ahead through the frozen shade of piñon trees. The lion had been heading toward the edge of an inner canyon. I hoped it knew the way to fresh water.

Cold as it was, I had not seen good water for days. Carrying a winter's camp on my back as I hiked west toward Utah, I melted a pan of snow for drinking every morning and every night. For several days I had been traveling alone among ruins of pueblos and small, scattered villages, their broken pottery slowly disappearing back into the ground. I had picked up the lion tracks a short distance back and now followed them to a shelf of rimrock dropping off to an inner canyon below. What looked like the remains of a classic, defensive thirteenth-century settlement appeared at the edge of the canyon, just heaps of masonry stones and the outline of a half-moon-shaped tower the lion had walked through.

From here I could see down tiers of cliffs to the canyon floor, where cottonwood trees stood bare. It was February. I did not see any water down there. The mountain lion tracks went over the rim, down along a narrow chute where a stone house had once collapsed. I followed.

Cliff dwellings were built into the bedrock eaves below the rim, and I walked under them, careful not to step directly on the lion tracks, a habit of respect or maybe just a whim of attentiveness. The lion's path led me along a ledge to the back of the canyon, where I found an overhang dripping with springs. I let my shoulders drop, relaxing. No need to melt snow tonight.

The springs had carved a shallow cave beneath the head of a cliff, an elliptical eye weeping into beds of stone and moss. I passed beneath winter-killed monkey flowers, where beads of water gathered at the tips of dead leaves and flower stems. Water croaked and mumbled. Drops fell onto bare rock. The fastest outpouring stuttered into a pool, falling from a bulge of moss hung from the bedrock ceiling. I would hesitate to call it a breast if it were not one. I touched it, gingerly, feeling the swollen cushion of water inside. The lion had come, too, and had left its tracks in wet clay below. It had paused at the pool, had raked water up with its tongue, paw prints planted at the edge. I moved to the same spot—still careful not to cover the lion's tracks with my own—and opened my mouth below the green, translucent nipple. My mouth filled even before I needed another breath.

I let my pack down and unbuckled my water containers. Holding each one up to this falling water, I listened to them fill, the musical sound of abundance. The Anasazi had done the same, I thought. Late in the thirteenth century, whoever lived in this local settlement gathered water here. We animals always come to the same places to drink.

The shadow of evening overtook the canyon. I needed to find my place for the night, a burrow somewhere to wait out the encroaching cold. I stowed full water bottles in my pack and walked back up through the ruins—coat, hat, and gloves on now, gratified by the weight of spring water on my back, enough for another couple of days. Whichever water bottles I did not keep in my sleeping bag tonight would be bricks of ice by sunrise.

Higher in the canyon I settled in a copse of half-lit junipers, took off my pack, and pulled out a down sleeping bag designed for twenty below zero. It would be barely warm enough tonight. As darkness came on, I stripped my clothes, my skin quickly cold in the brittle air before I constructed my night's layers: long johns, undershirts, a down vest, a wool serape, a coat on top of that. When I was done, only my eyes, my mouth, and the crest of my nose were left exposed. Stars coalesced overhead. Rigel and Procyon shone so cleanly they looked as if they might crack from their settings and fall to earth.

The assembly line of my camp kept emerging from my pack: a pot, a stove, sacks of food, crushed and dried pinto beans. With no moon tonight, I used my headlamp as I went around camp collecting juniper twigs. For later, for this sinking cold of stars, I would have the company of a campfire.

I started a pot of water to boil on a small stove. A cup of tea would be a good beginning to a long night, thirteen hours until daylight and everything frozen solid, even the mountain lion motionless somewhere, half-awake and dreaming of dawn.

. . .

Late that night I built a fire no larger than my open hand. I leaned my body over it through shackles of cold, still air. Dry twigs of piñon pine and juniper gave off no smoke at all.

I had finished dinner long before. A disk of ice lay in the bottom of my metal teacup. As I hunched over my fire, it struck me that winter nights would have been exactly the same at the end of the thirteenth century—a vast loneliness, scads of hard, wind-driven snow left here and there. The bold frame of Orion would have wheeled through the sky in the same way, slowly circling the North Star. For whoever was left, getting water from a spring as I had today would have been a triumph. The Great Drought hit this region in about A.D. 1276, and after that only the deeper springs kept flowing. Driven by necessity, or greed, or fear, the last Anasazi who had not migrated closed in around these terminal water sites, where they were trapped.

As I snapped another twig in my gloves and slid it into the fire, I thought of what Eric Hansen, a contract archaeologist working in this region, had told me. He had taken an interest in what kind of firewood people had used, trying to determine what plants had been most abundant and thus how much groundwater had been available long ago. Rather than looking at indoor kitchen hearths, Hansen had focused on outdoor fire pits, figuring that people outside would have been burning whatever was closest at hand. In the early years the ash and charcoal he found indicated the use of long-burning piñon and juniper. After a few centuries these two species were replaced by cottonwood, which burns quickly. Then, finally, came sage, a plant that burns like straw. He believed that he was seeing the steady deforestation of southwest Colorado.

Then Hansen noticed something he had not expected. At twelfth- and thirteenth-century sites people began burning cottonwood again, as well as greasewood, two plants that require high water tables. He had anticipated just the opposite, that while drought was setting in and populations were increasing, water would be disappearing. Hansen pieced his conclusion together: early deforestation must have allowed grasslands to prosper, and in turn the grass kept rain and snowmelt in the soil rather than letting it drain away. With the existence of a healthy water table during increasingly dry times, this part of Colorado would have been especially attractive to farmers. Perhaps this was why so many people ended up moving here.

The phenomenon that may have saved these people also was their downfall. Too many people had come to live and farm in this area, and when the rains ultimately ceased late in the thirteenth century, the whole cultural system of the Four Corners gave way. Some people ceremoniously departed from older pueblos atop the Great Sage Plain, while others had no such freedom and perished in warfare along the flanks of Sleeping Ute Mountain and elsewhere. In whichever manner they left, this is the period widely believed to have been the end, the fall of Anasazi civilization.

By the beginning of the fourteenth century, virtually no one remained in the Four Corners, at least not enough people to have left a record of themselves. I imagine some leftover families of hunter-gatherers, maybe a few ragtag households of short-lived farmers, but mostly solitary travelers tending their small fires back among empty canyons.

My fire burned down. I blew on the last coals, warming my face, and finally there was only the icy light of the moon.

. . .

In the morning I walked across drums of hard snow in a scrubby woodland. Yuccas stuck up from breathing holes in the snow. Piñon trees stood dead all around me, victims of bark beetles and a lack of rainfall over the past few years, their ruddy brown needles liberally sprinkled on the white ground. I had been seeing dead piñons all across the Colorado Plateau: in the Grand Canyon, along the Dolores River, on Cedar Mesa. A similarly widespread piñon die-off has been documented in the thirteenth century. Although it has often been blamed on Anasazi industry, it more likely resulted from a lack of precipitation and a subsequent invasion of beetles. Such cycles are common in this land.

When I came out of the bony trees at the rimrock edge of a canyon, I spied seven masonry towers across the way. They looked like melted candlesticks, some with only their right or left halves still standing.

These seven towers, fifteen or twenty feet tall, were the final, tattered banners of the Anasazi. I was startled by their dazzle, their brave stonework. I had not previously known of this site, although I knew I would be seeing towers as I approached Hovenweep, a region of round and square Anasazi pillars on the Colorado-Utah line.

Towers were the last form of architecture erected in the Four Corners, most of them situated to look over the best farming areas. They were not necessarily signal stations, like those of earlier times, but were defensive watchtowers built to protect the fields and the farmers who were still here in the late thirteenth century. Looking across at the daring way these towers broke the skyline, I was riveted by the message they delivered, hardly diminished in all these years: *We have spring water under this caprock, and farming fields all within view, and we will defend this place with fierceness and vigor to the very end.*

Anasazi towers frequently show signs of extensive burning, and not necessarily the kind seen in ceremonial departures. One excavated tower revealed the remains of more than thirty infants and children, who appear to have been burned alive. The positions of the skeletons suggested they had been taken to the tower's roof, where they had no escape, and then the tower was set ablaze. This event

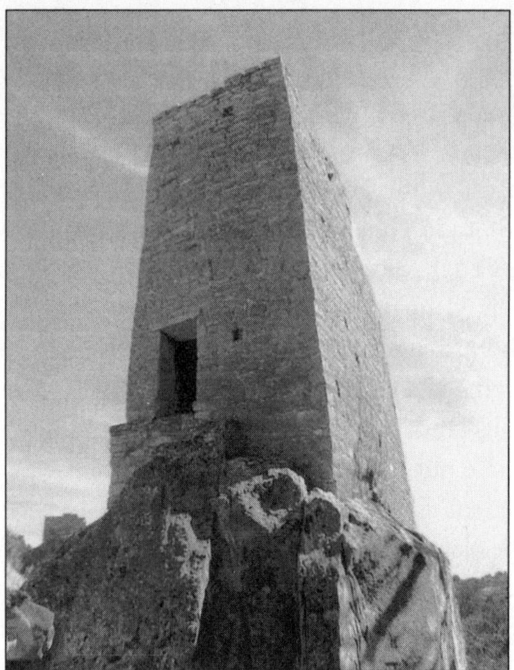

Three-story tower built on a boulder in the thirteenth century near the Colorado-Utah border. CRAIG CHILDS

cuts deeply into my imagination. I see smoke roiling intensely, black with grease, a sickening fist of flame crashing in as the roof collapsed, sparks bursting from splintered beams, the whole flaming turmoil plunging into the kiva below.

This would have been a fire signal meant to be seen from all around, an act of warfare shining across the land. It appears to me that it was a surgical strike intended to bring down an entire settlement at once, killing its children, what was most precious to the people, so that any survivors would flee, dispirited. The killers would have returned home, proud perhaps, and reeking with horror; brothers, fathers, and uncles turned to heroes, to monsters.

In a burned tower just inside Colorado, within a day's walk of these seven towers, the remains of eight men, three women, and three infants were found in the rubble. The excavator of that site reported finding the skeletons lying in confusion one upon the other. Beneath a T-shaped doorway in the wall of this tower, he uncovered a pair of infant skulls, the rest of their skeletons missing. "One skull," he wrote, "to our great surprise, was covered with hair, which to all appearances, was thickly matted with blood."

When these towers were no longer able to defend the land, they became torches marking the fall of one settlement after another, as if sending a message ahead: *Your neighbor's children have been burned alive, and yours are next.*

I pulled out my binoculars to study the seven stonework minarets, thinking this place must have felt very isolated in the last decades of the thirteenth century. Built in a time when most of the Anasazi had already fled, the tower complexes around Hovenweep were the last cultural strongholds. They would have been surrounded by the sounds of sharpening knives, hunter-gatherers constantly ready to lay siege, disenfranchised villagers and crop workers turned into scavengers and murderers in the country beyond. Everyone else had migrated out of here.

I pocketed the binoculars and started down into the canyon. As I reached the other side, coming through bunches of sage, architecture began peeking up around me—leftover walls, throngs of rooms, the ground cratered with kivas. Building stones were everywhere, thousands upon thousands of them. As I passed through these fallen structures, I pieced together in my head how these people might have gotten out of here. Perhaps the residents slipped out the back door, leaving their long-defended home to the vulturous tribes in the area, their departing caravan flanked by warriors as they headed toward rumors of a better place. Or they might have been surrounded and slaughtered before they got that far. However it happened, people finally left these towers empty.

I walked up to the nearest tower. It was big enough to have been a grain silo, its fat stone blocks neatly cut so that the remaining wall had a clean curve all the way around. Exterior faces on these stones were uniformly pecked in pointillist style, a decoration lending the tower a whitish appearance on the outside. The builders had certainly meant for these towers to be seen, giving them an ivory sheen in the sun.

Grass was growing inside the tower, the first green grass anywhere, spring coming soon. As I swept my hand around the outer stones, walking the full perimeter of piles of rubble, I thought about the people who had stayed here. Perhaps they were thinking, We should have left ten years ago. They had watched others depart before them, villages left vacant, and for whatever reason they decided to stay. Maybe they had young children, and the thought of months or years of walking, crossing the southern deserts to reach a foreign land, was simply too much for them. There was no guarantee that they would have found anything better than this. Maybe they thought they could weather the drought and fight off the marauders threatening them. After all, they had these glistening towers to protect them. But at some point they must have realized their error.

. . .

The question of why the Anasazi left has been debated since it was first discovered that they were gone. Drought has been the most popular theory. Wood specimens stored at the Laboratory of Tree-Ring Research in Tucson, Arizona, have revealed irrefutable evidence of the Great Drought. The land dried up, dendrochronology researchers surmise, and as it did, either people left or they stayed and perished.

But a closer examination of this drought has revealed that it may not be the smoking gun it was thought to be. Carla Van West, an archaeologist looking into the effects of drought, used the same tree-ring data to calculate the amount of soil moisture that existed in a 700-square-mile area of southwest Colorado during those dry years. Even in the depth of the drought, she discovered, there would have been enough water to have allowed at least a portion of the original Anasazi population to remain.

Drought played a role, according to Van West, but in the end it was not the most crucial role. People left, she believes, because of overriding social forces. These forces would have been powerful enough to uproot hundreds of settlements and send people away quickly. What exactly were they? The answer is not merely in the tree rings.

"The reality is that we can gather as much empirical evidence as possible," Van West once told me, "but we are missing the ideological and cosmological components of who they were and why they left."

Van West surmises that in the face of social turmoil and environmental strain, the Anasazi did what they had done for countless generations before: they picked up their entire culture and carried it off.

"We have to realize that people simply cannot live without each other," Van West told me. "We need other people in order to live meaningful lives, in fact just to function."

She went on. "It must have been getting very lonely for some people. If you weren't migrating out, you were left behind. There weren't enough people for mates anymore, not enough people to marry. If you want to maintain your culture, you need to go wherever your people have gone."

Van West offered herself as an example. She is Jewish but estranged from the Jewish culture. When her father died, she found herself trying to arrange various ceremonies and burial procedures without having the necessary contacts or personal knowledge. In her confusion she began to understand what it means to live far from your own people.

"For the proper religious ceremonies, you are required to have at least ten men in the congregation to recite the prayers," Van West said. "If you aren't near a Jewish community, you can't have a Jewish burial with the necessary rituals. They bathe the dead body in such a way and dress it in certain fine linens before laying it in the ground. You would have to find a rabbi to consult, one of your own persuasion. It seems like it might have been very much like this for people living in the Four Corners. Pretty soon there aren't enough of your own people nearby to keep the true heart of your culture alive. And then why would you stay?"

As communities began moving out during dry years, they took with them masons and farmers; fortune-tellers, priests, and healers; midwives, clan leaders, astronomers, and record keepers. Even if people could still grow corn and subsist off the last flowing springs, their elaborate cultural alliances had departed. It was only a matter of time before the final settlements caved in, detached and alone.

Van West said, "I think the whole spiritual, social business is very important for a cultural landscape. The environment certainly puts constraints on the physical facts of being alive, but people don't live simply as economic creatures. There are much farther, deeper relationships."

All that remained of these relationships in the Four Corners were garrisons of towers, the ultimate pennants defiantly erected over the Anasazis' last fields and springs. I walked through these standing hulks, wondering whether these people had felt abandoned, left to defend a homeland no one was coming back to. Grinding stones used for meal stabbed out of the ground around me. Snow huddled in the northern shadows of ruined towers. I walked through with a measured, pensive gait, as if passing through a cemetery.

. . .

At dusk I sat on a piece of capstone. I had walked into Utah now, or at least close to it, and from this isolated point of rock I could see clearly in all directions. Gloved hands stuffed deep in my coat pockets, shoulders drawn, I readied myself for the next round of stars. This quiet country and its empty houses seemed forlorn to me tonight, and I thought that the last people living here must have felt something like this, final hunters looking across these lands, feeling the press of emptiness, the tower complexes having finally fallen.

I looked south along the darkening aisles of the Carrizo Mountains, the Lukachukais, the Chuskas. This is where the land divides. Go to the left of these mountains, and you end up settling along the Rio Grande in New Mexico. Go to the right, and you enter a landscape of red sandstone towers and green mesas broken up with canyons, the country of Kayenta in Arizona.

The logic is simple. If the Anasazi left, they had to go somewhere. Their civilization did not end here, as is so often believed. Gone from the Four Corners by the end of the thirteenth century, they took many paths away from this place. A diaspora spread into the rest of the Southwest along ancient migratory routes and lanes of trade. The Anasazi moved on like a spectacular road show, carrying with them the foundations of their culture: signature T shapes, dazzling pottery, lofty architecture, and a penchant for corn. They did not disappear. In fact, a larger future lay before them, and they left a trail to follow to get there.

As I sat on this high dome of the Colorado Plateau, distant provinces of the Southwest visible on all sides, I imagined the question that must have been asked by many people eight hundred years ago: where do we go from here? Every village and pueblo, every family, had to make a decision. I watched as each horizon diminished into the indigo skyline, the white-crowned San Juan Mountains the first to recede. Next went the thorn of Shiprock, south near Chaco, and then Mesa Verde. Like lights going off in a house, room by room the Four Corners went dark as even the high peak of Sleeping Ute and its lesser attendant summits turned into yet another shade of night. The last to go were the Abajo Mountains in the west, a black nick against the stars.

Part Four

SOUTHEAST UTAH

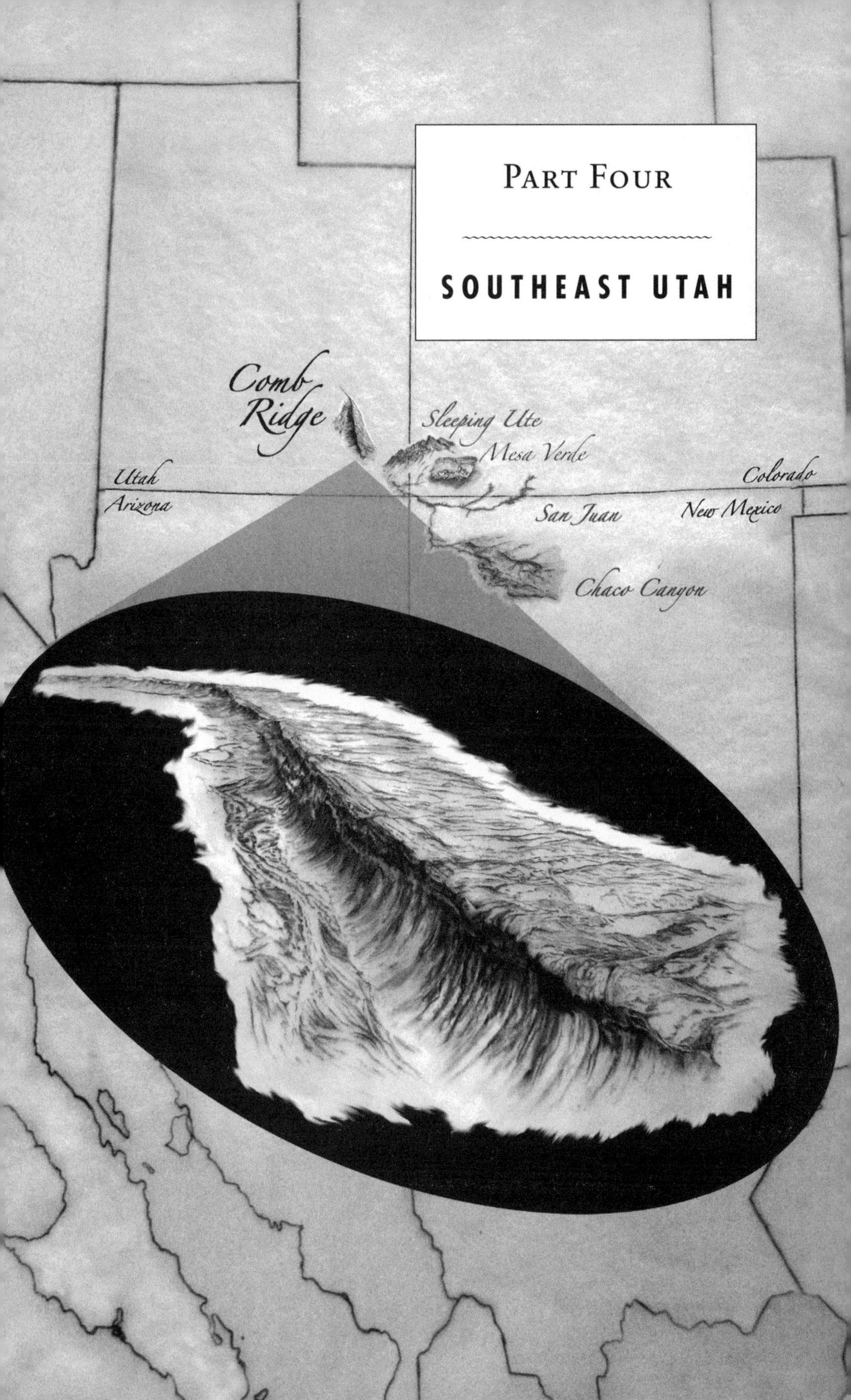

Escape Terrain

CANYONLANDS

This catwalk ledge runs midway along a cliff face. Following it an hour before sunrise, I pressed the weight of my body against the wall, the most stable posture I could manage. Glancing toward my feet, I noticed several beads of bighorn droppings. Very slowly I came to one knee, shoulder against the rock face, and reached two fingers down to touch the droppings. They were old, dry as wood, dropped maybe five years before. A bighorn had been out here, a stocky, agile animal that would not have come to this ledge if it was not a way to somewhere. I rose just as slowly and continued on, convinced I was not pinching myself out on this cliff.

There are few places to walk in this land of canyons in southeast Utah. You can follow the canyon floors, but they frequently end in impassable pour-offs, or you can stay on the rims until they whittle down to nothing, leaving you stranded on a distant point. Most of the time you end up here, not at the top and not at the bottom, picking along scaffolding cliffs and ledges. This ledge was not clean like a sidewalk, but was instead cluttered with broken rocks that were loose under my boots. An alarming sense of depth sailed below me into the canyon, dust raining down with every step.

For a couple of weeks I had been looking for a way up to the higher levels of this terrain, waking before Regan or Jasper stirred in our tent, my daypack loaded with a quart of water as I went out hunting for routes. The plan each morning was to make it back before Jasper woke.

There were no trails, just courses of geology, aprons of boulders pulled down by gravity and erosion, and fractures leading into back-door canyons. This morning I kept to this mid-level ledge, seeing how far it might take me. There was a fallen section ahead, the ledge gone. I grabbed what I could of the wall and stepped across, experiencing an instant of vertigo, the cliff gaping below me, before touching the other side.

The ledge continued, a tricky little path littered with bighorn droppings, each dry pile a word of encouragement. The cliff bowed, offering a place for me to climb to a high platform of bedrock balanced between two side-by-side canyons. From here the world looked as if it was falling apart around me, broken and heaved pieces of earth shaped into narrow fins. I had not found a vantage this high in nearly three weeks of poking around. I stopped under the open stage of the sky, the desert falling around me into impossible labyrinths. This was one of my home landscapes, Canyonlands, to which I returned often to walk the corrugated desert surrounding the confluence of the Green and Colorado rivers. I once spent an entire winter traveling and sleeping among the cliffs and frozen water holes here.

It is a place to disappear.

This is where the far Anasazi lived. Most of their remains date to the thirteenth century. These people came scrambling out of the core areas, some from Mesa Verde, others from Kayenta, another Anasazi bastion due south, in northern Arizona. I once saw an artifact from Canyonlands kept in a small Utah museum. It was a ceramic effigy of a bighorn sheep, its body the size of a kitten, long and hollow; its white surface was heavily embellished with tidy black spirals of paint. This artifact was found partially buried in sand and flood debris in a canyon, picked up by a couple of hikers. Its workmanship was classic Anasazi—careful details in the ceramic face, the ears, the horns, and the stub of a tail—not necessarily something one would expect from such a recklessly complex country. The artifact stood on four stunted legs atop a freshly unfolded bed of newspapers in the museum's back room, a new acquisition.

The same museum also has an older, more cherished artifact, a resplendently feathered sash that was found in Canyonlands. This happens to be the finest and most well-preserved pre-Columbian item made of feathers in the entire Southwest. Kept under glass, the sash is made of blue, green, and mostly scarlet macaw feathers woven into a soft gray padding of squirrel fur. It was found in a sandstone cave in the southern reaches of Canyonlands, an artifact with roots in tropical Mesoamerica. I have gone back to look at the sash a number of times, my eyes entranced by its knots and the awe-inspiring, almost phosphorescent red feathers, nearly unbelievable in this subdued, pastel desert.

These two artifacts, the ceramic bighorn and the sash, represent a geographic confluence between the north and the south. With their coiled, massive horns and acrobatic leaps through canyons, bighorn sheep are the quintessential beasts of the Colorado Plateau and especially Canyonlands, able to escape suddenly into the most imposing terrain. Depicted on tens of thousands of rock art panels, these animals must have held a prominent place in the minds of the people who lived here. Yet these people also must have been fascinated by the brightly colored feathers comprising the sash. These feathers no doubt came from the distant and perhaps legendary land of pyramids and jungles to the south. This broad spectrum is what it meant to be Anasazi.

. . .

As I stood on this high point of stone, burgundy cliffs of Wingate sandstone rose behind me to the west, forming a palisade called Island in the Sky. Not far to the southeast, beyond the steepled country known as the Needles, the Abajo Mountains stood robed in snow. To the southwest I could see the tips of a convoluted region called the Maze. I recognized places all around me, each view full of memories. For years I had hunted routes in this territory, yet I had never before reached this bridge of sandstone. For a moment I stood very still, taking it all in.

I was already too far along to get back in time for Jasper's waking. I watched the rising sun, then turned around and quickly descended, level by level, into the shadows below. Sunrise turned back into the fine gloom of dawn as I dropped lower, back toward the night that seems always to be lurking along the canyon floors.

I followed a canyon toward camp as it narrowed to a single pinch.

This was a route I had used off and on over the past ten years, a thin outcrop of rock over a free-fall drop, the only way through. It is the checkpoint through which all travelers must pass when moving from one region of Canyonlands into the next. Dangling off this rock shelf, I would have to inch across it, then jump down to another ledge below. I took off my pack—no room to climb down with it on my back—and as I turned to make the jump, I noticed above me pieces of a ruin I hadn't seen before, simple stones neatly placed, the grin of a low wall in an overhead cliff. I scrambled up to see if a human hand had really made this place. Teetering on the tips of my boots, trying not to leave footprints in the dust, I found a chamber filled with rubble, many of its facing stones having fallen away. It was Anasazi. Right above this pinch, they had built a guardhouse from which they could see anyone coming through, a natural bottleneck controlling the entire region.

Among the archaeological sites I have seen in Canyonlands, many are positioned in a way that makes me think the Anasazi were constantly checking their backs, keeping an eye on crucial points of movement in these canyons. Pressed by the thrust of war and overcrowding in the thirteenth century, they vanished into this hard, convoluted desert to escape the burning pith of their civilization. If you wanted to hide somewhere, guaranteeing no one would follow, this would be the place to go.

Perhaps the people living here were hunters and farmers who had lived in southeast Utah for generations. Only now there was no room for them to travel without running into danger—towers and pueblos burning in the distance. So they retreated into this warren of canyons, guarding its passages.

I turned around and shot down from the ruin, jumping over the edge of the pinch. I reached back up with the full extent of my fingertips to grab my pack, then disappeared down the deep, stone rabbit hole below.

. . .

Everybody was awake when I arrived at camp. The rounded shell of a small side canyon sounded like a nursery full of toddlers' echoes.

Friends had come to visit us in the backcountry, bringing their twin three-year-old boys down the Colorado River and up this dry canyon to camp for a few days. As I approached along a narrow, cobbled wash, the twins were pretending to be elephants, marching around and half-shouting, half-singing. I took Jasper, who was barely two, into my arms and kissed him good morning. Sweat still beaded on my brow, and the smell of climbing was strong in my clothing.

Once I had Jasper and the twins were marching a cacophonous circle around me, Regan threw me a smile and disappeared alone into the rocks and ledges beyond our camp. This was our daily routine—one person in, the other person out.

I joined Greta, the mother of the twins, who was cooking breakfast over a camp stove, our kitchen assembled under a slight overhang. While she stirred a pot of oatmeal, she asked me what it would be like to survive in Canyonlands. She thought that with the Colorado River nearby, a person might be able to live pretty well here.

"This would be one of the worst places you could choose," I said. "The Anasazi farmed here, but they were truly out on the periphery of their abilities. It took them several centuries just to get corn to the point where it would grow in sand off residual moisture from rainstorms, and I think even still, agricultural life was marginal when they tried it here."

She pressed on. "What if you tried to make a living off of drought-resistant crops—beans, amaranth, squashes, melons, corn? It seems like you could dig some ditches off the river and start up a nice life for yourself."

Greta, an attractive, sandy-complexioned woman in her thirties, was daydreaming, wondering whether she could make do out here. The desert was unfamiliar to her.

"You can't trust the river," I said. I did not want to undermine her daydream, but she had asked. "It would be hard to know how close to shore to plant from one year to the next. One year your crops will get washed away in high spring runoff, and the next year they'll be stranded and dry, not enough snow in the mountains to keep the river up. You'd be better off dryland farming at the mouth of a side canyon, where you can pick up moisture stored from flash floods, but then you'd have to plant fields everywhere, in every promising nook. Maybe one or two would turn out. The rest would get flooded out or wouldn't get any water at all. It would just be a hard place to farm, I think."

Greta seemed disappointed with my answer. I knew what she was asking, though. She and her husband, Paul, had been contemplating the decline of Western civilization, wondering what they might do if one day the cities fell. They had moved from the city themselves, working their way out to rural western Colorado, where they were now learning the intricacies of farming and irrigation. Should a true apocalypse occur, they were hoping for a place more remote, a sanctuary. They had responsibilities after all, children who might suffer if the world turned bad. In times of political turmoil and war, a parent is likely to consider such things. Greta and Paul were not driven by paranoia. It was simply a concern quietly nagging at them. They wanted to be prepared for a dire recession, or martial law, or an unfavorable new world order. They had both been born to East Coast affluence, and Paul had worked in corporate America. He had assured me that if things turned sour, people below the top one percent of earnings were going to be left out in the cold. He knew well the gap between the chosen few and the rest of us.

I was pretty sure Greta and Paul could not make it in Canyonlands, even as hardy as they seemed. Regan and I probably couldn't either. At the moment we were all just explorers in this desert, with our space suit gear, our little bags of organic nuts and tins of fish ready to satisfy the slightest hunger. These convoluted canyons of bare stone would not yield easily to subsistence. Only the desperate, the terrified, and the truly adaptable would turn to this landscape as a place to live.

Greta kept stirring the oatmeal, and she asked me about the Anasazi. We had found an arrowhead the day before, so she knew people had once been in these canyons. I told her that the Anasazi, at least the ones residing or passing through Canyonlands, had made a living from part-time agriculture and probably full-time hunting and gathering. There were probably other people here to contend with, the more northern Fremont culture reaching this far south. They had to work hard to survive here.

"You find their caches every now and then," I said. "Little masonry granaries full of corncobs the wood rats have eaten clean. They left things all over the place, even out here—broken pottery, abandoned villages."

They left things about, signs of isolated settlements, but now no one was here but us. In the end this place did not work for them.

. . .

At nap time the side canyon fell silent. Regan offered to guard the tents and the sleeping toddlers while I showed our guests around. Greta and Paul wanted to see a bona fide Anasazi ruin, one not touched up by stabilization crews or reached from a marked trail. They wanted to see the real thing back in the wilderness. The closest site I knew was across the river.

We uncovered a canoe that Regan and I had cached down in the main canyon among shedding tamarisks and whips of willows, and used it to ferry across the Colorado River, swollen with spring runoff. On the opposite shore under high red cliffs, we tied up to the arm of a box elder.

We headed up through thickets of char-barked tamarisk trees, ducking down to our knees, clothes dusted with spiders and ants and powdery detritus. Continuing on through walls of desert olive, we reached an open bottomland of sand, saltbush, and greasewood, where lizards darted away in the light. I told Greta and Paul the site was up ahead, a place I'd found many years back while exploring the base of a teardrop-shaped butte.

The butte hung over us, the slopes beneath it littered with thousands of boulders ready to move at the slightest provocation. We took a cut where the wind had hollowed a slender, dim passageway out of the rock, our shoulders brushing the narrow sandstone corridor.

As we walked along a bare floor of sand, Paul craned his neck to look up at cracks of daylight overhead. He asked me what kind of archaeology I had found in the area.

"If you go straight up about eight hundred feet, there's an old hunting camp, probably pre-Anasazi, very hard to get to," I said. "It's on the top of the butte, escape terrain where bighorn sheep go to evade predators. I figure it was an ambush site for hunting sheep—some spear points and stone skin scrapers, a bunch of flaked stone, a few outdoor fire hearths. You see that sort of stuff around here.

"On the opposite side of the river, there's a ring of stones where a cliff dwelling collapsed, and it marks one of the few routes where you can actually get from the river all the way to the upper canyons."

"Do you have these places marked on a map?" Paul asked.

I shook my head no and explained that these were just small sites, places better committed to memory than paper.

"You don't tell archaeologists?" he asked.

"This is the middle of nowhere," I said.

"And you know they were Anasazi?"

"No one else was ever here," I said. "Fremont Indians, but it's hard to tell the difference between their cultural remains sometimes. There were some uranium miners in the 1950s, but they didn't even come this far back. The only ones before them were Anasazi in the thirteenth century around the time the cultural shit was hitting the fan in the Four Corners. They were looking for a place to hide."

Our passage opened to a tablet of cliff that had fallen facedown like a monolith toppled from a Greek ruin. We climbed over it and saw a natural hollow eroded from a cliff. In the back was a slim granary. Greta saw the structure as soon as I pointed it out; Paul had more trouble. It was unevenly built with large, uncut stones taken from the immediate vicinity and mortared with local silt turned into paste so it would look like all the natural jumbles of red rocks around it. For the most part, granaries you find in Canyonlands are the size of household refrigerators, sometimes as small as the average freezer—enough storage for a family or two.

Eventually, Paul coaxed the granary out with his eyes.

"There's a bigger one around the corner," I assured him.

We climbed past the first granary, its darkened, rectangular entry situated on the opposite side, so it would not stand out to anyone passing by. I pointed out to Greta a large corner stone that had fallen from it within the past five years. The fall had left a big, fresh socket of mortar behind.

As we walked farther into this natural cove, I said, "Over there you can see the bigger granary."

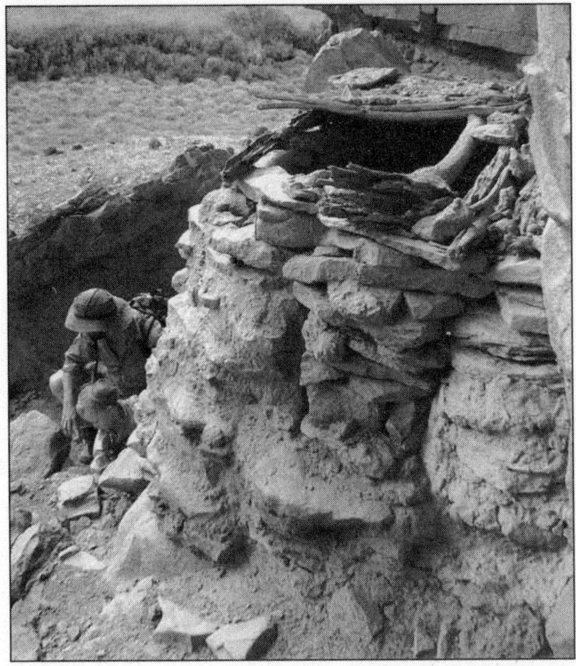

A well-concealed granary above the Colorado River. REGAN CHOI

Paul paused for only an instant before he saw the masonry chamber across from us, as large as a Dumpster. Its rounded walls were made of red stones and mortar. Paul quickened his pace once he recognized it, crossing boulders and a thin gray ledge of limestone to reach it. I stopped to watch him, his demeanor, trained for authority and poker games, suddenly turning to that of an inquisitive boy, long legs and arms springing forward, greeting this ruin with arms spread wide. It was a subtle structure, nested into the cliff, hard to see, though large. It still had a roof, or part of a roof, made with slabs of mortar and narrow beams—a little crooked, but as straight as they come in this desert. Seeing the remains of the roof, Paul glanced back at me once with an inspired grin, then got about his business of exploring. Here was something he could appreciate—fine, inconspicuous handiwork.

Greta approached the ruin more slowly, admiring the structure. I paused at the granary's rough clots of mortar, each dimpled by fingertips eight hundred years ago, the whorls of fingerprints still apparent on some. I had been here six or seven times over the years, but I couldn't get enough of this large granary, an endeavor of people living on the far edge of their civilization, someone's final hope.

Paul asked what purpose it might have served.

"A storehouse for a small community," I ventured. "They had set up shop at the foot of this cliff."

"And this wood," Paul said, studying what remained of the roof, "how old is it?"

"Eight hundred years," I said. "The dryness protects it. It takes forever for wood to decay."

Paul considered this and touched the wood with his hand. He nodded thoughtfully, understanding the wood's antiquity through its feel.

In front of the granary I squatted near a small chute, framed with two short wooden uprights. The whole granary looked like a prototype of a modern silo. But there was no grain inside, a surprising absence of corncobs for a building in such good condition. In fact, there was a dearth of any artifacts, only a smattering of broken pottery, indicating that occupation of this site had not been long.

Canyonlands offers glimpses of life—some broken pottery, a few corncobs, the circle of a shield bearer painted on a bedrock wall—but rarely more. There are no great houses or roads, no T-shaped doors or truly D-shaped buildings. This was the northernmost dead end for the Anasazi. Some had come this way, but they did not stay, and they were not here with their full cultural complement. These refugees' bloodlines may have finally ended here.

Most archaeologists who have spoken to me about this region have a bias against the hard barrens of southeast Utah. When the map of Anasazi occupation is drawn in academic papers and textbooks, it barely reaches this far north. This region is thought to be too cold, too hot, too dry, and too remote. If you are looking for grander traces of the Anasazi, you must go south, across Salt Creek, with its painted handprints and carefully constructed granaries; over the high ground flanking the Abajo Mountains and farther into southeast Utah, along the looping, pale meanders of White Canyon, where kivas begin to appear, some with their original ladders still in place; then along Comb Ridge, toward the Neapolitan sandstones of Cedar Mesa, where murals painted inside cliff dwellings have a surprising freshness. Nearby you will find the last of the great houses and the path many Anasazi took when they finally exited the Four Corners. By the end of the thirteenth century, even the refugees who had fled to Canyonlands were gone, their granaries deserted. Their bid for survival in this complex landscape failed as the core of Anasazi civilization marched south, leaving this place even more remote than ever before.

. . .

As I wandered through natural rock rubble beneath the granary—boulders shattered wide open where they had fallen—I noticed an ivory curve in the ground. I flicked it out with my fingers, startled to see it was a seashell. A little olivella as delicately scrolled as a shaving of white chocolate, it had come from the sea seven hundred miles away. In all these years I had never encountered a single shell artifact in Utah, and now I could not suppress an astounded smile, the rush of promise quickening my blood. In my imagination lines of trade routes suddenly fired across the continent, long threads winding through deserts, over austere, cracked mesas to arrive here. It completed a triad for me: feathers from Mesoamerica, bighorns from the canyons, and a shell all the way from the sea.

I rolled the shell into my palm, thinking it had come from a necklace, someone's prized possession carried through who knows how many years and villages and hands to end up in Canyonlands. Its string had snapped one day, a tinkling of a hundred small shells on the ground. The owner had crouched to pick each one up like a grain of rice, recovering all except this one, which had rolled under the nearby couch of a boulder, impossible to find until it washed out eight hundred years later.

Looking for this? I asked silently, holding the prize between the tips of two fingers.

I showed my find to Greta and Paul. They detected the excitement in my voice, understanding how far we were from the nearest ocean, perched on a high desert plateau landlocked in the Southwest. I slipped the shell back into the ground, and the three of us sat on boulders below the granary, looking across the dry mouths of farther canyons.

Paul mused that if people had shell necklaces, they must have had good lives. He said that maybe a family could be raised in this hard country.

"What finally happened to the Anasazi who lived here?" he asked.

"They didn't last," I told him. "Not out here. I figure they had some good days retiring in the cliffs, watching the river pass by. But now they're gone, so the evidence is pretty clear that they didn't make it."

"They could have made it, maybe," Greta said, always hopeful.

I shrugged. "I'm sure they could have. I think it's a case of bright lights, big city. I mean, if this is your refuge, you're safe, but you're out of reach, far from contact with civilization, and you still remember what it was like in the big city, living at the glorious heights of your people. No movie theaters anymore, no cafés; no bustling trade routes; no churches with full congregations and altars crowded with ancient ritual objects. Just a prized shell necklace you brought with you to remind you of the old days. They got away just in the nick of time, and maybe they barely made it out of the great abandonment alive. But I imagine once they got themselves settled here and dusted off, they looked around and said, *Now what?*"

Paul said, "I wonder if we could do it. I mean, if we had to."

I just breathed, wondering if the Anasazi of Canyonlands enjoyed their last years in seclusion, imagining them alone, their children gone to find what happened to their civilization. Setting traps to catch wood rats and lizards, tending marginal crops, painting shields on walls to frighten enemies away—maybe they had a good retirement in this dead-end landscape I so adore.

If we had to, I thought, maybe we would be able to survive. With a pair of twins and Jasper growing up strong and sticking around at least for a little while—and with some other skilled companions for making tools, tending check dams, and hunting rodents—maybe we could maintain a viable community in this beautiful oblivion of canyons. But often, I also thought, I would find myself pausing at the tops of the high buttes, looking beyond our local ring of snow-capped mountains, wondering whether civilization was still ticking along.

Red

THE HEAD OF COMB RIDGE

Two mirror-image buttes stood before us in a high basin dotted with piñon and juniper trees. The buttes looked like a pair of salt and pepper shakers arranged on a table. Rings and mounds of ruins surrounded them and were even stacked upon their two flat heads. The place looked like the remains of a crowded citadel out of a Tolkien novel, a Rohan capitol. Behind the two buttes stood the awesome white gnomon of the Abajo Mountains, glazed in a fresh spring snow.

As we emerged from the woodlands, we lifted our hands to shield our eyes from the mountainous brightness, high and distant snow gleaming in the sun. We stopped and stared at the perfect assembly of buttes before us as if they were statues, twins turned to stone right where they stood. We were a small group of travelers, archaeologists and friends out walking for several days around the northern end of Comb Ridge, about fifty miles south of Canyonlands in Utah.

Many archaeologists have dismissed this area as culturally underprivileged, an empty quarter, but we were seeing otherwise. The Anasazi had once come here in significant numbers. This morning we had already found the remains of a great kiva among the piñons. We had seen vestiges of ancient settlements nearly everywhere we walked—ruins sometimes mistaken for hills back in the woods, masonry structures shouldered with sage on high points between canyons. Some with fallen towers looked like thirteenth-century Hovenweep; others resembled the terraced eleventh-century great houses of Colorado and

New Mexico. Civilization had once taken hold out here, not strings of loosely affiliated settlements, but communities packed with public architecture. A place thought to be isolated and nearly off the Anasazi map turns out to be an entire map in itself.

This must have been some sort of city, I thought as I walked, aiming for the space between the two buttes. Not a city like the ones we think of now, but a city for its time and place, an industrious center inhabited for centuries by many different peoples. The pottery I saw on the ground, gray pieces of kitchenware and black-on-white sherds scattered around my feet, came from numerous different ages. The most visually striking ceramics were red wares with candied-apple surfaces. This color must have stood out in its day among the customary whites and grays.

I knelt and flicked up a piece of broken pottery as red as lipstick. Painted black designs crossed its curved face, exactly the same geometric images one would see on an Anasazi black-on-white vessel, only on a much different-colored canvas. Red is the color of a specific geography, maybe a different people: the western range of the Anasazi, sister to Mesa Verde, cousin of Chaco. I had not seen much of it in the east, in Colorado or New Mexico. It was new here.

Around A.D. 725 people in southeast Utah began making this striking red pottery by using iron-rich clays and slips and by allowing excess air into their kilns, oxidizing the vessels to an amber, pink, or tomato color. When you see this kind of pottery in Chaco or around Mesa Verde, it generally means it was acquired in trade. Finding so much of it beneath the twin buttes told me I was moving into new territory, where red wares had been manufactured over a span of about four hundred years.*

Production of red wares ended in the twelfth century, at about the time populations were moving out of the Chaco region and into the Four Corners area, where they built up places such as Mesa

* In southeast Utah, Abajo Red-on-Orange dominated between 700 and the mid-800s, followed by Bluff Black-on-Red from 800 to the mid-900s, and finally Deadman's Black-on-Red from the 800s into the 1000s. The production of red wares ceased in Utah by the twelfth century. They were replaced by the rise of Tsegi Orange Ware in northeast Arizona.

Verde and the Great Sage Plain and began erecting great houses in the far country of southeast Utah. At that point red ware manufacture moved a couple of hundred miles to the south, into the Kayenta region of northeast Arizona. The next type of red pottery to appear was Tsegi Orange Ware, which emerged in the twelfth and thirteenth centuries. Unlike the red wares that preceded it, which were tempered with rock, Tsegi Orange Ware was tempered with fine bits of crushed pottery. New ceramic techniques and the movement of production to Arizona suggest some sort of cultural shift to the south, the appearance of a new center away from the bustling Anasazi core. Looking for the escape route the Anasazi had used, I found a passage to follow in this red pottery, an arrow pointing to the south.

Back at the head of Comb Ridge, I rubbed my thumb on a sherd's smooth red surface, tracing what had once been the inside of a Deadman's Black-on-Red bowl. Red may represent an old, western lineage of Anasazi. This kind of pottery was made by people who once lived out on the edges of Chaco in this red sandstone country, staying away from the urban hubs but carrying on trade with settlements in Colorado and New Mexico. When the eastern populations sprawled in this direction, bringing great houses and municipalities with them, the red ware makers left, moving south. I returned the sherd to the ground, fitting it back into the mosaic of thousands of other sherds, wondering whose territory I had entered.

. . .

As we continued toward the paired buttes, it dawned on me that I had seen such sites before. I knew of buttes topped with ruins around Chaco, right along the Great North Road. And Chimney Rock in Colorado had its own great house, vaulted above everything else. I also had encountered numerous ruins perched on buttes and high rock stumps all across northwest New Mexico and southwest Colorado. Here in southeast Utah the Anasazi were up to their old tricks, building on the most remarkable and elevated pieces of land they could find, as if stepping onto a soapbox to announce their presence. The red ware on the ground indicated a regional variation, but the daring style of settlement told me these people were pure Anasazi.

The Anasazi around the Four Corners had many provincial differences, such as the scrupulous masonry of Chaco versus the slightly looser stonework of Mesa Verde. The farther west one travels, the less regimented the masonry becomes. Perhaps the Anasazi of Utah and Arizona were more rural, less interested in the urban edicts and niceties of Chaco.*

Different as they may have been, the Anasazi were also a single entity, held together by corn, kivas, T shapes, and intensely geometric pottery designs. I was following a collection of many people bound together by a civilization, similar traits shared across a vast landscape. I was tracking a cultural organism.

The ruins ahead of us were trademark Anasazi. They stuck out of the ground as I walked, surges of walls and inner chambers mostly buried by soil and sage. Hundreds of rooms encircled these two buttes. Jonathan Till, one of the archaeologists in the group, was convinced that this was the site of a great house similar to those of Chaco. It was a western great house, he said, a red ware great house.

Till paced out grids on the ground ahead of me. He had been to these buttes before, but he was still not able to define exactly which cluster of ruins represented the great house he believed was here. He walked back and forth with potsherds in both hands, his eyes tracing the footprints of buildings.

Till was interested in twin features in the landscape. He had been roving this region surveying sites and finding significant archaeological remains wherever a noteworthy set of geological twins appears—matching pairs of buttes or boulders or alcoves. He felt as if he was getting into the psyche of the landscape, beginning to understand some

*Regional diversity among the Anasazi is perhaps best and most delicately revealed by the way murals were painted inside kivas in different places. The eastern Anasazi in Colorado and New Mexico tended to paint kivas to look like the inside of a decorated ceramic bowl, the encircling walls bearing the same designs you would see within a vessel. By contrast, in the west kiva interiors were painted with designs more common in baskets and on textiles. The physical construction of kivas was more or less the same across the board, but the different decoration techniques imply ethnic or social distinctions, perhaps divergent bloodlines between the eastern and western groups.

aspect of how people once related to their geography. His pet theory was that these western Anasazi had aligned themselves with twins on the land, going to great lengths to build their settlements and shrines to look through natural goalposts and gateways on the horizon.

Till felt that these twin buttes were a major landmark in the western Anasazi pantheon, where people's eyes turned not back to Chaco or Mesa Verde, but back to the flare of Monument Valley in Arizona and Utah, maybe to the swollen, redbrick bends of Canyon de Chelly, and across to the high, pine-covered mesas of Kayenta. We had been teasing Till about his theory—pointing out twin beer cans abandoned on the side of the road, peeping between twin tree stumps in the forest—and he laughed with us, a gentle man in his thirties, short kinky beard framing a white, freckle-peppered face.

I followed Till as he scrambled up a rubble slope to the top of the easternmost butte. The coral-colored bedrock around the butte's rim was punctured with drill holes, places where timbers had been inserted into stone so buildings could be erected out to the very edge. These buttes must have been impressive to look at, I thought, geologic twins rising into multistory masonry blocks surrounded by a mosh pit of kivas and housing complexes below.

"Maybe it doesn't matter if there was a great house here," Till said, his voice buttered with a Tennessee accent. "Maybe the whole place is a great house."

Till was hoping to convince Susan Ryan, one of his closest colleagues, that this region had been loaded with riches—not some Anasazi backwater, but a bold and populous center. Skepticism came naturally to Ryan, who came up behind us and crouched among the ruins, her eyes scanning the floor plans around her. As Till crouched beside her, she conceded that she was surprised by the extent of settlement here.

"They definitely had a way of building," she said, gesturing with her head in Till's direction. "They're aligned with the landscape."

. . .

Over the coming days we moved south by several miles, and the Abajos began leaning behind us. Along the way ruins stuck up from the ground like gravestones. We found red pottery at nearly every site, rose petals lining the path. The pottery led us through ranks of great houses built around the head of Comb Ridge in the thirteenth century, the last of the Anasazi great houses. They seemed to be a mix of eastern, Chacoan architecture and western pottery, perhaps the final expansion of an old guard civilization into the hinterlands before falling apart.

Till led the way among gullies and sagebrush-lined washes, showing us up steep, terraced slopes on the side of a hill. Partway up I realized this was not a hill; it was yet another great house. They were everywhere it seemed. The terraces we climbed were built by hand, each one littered with the remains of masonry structures. This was a stout, pyramidal building, part natural rise, part earthen fill, and part stonework, erected so that it could be seen from miles in all directions. Its bare, ruined frame reminded me of unexcavated Mayan temples in Guatemala or Honduras, suggesting a connection to a much larger civilization—a familiar shape from Central America and Mexico.

Ryan sat beside me at the peak of the great house. She twisted a piece of dry ricegrass between her teeth as we watched Till pacing through sage below us, hunting for shapes in the ground. He stopped every once in a while and looked up for a long time, framing the horizon around him. Looking for twins, I thought.

"He doesn't stop, does he?" I asked.

Ryan shook her head.

Eventually, only the three of us remained on this southward journey. Till, Ryan, and I were the last of the group. We moved through sage lands where reddish sandstone bedrock began to appear beneath our feet. The gentle downslope of erosion unveiled more bedrock, until the sage disappeared entirely. Small, naked washes cut beneath us into rivulets that we followed into dry streams and, below them, cascading wells of stone. Discreet cliff dwellings began peeking out of high coves, the hermit crabs of the Anasazi world. My eyes traced bare-boned ledges and fissures in the rock for routes connecting one unlikely place to the next.

Canyons rose around us blush red and gaping, until we were at the bottom, pushing through tamarisks, seep willows whipping at our hands. Till knew the particular side canyon we wanted, one of many. He took a turn at its mouth and led us along a quickly narrowing passage filled with spattering sounds of springs. We heard musical echoes, the sounds of dripping and running water rising into the rafters of cliffs above us. At the back of this side canyon, the walls were round and smooth as eggshells.

Here the Anasazi had carved and painted numerous images and symbols. It was as if we had walked into an open book, words printed around us. We moved slowly under these rock art messages, our heads tilted back, finding faces painted above us. The faces were set in a row, their eyes watching us pass, and nearby was a human figure bearing a bird on its head—a duck it seemed.

Just beyond the rock art, a pale arc of sandstone rose out of sight

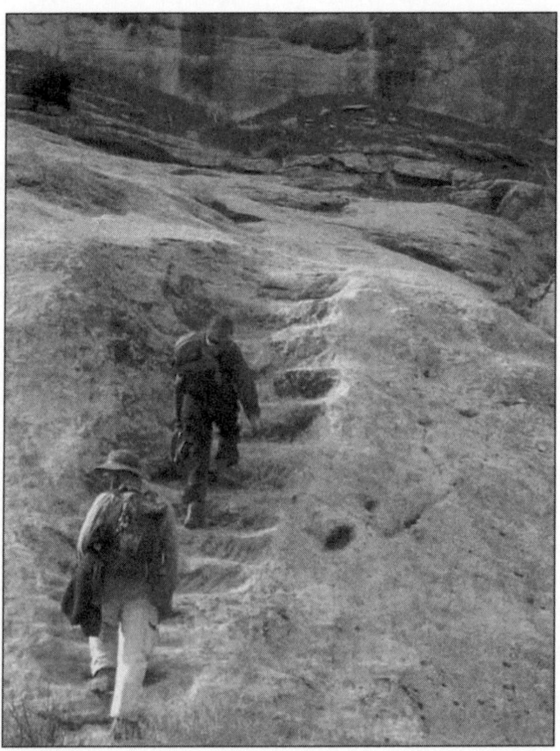

Susan Ryan and the author ascending stairs carved into a rock face near Comb Ridge, southeast Utah. JONATHAN TILL

above us, the end of the canyon. But it was not the end. Directly up the face was a hand-carved stairway, its steps as deep as cabinet shelves. It looked much like the staircases I had seen carved up the walls of Chaco Canyon, reaching toward roads above. The three of us stopped, eyes traveling along the clean steps cut in the bedrock.

Till looked at Ryan.

Ryan nodded, impressed to see such a bold and ancient path.

"After you," Till said.

THE GREAT WALL

COMB RIDGE

This was the clearest pre-Columbian road I had ever seen. Walking along its faded trough, I could not tell whether it looked this way because my eyes had grown accustomed to discerning obscure Anasazi features or it was actually the bold, straight road it appeared to be.

Jonathan Till assured me that it was the latter. Along with Susan Ryan, we were following this ancient road across a rolling plain of blackbrush east of Comb Ridge. As we went, sage sparrows scattered from the brush before us. Miles ahead Comb Ridge stood in a line all the way from the one visible horizon to the next. It looked like a stone tidal wave rolling across the land, solitary and enormous. This road was leading us there.

That is not to say that the road was especially easy to see in the light softened by low and swift storm clouds riding in from the west. The road was several hundred years old and badly weathered. Where it seemed to disappear, we had to crouch to get it back, framing the low-angle horizon with our hands. When we found it again, we kept walking, noticing the way that cheatgrass shimmered around old cuts where the road had been built, patterns of low chops in the ridges.

Till had discovered this road a few years back from an airplane, flying low in morning light when he could best read the topography. When he saw it, there was no doubt in his mind what it was, a human-made stroke across a blackbrush plain. As soon as he could, he verified it on the ground, mapping the longest, straightest procession of its kind known in Utah. He planted survey flags so that he could turn around and look along four miles of little orange banners behind him.

When Till first told me of his find, I mentioned it to a few archaeologists working in the Chaco area. They assured me that no such roads existed in Utah. Although they had never been walking in Utah, these researchers authoritatively explained that Utah was too far away to have "Chaco roads." Ancient foot trails maybe, but not roads. I saw now they were wrong. A straight clearing stretched in front of me as plain as day. It was about thirty feet wide, as big as any Anasazi road made in Chaco.

The presence of this road meant that Anasazi labor had been organized on a massive scale in southeast Utah, not only to erect great houses, as we had seen around the head of Comb Ridge, but also to cut and fill this impressive thoroughfare before us. Till told me that there were many more roads. This was no backwater. Chaco, or at least the ideology that gave rise to Chaco, had reached its long arm into this desert. The road was slightly more recent than those in northwest New Mexico, a twelfth-century development, maybe even thirteenth-century, marking a later spike in Anasazi civilization.

Ryan pulled out her camera, angled it for several pictures, and then returned it to her pack. She knelt and kneaded the sandy soil with her fingertips, contemplating the width and directness of this feature, realizing that she had never before seen such a clear road in the Southwest. Her face was full of thought as she plucked up a few pieces of chipped, sulfur yellow stone, debris from someone's toolmaking many centuries back.

She stood and looked at Till.

"It's a road," she said, as if it should have been known long ago, as obvious as an ink mark ruled across white paper: a long, straight road out in the western Anasazi netherworld.

. . .

In the afternoon, as low gray clouds poured across the crest of Comb Ridge, Till walked in a halting sort of way. He kept stopping, hands hanging limp but open, as if he were feeling the air. To a stranger watching him, Till might have seemed lost, sometimes walking back on himself before turning around again, or pausing for long minutes without moving. I recognized this way of travel, the same way I get about, responding to the many glints of light, unaccountably kneeling to feel grains of ricegrass between my fingers. It is how one reads a place.

The air suddenly cracked with thunder, and all three of us stopped in the middle of the road to listen as a rumble played across the miles. It was the first thunder of the year, spring thunder. When we moved again, it was to pull on rain gear, and we continued under a light patter of drops, the air smelling like cold metal. The road kept going, though I could hardly see it anymore. Till knew where it was, and he followed it, leading us toward the only tree within miles, a gray fist of a cottonwood that was just beginning to bud. It marked a damp spring coming out from an undercut.

At this tree the road ran onto a hump of bedrock, the first time so far it was not cut into blackbrush and the gritty soil of stabilized sand dunes. Where it ran across bare rock, nothing of the road could be seen except one long groove cut into the rock, a thread meant to maintain the road's continuity until it could resume in the soil on the other side. I crouched and swept a hand out from under my poncho. I ran a finger down this wet groove, thinking it looked exactly like grooves found in the bedrock of Chaco Canyon, a furrow carved in a straight line no more than one knuckle deep or wide. No one knows what these grooves were for, but they appear only in association with roads.

I stood and turned to look at Comb Ridge, still a couple of miles away. From this vantage it had the appearance of an ice palace—its white sandstone slick with rain—and canyons melted out of its face. Till and Ryan were already moving ahead, a long way left to go with evening on our heels and the storm growing. I picked up my pace so I would not lose them.

In the very last light, rain sheeted down my poncho, and I walked with my arms partly extended, collecting a basin of fresh water and then throwing it off so it would not drain down into my pant legs and boots. It was no use; I was amply wet. Till and Ryan also were wet. We moved swiftly.

Coming down a gully of mud, Till turned around in front of me and crouched down on his haunches, where he paused to study a rock in the ground.

"What is it?" I asked.

"Basketmaker cist," he said.

He reached out a hand and wiped the mud away so I could see more clearly. All I saw was a rock.

Ryan came up behind me and asked, "What do we have here?"

Till said the same to her, Basketmaker cist, and she nodded sagely.

"It's just a rock," I said, not so much to point out the obvious, but to elicit more information.

"There will be another one here," Till said, moving his hand over and wiping off more of the clay gumbo.

Just as he predicted, there was another rock, same shape and size as the first one. Till kept wiping his hand, smearing away the thin surface of mud, until the tip of a third and then a fourth rock appeared, beginning to outline a broad circle in the mud. I recognized it now, a storage pit, a cist lined with rock slabs, typical of the early Anasazi, known as the Basketmaker culture. This was a granary from the sixth century A.D., or maybe the eighth century. Whatever century, it long predated roads built in the Southwest. I looked around in the rainy dusk, seeing no geographic reason for a person to build a storage chamber here. According to Till, the road we were seeing, at least in its largest form, was built around the twelfth century. Certainly, the Basketmaker people did not have this landscape officially surveyed, as the later Anasazi might have. They would not have built granaries along exact lines across the land back in the sixth or eighth century, would they?

Till just shrugged in his raincoat when I asked this. He swamped mud back over his find until only the first rock was visible. Then he stood, rubbing his hands in the rain to clean them.

"I think they were using this lane of travel long before there was a road engineered through here," he said. "The road was just a formalization of whatever was here to begin with. Don't forget, they lived here for a long time."

We followed the road as far as we could in the dark, although after a while we were just guessing. No moon tonight, the clouds racing over us as black as ink. We finally stopped at what Till assured us was the foot of Comb Ridge. We got out gear and heated tea over a stove. For a long time we stood sipping from our cups. We slipped on gloves and warm hats so that we could erect our tents, constructing a brief little hamlet along this nearly forgotten road. There we slept, sheltered from the rain.

. . .

In the morning coyotes howled from creases in the land, down between gullies and shields of standing bedrock. Pups yipped with their high voices, and they danced, perhaps amused at us walking with our clown suits of pants and coats, our packs, notebooks, and water bottles. We stopped and listened, somewhere around sunrise, mist hanging among the canyons of Comb Ridge. The rain had ended, broken into drifting clouds. The ridge now looked like a mountain before us, thousands of feet of raw, seamless stone angling toward the west. When the coyotes stopped their morning announcements, we continued moving. With no more road to be seen, we were now following Till's projection, an invisible line pointing us up one of the many canyons cut through the raised back of Comb Ridge.

Usually bone-dry, Comb Ridge was inhaling the previous night's storm, and now it slowly let water back out through its porous sandstone, dribbling from seeps and springs where maidenhair ferns grow. The canyon we were following steepened across clear pocks of water holes, finally leading us up into broken ledges where boulders were chopped all over each other and we had to climb hand over foot. Every several steps a rock would slide—nothing bone shattering, just a disquieting clamor as it tumbled for one or two seconds.

As we stopped to rest midway up, Till pointed to show us a cliff dwelling tucked high over our heads. It had a single, T-shaped door facing down at us like a banner, an arcane cultural message that perhaps let people in pre-Columbian times know to whom this passage belonged. People of the T. Curious how they had even gotten up there, I pulled out my binoculars and scanned the cliff face. I saw ladder rungs carved into the rock, footings perhaps for a wooden

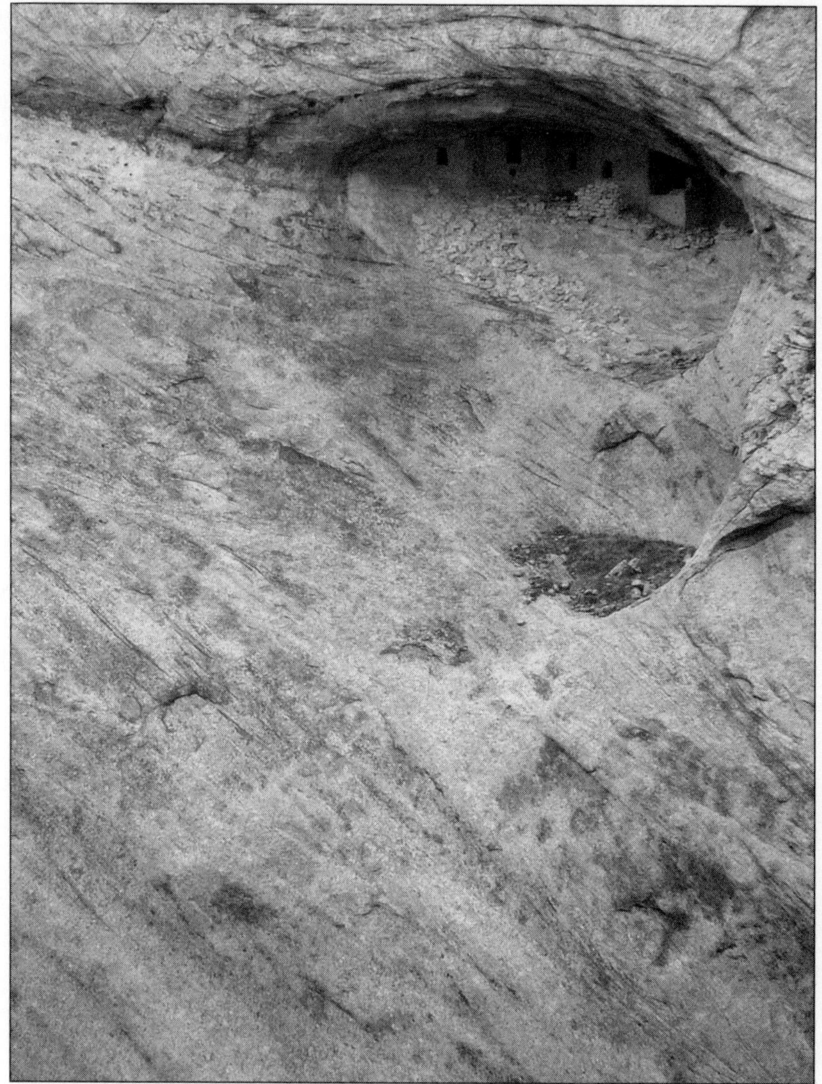

Small thirteenth-century cliff dwelling on Comb Ridge. REGAN CHOI

stairway that would have accessed the site, postholes drilled into the cliff. The place looked like a guardhouse, its T-shaped eye keeping watch over all who passed below.

We started back up the steep planes of rock and reached a point where the curve of the planet became visible around us, high enough now that I could see Sleeping Ute Mountain in Colorado to the east, and just beyond it Mesa Verde. We were climbing a bell tower, it seemed, rising to where the wind busily cut across nude beige stone. As we cleared the top of Comb Ridge, the entire earth opened around us, gaping distances filling our senses. We saw not only the landmarks of the Northern San Juan Basin behind us but also well into Arizona to the south. To the west canyons streamed through the woodland bands of Cedar Mesa, the cliffs there alternating between salmon-colored and cream, places I knew were loaded with cliff dwellings. Beyond that my eye was drawn to a set of high twin buttes known as the Bear's Ears. The space between the ears was the target of Till's projected line, the destination of this road.

Till shouted in the gusting wind. He pointed at the remnants of a small masonry chamber worn almost completely away, a site that had once been a stone box. Till told us to take note of the color of the stones, pinkish, oxidized by fire. Someone had built a big firebox between the eleventh and thirteenth centuries, what Till calls "late Pueblo Anasazi."

Till was convinced that this spot, with an entirely unobscured view of most of the Anasazi world, was a fire signal. What else could it be? A fire ignited at the pinnacle of Comb Ridge in Utah could be seen deep into Colorado, New Mexico, and Arizona. How many other signals are out here? I wondered. At Chaco it took a century and scores of ground crews poring over the desert for archaeologists to figure out the relay system. In this part of Utah there are only a handful of dedicated archaeologists. What cunning mechanisms have yet to be discovered here?

Till never raised his voice excitedly, never demanded undue attention, but he wanted Ryan to notice certain things about the view from this fire signal. With one hand stuffed into his overalls pocket, he used the other to gesture across the horizon, pointing at the Bear's Ears. Winston Hurst, a prominent local archaeologist with whom Till worked closely, had led him to a great kiva over there in the canyon-cut striations north of Cedar Mesa. Seeing this isolated great kiva, Till plotted his line even farther, straight through the kiva toward the gap between the Bear's Ears in the distance. The kiva was built there, he surmised, to lie within an important cultural and geographic alignment. He turned and pointed the other way, back toward where we had started walking on the road yesterday. He said that if you follow the road's trajectory, it goes right down the carved stairs to the rock art we saw the day before. If you keep going, you will find a set of natural twin towers standing above the largest great house in the vicinity. The projected line ends directly between two symmetrical alcoves in the face of a cliff. Beneath these alcoves is a noteworthy boulder split right down the middle, surrounded with broken pottery, and with two holes of the same size chiseled by hand in the rock face on either side.

"Let me guess," Ryan said. "Twins."

"Twins are all along the road projection," Till answered matter-of-factly as he peered into the distance. "Both human-made and natural."

Till envisioned a pocket of finely orchestrated civilization, great houses tethered together by ancient roads, and the slice of Comb Ridge passing straight through them. When Chaco became the Anasazi center in the eleventh century, yet another center was beginning to form in this western landscape of twins. It was more spread out than Chaco, and with smaller sites, but it had the same hallmarks of alignments, great houses, roads, and fire signals. Whatever civilization was emerging on the Colorado Plateau then, it reached clear out to Comb Ridge, and eventually this branch of the Anasazi outlasted those living in Chaco. The great houses in this part of Utah were the last of their kind to be occupied.

Ryan's body was bunched together, arms crossed, one hand up to keep her hat from blowing away. She could see Till's point. This road was connected to larger landscape features, lined up with geography the way people back in Chaco had aligned themselves with the heavens. Perhaps this place was the yin to Chaco's yang, the earth to the sky. She turned slowly to take in the horizons: Hovenweep quilted with towers; the slums and citadels of the Great Sage Plain, where she had been excavating; Mesa Verde beyond that, full of secrets. The old guard centers of Aztec and Chaco lay farther off, unseen. Behind her, over a rise, lay Canyonlands, with its granaries built in the cliffs like kitchen cabinets. All of this was Anasazi. It was bigger than even Ryan had imagined, a civilization busily stretched to the horizons.

From there we turned and started down the other side. In spaces between tilted planks of sandstone, the wind died down, and Till told us that his road projection passes through here directly between two circular sites that must have been shrines of some sort. Walking among twisted juniper trees, we reached the first shrine, an extensive halo of cut and laid stones now fallen around one another.

As Ryan paced around the circle, she said, "Maybe a great kiva."

Till nodded, seeing that she could be right. He took us to the second shrine, which Ryan also believed to be a great kiva. We stopped there for a bit, out of the wind, as the sun broke through the spring storm. Ryan draped her body over a south-leaning boulder and lounged on it as if it were a bed. Warmed by the sun, she let her fingers fiddle down into the soil. She lifted out handfuls of potsherds, then let them spill out onto the ground. She seemed to be dreaming.

"Twin great kivas," she said, pondering.

Till found a place to sit on the other side of the boulder. "Twin great kivas," he repeated, also to himself. "Positioned at the top of the highest place around with the road passing right between them."

They were both seeing a larger landscape, its impressions forming in their imaginations: twins and lines, the Anasazi embroidering their geography with roads and alignments of kivas and storage chambers.

. . .

A short distance away we were faced with a harrowing palisade—the entire western flank of Comb Ridge a seamless cliff falling out below us. Till paused, rubbing his beard, his eyes studying the cliff edge. "The way down is right around here somewhere," he said.

A colossal block of cliff was separated from the face of the ridge. Coming down behind it, we squeezed into a tight space that dropped like a rope. There was open space below, nothing but air. Till led us down to where flat stones had been wedged, forming a staircase, some of the steps now gone, fallen into oblivion. Till reminded us to be careful. He was talking not about preserving our lives, but about not dislodging any of these placed stones, protecting the route. It had been used rarely in the past eight hundred years.

The crack let us out onto the western face of Comb Ridge, a blank wall of sandstone that was nothing like the comparatively gentle eastern incline we had just ascended. All along this side of the ridge Anasazi toeholds had been chiseled like rope ladders, the only way to get up and down. Many of these toeholds were so old and weathered that they were hard to see, much less useful for survival.

We spotted toeholds below us, faint marks in the cliff where people had once chiseled their way up and down. The face of Comb Ridge felt tremendous around us, a solid stone wall extending as far as we could see north and south. We traversed a ledge—not a particularly flat or wide one, but good enough—stepping gingerly around fallen stones that barely held purchase. Every now and then a stone slipped free, causing us to freeze as it skittered down the bend of the cliff and disappeared, not a sound to be heard.

We finally reached a ladder of little oval rungs the Anasazi had cut into the rock. The rungs were slim as soap dishes, hardly wide enough to feel with your fingertips, and they trailed out of sight straight below us. I could hear Ryan breathing deeply. Till wiped his palms on his overalls, drying the sweat.

I was out front, so I went first, moving onto the steep exposure. The rock formation had a good, solid grain to it, a sturdy grip for my fingers as I lowered myself down the face. Ryan followed, and Till after her, the three of us forming a string down the wall. I reached the spine of a jutting cliff flake, where toeholds were carved as if along a steep little bridge in a Japanese garden. I followed the toeholds, step by step, until the bridge came to a sudden end.

The rock below me had broken away, and the last step led straight into empty space. There had been an accident, a catastrophe long ago, when the remainder of the steps had collapsed. I shot a look up through Ryan's hands and legs, spotting Till above her.

"This is it?" I asked, startled by the abrupt end, the bridge out.

Till did not respond, focused on his own descent, patting at the holds, his face flat against the rock. I looked back down, thinking this break looked old, weathered, something that must have happened under the Anasazi's watch. If it was such an important route, tied into a great road, they must have repaired it. I glanced to the side and saw a fainter set of toeholds carved horizontally for a short distance, then down. They were not as well crafted as the originals, made more quickly and with less care, not quite so deeply cut.

Till had found a stable place and now rested against the bedrock.

"There's another way," he called down to me, his voice shaking, the route more difficult than he had recalled. "Don't try the route straight down; it's a dead end."

Right.

I inched onto the detour, my cheek dragging down the grainy stone. It was by far easier to go first, not having to watch the others. The last climber to go is always shaken. Twenty feet from a solid ledge, the holds were faded, worn away by wind. I lowered myself as far as I could, then simply let go, my body sheeting down the rock face. I stamped to a halt on the ledge, planting my weight.

I forced a grin up at Ryan and told her it wasn't bad.

Her face was like marble as she peered down at me.

"Send your pack down first," I said. "I'll catch it."

Ryan climbed as far out as she could, letting her pack dangle by a strap until she let go. The pack skidded over the smooth rock and slammed into the ledge, where I slapped it still with my hands and prevented it from catapulting away. She came down exactly as I had, move for move, letting go at the same place and landing on the ledge beside me.

She forced a smile. "It's really not that bad," she called up to Till. "Once you're down."

Till sent his pack sliding down behind her, but it struck the ledge cockeyed and launched clear of my hands. It sailed into the air, hit the next level down, and then cartwheeled into a slew of boulders far below.

The blood drained out of Till's face.

"Go now," I called up to Till. "Just move on it, quick as you can."

He did, right out onto the face, his breath huffing against the rock. He chewed on his lip as he peered down between his boots, repeatedly saying, "Shit, goddamn it. Shit, goddamn it." His face lost all control, expressions rushing over it in panic. I gave him whatever encouragement I could, but after a while I sounded desperate. Silence was best. He clawed the last twenty feet down, half-falling, half-glued to the rock, landing hard. Balanced on the ledge, he crept back up to where he could stand.

Till swallowed quickly and apologized for his fear, for the sloppy climb. Ryan reached over and touched his shoulder.

"No apologies necessary," she said.

Ryan and Till started moving down the slope of rubble where a stately ramp had once been built, its path lined with heaps of broken pottery and rock art carved into boulders, the route decorated. I waited for a few minutes before following them. I leaned against the cliff base and spread my arms across it, palms open, sensing the weight of Comb Ridge against my back.

This is one of the more prominent landmarks in the Southwest, a long cliff that seems to go on without end from north to south. Knowing how nimble the Anasazi must have been, this would not have been so much a physical barrier as a mental one, a great wall in the middle of the desert. I looked along it to the north, where the cliff vanished in the distance, and then to the south, where it vanished again. It occurred to me that Comb Ridge is a barrier only if you are traveling east to west. North to south, however, it is a compass line, a dramatic course set across the earth. As much as it is a great wall, Comb Ridge is also a great road. While Till and Ryan rambled through the boulders below, I peered south along this cardinal line, this bolt of red sandstone pointing the way.

Walking the Line

CHINLE WASH

Comb Ridge bows politely where it meets the lower San Juan River. Then it rises again to the south, where it becomes entangled with the canyons of Chinle Wash. My stepfather and I walked these canyons in the relentless heat of July, Comb Ridge riding high next to us. All day we had been napping uncomfortably in what shade could be found, then rising and making time again. We walked among upwelling rock formations, the colored slabs of Comb Ridge painfully vivid in the sharp summer sunlight.

My stepfather, Dick, is a geologist, and when I asked him a question about strata and fault lines, he answered by dropping to one knee, sweat dripping from his face, and wiping clean a space in the sand. Using the point of his hand, he drew a map on the ground, making a cross section of the earth, with the mantle and then the core, where diamonds are born under heat and pressure and are thrown up along deep fractures, such as those along Comb Ridge, cracks down through the basement of the planet.

Dick's vocabulary often ventured into an imagined underworld, the underpinnings of the earth where massive faults and continental fractures mingle. He named the odd species of minerals inhabiting such depths, the ones mysteriously forced up into daylight along parts of Comb Ridge: *sodalite, alkali pyroxene, britholite, lujavrite, phlogopite.*

When his cursory sand map was not enough, he emptied his pack and unfolded a map as large as a dining room table. All of southern

Utah and northern Arizona spread before us, propped up by paper creases, and he tapped his finger on our position on the Navajo reservation near the Utah-Arizona border, the place where Comb Ridge bends away from the San Juan River, where Chinle Wash comes snaking north through a region of cliffs. His map showed jigsaw colors of geological formations, cryptic symbology of strikes and dips. I listened and watched, resting on my haunches beside him, heat radiating off the ground, through my boot soles, and up my leg bones.

In Dick's eyes, everything on the surface of the earth has meaning, each hump and shove of the ground tied back to some process of uplift or erosion. I enjoy traveling with him. Every few years we found our way into the desert, where we could indulge in fantasies of geology, cracking open rocks to see what is inside, following fracture lines for miles out of nothing but pure curiosity. Now we were on the line of Comb Ridge heading south, trailing one of the most striking geological features on this part of the continent.

While my stepfather carried the geological maps—was there a need for any other kind?—I carried our official papers, stamped and signed, acquired through a tribal agency in the town of Window Rock, giving us permission to walk the Navajo reservation. In these backlands, though, our documents were virtually meaningless. To the few Navajos who live around here, a tribal decree from Window Rock is a near-worthless piece of paper, if not an insult. It does not replace talking in person at the door of a hogan or sitting down to coffee with a local. But we saw no one to talk to here, only rocks.

Dick looked awful in the heat, hair smeared by sweat and now dry. I'm sure I didn't look any better. We were traveling through temperatures unseasonably high even for summer—118 degrees in the air, 130 degrees on the ground. On our backs we carried several days' worth of gear. Even without sleeping bags or much water, our packs felt heavy this afternoon, like sacks of lead. I had promised him water—springs leaking out of the Navajo sandstone alcoves, or at least a murky trickle along Chinle Wash—but I should have known better. I had hardly been touched by rain in months. Dick and I had not been able to find any of the customary water holes, pots and pans carved out of bedrock half-filled with old rainwater.

Everything was dry. Late in the day we entered the wash, which had no water at all. We looked both ways. Salty tamarisk shoots crowded the wash's outer banks. I had expected at least a warm, greenish trickle, a few pools rippled by dashing water striders. I knelt and pinched the ground between my fingers. It had not seen water for months.

We climbed to a high flood terrace, where we could look across the country. There I dropped my pack and told Dick to rest. I said I would have water for him by dark. I turned and walked toward a nearby canyon, which opened like a gateway.

. . .

Pieces of curled, dried mud popped beneath my feet like sticks of chalk. High red walls fell into shadow around me, relaxing finally, letting down their hot shoulders after a day in the sun. As I walked through the parting cliffs of this canyon, my own shoulders sloped toward the ground. In the shade the air was a few degrees below scorching. Just taking my pack off felt good. My body seemed to float along the canyon's rubbled floor, where stones had once been driven by a flash flood.

How long ago was this flood?

I lifted one of the rocks up with the toe of my boot.

Too long ago.

Every light step I took echoed among the walls. Panels of rock art came into view, unveiled as I passed around a bend. Petroglyphs were etched and pecked into red rock forty feet above the wash floor on my left. I walked with my head lifted, seeing fine geometric carvings go by—human figures with hands upraised, and spirals, and creatures with horns. I was too directed toward finding water to pause, so I just watched them pass, thinking simply, People were here—a long time ago.

Some of the zoomorphic drawings—a bighorn sheep with two other sheep set inside its body and some sort of canid below its front legs—came from a tradition of rock art known as the San Juan Style, a thousand years old, give or take a few centuries. In this style people are portrayed in events of the day—hunters and dancers dressed ceremonially, the pecked likeness of a man pulling back a bow before the arrow flies. This part of southern Utah is awash in rock art, a pre-Columbian archive with representations shelved by the thousands on cliff faces and boulder clefts. The day before, Dick and I had seen San Juan Style giants carved into another rock wall, manifold human figures taller than either of us, their bodies marked with clothing and jewelry, their hair composed in particular fashions beneath elaborate headdresses.

Some stories told by these panels are obvious: the dances, the hunts, people walking in lines with loads tied on their backs. But there are more specific tales, harder to read: insignias, ranks of geometric symbols, repetitive icons. Rock art in this area looks like a lettered narrative of some sort: clan symbols, society symbols, perhaps the names of places left in a forgotten script.

An eye-catching figure appeared above me. I stopped to look at it for a moment, my mouth tipped open in the warm canyon air. A spiral had been methodically pecked to reveal paler stone within the bedrock. It had been done with laborious attention to detail, its curves no more than half a finger width apart. Two bighorn sheep had been carefully installed at the start of the spiral, both sheep seeming to be in motion, positioned as if traveling toward the spiral's center. One of the sheep was actually standing on its hind legs as if walking upright, part human. I took the figures as a story of a journey. Was I seeing a record of an event, a document of migration where a clan once set off in search of a promised land? Was it mere decoration, a tale told in code, a clever signature? I have asked these questions countless times in this decorated wilderness.

A man named Joe Pachak lives on the other side of the San Juan River in Utah, where he has been studying local rock art. Pachak once told me that he felt many rock art panels were places people migrated to, pilgrimage sites where they came to embellish very specific stories. A specialist devoted to cataloging ancient images around the Four Corners, Pachak has an old army barrack in the town of Bluff where every surface and shelf is overloaded with his drawings and photographs. Pachak has come to recognize the representation of Venus when he sees it in rock art, as well as the cipher of particular clans and the ubiquitous appearance of twin figures who must have played a role in Anasazi mythology. He is an antiquarian pacing through a library, thumbing through rows of canyons, finger

Detail of two bighorn sheep walking a spiral on a rock art panel in Chinle Wash. CRAIG CHILDS

lifted in the air as he silently reads captions and pictograms; images of carved faces, shields and weapons, animals, bird-headed people, star charts, insects, women giving birth, and men cutting off each other's heads. If there is a question about rock art near the San Juan River, researchers turn to him.

I once spent an evening in Pachak's barrack, and there, for the first time, I grasped the scope and codified nature of Anasazi rock art. He unrolled wall-size sketches and showed me exact patterns reproduced in many places. Certain Anasazi petroglyphs and pictographs are consistently stylized regardless of where they are found, rhythmic like primitive ogham characters from Ireland, and representational like the earliest pictograms from the ancient Middle East. For the most part Southwest archaeologists have disregarded rock art's usefulness.

"Archaeologists look at it as too difficult to handle," Pachak once told me. "Too complex, too ambiguous."

But for Pachak the purpose of rock art has become almost transparent. "It holds incredible information about prehistoric culture," he said. "You can demonstrate theories with rock art the same as you can in an excavation. You can compile data that will say this rock art image is part of something bigger—it appears in four thousand rock art panels in this region, a reoccurring motif that tells a particular account. It's demonstrable. No doubt in my mind."

Pachak sees an Anasazi narrative recorded in this art, specific stories being told. He said, "I'm very interested in T-shaped doorways for that reason." To show me why, he pulled out some rock art images and tapped his finger on representations of T shapes—not just physical portals, but artistic portrayals of Ts painted and pecked into cliffs and boulders. His voice accelerated as he explained that these Ts evolved from some of the earliest cultural icons on the Colorado Plateau. He excitedly said that he believes these symbols are associated with a very old legend, one that as far as he can tell involved twins and a passage between two worlds, a creation story.

"The T shapes are not doorways at all," he explained. "They are windows, entries and exits. They're holes of emergence. They are sipapus in the architecture. People would have been reminded of their story daily, going in and out of the house, emerging into the world, then going back inside. Rock art symbols were integrated into architecture to illustrate a creation mythology."

Like any culture, the Anasazi appear to have been living within the emblematic framework of their own story. They wrote this story into their architecture, in the weave of their textiles, on their decorated vessels, and on rock faces.

Looking up from the canyon floor at a tightly bound spiral and the forms of two traveling bighorn sheep, I wondered, What tale is this? Pachak might know. And he might not. I thought of the way his voice had quickened when he told me of his findings, the same animation professional archaeologists have as they piece together codes hidden among artifacts and ruins. It is all storytelling, I thought. Flights of imagination and science. I was convinced that this scene overhead was a legend of migration, telling of a journey, but I was not an impartial judge. I had distances to cross myself.

. . .

I stopped looking for rock art and turned all my attention to water. My stepfather and I had barely enough to last until sunrise, even if we restricted our drinking. I sharpened my eyes, scanning any small, incoming drainage or shaded cleft. An ample depression appeared in the floor fifty feet ahead, its bedrock slopes stained with a white bathtub ring. I walked into it. Dry.

Damn you.

I stammered to a halt.

In the bottom of this hollow lay a dish of dark clay. I knelt and shoveled a hand down to reach a layer of slightly moist black matter that smelled like a rotting carcass. In the past I had coaxed water out of this sort of half-dry mud, but I was hardly in the mood to suck on a wretched ball of clay. I doubted that my stepfather had even imagined stooping to such an extreme. I walked on, wiping clods of clay on my pants. I abolished any wish for water. I just stared ahead.

A few minutes later I came to a pool of rot-green water. It was black down in its depths. Bubbles of methane troubled a gray film on the surface, where six fingerling fish floated, dead, an array of white bloated bellies. The fish had ridden the last flow of Chinle Wash and had taken whatever refuge they could find when it dried up, waiting for the next flood, which never came. I dabbed my fingers into the warm water and touched my lips. It tasted like a poorly kept aquarium. This was our ticket, I thought, our permission to keep going. I had promised Dick water, and here it was.

I slid my boots into silvery mud and reached out with a plastic bottle. I sank its wide mouth beneath the surface, hoping for better water two inches down. After gulping the bottle full, I brought it back and poured it into a canvas-lined bladder. I spent about half an hour gathering what I could carry, six gallons of bladders laid like dead seals at the edge of the water hole. As a final act I dumped a hatful of water over my head, stunning slices of coolness tracing all the way down my body, under my shirt. I walked back dragging a wet trail, as if I had just crawled out of the sea.

At a twilight camp I found my stepfather flicking red ants off his legs.

"Good news and bad news," I said, dropping the weight of my pack onto the ground.

He could see from the way the pack landed that I had found

water. I sat and pulled one of the bladders into my lap. I unscrewed its lid with one hand and with the other opened a small glass jar of iodine pills. I shuffled five tiny green pills into my palm, then dumped them into the bladder's open mouth.

"I found plenty of water," I said.

Dick nodded. In the past everywhere he and I had traveled together we had found ample water hidden in desert springs and holes, but now he was about to witness the other side of walking here: drinking foul, black water purely out of need. Part of the reason I had asked him along was because he is my stepfather, and I wanted him to see my life as I chased trails of ancient migrations into the wilderness. Most members of my family had no idea what I did for a living or how I filled my years. This was like having him over for dinner, showing him around the place.

I capped the first bladder and opened another.

"It's pretty nasty-tasting stuff," I said. "But it's water. It's not putrid, and the iodine should help the taste a little."

He took this in, saying nothing.

"Just so you know," I said, "there were dead fish floating in the hole."

Dick repeated flatly, "Dead fish."

"It'll be hard water to drink," I said. "But it'll be good enough until we find something else. We've got a good three days' worth here."

Dick wiped dust off his knees and looked into the fading western sky—hot, bare stone as far as he could see.

"How bad is it, really?" he asked.

"I'm sure we'll find better," I said in reply.

. . .

The next day, with this water heavy on our backs, we dropped into the sparse, dappled shade of a cottonwood tree that grew in the wash. We slipped our tired bodies onto the ground, jaws open, hands slack and pulling out gear that we could use as backrests, hard pillows. We had walked a number of miles already, and it was time to rest. I uncapped a bottle and drank. The water was hot and tasted bad. I stretched out on a thin bed of dry cottonwood leaves and squinted straight up through the sporadic shade and blistering green light between the branches above us.

Some modern Pueblo people in the Southwest still use the kiva as their holy chamber, and among those who speak the language of Tewa, the kiva is called *te'i,* "the place of the cottonwood tree." The kiva is thought to be a bridge between the underworld and the world above, and the hole traditionally placed in the kiva floor, just beyond the deflector stone and in front of the ladder, represents a place of emergence. In Tewa this hole is called *p'okwi koji,* "the lake roof hole," which leads up from a mysterious underground lake. The kiva is where a radiant green tree grows in the sparseness of the desert, as if it were a flag raised on barren ground announcing the presence of water below, a sign of hope and fertility.

On this July morning it was easy to envision how a cultural cosmos would be structured in this land, the most salient green of the desert luminous over my head, water pumping from vaults far below into thirsty cottonwood leaves above. This tree is a heavy drinker. It will wither without a steady, daily source of water. I lay beneath it, imagining an underground lake below my back. There was water down there, out of my reach but made apparent by this tree.

The few flies that came by were exhausting to watch. They darted and spun around our bodies, landing to sip sweat off our forearms and cheeks. Ants mapped the skin of my hands, the rim of my right ear, and I did nothing to dissuade them. Unable to sleep but not quite awake, I lay on the ground as flies bit little plugs out of my flesh, my hand lifting to shoo them away now and then, my mind wandering into the long stillness of the day.

For hours I watched the sun creep overhead. Thin tree shadows wheeled around my body. I did not carry a watch these days; there were enough markers of time on the land. But at one point the sun seemed to stop, the shadows no longer turning. High noon. I got up and drew on my hat. My stepfather lay half-asleep nearby. I walked into the open light across grill plates of bare rock, the underside of my hat brim glowing from sunlight reflected off the stone beneath me. Slight remnants of eight-hundred-year-old granaries hung from the cliff overhead, mortar footings and a few squares of abandoned stonework. Just down from these were tablets of rock art—markings of a mobile people, travelers who spent their years passing up and down Chinle Wash and all along Comb Ridge.

I once worked at an excavation with an archaeologist specializing in the Hohokam culture, a desert people from far southwest of here, where the city of Phoenix now stands. The Hohokam were irrigators, large-scale farmers who did not move so much. My colleague had come to work at an Anasazi site in order to learn field skills, but he made it known that he believed these Colorado Plateau folk to be inferior to his Hohokam, who had developed an advanced social and political domain in order to properly allocate river waters among numerous irrigation communities. He saw these southerners as corporate entities—making decrees, balancing powers—while the Anasazi lived on the dusty edge of the world, honorable people no doubt, but bound to a desperate landscape. For as sedentary as the Anasazi might seem with their great houses and pueblos, they were still nomads, which lessened them in the eyes of my colleague. They were dryland farmers who rarely employed irrigation. In my colleague's mind this northern desert, so bitter with its droughts and its few unpredictable rivers, did not allow them to become a great people.

One day while we were eating lunch under a shade tarp at the excavation, I mentioned to him that it was their ability to move that made them great. Their resource was not annual irrigation water, but daily drinking water. Their decisions had to be implemented immediately. Whole communities had to be prepared to disband at the drop of a hat, while preserving an inner social structure that would allow them to come seamlessly back together years or decades later when conditions improved. I had my own bias, respectfully suggesting to him that this was a civilization on a sliding scale, able to contract or expand at a moment's notice, abandoning regions for tens or hundreds of years before returning and building again as if they had never left. The people had a continuity that stretched beyond generations, a coherence of cultural practice surpassing time and place, calling upon memory, the very rudiment of civilization.

My colleague stuck to his premise that civilization meant big business, booming agriculture, fields of irrigation canals. Civilization is defined in different ways by different people. To me it means an overarching social organization consistent across long spans of time and space. It is the formation of a cultural entity, incorporating diverse ethnicities and languages, where there is a single, standardized symbology—for example, the symmetrical geometry painted on pottery, or rock art images left all across the Colorado Plateau. This landscape engendered its own form of civilization, one tied inextricably to the chance presence and absence of water.

Now, as I walked away from Dick's and my resting spot, I watched for etchings in the cliffs and on boulders. More than that, I probed for any dark stain high in the rocks, maybe a tuft of greenery, some mark of water. My slow steps broadcast every turn of gravel, every soft press of sand. Time seemed to stand still. I came to an opening, a bend in the cliff where I could see most of the sky. Isolated thunderheads roamed in the distance. I stopped to watch these vaporous lakes glide by, while down here on the ground creatures like me were slowly dying, skin pulling against our bones. The thunderstorms were inaccessible, too far away to offer even the hope of shade.

Did the Anasazi call to these lakes in the sky? I wondered. Did they cry the very name of rain, shamans mumbling in their dark rooms, while young, vigorous dancers sweated in woven, shell-stitched kilts, their steps sending them out of their minds, into a dream flying upward, a request sent to rain gods to please consider relinquishing their precious stores?

I stood alone, my shirt in tatters, thinking my voice too small and far away to ask these distant storms to come to me and collapse upon the ground. The only sound I heard was the bumbling passage of a fly. It zigzagged along the canyon and flew a quick inspection around my head. Just as fast, it was gone, like a missile along the cliffs. Water, I thought. Water, somewhere.

A spring, enough to sip or pat with my tongue. If not that, the carcass of a lost Navajo cow, its belly churning with maggots, a water hole in itself, if only for flies.

I walked back to the cottonwood shade, where Dick barely

opened his eyes. I slumped to the ground, giving myself once more to the crinkle of long-fallen cottonwood leaves, my body turned back into a riddle for the ants.

. . .

When the sun finally moved from the peak of the sky, the cliffs began showing their shadows. Dick and I sat up and spoke a few cursory sentences to each other. We rose to this broadening light and cooked a macaroni and cheese dinner in a battered, blackened pot. After scraping the last burned flecks of pasta out of the pot, leaving it unwashed for the lack of water, we continued to move south.

Dick was interested in the bedrock, in its composition, how it had originally been laid. His was not a stable earth, but one covered with rising blisters and sinking wells, and as we walked, he could see the ramifications of these actions, pointing across long arcs of thrusts and faults where global geological processes were making themselves known. Comb Ridge lifts out of the earth along a crack that goes deeper than any geologist has ever been able to see. There are unknown regions down there, monsters inside the earth that eat the charges of seismic waves we thump into the ground.

In the past few days along Comb Ridge, Dick and I had walked by chunks of rock the size of buildings coughed up from the earth. Isolated volcanoes seem to have sprouted between the seams of the ridge—not volcanoes per se, but upwellings from deep in the earth, features known as diatremes, which erupted from below the level of magma where stone is no longer molten but plastic. In these diatremes we found beautiful little squares of garnet crystals and threads of greasy green serpentine that had been spewed up from 150 miles below the earth's surface. With the tip of a sewing needle, we had plucked out a minuscule pinkish gem that under a hand lens appeared to be a diamond, something found in diatremes. Comb Ridge impressed my stepfather. It represented the mechanics of the underworld.

Late in the day, as we walked along the scrolling meanders of Chinle Wash where it touched in and out of Comb Ridge, Dick told me that some people believe if you could drill a hole to the very core of the earth, the planet would explode, like a balloon popped with a needle. There is so much pressure in the middle that the earth might suddenly just blow up.

Dick saw around us fractures caused by migrating continents, welling plates of stone moving across beds of molten rock. He told me that he used to take gravitational measurements, traveling to different places to read the shifting pull of the planet, and that the differences he noted were not just from place to place, but from hour to hour. Gravity, he discovered, changes within the earth as if tides were passing through the planet, waves of liquid rock rising and falling. He concluded, like so many geologists before him, that the ground is not solid. It is a thin sheet of fabric thrown over a heaving interior. Thus we see all of this at the surface—Comb Ridge tossed up, cliffs drawn along its edges, matter thrown through semivolcanic fissures. The Colorado Plateau, which Comb Ridge splits nearly down the middle, is a precise expression of movement, its solid bedrock a thin facing that reflects every change below.

Like the cottonwood tree, I thought. The underground lake. The cosmology of this desert is constantly revealed in different forms. I looked up and saw rock art unfurling down a sunbaked cliff, and bits of fallen cliff dwellings hanging from shallow alcoves. The movement of people is one of these thin veneers across the planet's surface. Flowing over the geologic ripples of the Colorado Plateau, people once slipped into these convenient spaces, journeying between gaps and along ridges as the earth flinched and rolled around them. The climate also nudged them along—rainy summers swelling their staying power, longer than average winters freezing them out of the high country and sending them down into the deserts. They must have felt the constant pressure of these boiling, dry storms and of the solid stone undulating beneath them. The hands of the world were touching them, leading them first one way and then another.

. . .

It was an archaeologist named Nieves Zedeño who told me I should come walking along this line where Chinle Wash runs. Meeting her for lunch, I was prepared to take notes in my journal and record our conversation on tape. She told me to put away my notes. I looked up at her—Ecuadorian accent, dark almond eyes—and said, "Of course, whatever you want. May I use the recorder?"

"No," she said. "Just listen. I will send you the data. Just listen."

Zedeño pushed her salad out of the way and with her fingers drew an imaginary map on the table. "People were moving all the time," she said. She laid out the geography for me, the southern and northern basins of the San Juan River, the Chuska Mountains, the mesas in the Kayenta region of northeast Arizona, everything that was Anasazi.

She told me that she learned how pottery had moved throughout this region. Zedeño's work was much like that of Donna Glowacki around Mesa Verde. Like Glowacki, she was performing neutron activation analysis on ceramic remains, determining where pots were made and recording where they finally came to rest. Whereas Glowacki had uncovered intricate movements within the confines of the Northern San Juan Basin, Zedeño's research took in nearly all of the Southwest. The migrations she described to me sounded tidal, not happening all at once but occurring at increasing and decreasing intervals.

"It was truly organic," Zedeño said. "Almost beautiful."

As she spoke, her hands moved across the "map" she had made, defining larger cultural movements as waves of people drained off the Colorado Plateau late in the thirteenth century. In Zedeño's mind, in her hands, was the entire geography of the Southwest pressed through a fine gauze of centuries and reconfigured based on data she and her colleagues had gathered on ceramics. Zedeño described for me the growth and subsidence of communities and cultures in this landscape, pueblos buried in sand, one by one, from north to south. By the fourteenth century, nearly everyone in the Southwest was moving, the whole culture upended. Something big had happened: drought. But more than drought. A call had gone out. It was time to go.

Zedeño detected a strong southward movement of ceramics, entire households of pottery carried hundreds of miles from where it was made. People were vacating their homelands and heading for new population centers in the south, where they would have a better chance of growing crops. Along the way they left lines of pottery connecting one place to the next. These migrations, she explained, probably went back and forth, not a singular movement but an ebb and flow.

Zedeño centered her hands on the table and named the key archaeological areas there: Cedar Mesa, Canyon de Chelly, Chinle Wash, Chavez Pass, Chodistaas, and so on. She described populations pushing through desert canyons and gathering on high mesas, surging back and forth, two steps south, one step north. Then she drew her finger straight down the middle, inscribing a line.

"There is this blank area here," Zedeño said. "I think if you looked closely along this line, you would find strong signs of movement. We just haven't been able to devote the time that is needed."

The line she had drawn on the table was Chinle Wash, a north-south meridian starting in southeast Utah and cutting straight down through northeast Arizona.

"I've been walking there," I told her.

"It would help many of us just to hear what it is like," she replied.

"This line's a hundred miles. Three hundred if you follow it clear out. I've only walked small portions of it," I said.

"It's a long way," Zedeño agreed.

"I've often thought about taking some serious time there," I offered.

Indeed, I had maps of this region on my walls at home, aerial photographs from the U.S. Geological Survey (USGS) pinned floor to ceiling. My study looked like the den of a madman, clear plastic sheets draped over wall maps so that I could connect place to place with penned red lines of genetic traits drawn from prehistoric skeletons, blue lines of ceramic distribution, green lines of architectural styles. I had delved into the geology of this region, seeing the surface of the earth there like a glass windshield and the landforms as hairline cracks creeping along it, arcing over hundreds of miles.

I looked down at the table, coyly, as if letting her know the hardship, the weeks, the months it would take to fully examine this line of hers, to do her dirty work of walking. I studied the line she had drawn across the table. A dry place, I thought. Reservation land. Remote country. I had barely touched the place, just enough to know it was full of potential.

When I looked up, I noticed that Zedeño had finished her salad. Mine was hardly touched. I told her that I would go there and walk. I would let her know what I found.

. . .

I took many journeys along the length of Chinle Wash, and at different times, in different reaches, I came upon many archaeological sites—a D-shaped building still standing in the open, and numerous cliff dwellings tucked into recesses, some with roofs still intact, T-shaped doorways peering across the land. I saw strands of rock art all the way down Zedeño's line, individual boulders marked one after another like signposts. Trails of broken red pottery denoted the movement of red ware production to the south from the thirteenth into the fourteenth century as people fled the Four Corners, taking their industry with them.

By far the hottest, most desolate journey was with my stepfather. Every day was the same, hiding from the sun after a few hours of morning travel, then waiting in overpowering silence for the sun to sink so that we could move again. One morning we climbed into the cliffs looking for shade. Ancient steps had been carved into a rock face, and we followed them toward a vaulted circle of shadow towering over us.

The massive sandstone formations of southeast Utah tend to erode into concave shelters known as theater-heads—enormous round alcoves, ceilings one hundred, two hundred feet high. Breathing hard, veins standing out in our faces to shed heat, we reached the shade of one alcove, where we climbed into a hollow space the size of a concert hall. Boulders lay around us, and nearly all of them were scored with designs—snakes and spirals and enigmatic symbols the likes of which I had seen throughout the Anasazi realm. I thought, They spent their days here, too, getting out of the sun and lazily pecking at the rock. Some of the images were San Juan Style, and some were older, Glen Canyon Linear, designs cut like the rib cages of insects, centipede-like imagery. We peered upward and saw more figures inscribed along the back wall as far as a person could climb. Some were not so old. Domestic Navajo horses had been painted in white, looking fifty, eighty years old at the most. The horses had been painted so that they ran with heads lifted, trotting and alert, manes flying like banners. (The Navajo are unrelated to the Anasazi, having come from the north late in the game, after this place was essentially cleared out.)

I peeled off my sunglasses in the shade and wandered along the curved wall, finding among designs of pre-Columbian headdresses and bighorn sheep the image of a colt walking beside its mother, one of the most pleasing sights in a rancher's life. Humans have been coming to this shelter for some time, I thought, leaving marks of our aspirations on the wall, on fallen boulders. I dabbed two fingers of sweat from my forehead, planted them on the rouge bedrock, and made a smudge that faded slowly.

Dick and I sat in the shade together, cradled by this huge mouth eroded from the cliff. From here we looked across the white heat of the land outside, and my eyes tracked over various stone shapes in the distance for any sign of greenery—a drip, a seep. There was no water anywhere. A teardrop of a butte stood maybe five hundred feet below us, half a mile away. After studying the butte for a minute, I pulled out my binoculars and handed them to Dick.

"You see something circular down there, on top of that butte?" I asked.

He adjusted the binoculars for a bit, asking me where, and finally said that yes, he saw something round in the center of the butte.

"Does it look natural?" I asked, recognizing immediately the foolishness of the question. What out here is not natural?

"Hard to tell," my stepfather said. "But it doesn't look quite right. Something's out of place."

He handed the binoculars back to me and waited. He was willing to go about anywhere with me, walking for hours in the sun if necessary to escape another day of half-sleeping in hot shade. I steadied the binoculars, my forearms resting on my knees.

"It's something," I said. "I'm going down there. You can stay up here if you want. I'll come back for you."

I left him there and climbed down the carved toeholds, where I stepped into stinging sunlight. I side-hilled along balconies of sandstone, using my hands for balance on the hot, parched soil. Rocks clattered above me, dust kicking up. It was Dick coming down behind me.

The butte stretched ahead of us, rising slightly where I would expect a rise if people had built here. I began to notice pottery, broken pieces growing in number, thickening the sandy orange soil the closer we got to the rise, which started to take on a circular form. Larger sherds appeared, half sections of bowls, red ware necks and bases. Gardens of red pottery spurred me on, as I quickly scanned the ground, seeing the remains of rooms, shapes in the earth. In the center was the dish of a kiva.

I stepped to the kiva's edge while Dick made his way over. It was not an ordinary kiva. It was at least fifty feet across, a great kiva, like the ones I had seen around Chaco and north of here near the head of Comb Ridge. I had not been expecting to find anything this large in the area. All of the great kivas in this part of the world had been mapped, I thought; not excavated or even measured, but at least recorded; spotted from airplanes, walked upon by ground crews, described through archaeological rumors. There was never any mention of a great kiva out here. This was right down the middle of Zedeño's line.

From just a cursory glance at the pottery, it was obvious that this had been a substantial regional center in the twelfth and thirteenth centuries, a place where many people had gathered in the dry hell of what was to become the Utah-Arizona border. I was impressed. That anybody had ever lived in this fractured topography was a monumental accomplishment, let alone a people who could afford shapely pottery and break what looked like hundreds if not thousands of vessels around the ring of this kiva.

Dick walked up with a grinding stone in his hand, studying it through a hand lens as he approached.

"Oh, yeah, that's granite for sure," he was saying. "Mica... quartz...feldspar...this had to have been brought from some distance. I don't know any granite from around here. Probably it came up through one of the diatremes."

A geologist, he was thinking in longer time frames than I, his mind trained for a realm in which matter creeps indiscernibly, centimeters accumulating into mountain ranges. His scale was in billions and millions of years, mine in thousands and hundreds, yet the processes we studied were inseparable, the earthen crust and human civilization hardly different in their uplifting and falling but for the time involved. He handed the stone to me. It was as smooth as a rolling pin, a mano used to grind corn, amaranth, dried beans. I told him what it was, said that people in the area probably mined the diatremes for good, hard rocks that would make durable grinding stones. I slid my palm across the stone's flattest, polished surface and then used it to point around us, explaining that the circular depression in front of us would have been an underground ballroom, maybe with quarter-ton timbers holding up an audacious wooden ceiling.

"Can you imagine something like that here?" I said. "It must be sixty miles to the nearest good tree."

I told Dick that I knew of only four great kivas documented over the next fifty miles north of here and one at the Twin Towers in New Mexico to the east. Just about due south there was one at Antelope House in Canyon de Chelly sixty, seventy miles away, another south of there near Ganado. The closest one I could think of was at the point where Comb Ridge touches the San Juan River in Utah, an auspicious site marking a change in the landscape. On the map, the four nearest great kivas form a ring around a blank spot where no great kivas have been recorded. The center of that spot was where we were standing now, where this ceremonial chamber lay collapsed and mostly buried like a mouth forming an O fifty feet across.

"Found yourself a missing link," Dick said.

I handed the mano back to him.

Zedeño would want to hear about this, I thought, an undocumented great kiva out in the arid path she had traced on that table. This was a phenomenal find in an era when it was said that all the big sites had been documented, that there were no more startling architectural discoveries to be made in the Southwest.

Surrounding this kiva, its interior as shallow and round as a dinner plate, I could see an attached cluster of rooms, their shapes pushing up through the soil. This is where they kept paraphernalia for the dancers, I thought. In the great kiva they must have begged the gods to open the underworld lake and let a little water back to the surface, the dancers' feet shaking dust down from the rafters.

Dick and I circled the kiva through the heat of the day like antelope grazing in tall, dry grass, our motions uncomplicated, difficult to detect. My hand drifted to the ground to lift the handle of a jug, then a red-slipped quarter of a jar, then a corrugated rind of red-painted pottery. We walked circles around the top of the butte. Every fifteen minutes or half hour our orbits would cross. Then Dick would lead me over to wildly colored pieces of carved chert (a type of rock), aqua and bloodred, and I would point out to him the base of a gray corrugated vessel, its coils winding inward in a graceful spiral. Then we would break away from each other again and drift back into our own universes beneath the sun.

You could die here, I thought. You could rove the ground until thirst is forgotten. The skin on my hands was cracked and brown, my wrists blushing with sunburn from holding these sherds up to my eye and exposing the undersides of my forearms. The volume of ceramics was outlandish. Were the sherds candy wrappers and popcorn bags stampeded to the ground after a ball game, or were they coins serene in a shallow fountain, left as offerings? Whatever they were, they indicated the presence of a sizable, or at least a well-supplied, population, many pots and people moving through this desolate place.

By the time I stopped, my movements were languid, inaccurate as I wasted in the heat. I had begun picking potsherds up and not returning them the way they were found, just lowering my hand, relaxing my grip, and letting them fall to the earth. Dick headed elsewhere, looking for shade. I drank from my bottle, a searing taste of iodine and death, and I let the bottle down, empty, hanging from my hand. I looked up toward the horizon, my eyes sweeping a country of stone spikes and ridges, Monument Valley in the distance, absolutely dry. Everything dry. I wished for summer to end, for this oppressive sun to fade. I wished for water, please.

Part Five

NORTHEAST ARIZONA

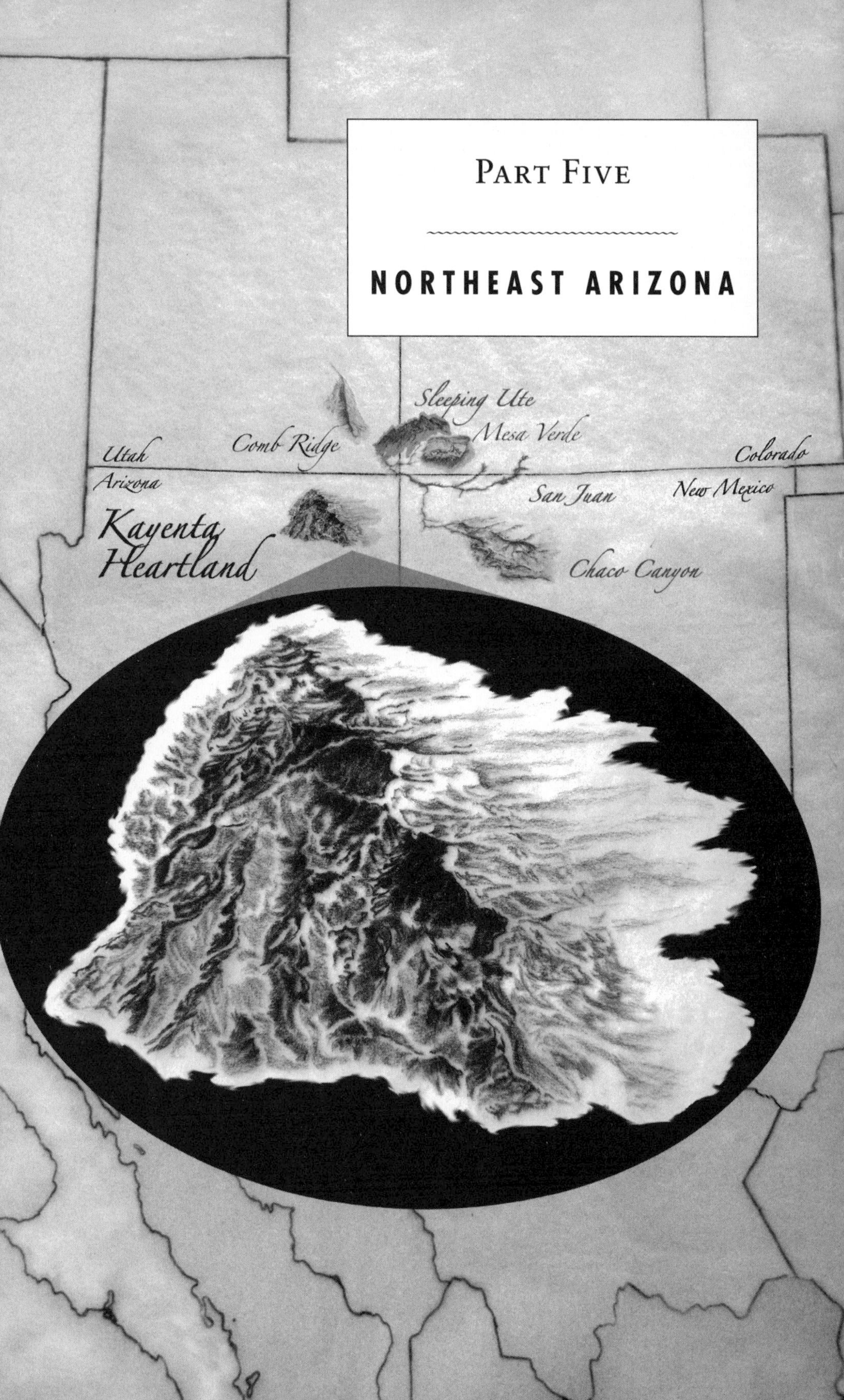

Retreat

NEAR MONUMENT VALLEY

For a short time Comb Ridge and Chinle Wash are on top of each other, riding along the same north-south trend, one a tightly meandering canyon and wash, the other a long and imperious crest of rock. Near the Arizona border they divide and follow two different geological destinies. Chinle Wash keeps its cardinal path straight south toward Ganado Mesa, while Comb Ridge strays westward, forming an elegant arc across the northern Arizona desert, a curving wall made of peach-colored sandstone. Crossing through the Navajo reservation, the ridge becomes a backdrop for the voluminous red buttes of Monument Valley. Hardly a living thing is to be seen but wind-raked snubs of blackbrush.

Storms in the winter roam through Monument Valley like herd animals, low to the ground, enveloping one butte in clouds, revealing another. Cold wind scrapes and hisses across the bare red earth. On this day I was riding in the back of a pickup with a companion, a traveling man in his twenties named Colin. Dry bits of snow flurried across the highway as we watched Monument Valley recede over the tailgate, our gloved hands stuffed into our coats, our faces huddled down into our collars. Our two packs lay like carcasses in the bed with us. We had been carrying their winter weight through the Navajo wilderness when we reached this highway and hitched a ride. Colin looked weatherworn, his boots and pants wet from breaking through stream ice, his face unshaven, reddened and chafed.

The pickup wobbled a little on its battered frame as we passed mudded domes of Navajo hogans. Fence gates were left open where abandoned tires were stacked on top of each other, used as signposts, their bald black rubber beginning to gray from too many seasons in the sun.

This desert must have stretched into eerie isolation several hundred years ago, ghost towns of wasted jacal and stonework that had once been stopovers for extensive trade networks. People retreated across this land in the thirteenth century, pulling back their settlements for more than a hundred miles in all directions to hole up just down the highway from here. It was an impressive movement of far-flung populations, like the electric snap of a tendon yanking them back home, leaving kivas and villages empty in the hinterlands during a time of drought and conflict.

The same thing was happening around Mesa Verde as was happening in northeast Arizona. People were scrambling for shelter, for highlands. Here they settled in valleys and high basins just above the desert, a territory known as Kayenta, analogous to the Northern San Juan Basin in Colorado, where farming was more tenable during the Great Drought. And if one needed an escape, a pair of precipitous, forested mesas stood nearby, Arizona's own Mesa Verde. Kayenta was a haven.

The towering buttes of Monument Valley shifted past each other as we traveled at a processional pace, forty miles per hour in a pickup. A raven perched on a fence post, wings pulled in like a coat against the beleaguering wind.

The huge black bird startled when we drove by, its bolt of a beak coming up, wings trimming back to launch as it went up on its toes. Sitting cold in the pickup bed, I was glad to see that the raven didn't fly, but instead settled its feathers. It was a cold enough day, no need to take off into the wind if it didn't have to. I watched the raven recede, eventually becoming a comma in the distance, overtaken by banners of black trash-bag plastic flying from barbed wire fences.

We were nearing the town of Kayenta, a mostly Navajo community with a high school, a post office, a Bashas' grocery store. To this town and its vicinity, the Great Drought brought waves of thirteenth-century migrants looking for farming opportunities and for cultural alliance, neighbors to live by. Many clans of Anasazi converged here.

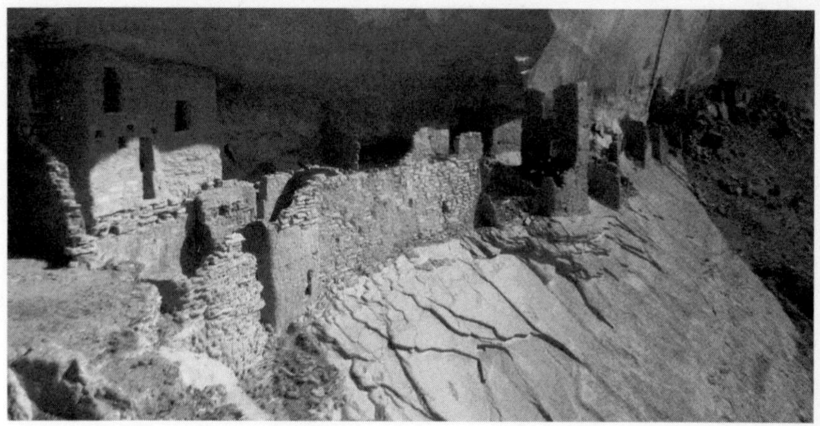

Half Mesa Verde, half Kayenta cliff dwelling near Monument Valley. REGAN CHOI

In that time a great cliff dwelling was built on the eastern margin of Kayenta, its windows looking out at Monument Valley in the distance. The floor plan of this site—one of the larger cliff dwellings in the Southwest—is partly based on Mesa Verde styles, while its rockwork is that of the more western Kayenta Anasazi. It is believed that this cliff dwelling represents the larger intermarriage between Anasazi from the Four Corners and those from Kayenta. Wives were producing pottery (traditionally a female task) in an eastern and northern Mesa Verde style. They lived with husbands who wove textiles and built structures (both believed to have been male roles) in a western Kayenta fashion.* Half of the pottery found at this site derives from Four Corners traditions, and the other half consists of red wares and intricately hatched black-on-whites from Kayenta. One team of archaeologists documenting this cliff dwelling referred to it as "a Mesa Verde pueblo with some Kayenta affiliations," while another team called it "a Kayenta outpost with many Mesa Verde connections." In a time of escalating migrations, at least some distinct groups of Anasazi seem to have found common ground.

*Because the Anasazi appear to have been matrilineal, women lived in houses formed like their mothers' and grandmothers', while men left behind the houses of their families when they married. In the case of this cliff dwelling, Kayenta men may have been using their own masonry techniques to replicate the structural forms of Mesa Verde for their wives and their families.

Prior to this the Kayenta Anasazi had been evenly scattered, some living in great-house communities around Comb Ridge, most occupying isolated farming households across northeast Arizona and southeast Utah. As drought came on, these people migrated to just south of Monument Valley looking for sanctuary, skyrocketing the local population. Around the modern town of Kayenta, small thirteenth-century colonies quickly expanded into large, centralized pueblos with courtyards and plazas. At first these villages had no more than fifty rooms, but as people arrived from the surrounding country, they grew to more than three hundred rooms and were soon ringed by satellites of encampments and small communities.

Bruce Anderson, a prominent elder field archaeologist of the Kayenta Anasazi, once told me about surveying this region. In his slow western drawl, Anderson explained how he had excavated along the path of a new railroad across the Kayenta heartland. There he unearthed the remains of pueblos packed tightly together, large residential sites no more than two to three miles apart.

Along this planned railroad, Anderson clipped through a burial plot in front of a pueblo that had all but vanished under blowing dust and sand. There he dug up fifty skeletons within the thirty-foot-wide space of his survey corridor. Among the jewelry and many ceramic vessels he uncovered was a burial assembly of five wooden flutes, each a foot long and painted an alluring blue. Maybe it was the mark of a special society, he thought, a member of a Flute Clan, or a musician's burial. He kept digging and finding more remains, proof of a high culture archaeologists had not expected in this region. Since Anderson's work, evidence of vigorous trade in the area has been unearthed, trade that stretched into distant regions at a time when long-distance exchange all but ceased in the Four Corners.

"If I could get a hold of a time machine," Anderson said, "I would go back to Kayenta in the twelve hundreds. Out of any time or any place in the Southwest, that's where I would want to see."

Many of the larger pueblos in the Kayenta region went up on the highest points around, establishing line-of-sight networks so that one settlement was usually in view of at least two others. In one case a notch was manually chopped into the terrain so that two key pueblos could see each other. In another case an unbroken corridor of visibility was established by way of relays between a site on a valley floor up to a nearby mesa and from there into a canyon on the other side. These people were making eye contact with each other across great distances.

A compact social matrix is revealed by the settlements themselves. A litany of dedicated architectural forms came into vogue in the twelfth and thirteenth centuries around Kayenta. Large residential quarters were built, accessed through low-silled doorways with specialized vestibules. The walls were neatly plastered, the floors prepared with wet clay and sand. Small niches and shelves appeared in corners and on walls. Arrays of ceremonial and secular gathering places were constructed—kivas, plazas, and food-processing areas with batteries of stone bins for sorting cornmeal—were left unroofed and open to the public, implying that they were community property, places to kneel and grind corn together.

Many different people were being thrust into these communities, and yet order was kept. Kayenta could easily have become an unruly shantytown, a refugee camp unable to survive even a decade without spiraling downward into conflict and famine. Instead the people were able to integrate to the point where one can seen hierarchical layers of households bound into federations of local pueblos. Isolated farmers had somehow consolidated into urban planners. Something in the Anasazi ideology, perhaps a rising and falling history of contraction and expansion, allowed them to shift seamlessly into whatever pattern of organization was needed. This was a civilization of incredible potential.

. . .

As we arrived in the town of Kayenta, the pickup listing badly on its unevenly worn brakes, we drove past the Burger King with its World War II Navajo Code Talkers display. When we pulled into a gas station, Colin and I jumped out and hoisted our packs behind us. We walked around to the cab, where a middle-aged Navajo man with a bit of plump Hopi in his face sat crammed with his two kids and his wife. I quickly smoothed a rumpled five-dollar bill between my palms and handed it to him.

"Thanks for the ride," Colin said.

The round-faced man, small and beaming, told us to take care.

Colin and I walked to the highway just as evening lights flickered on at the gas station. We stood quietly, enjoying the sense of rebirth that inevitably comes from getting out of the back of a pickup and having it pull away behind you. We could go anywhere from here, the book of our lives not yet written.

For a minute we stood saying nothing to each other, assessing the world around us. Black Mesa rose roughly over the town, with an ivory band of cliff across its top. Beside it Skeleton Mesa bent up through arcs and precipices of red stone. The interiors of both of these mesas are gutted by high canyons we could not see from here, and inside of them are Anasazi cliff dwellings marking a turn for the worse late in the thirteenth century.

The Last Cliff Dwellings of the Anasazi

MESAS OF KAYENTA

By midnight Colin and I were walking under the full moon, crossing miles of ivory light, the ground mostly barren, eaten back by cattle. Far from any road we stopped at the rasp of a solitary juniper tree, where we laid our bags and slept in the frozen dark.

At the very first glimmer of dawn we broke our camp. I snuffed out the tea stove while Colin slipped our only pot into his pack. We gathered gear snugly on our backs and began moving. Sunrise touched a long cliff above us, lighting the face of a high mesa. Below it we walked through wracks of fallen boulders and mounds where hundreds upon hundreds of potsherds were barely exposed at the surface, signs of thirteenth-century congregations. Figuring the pottery marked a route, we struck from there directly up the mesa, climbing its steep skirt, working the cold out of our bodies with hands reaching ahead and pulling on stone handholds that felt as if they were made of ice.

Water was frozen in some of the crooks, seep springs and water holes turned solid, their surfaces delicately feathered in ice. I worried about not being able to find available, unfrozen water. We could melt whatever we came upon, but that would take time. Maybe back inside this mesa we would find what we needed.

My pack felt like a beast clutching my back, where it draped its arms over my shoulders and wrapped its legs around my waist, moaning in my ear to keep going, to carry it into some vast country far away. Heavy with winter-weight gear—a rolled wool serape, many thin layers of clothing made out of petroleum, a down sleeping bag, a good pad, a tarp, fuel, and food—I wanted to drop the pack, let it sail into the fall behind me, leaving me free to move. Instead I took long, sharp breaths, heart pounding as even in the frozen dawn, sweat touched cold skin at my forehead, my wrists.

We used our fingers in the rock cracks, gloves tattered down to our knuckles, climbing through broken bedrock. A sandstone boulder the size of a desk was balanced above me, and I climbed over it, trying to match its weight with mine. It tipped and fell out from under me. Sputtering a curse, I grabbed the root of a hanging juniper tree. I caught it at the full length of my arm, scrambling on boot soles as the boulder slid off into space. It crashed into ledges of frozen soil, where it ripped up more rocks. They all smashed to pieces against a cliff below, then showered to the earth, where I could no longer hear them. I scrambled up the juniper root and stopped when I found solid footing.

I glanced up and saw Colin watching from a high edge, his body crouched a hundred feet above me. I had broken the morning's silence. Colin nodded to me, knowing that I felt like an idiot right now, waking up the dead. We kept going and soon crossed the meridian of sunrise. An orange sheet of light came across the desert and cropped the top of the mesa. The sun was suddenly warm on our backs. We climbed a bright block of stone at the mesa's full height and stopped there, turning to look back down into the country we had slept in the previous night.

We could see everything from this point. Above the lid of the Great Sage Plain far away in Colorado stood Sleeping Ute Mountain. Beside that lay Cedar Mesa, a cool, green scrim across Utah, and upon its head the twin buttes of the Bear's Ears. Out of this array of landmarks Comb Ridge came over the earth like a gigantic, bony snake, dipping to let the San Juan River through, then rising again to turn west into Arizona, passing forty miles away from Chinle Wash around Monument Valley. After one hundred miles of crossing the desert, Comb Ridge finally ended below us, where the town of Kayenta glittered in the sun like broken glass.

We lingered on the rock tip for a while, admiring the country, nearly the entire Anasazi range laid before us. Chaco was barely blocked by a chain of mountains to the east—the Carrizos, Lukachukais, and Chuskas—the places Chacoans had cut their timbers. The land between here and there lay pale and barren. I could see the Anasazi pattern, where they were born from the reddish dust of the Colorado Plateau and where they once spread across the horizons with their pottery, their great houses, their jacal villages. And I could see them pulling back during a long drought, a century's race of desert people threading through stone pillars and canyons, lurching over plains of dry earth, to return to this land of high mesas upon which we were now sitting. They paused in the country below, setting up a hundred years of pueblos and line-of-sight citadels. But they did not stop there. They teetered as long as they could upon their prayers for rain, but the climate only became drier, and they went to their fallback, taking refuge in canyons falling into the mesa behind us.

I turned to face south. The mesa was thrown open where big-hearted forests draped into canyons. This is where the residents of Kayenta went. This was their stronghold, where perhaps they believed they could wait out anything, drinking from springs in the rock. I had not seen such a place since Mesa Verde, such lush secrecy standing over the desert.

I turned my gaze north and back south, then north once more to stare across the desert, as if I were unsure where to focus my attention. North was the Four Corners, familiar country, the realm of Monument Valley, Sleeping Ute Mountain, and Comb Ridge. But the future of the Anasazi lay to the south. Once they moved into the canyons behind me, they left the landscape of their birth behind.

Colin began walking in that direction. He started across a narrow flank of stone, a natural walkway between two competing canyons. Cliffs pinched beneath him, eroding from opposite sides, leaving just enough room to travel straight ahead.

Cold cliffs lay beyond him, where dense forests of pine and fir spilled into plump canyons. In there were the last fallen cliff dwellings of the Anasazi. I looked once more at the desert panorama, then shouldered my pack and quickly moved across the slender passage after him, cliffs eating at my feet.

. . .

We wandered into the earth. Canyons fell into canyons, eviscerating the mesa's insides. In deep shade Douglas fir trunks stood as big around as palace pillars. They grew straight out of bedrock fissures. Where a canyon plunged, it left a barrel of a hole carved in bedrock at the bottom. We found water inside, a still pool somehow completely free of ice. We shrugged off our packs and dropped head-to-head, our lips touching the surface to drink.

There we set camp. In the morning we moved again, sliding down a chute of bedrock with our packs and landing along an interior ledge. Packs went down hand to hand. Finally we reached a deep gulf in the canyon below and scouted it for a while, finding no way around. I tied a rope to a tree root and lowered our gear to Colin, who had climbed down. He stood fifty feet below, hands outstretched to catch the first descending pack, then the second. He gave the rope a tug, and I untied it, then let it go. Its tail snapped on the ground as it landed. While Colin coiled the rope and stowed it in his pack, I worked my way toward him, hand under hand like descending a pole, slowly sending my body down rock-crack handholds and shelves. Halfway to the floor I noticed the light was becoming frailer. We were tumbling into a well, the inside of the mesa deepening.

That evening we spent an hour looking for a place to set camp, but few flat spaces could be found, everything crammed with toppled pine trees and boulders. Finally we came upon a clearing and in the night set a small fire to keep the freeze off.

. . .

A storm arrived before dawn, soft waves of snow, and in the first light we packed up and pushed farther. A side canyon opened above us through the clouds, and we turned into it looking for morning shelter. As we walked through fresh snow, the side canyon blossomed into a massive alcove, a natural stadium recessed into the cliff. This part of Arizona is known for its theater-headed canyons, giant alcoves containing some of the largest cliff dwellings in the Southwest, rivals of Cliff Palace and Spruce Tree House back at Mesa Verde. The fortress of Kiet Siel is within the Kayenta mesas, not far from a large, precariously perched ruin known as Inscription House. Betatakin, with its racks of wooden ladders, sits in a huge rounded alcove that feels like the inside of a hollow moon.

The snow ended suddenly, as if we had stepped beneath an eave. We looked straight up and saw that we had crossed into a yawning hoop of bedrock, a natural cave with a ceiling hundreds of feet over our heads. In the back of the alcove stood an ancient masonry village built along a high ledge. It was an abandoned hamlet full of windows and doorways.

We walked across a dusty, settled bay, and there we sat among boulders and broken pottery. We stared at the ruins as if we had just come upon a bear sleeping in its cave. Startled, but not surprised to find it here, we sat in fine wind-sand with our arms resting on our knees. The site seemed perfect, a tight package of masonry structures. One of its larger chambers, a kiva I assumed, stood out front, its roof still in perfect condition. The site seemed secured from time, untouched.

"Jesus," Colin said.

I just sat, arms hanging across my knees, unable to look away.

"It's a beautiful thing," I finally said.

Colin slipped off his pack and opened a zipper. I heard him unwrapping plastic next to me, the cock of his knife opening. He reached across with a palm full of whittled cheese, and I took it, saying thanks as I looked at the fine sand around me, where potsherds poked up. I dusted one out, a red piece, and lifted it up like looking through a lens.

Here you are, I thought. The red people, the migrating Anasazi heart, hidden in these mammoth, winding canyons so no one would find you. The site across from us would be only the first settlement to explore, where we would find fragments of woven turkey feather blankets and a kiva with its ceremonial furnishings in place. In the following days we would come upon more villages built in the cliffs—

spectacular masonry settlements soarting over our heads—the late-thirteenth-century sanctuary of Kayenta.

. . .

Days passed. Colin and I turned along one canyon and then the next, walking through an eroded maze of cliffs, where one afternoon we spotted a spangle of running water. When we reached it, we looked straight up and saw the largest dwelling yet. It was high in rusted bends of sandstone, where entire wooden roofs had fallen and what remained of them was caught on ledges, beams left in acrobatic disarray. We climbed past these broken timbers by the skin of our boot soles, fingers testing the holds above us. The Anasazi had erected supports to mount the cliff, pitches of wooden ladders and walkways rising over our heads. Not much was left of them, some rungs and long staffs. We did not touch their fragile remains as we climbed past them, carefully, rising along handholds carved centuries ago into a concave dome of bedrock.

A pueblo had been erected in this lofty space, enclaves and neighborhoods built on various levels. Every stab of rock above us was topped with a cherry of a ruin. This was a cliff dwelling in the truest sense, its buildings balanced on spans of timbers and rock ledges. The settlement looked like boxes put on narrow shelves, a reliquary of stonework, some of the square houses and towers fully intact, some caved in.

When we reached the main avenue of ruins along the alcove's high midriff, we saw grain houses and dwellings, fifty or sixty rooms I guessed at first glance, many in impeccable condition. There we separated, as Colin took a route across the length of the ruin, and I climbed higher to where a patio had been constructed. I found a court of public mealing bins, boxes made from vertical slabs of rock. Around them were scattered grinding stones, left where they were once set down. The Anasazi had been on their knees in this spot, the winter work constant when dried corn needed to be ground into meal and flour.

From ethnographic studies it is believed that Anasazi women did most of the grinding work. As I stepped along a mealing bin, I

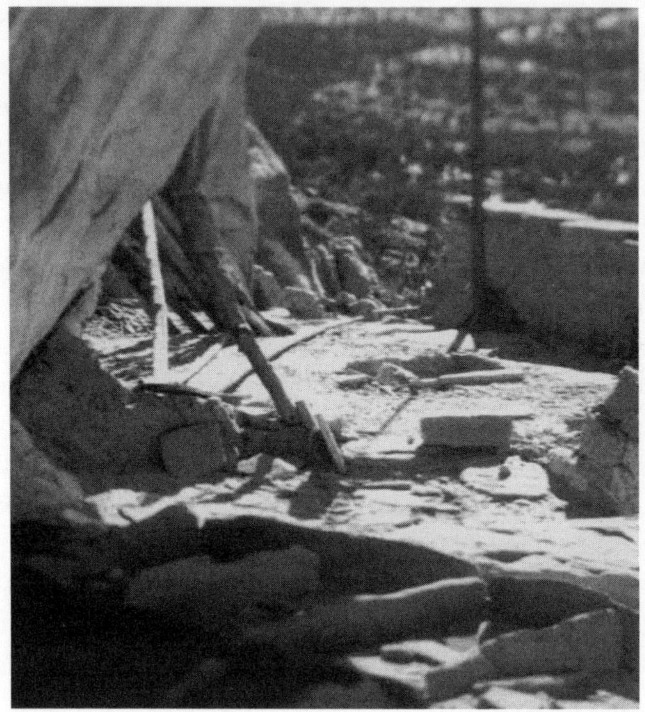

Set of mealing bins in a Kayenta cliff dwelling. CRAIG CHILDS

thought that in this place grandmothers had once paused to rest their arms and backs, while daughters and granddaughters kept on grinding. I imagined this as a place of social exchange. Conversations would have occasionally arisen while the women worked their grain, a question asked, a story told, advice given.

I bent down and touched the grinding stones, where I felt the glacial wear of women keeping this place alive. I wondered if they spoke of their fears during their work. They were, after all, living high in the cliffs in a place that felt like desperation. It was the very end of the thirteenth century, a time of powerful change, of migrants fleeing this way and that. The smell of war drifted in the air from the north, from the Four Corners.

A number of researchers see these late Kayenta settlements as fortresses, their line-of-sight networks designed to warn of invasion. Threats may have come from neighbors, or from Mesa Verde refugees looking for a canyon to claim as their own. Probably a mix of people was showing up, some bringing warfare with them, others just hoping for a bit of water, a small plot of land. The strongest evidence researchers have of conflict is the way the people were living, their ascension into the cliffs, and the seemingly defensive postures of their villages and pueblos.

I envisioned women talking about their concerns as they ground back and forth on their slick, deep stones, parsing meal into bins. One day they might have stopped grinding altogether. Their conversation may have risen above the daily work as they agreed that their predicament had gone on too long. Surrounding lands had erupted into conflict and mass migrations, a diaspora of Anasazi farmers, fugitives, and warriors heading south from the Four Corners. No telling when a clan of marauders might take one of these mesas by siege. Their cliff dwelling was no longer a safe place, the springs going dry, the wood supply running out. Corn was becoming less reliable as water tables dropped in the fields. Game animals were more and more scarce.

These very mealing bins may have been where the decision was made to move again: the families must be gathered, and the men must make their laborious proclamations down in their kivas. Then, the women agreed, we will leave this place for a more secure land, some distant country of better water.

I reached down into one of the stone bins and picked up the hull of a broken vessel, one with a clay loop where it had once been hung from a ceiling rafter. I tilted the piece into the sunlight, a quarter of a jar. Are your voices recorded in this clay? I wondered. Is this where you put your final fears and your decisions to leave this place?

. . .

Colin and I spent most of the day at this cliff dwelling, hardly speaking to each other, just moving from ruin to ruin—some hardly ruins at all. I eventually made my way to a set of three kivas built at the edge of a precipice. They were sunken next to each other, each broken open, with their fine southward facings gone and their roofs fallen into the canyon below. I stepped down into the first kiva, its deflector still in place like a gravestone and one of its ceiling posts still standing. I walked to this upright timber and ran a hand down its gray and ancient surface, kneeling as I felt all the way to its base. There my fingers stopped at a change in the wood's texture. I felt a space the size of a quarter on the post's backside, a plug of cork used to cover a hole, a message someone had left.

To determine dates of construction for various sites, an archaeologist walked through this area in the 1970s gathering viable wood samples. Tree rings from extracted cores were read like bar codes, revealing the exact date that a tree was felled for construction. I felt the plug's smoothness, how it was hammered in and then carefully sanded flush so it would not be obvious. I knew who put it here. Jeff Dean, head of the Tree-Ring Lab in Tucson. Now I knew where I was. This canyon previously unnamed in my mind was Waterlily Canyon. The cliff dwelling had been called Pine-Tree House by an archaeologist who had come through in 1910. To the Navajo it is Dogoszhi Biko, a remote canyon of ancient death. Few Navajo come to these places. They are too full of ghosts—someone else's ghosts. The Navajo have closed these canyons off, as if boarding up rooms in a house where terrible things once happened, where human skeletons slowly erode out of steep graves. Dogoszhi Biko is hardly a place to be visited.

Jeff Dean had inserted this plug while roaming these canyons, taking copious notes pertaining to cliff dwellings, and drilling cores out of choice pieces of wood. He took cores back to his lab in Tucson, where he put together the most detailed prehistoric time line ever deciphered in the Southwest. Among Kayenta cliff dwellings he found two decades of steady growth through the 1260s and 1270s, followed by a final flurry of small-scale construction. The flurry ended suddenly and by 1290 it was over, the last pieces of wood cut.

Overseeing a collection of sixty thousand Southwest wood specimens that show in their tree rings not only dates but also climate fluctuations, Dean is the quintessential time and weather keeper for the Anasazi. When I spoke with him about the abandonment of Kayenta sites, he told me that climate and social factors had been delicately balanced against each other, as was always true for the Anasazi. But there was no resisting the Great Drought of the thirteenth century. After it hit, there remained enough water to keep some meager population alive. Just as in southwest Colorado, some people could have stayed, but none did. This was simply and suddenly no longer a good place to live.

"In the Kayenta region what actually drove agricultural success was not so much rainfall as a combination of deep floodplain sediments and a high water table," Dean told me, tilting his body back in his office chair at the lab, fingers clasped thoughtfully at his barrel chest. "That's why they were originally able to live in as many different places as they did. But when the water table dropped and you had erosion—like we do these days—precipitation became the dominant driver, and rain is just a lot less reliable. So it happened that you had not only the Great Drought, but you also had eroding farmlands and falling water tables. This huge environmental whammy hit just as populations were right at the carrying capacity of the land. That was when you start seeing cliff dwellings, and right after that Mesa Verde, all of the Four Corners, and finally Kayenta fell through."

According to the tree-ring dates Dean and his colleagues assembled, the cliff dwellings just west of Comb Ridge, in Utah's Cedar Mesa, were the first to be abandoned in the 1260s and 1270s. The next to go were the dwellings at Mesa Verde, which produced no tree-cutting dates after 1280. Finally the large Kayenta sites of Kiet Siel and Betatakin saw their last construction in 1285. The final tree-ring date found among the mesas of Kayenta is A.D. 1290. The Anasazi made their last attempts to hunker down, and finally no one was left. Ten years after Mesa Verde fell, Kayenta went down right behind it, like the successive toppling of dominoes, a wave of immigrants and abandonments heading south, pushing down walls as they went, uprooting everyone.

As I felt the plug that Dean had placed in the kiva timber, I thought of Anasazi women talking around their mealing bins. I imagined their eyes cast toward the ground, hand-polished manos resting in their laps as they agreed they could hold on no longer.

They were the last surviving people in these mesas. Everyone else had fled south already. It was time to go. After that, all these cliff dwellings stood empty.

. . .

I used to have notions about there being a cliff dwelling in the most isolated reaches and people still living there, speaking a dialect of Hopi or maybe Tewa. I can frame it in my mind, winter smoke rising from a cluster of masonry rooms, the roofs freshly mended. These people would be casually armed with rifles to keep out wanderers such as myself, and they would be carefully tending their plots of corn in the canyons through the spring, summer, and fall. In the 1930s a small faction of Hopi were politically driven out of a pueblo south of here and contemplated moving into one of the great abandoned cliff dwellings of Kayenta. The faction did not make it that far. Instead they settled only a few miles from where they were banished. But the fact lingers that they did discuss moving into a cliff dwelling that had not been occupied for eight hundred years, an implication of cultural continuity, of connection to a place. The notion will probably be spoken of again. Someday I may round a corner and freeze, seeing smoke coming out of a cliff dwelling, fabric covering the windows, and a man in a denim coat shuttling a pail of water back into one of the rooms. In some of these dwellings eight hundred years of decay could be swept clean and patched in a matter of months.

For now Colin and I saw no one as we continued through the canyons. People had not lived here for a very long time. One morning we climbed out, finding our way into the open sky above. We reached rolls of bedrock on the mesa top and groves of winter-bare aspens. On a high knob of rock we paused over the next canyon that cut across our path, its cliffs furrowed with alcoves. Inside one of these alcoves stood bright faces of masonry buildings, a cliff dwelling bearing well over a hundred rooms. I pulled out a pair of binoculars and peered down into what seemed to be alleys and streets where a courtyard was built nearly two hundred feet along a masonry retaining wall. No smoke came out of the hatchways, no signs of life.

Eight hundred years ago large portions of the Kayenta population had already launched into long-distance migrations. Only a skeletal society of cliff dwellers lived here, and perhaps those who remained until the last moment actually vanished in the fabled way, stepping out of their doors and never walking back in. By A.D. 1290 everyone had moved on to catch up with the others, and these canyons were vacant, places of stories and shrines left behind.

I handed the binoculars to Colin. As he studied the cliff dwelling, I looked out to a ramp of descending mesas heading south toward lower, more arid country. That is where they went. South. Looking for rain and better days.

The Great Pueblos

ANTELOPE MESA

Antelope Mesa is the last high edge above the Painted Desert of northern Arizona, the final place of reasonable water before bolts of black buttes, before a bleak, rippled basin that goes on for a hundred miles. I was escorted across the mesa, some seventy miles south of Kayenta, in a large government truck with a V-8 engine. Tires gobbled at paprika-colored sand as we gunned our way toward a far corner of the Hopi reservation, the plant life far less lucrative than back at Kayenta. Dusty green tufts of junipers blocked our view of the horizon, so that I could not quite see where we were. I had never been here before, but I knew Antelope Mesa from glimpsing it at a distance—a long, pale block of land rising from a seemingly endless desert.

Antelope Mesa belongs to a configuration of four principal mesas spread over some thirty miles. The Hopi people dwell on the other three mesas north and west of here, which are home to many clans and several thousand residents. Meanwhile, only a handful of isolated families live on Antelope Mesa, where there are no phones, no addresses. It has not always been this way. In the fourteenth century, Antelope Mesa was a cultural center, a bastion of great pueblos bustling with trade, manufacture, and incoming migrants. By far the largest pueblos in the Southwest were once built here—up to three or four thousand rooms each, more than four times the size of Pueblo Bonito at Chaco.

We were driving out to one of these abandoned pueblos buried along the mesa's edge. The driver, Mike Yeatts, an archaeologist for the Hopi tribe, was telling me that Antelope Mesa had once been a major trade center famous for cotton textiles and multicolored pottery. Yeatts said that in a way this single mesa had been a city in itself.

"I think this was the hub," Yeatts explained as he drove. "You see a lot of prehistoric pottery from this region traded throughout the Southwest, and the sourcing indicates it was coming from here. I believe these people were involved in a major trade network getting their pottery down to the Phoenix basin and over in the White Mountains, and west into the Grand Canyon. It seems like a regional market society where they specialized in pottery and cotton textiles, and a population grew up around it."

Yeatts turned left onto an unmarked road, then right onto another inconspicuous two-track of sand. The roads came and went, yet I saw no sign of anyone living here.

"What are all these roads for?" I asked.

Yeatts shook his head. "I don't know," he said. "Cutting juniper wood maybe. Looking for cattle."

Yeatts took a sharp left onto a track of blown sand. The truck sank into the ground, the sheer weight of the vehicle pressing the sand down as Yeatts punched the accelerator to get us through. At the next fork he turned left, and then right after that between plumes of stunted juniper trees. There was no use in trying to memorize the route. Maybe this was Yeatts's way of blindfolding me so that I would not be able to find my way back on my own. This is sensitive territory. There were massacres here long ago, and the Hopi have left this place quiet.

We drove through groundswells of dunes tied down at their edges by rabbitbrush and ricegrass. In a tuck between two large billows of sand, Yeatts stopped the truck. He shut off the engine and opened his door with an easy manner that suggested it did not matter if we were blocking the road. No one else would be coming by.

We were about half a mile inland from the mesa's edge, where the wind bustled up through juniper trees. It was a warm spring wind. As we walked, approaching the open sky beyond the mesa, the dunes shrank. Bedrock appeared from under the sand, whales of reddish stone barely breaching the surface.

Yeatts stopped on a long, exposed floor of bedrock. Incised

straight across it was an inch-deep groove running out to where blown sand had recently covered it. The groove looked like the trail of a finger through soft butter, something that had been neatly chiseled into the rock. I knelt and ran a finger along it.

"You've seen these before?" Yeatts asked.

"Yes. In Chaco Canyon and in Utah, usually associated with prehistoric roads. Do you know what they are?"

Yeatts shook his head no. "Just something I noticed. There are a number of these grooves around here."

Chaff from dried, wind-tumbled oak leaves had collected along the groove's slender course. Blue-green juniper berries had fallen in, all of them lined up in a row. Obviously, this served some Anasazi function, manifesting a connection between one place and another, setting a line to walk or run along, although no one seems to know exactly what these grooves were.

"I don't think they're well known," Yeatts said.

"I think of them more as a Chacoan phenomenon, not something you see over here," I replied.

"Maybe this is the boundary," Yeatts said. "Maybe this is where Chaco met the west."

The larger route I was taking across the Southwest had brought me back near Zedeño's line, the division where Kayenta in the west once rubbed shoulders with Mesa Verde and Chaco in the east. If these enigmatic grooves were going to appear anywhere else in my travels, it would be here.

"There is plenty of Kayenta pottery found here, so you know there was a strong western influence," Yeatts said. "Then you get iconography showing up that really stands out—images from New Mexico, from the Rio Grande. The ceramic designs painted here are radically different from what precedes them. There is something new going on in the fourteenth century, and I think it's a result of migrants."

In the early fourteenth century, populations around Antelope Mesa exploded as people swarmed in from the surrounding country. Kayenta migrants were coming from the north and west, while those from Mesa Verde and whatever was left of Chaco arrived from the north and east.

Yeatts and I followed bedrock grooves along the edge of the mesa, the desert extending pallid and almost featureless beyond. I began noticing potsherds on the ground—luminous yellow-orange pieces, a color I had not encountered at any previous site. They looked like little suns rising out of the ground. I reached down and picked up one of the larger sherds, a piece of a bowl. Its warm, egg yolk hue was completely unlike the cherry-colored red of the pottery I knew from north of here, and a far cry from the sharp black-on-white pottery that dominated the whole Colorado Plateau for seven hundred years. This pottery marked the arrival of the fourteenth century.*

As I studied the sherd, I commented to Yeatts on its luster, its solidness.

"You find prehistoric coal mines below most of the sites out here," Yeatts said. "They were using coal to fire their pottery. It was a technological shift that took them from red wares and black-on-whites to these yellow wares."

"The coal affected oxidization during firing?" I asked.

"Both oxidization and how long a high temperature was maintained," Yeatts replied. "Wood burning reaches the peak just as it is about to collapse and after you've lost your main flame. Coal holds its shape, so you can get that heat and keep air going into it for a much longer period of time. That is what gives you this wonderful color. Potters were probably using the same clay as that used for white wares, but it's the technique that is different."

This new coal technology created an exquisite style of pottery, a hardness never before seen in Southwest ceramics. Yeatts picked up two pieces and clinked them together, producing a melodious chime.

"Nearly porcelain," he said.

It is no surprise that a new style of pottery appeared on the border between east and west at the moment that late-thirteenth-century settlements disbanded north of here. Mesa Verde had come apart at

*The lineage of colored pottery comes clearly from the north, beginning with San Juan Red Ware in southeast Utah in the eighth century, followed by Tsegi Orange Ware in Kayenta in the twelfth and thirteenth centuries, then yellow ware and polychromes farther south in the fourteenth century. This forms an apparent cultural shift from north to south across this time span.

the seams and was left empty. Kayenta, which had earlier witnessed a mass retreat to its core, also had been vacated. Heading south, the people of Mesa Verde and Kayenta no doubt mixed in their exodus. Antelope Mesa would have been hard for these travelers to resist, its edges studded with huge, highly visible pueblos. Even today the Hopi remember the place for once having high-quality textiles, beautiful ceramics, and busy ceremonies. As much as drought was a push factor urging people out of Kayenta and the Four Corners, the lure of growing civilization here in the south served as a strong pull factor.* Migrants were in motion like never before, carrying with them objects and ideas. Where travelers mingle and cultures touch one other, imagination and invention flourish. For instance, the katsina religion, which would eventually come to dominate the western Pueblo cultures, got a foothold around Antelope Mesa in the fourteenth century. At the same time, new images of water serpents, stars, clouds, and animals began to appear on pottery and in rock art here. This area became the nexus of the times, analogous to similar centers that were at the same moment being established in the Rio Grande area of northern New Mexico.

From the eleventh to the fourteenth centuries, the Anasazi rode an escalating course of history, each gathering larger than the last, each new center containing more people, bigger cross sections of ethnicities and distant societies. Antelope Mesa was the ultimate unification of the Colorado Plateau, the two Anasazi halves of east and west coming together.

As Yeatts and I walked, the pottery at our feet increased exponentially, not just exposed from the ground but actually *becoming* the ground, more sherds than I had ever seen before. Pieces of broken pots showed like teeth. Our pace slowed substantially, every step delicately negotiated. The terrain rose into a hill at the edge of the mesa. The hill was a fallen pueblo, and Yeatts moved onto it ahead

---

*The entire province of mesas in northeast Arizona was a key gathering place for migrants. Although Awat'ovi, the principal pueblo on Antelope Mesa, may have had the most complete ceremonial cycle and thus the strongest regional lure, the pueblos of Oraibi and Shongopovi on the nearby Hopi mesas each attracted their own migrating clans at the time.

of me, drawn by his own enthusiasm as he kept turning around to point out walls and rooms and plazas that I could hardly see. The pueblo was buried, only bare shapes showing on the surface.

Yeatts and his colleagues had been working for years putting together a map of the site, recording evidence of thousands of rooms contained within a series of perimeter walls. Even so, this was not the largest pueblo on Antelope Mesa. It was simply the one he had come to know the best.

The hill rose to a single, artificial peak, a high ring of rooms where I stepped over at least a hundred broken ceramic ladles, passing by rims and basins of bowls painted with ornate black images unlike any I had seen before—wildly involuted designs full of arcs and geometry, and broken images of animals that looked to be influenced by prehistoric groups living in New Mexico at the time. Yeatts reached the high point first. He turned to face me coming up behind him. "I think it looks kind of like a great house," Yeatts commented.

I stopped and peered at the rise ahead of me. It was built like a huge throne. Yeatts was right, although I had not noticed this until he mentioned it. The site looked like archaeological mounds from the eleventh and twelfth centuries found all across the desert in northwest New Mexico, in the core territory of Chaco.

"I have nothing to back it up," Yeatts said. "It just strikes me as a great house."

Whatever it was, this pueblo was a major site. The first wide-scale construction appears to have taken place in the eleventh and twelfth centuries, as evidenced by the abundance of black-on-white pottery from that age cropping up between the yellow ware sherds. The pueblo later blossomed into a center for trade, textile work, and coal-fired ceramic production. The exchange routes to and from here were obviously expansive, with locally fired yellow wares showing up all around the Southwest.

I walked to the top of the ruined pueblo, enthralled by the possibility that an ancient and far-flung great house had become the nucleus of a village and then a massive pueblo into the fourteenth century that continued to prosper until as late as the eighteenth century before it was finally abandoned.

Unlike most Anasazi settlements that have been empty for many centuries, pueblos on Antelope Mesa and the Hopi mesas have been occupied well into historic times. In fact, Hopi pueblos that have been around since ancient times—Walpi, Oraibi, and Shongopovi—are still lived in today. That is, the Anasazi never left them.

The Hopi are direct descendants of ancient pueblo dwellers. They have old names for the places I had been traveling, Hopi names: Kawestima (Kayenta), Pokanghoyat (Comb Ridge region), Waakiki (Hovenweep), Tawtoykya (Mesa Verde), Hoo' ovi (Aztec), and Yupkoyvi (Chaco). The famous question of what happened to the Anasazi is partly answered here. They are now called Hopi, living on an island of a reservation, a cluster of mesas settled long ago. They are the ones who did not leave.

Antelope Mesa and its sister mesas of Hopi stand like castles in a moat of desert. Approaches from the south, east, and west are guarded by barren, difficult ground as far as the eye can see—formidable land for any army to cross, with little protective cover. In the seventeenth century, during the Pueblo Revolt, a number of native pueblos in New Mexico were briefly abandoned as residents fled to the Hopi mesas, escaping the wrath of well-armed Spanish troops. Though they had dissimilar customs and spoke languages far different from Hopi, they were given refuge here, offering their ceremonial, agricultural, or military services in exchange. This region has long been used as a stronghold when people were in motion, slipping out from under drought or war, looking for sanctuary or a prophesied center place.

The clans that now live on the Hopi mesas near Antelope Mesa each came to this part of Arizona along its own migratory path, arriving any time over the past thousand years; clans named Flute, Sand, Corn, et cetera. Some came from Anasazi heritage on the Colorado Plateau, and others arrived from as far away as the Phoenix basin or even Mexico. Some tell of tribulations in southwest Colorado, where they barely survived an onslaught of thirteenth-century butchery and warfare before making it to Hopi. Others remember walking from New Mexico with their families centuries ago, carrying what pottery and blankets they could, bringing their own ceremonial inventory to add to these isolated pueblos.

The ancient Hopi symbol for migration is a spiral or a swastika, an icon seen in rock art and pottery all over the Southwest: arms turning round and round leading toward a focal point, scattered clans finding their way to a foretold center. After years of searching, after Chaco, Mesa Verde, Kayenta, and regions far beyond, the Hopi say they finally found the center of the universe here in northern Arizona, which explains why they have not left.

. . .

I once met with a council of elders at the Hopi town of Kykotsmovi, not far west of Antelope Mesa. A well-spoken middle-aged Hopi man translated for me, passing my words into the staccato consonants of the Hopi language. Everyone understood English. They used a translator to give them time to think and discuss how they wanted to respond—or not. I was here to let them know that a white man, a *pahana,* was passing through their reservation, traveling along their ancestral routes. Coming to tell them this seemed the proper thing to do.

Old men looked on, most regarding me as if I were a passing cloud. Unfolding the origami of my words at a wooden table, I explained that I had spent my life traveling through the far reaches of the Southwest, where I inevitably found the remains of a buried civilization—ancient roads and villages, burned ceremonial centers. I said that I disturbed these sites as little as possible, but I had questions, needling curiosities. I did not avoid these places. I walked straight to them.

"The Southwest seems to be a landscape built for migration," I said. "In my mind it is all about movement, about erosion and drought and places where you search for water."

I looked around the table, hoping for recognition in someone's eyes. The translator said a few things. Someone asked a question in Hopi. In answer, the translator simply shrugged. I had no idea what they were saying to each other. Some of the old men looked back at me. Some, in their seventies, eighties, and even nineties, seemed to be looking at nothing.

I told them that I had seen recent shrines left out in the desert. I knew the Hopi had been there. I recognized their *pahos*—painted prayer sticks strung with feathers fluttering in the wind—which had been placed near ancient ruins as if marking ancestral territory. Along supposedly abandoned Chaco roads around Yupkoyvi in New Mexico, I had found broken Hopi vessels not more than a few centuries old. That told me that people had been traveling to these places somewhat recently, centuries counting for very little in this landscape. In Utah, around Pokanghoyat, I had come upon colorful fifteenth-century Hopi potsherds left like wishing-well coins atop the ruin of a twelfth-century great house. I had seen fresh turkey feathers hanging from a *paho* no more than a month old at the mouth of a spring below a thirteenth-century cliff dwelling in Arizona. I said that these places were not as abandoned as one might think.

The translator said some words. I waited for a response. No one asked anything. Grizzled corn farmers, long-fingered weavers, and sturdy stockmen looked at me, and their silence grew too long for my comfort.

I spoke again, saying that my principal interest lay in geography, where I was beginning to understand how landscape and climate have always ruled the comings and goings of people, controlling, it seemed, my every step. I called it a landscape of motion, saying that the science of archaeology has been hampered by an inability to comprehend even simple distances. It is crucial that one walk across the land to earn a true sense of how people might once have traveled.

"I've been trying to understand the qualities of distances out here by actually moving across them," I said. "It seems that a person should learn about the landscape by sleeping on it, by waking up in the morning in December and August and March to see sunrises from different seasons in the same places—traveling by foot, drinking from springs and water holes."

After a couple of sentences of translation, one of the older men made a sound with his closed mouth, and the others responded, attention turning slightly as if the air had changed in the room. The idea of walking and living on the land seemed to ring a bell with them.

"You never hitchhike?" asked a younger man wearing a feedlot baseball cap, his English only shortly cropped by a Hopi accent. He looked to be in his late fifties, early sixties.

"A few stretches, yes," I said. "Coming down from Monument Valley, and through Marsh Pass. Here and there."

He nodded his head.

The conversation went on slowly, the translator and I doing most of the talking. There was only a brief eruption, when one man irritably told me in English that there was no way a *pahana* such as myself could ever grasp the ancestry of his people. I stared at the table's wood grain. I looked up and said that I could only tell the story that I knew, what I have witnessed on the ground.

The man who charged me muttered, "*Pah!*" He waved his hand in the air, dismissing me.

I was well aware that I was treading on very sensitive ground. Hopi society is one of the most secretive societies in the world. Rites performed inside Hopi kivas are concealed even from other clans. The most valued currency is ceremonial knowledge, which is based, in part, on geography, on distant customs brought to the Hopi mesas centuries ago.

A prominent ethnohistorian once told me that he had never experienced so small a culture with such a vast cultural repertoire. He said it is as if the modern Hopi preserve an ancient civilization in their social structure and ceremonial makeup. The entire population is no more than that of a small American town, yet different Puebloan languages are spoken on this isolated reservation, and even those who speak the same tongue do so with sharply different accents, telling of divergent heritages. There is far more to the Hopi than meets the eye.

After quiet set in again around the table, the man who had asked me about hitchhiking leaned forward in his chair. He seemed to like me; he had a lenient voice.

"If you could ask one question," he said, "what would it be?"

I glanced around the table and swallowed. I had many questions. I wanted to know about Antelope Mesa, why no one lives there anymore when it was once the apparent cultural center of northern Arizona. I also wanted to know about the T shape I had seen in so many Anasazi sites. If it was a symbol, then what did it symbolize? But I did not want to waste my question on a taboo topic or on architecture.

Instead I said, "I wonder if you know of any clans who went south from here and never came back. Any lost clans who kept going. Back in the fourteenth century or so."

The room was quiet again. I said, "That's what I would ask."

I wanted to know where the rest of the Anasazi had gone. Certainly, they did not all end up here. Besides the pueblos of Hopi, there are numerous other pueblos in northern New Mexico that carry Anasazi ancestry, such as Zuni, Acoma, Cochiti, and Taos. A whole civilization once rose in this landscape. Only scattered populations remain.* Where had the others gone?

The man who had opened the door a crack for my inquiry leaned back in his chair. Tension eased in the room as some of the elders shifted in their seats. The conversation was over.

Relaxed talking began among the men. The man who had been translating turned to me and said, "It would take about a year to answer your question."

Some of the men got up for coffee, pushing their bodies out of their chairs, helping each other by taking each other's arms. The translator stood up. I was left in my chair, tired, as if I had walked a very long way to get here.

. . .

As Yeatts and I walked through the ruins, I asked him about ancestry—the relationship between Hopi and Anasazi. But when I used the word *Anasazi,* Yeatts put his hands in his pockets and looked uncomfortably at the ground.

"I'm sorry," I said. "I wasn't thinking."

Yeatts shook his head as if to say it was nothing, but I knew better than to use that word here. Yeatts reminded me that the Hopi

---

*Each region of modern pueblos in the Southwest has its own kinship structure, language, governing organization, and ceremonial focus. The western pueblos of Hopi, Hano, Laguna, Acoma, and Zuni engage heavily in a katsina religion and hold ceremonies known for rain making and weather control. The eastern pueblos of Tesuque, Nambe, Pojoaque, San Ildefonso, Santa Clara, San Juan, Taos, Picuris, Sandia, and Isleta are less involved in katsinas and are better known for ceremonies dealing with curing, hunting, and warfare.

prefer the word *Hisatsinom,* a Hopi term for their ancestors. *Anasazi,* I knew, was an insult.

The word *Anasazi* was crafted by the Navajo, who in the 1800s were paid by white men to dig skeletons and pots out of the desert. The Navajo who came up with this name probably did not arrive in the Southwest until the sixteenth century, nomads from present-day southeast Alaska and British Columbia moving into a land left mostly empty by the departure of the previous civilization. Their reservation now dwarfs the Hopi reservation and surrounds it on all sides. Understandably the Hopi do not like having their ancestors named by the Navajo. For a long time *Anasazi* was romantically and incorrectly thought to mean "old ones." It actually means "enemy ancestors," a term full of political innuendo and slippery history.

In Navajo, a notoriously complex and subtly coded language, *'Ana'í* means "alien, enemy, foreigner, non-Navajo." *'Anaa'* means "war." *Sází* translates as something or someone once whole and now scattered about—a word used to describe the final corporeal decay as a body turns to bones and is strewn about by erosion and scavengers.

"You understand why it is an unpopular term," Yeatts said. "It is not a name the Hopi chose."

"I understand," I told him, aware that the word suits the needs of the Navajo by implying that these previous people are dead and gone, the land abandoned, available to whoever wants it.

"But *Anasazi* is also a very rich term, full of history," I said.

"The Southwest has many conflicting histories to contend with," Yeatts admitted.

I told him that I could find no easy solution for what to call these people I was following, that I understood naming the past can either connect people to their ancestors or alienate them. I politely suggested that although *Hisatsinom* is an adequate word for the Hopi, like *Anasazi* it does not take into account other names and languages. How do the Zuni feel about using a Hopi word for their ancestors? What about the Pueblo people of Jemez, Santa Clara, Sandia, Acoma, Santo Domingo, Zia, Taos, Isleta, Tigua, Tano, San Felipe, and Tesuque? Four isolated language families are now spoken by the modern Puebloans who represent what is left of the Anasazi. Among those language families are numerous dialects, some of which are mutually unintelligible even if they belong to the same family. The linguistic background of the Pueblo people points to incredibly different histories, which are glaringly oversimplified by the word *Anasazi.*

I spoke to many people—natives, scientists, wilderness travelers—in search of a consensus about what to call these ancestors, but I found none. Most archaeologists and Pueblo people implored me to switch from *Anasazi* to *Ancestral Puebloan.* One could argue that this rather bleak term is a combination of English and Spanish, neither having linguistic roots in the ancient Southwest. However, none of the Pueblo people would accept another tribe's name for themselves or their ancestors, and this is as neutral a term as they will ever find in the current political environment.

Each name is history—or prehistory—seen from a particular vantage. *Anasazi* is a purely material, diagnostic point of view made of pottery and ruins, lacking ethnohistorical interpretation. *Hisatsinom* is Hopi ancestry, direct kin relationships with ancient people. *Ancestral Puebloan* is the whole package of Pueblo ancestry bundled up with the Colorado Plateau as its home. Each is a tool with its own limitations—inadequate in some senses, revealing in others. The most common denominator is the name Pueblo. Referred to now or a thousand years ago, these are the Pueblo people, a culture based on corn and kivas, their masonry rooms butted against one another, forming compact pueblos, an architectural hallmark. Though it is a Spanish word, an outsider's term, *Pueblo* reasonably encompasses both history and prehistory, telling of a people who have been here since the beginning.

Yeatts stopped atop a hill of broken pottery, at the peak of this buried pueblo. We stood beside each other gazing south across dry, maize-colored washes, a brindle expanse. He said, thoughtfully, "Maybe it's more than Anasazi you're looking at."

The desert spread a hundred miles into the distance. Everything looked so deathly dry that it seemed no one could possibly live here. Yeatts is right, I thought. This was not a mere culture I was following, at least not in the common use of the word. It was a form of organization carried across a landscape, a means of orchestrating a mobile civilization in the face of a marginal, unstable climate where geography presents boundless possibilities. It was an umbrella covering many heritages and clans, something that could be traded, incorporated, fought for, resisted. It was a time, a place, and a way of living. I see why we cannot agree on a single term. There probably never was one.

THE CHOICE

PAINTED DESERT

T. J. Ferguson is a man of brief but rich smiles. He is very white, both the full hair on his head and his roomy beard as brilliant as snow. In an even-tempered voice he told me that it is a mistake to see prehistoric archaeology and Native American history as being separate.

"It's an unbroken chain," Ferguson explained, his soft, glacial-blue eyes peering into the desert as he spoke. "You can't look at one without looking at the other. And if you're following paths of migration, you'll find them in linguistics and in oral traditions. They are still very much intact."

Ferguson, an ethnohistorian, works a delicate line as a liaison between modern tribes and the scientific realms of archaeology. He is a repository of so much sensitive cultural information that I had to acquire permission from the Hopi tribe before speaking with him about matters of migration. Permission was granted.

We sat in his backyard just outside Tucson in the warmth of a spring morning. His perfectly white hair was dazzling in the sun, and a single, tightly strung braid of white ran down the middle of his back. He told me that *Anasazi* is a limiting term, that the people I was studying had been far more than a constellation of archaeological traits. Names, he said, are troublesome, placing sometimes false boundaries. Names also have power, and one should be careful when using them.

I asked him what name I should use, and he gave me no answer. Calmly, almost generously, he said it was my dilemma.

"But there is some entity that I am following," I said. "A belief system or a cultural faction that left tangible remains as it went. I feel like I'm stalking someone through a crowd, cultural groups coming and going all around me, while I'm right on this one trail south, a big group of people in motion."

Ferguson merely nodded.

I asked him about oral tales of migration, and he reminded me that only initiates of certain Pueblo societies are entrusted with the full stories. These are sensitive matters, he told me. The oral traditions of Pueblo people contain information of a different quality than what archaeologists have assembled. Ferguson said that from the Zuni tribe, a Pueblo group now living in northwest New Mexico, the most rudimentary stories of migration would take all day and well into the night to recite, and in some cases would be unintelligible to me. Stories within stories tell of people leaving one place and then another, directed by omens and hardships and the advice of ancestors. Each clan has its own narrative expressing a different path taken across the Southwest to arrive where the people live now. These stories are a form of cultural validity, naming people's places in the heredity of this landscape. Perhaps this was why I sensed so much movement, a crowd of cultural groups. People had, indeed, been going in many different directions, moving in and out of one another. Their stories keep track of these directions, forming a map.

I was struck by Ferguson's hushed equanimity, his gentle but authoritative voice. He seemed at ease in his place balanced between archaeology and a people's remembered history. He explained how he had accompanied various tribal members far south of the Colorado Plateau, where he walked with them among ruins, showing them what archaeologists had reported there. He listened carefully to what the tribal members had to say, their *hmms* and *ahs* as they looked into the pits of abandoned kivas, picked up pieces of pottery, pleased but not surprised to find evidence of their own ancestors so far away. Ferguson was impressed by the specificity of their responses. A person representing Zuni was drawn to the more colorful pottery found lying about, while those of southern tribes such as Tohono O'odham passed over the same pottery, preferring undecorated wares of brown and gray. To Ferguson this meant affiliation, memory. Different kinds of pottery had belonged to different groups of people, and those people had bloodlines stretching directly from a thousand years ago to today.

While Ferguson traveled with these representatives, a Zuni man told a story. It was about something that had happened near the Little Colorado River, in the country of the Painted Desert, south of Antelope Mesa.*

People there were given a choice of two eggs, the Zuni man said. One was dull and buff-colored, the other brightly chromatic. One group chose the colorful egg, and out of it sprang a dark bird, a raven. From this they knew they were to remain on the Colorado Plateau. The second group chose the plain egg, from which hatched a rainbow-colored parrot. These people were told, "A'lahoankwin ta'hna ton a'wanuwa" (To the south direction you shall go).

As Ferguson retold the story of the two eggs, I thought, There you are. Pushing through a crowd of ancient cultural groups, I caught a glimpse of the people I was following, the ones who had vanished. They were just turning a corner when I saw them, passing through the Painted Desert late in the thirteenth or early in the fourteenth century on their way south.

The metaphors in this story were clear to me. The people who chose the raven were meant to stay in this northern land. Ravens are icons on the Colorado Plateau, black jesters echoing in the canyons and across arid plains. The colorful egg from which the raven sprang may have represented the rise of fourteenth-century yellow wares and multicolored pottery on the Colorado Plateau. The dull-colored egg might have indicated a tradition of buff pottery known from the same

*One might imagine that nobody ever lived in the country where this story took place, an expanse of stark, colorful clay and bleak, rocky buttes. But archaeological surveys done in the desert south of Antelope Mesa have revealed densely packed settlements now buried by dust and sand. When excavators cut trenches for a gas pipeline expansion across this region, their backhoes kept unexpectedly revealing kivas and blocks of rooms. Nearby, a great house was found among trunks of petrified trees 200 million years old. The few exposed rock faces are riddled with ancient art. This story came from a well-populated place in pre-Columbian times, a significant cultural juncture.

era far south of here, in the desert of southern Arizona, land of the prehistoric Hohokam culture. The parrot that came out of the second egg is strictly a southern bird, the colors of Mexico and Mesoamerica. For more than a thousand years, parrot feathers, like macaw feathers, have been prized in the Southwest. The raven and the parrot are symbols of two places, two different courses of history.

Ferguson warned me not to read too much into these stories. They are told in a far different language than the one I understand—not just different words, but a whole other way of communicating. This is a civilization other than my own, with unseen rules and agendas, a phonetic memory unfamiliar to me. Even if I comprehend the words, I am likely to muffle their true meaning with my own projections.

Then Ferguson said, "The Zuni have a tradition of Lost Others."

"Lost Others?" I asked, suddenly even more alert to Ferguson's voice.

"The Zuni consider them to be ancestors," Ferguson said. "Still part of the Zuni body."

I had asked the Hopi about any lost clans that went south and did not return but had not thought to ask the Zuni, who have just as old an ancestry in the Southwest as the Hopi.

"Is there any remaining contact? Do they have any idea where these people went?" I asked.

"Not exactly. Somewhere far to the south."

"South," I repeated. "Any idea how many people?"

"Maybe many," Ferguson said, his tone of voice suggesting it is not possible to know, or it is not my business. His tone also belied an unanswered question in his mind, the same question that was sending me searching across this land: where did these people go and why? This question is not simply answered with words such as *south* and *drought*. Edicts and cultural imperatives had been in place, groups of people directed this way and that. Something had happened once in the rippling badlands and tightly packed settlements of the Painted Desert, a choice made between two different eggs, one telling people to leave, the other instructing them to remain. I mused that the Little Colorado River would have been a good place to make such a choice, a thin ribbon of water passing east to west, a boundary at the edge of the Painted Desert. North of the river lies the bulk of the Colorado Plateau, a landscape of high desert and scattered green mesas. To the south the land rises steadily, finally consumed by broad alpine forests, the world changed completely. The people would have gathered at this river and made their decision there.

Outpost

LITTLE COLORADO RIVER

It is hardly a river. A death rattle of water, more like it. I have tasted it before, as gritty as the water on a potter's wheel. Barely wet enough to be called a river, it is named the Little Colorado. During the few weeks that it runs high—in late winter and again in July—it is a bloody froth of silt. Running toward the west, it falls into a quicksand gorge and then into the Grand Canyon, where it indelibly stains the greater Colorado River, turning it a turgid red.

It is the quixotic cousin of a river, never obedient, killing crops with drought before sinking their stalks under three feet of flood-driven mud. I carry a loyal respect for this river, admiring its capriciousness, its ruthless floods, and its long stretches where the bed lies as dry as cornstarch. It passes about sixty miles south of Antelope Mesa through a yellowish, empty valley 150 miles wide. The surrounding vistas are a still life of distant, lonely landmarks, some buttes sprinkled on the horizon, the bat wings of the San Francisco Peaks barely visible far to the west, and ruins standing on prominent points all along.

In the center of this desolation the Little Colorado River passes a cluster of buried pueblos dating from the thirteenth to the fifteenth centuries, a place known as Homol'ovi. This is a Hopi word describing something mounded up, the mounds marking an ancient colony.

For three straight days a windstorm pumiced Homol'ovi. The hot dust of summer hissed across the backs of excavators unearthing one of Homol'ovi's buried pueblos. The place looked like a refugee camp with its tarps snapping in the wind. Some twenty people crouched into their digs, the shields of their backs all facing southwest against the gale. Once or twice a day someone's hat fled the scene, catapulting off the peak of this five-hundred-room mound. It would skate over an expanse of broken pottery below and be caught several hundred feet away on a sharp sprig of greasewood.

We looked like rumpled hoboes milling about, wearing bandanas and sunglasses, faces darkly peppered, rarely glancing up. Earlier in the day I had sat with two women who were up here taking a break from their more frequent work in Mesoamerica. They pulled their bandanas down, faces caked with dust, and said it takes a while to get used to all the sediment here, digging in dry holes full of dust and rocks. But they liked the break. Too much royalty in Mesoamerica. One woman said, "It's just about kings, kings, and kings down there." In the Southwest they could study households, the individual lives of families. They were thinking about staying here, maybe acclimating to desert excavations and not returning to the more familiar jungle temples of Mesoamerica.

Most of the time I spent in my own half of a trench, where I passed maddeningly slow hours prying at the ground with the point of a trowel. I was slowly revealing a masonry wall, chipping and scratching at it, and when part of another evenly laid construction block began to appear, I set down the trowel and reached for a whisk broom behind me. Sand ripples were gathering against my newly cleaned wall. No wonder these archaeological sites are always buried, I thought. If people were not working every day, this place would be full again in no time, its mouths of rooms choked with dust and sand. We were cleaners here, busy wrasses.

I leaned back onto my heels. My cheekbones prickled in the gale. I needed a dustpan.

Leaving my tools, I stepped out of the trench—three feet deep—and went off looking for one. I walked over a maze of chambers being dug out of the ground, heads bobbing to tasks, a woman ticking at a fallen ceiling beam with a dental pick, her face right down on the wood.

I stopped over a room that on the initial site map was being called a kiva, although the dig had not gone deep enough to confirm this.

With small movements and tiny tools, three people raced the wind eight feet down in the hole. They were doing a particularly fine job, their trowel skills sinking them into a flawless cube of red soil, morsels of pottery showing through the walls. No sense in asking to borrow a dustpan here. This was a busy trench, discoveries made quickly, the dustpan used every minute or two.

Charles Adams, one of the directors of this dig, stood over the top of this room. He looked like a falcon—compact body, small facial features, and a ceaseless stare. I asked how things were going, and without taking his eyes off the work below, he told me if they didn't find a ventilator shaft, a deflector stone, a bench—some characteristics of a kiva—he was going to become very frustrated.

So much hope here, I thought. So much anticipation of discovery. The kiva, an icon of Pueblo ancestry on the Colorado Plateau, would give Adams that much more of a grasp of what had happened here, who these people were. And when you're digging, a ceremonial kiva is a nice feather in your cap.

Adams had focused a great deal of his life on deciphering Homol'ovi's remains, working on its pueblos summer after summer under this clear, burning sky. He saw a thirteenth- and fourteenth-century ascension along the Little Colorado River, where elaborate katsina ceremonies became the rage, with masked dancers wearing feathered, shell-stitched gear and directing prayers to animalistic rain gods. These colorful gatherings had attracted people down from the north, urging them to leave their dwindling settlements around Kayenta and the western reaches of Mesa Verde and come to where the action was.

When I was in high school in Arizona, I went to hear Adams speak on his research at Homol'ovi. His description of up-and-coming prehistoric colonies at the edge of the Painted Desert riveted my attention. His studies in the katsina religion made it sound as if these colonies were almost religious protectorates, enclaves of an ancient rain god cult. Listening to him as an eager, young student, I was excited merely to taste the word *Homol'ovi* on my tongue, captivated by Adams's scientific stature.

In his early work Adams found that the first Homol'ovi pueblo was settled around A.D. 1260, at about the time migrations were beginning out of Kayenta and the Four Corners. Although it stood magnificently upon a lone butte, this early pueblo lacked the expansive interior plazas that would appear in later sites, and its rooms were relatively small and close together. It was an outpost on the southern frontier.

This first site was abruptly abandoned at the end of the thirteenth century. Five new pueblos then popped up to replace it, as if to handle the many migrants moving south across the Painted Desert. Evenly spaced, each controlling identical units of floodplain, these five pueblos represented a strategic burst of growth. With this expansion from one founding pueblo into five, residents of Homol'ovi now had 400 percent more land under their control. The orderliness of this expansion—seemingly without conflict, the land evenly divided—appears to have been carefully managed. It could have resulted from an edict passed down from a higher power, perhaps from the pueblos north of here, at Antelope Mesa. Or maybe the people made up their own minds, a group of outcasts or refugees establishing their claim on the Little Colorado River.

Construction at Homol'ovi was swift and efficient. Thousands of new rooms went up around plazas and kivas in a matter of years or even months. Pueblos were erected on tall, artificial mounds that would have lent them an august air of authority in this flat, drab landscape.

One evening after we had pried off our sunglasses and taken showers from a day of digging, Adams told me, "I think they were down here securing this area during an unprecedented time of abandonment and migration. Locals came to consolidate their territories, claiming this place before migrants could get here and take over. It looks like it was a matter of politics and power."

Pueblos were being moved like pins on a war room map, outposts established to maintain crucial resources, to act as stations for traders, gateways for migrants, homes for cotton growers.

Homol'ovi rose as a cotton-growing capital, its budding white fields spreading rapidly along the banks of the Little Colorado. Raw cotton was transported north to Antelope Mesa, where textile workers manufactured it into woven goods that were then traded all across the Southwest. As payment, it seems, yellow ware vessels were sent south to Homol'ovi by the tens of thousands, most of them a certain size and shape so that they could be nested into each other for convenient shipping. From there the vessels were traded for hundreds of miles, becoming collector's items across the fourteenth-century Southwest.

Along with yellow ware ceramics, there came substantial numbers of pots from the Kayenta region as people moved south out of their cliff dwellings. Specific and peculiar forms—shallow dishes with perforated edges previously known only in the cliff dwellings and pueblos of Kayenta—began accumulating here, a sure sign of migrants. People were knocking on doors, looking for places to live, beseeching relatives. They brought their pottery with them out of the north, offering it as payment to stay at these new pueblos.

. . .

Standing in the wind and heat, Adams perched hopefully at the edge of his excavation, posture rigid, the wooden handle of a digging trowel gripped in his hand. I was not going to borrow a dustpan here either. I walked on.

People appeared to be praying into the ground all around me, their bodies cupped over the smallest of objects. I paused above a trench where I noticed a dustpan set aside. I asked if I could borrow it. A man on his knees looked up and then looked at the dustpan. His cheekbones were dark with sweat and dirt, the rest of his face a mask of a bandana, sunglasses, and a hat brim. It was a lot to ask, I knew, like walking into someone's office and asking to borrow the telephone. During long hours of work each trench becomes a very private space. He said that he was using his dustpan, apologizing that he could not get his work done without it. He thought that Room 266 might have an extra one; the excavators there seemed to have extra gear all the time.

He went back to his tiny, mind-numbing task. At Room 266 I approached two students in their early twenties who had an entire court cleared down about four feet. Two dustpans were set off to the side.

I dropped to one knee, looking in on their dig. They had exposed

Multistory masonry ruin near the Little Colorado River. CRAIG CHILDS

almost all of a coal-fired yellow ware bowl. I could see in the bowl's placement, in the way it lay among decayed wood and cobs of adobe, that it had last been set on top of a roof. The roof had caved in, and the bowl was tangled in the debris, broken into a few pieces but mostly intact. It glowed a pale peach, a sun rising out of the red earth. Inside it was a message painted in brownish black pigment—fourteenth-century geometry, an import from Antelope Mesa.

I asked the women if I could borrow one of their dustpans. They both looked up, faces haggard, eyes boggled as if they had been studying something microscopic for too long.

One of them quickly gathered herself, becoming suddenly professorial. "Sure, we can do with one," she said.

I thanked them and took it, then began walking back toward my own little dig. Heavy sifting screens swayed from their wooden tripods around me. One of them was in use, a woman palpating the screen, dry-washing a bucket of soil with her fingers, plucking out turkey bones and ticks of charcoal. Dust from her work raced away in the wind.

. . .

I scratched my trowel along a masonry wall and brushed the debris into my borrowed dustpan, then dumped it into a pail. My trench was shallow. It would take weeks to dig all the way to its floor, where solid artifacts might be found. Picking through rubble and sniffing along underground walls was bitter work, very little to be found except rocks and dirt. Meanwhile, about three feet away from me a ceremonial chamber was in the process of being opened, the dig only hours away from reaching the floor. The hole was covered by a tarp to keep out the hail of dust. I could not see inside.

In other ceremonial rooms at Homol'ovi, floors had revealed macaw skeletons, beautiful vessels, rare stones, copper bells, and fetishes carved out of shell. Long-distance trade networks had been alive and well here in the fourteenth century. There was much talk about what exotic items might be found on the floor of the ceremonial room next to me. At lunch the room's excavators decided that once the floor was uncovered, they would take off their work boots and walk barefoot on the flagstone surface, the first flesh to touch the floor in seven hundred years.

The tarp thundered beside me in the wind, its grommets straining. Suddenly, a man was standing over me. I squinted up at him, seeing that he was one of the excavators working under the tarp. I had been lost in a dream, scraping broken pottery out of the ground, but I composed myself and asked him if they had reached the floor yet. He said they were just now uncovering it and that bone had been found.

"Bone?" I asked. Other such rooms had contained the painted skulls of bighorn sheep and pronghorn antelope. "What kind of bone?"

He bent over, holding something small in his fist. I pulled off one of my leather gloves and extended my hand. He dropped a tooth into my palm.

I recognized its long ivory roots immediately. Human. The roots looked like porcelain tentacles. It was a molar. I brought it closer, sheltering it in the cup of my hand so the wind would not steal it. The tooth's surface was worn as smooth as glass, belonging to someone who had tasted a full lifetime of sand in this desert.

The room beneath the tarp changed in that instant, darkening in my mind. There would be no walking barefoot on that floor.

I looked up at the man from my trench. He explained that it was a disarticulated skeleton, indeterminate sex. Maybe after the place was abandoned, someone had died here, the skeleton worried into pieces by coyotes and wood rats. Or a murder. Who knows? It was clearly not a formal burial. The bones seemed to be everywhere. Excavators were trying to work around them, trying to make the best of things. After having dug gingerly for weeks just to get to the bottom, they did not want to be turned back now. Current laws regarding dead bodies in the United States prohibit disturbance.

"We're being careful, but I don't know how much we can do at this point. This room might be off-limits," the man explained.

I understood. This was a Hopi ancestral site; the dead were not to be bothered. If a margin could be found without human bones, they could keep digging to see what else might be on the floor. Otherwise, they would have to backfill the chamber, close it off.

He asked if I wanted to go in and help. The work would be delicate to keep from disturbing the skeleton.

With the tooth in my hand, I considered his offer. The thought of knowingly digging around a dead person was disquieting but at the same time alluring. I was following people, after all, and might as well acquaint myself with at least one person's remains. Maybe my hesitation was only superstition. I remembered a woman telling me about excavating inside a bell-shaped storage room so deep and narrow that the ladder had to be pulled up behind her to give her room to work. She had found a skeleton down there. Alone in a hole, no way out until they brought the ladder back, she said she had been able to keep herself calm for a while—uncovering the back of the skull, some of the jaw—but eventually a wave of panic had overwhelmed her scientific sensibilities. She had backed up against the wall and begun shouting for help, for someone to bring a ladder and get her out of that grave.

I handed the tooth back to the man and told him I would help dig, thanking him for his trust.

I pulled back a flap of the tarp and peered down a ladder into the gloom. A woman was at the bottom, picking at the ground, and a man crouched beside her, writing on a clipboard. There was not enough room to stand under the sagging, whipping tarp. The man looked up and waved me in.

I descended the ladder; the flap closed above me. The room was strangely still. I had not been out of the wind for hours, and I could hear everything inside this hollow room: my dry hands rasping down the rungs, the creaking leather of my boots, the pinpoint sound of steel where the woman plucked with her trowel through hardpan. I crouched on the floor, careful about where I put my feet. The tarp drummed over my head. Hourglass sand poured through seams above us, forming little pyramids on the floor.

The man with the clipboard told me we needed to keep quiet about these human remains. At least for now. If word got out too quickly, it might filter through to the nearby town of Winslow. There were pothunters waiting for notice of a skeleton, coming out at night to check whether a burial had cropped up with its numerous funerary artifacts that could be quickly dug up by lantern light and spirited away.

"It's definitely not a burial, though," he said. "Just a place where someone died or where a body was dumped. Whatever it is, this close to Hopi you don't want to make any mistakes."

I agreed. We were digging in a graveyard, a strange enough thing to be doing without speaking out of turn about it.

The man used his pen to point out what they had found. A disarticulated spine here. A pelvis over there. Leg bones. Foot bones. Some ribs. No skull. But one tooth, so the skull must be in here somewhere.

The person lay scattered all over the floor, as if she or he had simply burst apart. The bones were tanned by iron in the soil. The man pointed to where he wanted me to work.

"If you hit bone, just go the other way," he said. "Let's see how much of this floor is still available to us."

He said he needed to speak with Charles Adams in order to decide what to do here. He climbed up the ladder and slipped through the tarp back into the wind.

I dropped to my hands and knees to start my work. The woman

glanced at me and nodded a greeting. She was an archaeologist from Jalisco, Mexico. She told me in her accented English that she thought what we were doing was a pain in the ass. In Mexico there are no such regulations, none of this guarded language. Bones are bones. Death is death.

I said nothing.

Bones stuck up around me like bedsprings. I tapped lightly at the ground with the edge of the flat-bladed trowel, listening for hollowness. Finding the right place, I picked at the soil, loosening pieces with the trowel. After several minutes I had revealed another few inches of the floor. It was made of flagstones, just as the excavators had thought, the stones smooth and jigsawed together. It would have felt pleasing to step on them barefoot. I kept hearing the hiss of sand slipping in through the tarp, slowly filling the room.

As I worked, I thought of another story I had heard, this one from the thirteenth-century bloodbath of southwest Colorado, beneath Sleeping Ute Mountain, where signs of cannibalism and extraordinary violence had been uncovered. Excavators had found a kiva packed like a barrel with human bones, apparently victims of a prehistoric massacre. They had strung a tarp over the kiva for shade in the summer heat. The day had been absolutely calm, not even a breeze. The digging crew had been taking a break for lunch when out of nowhere a dust devil rose straight into the sky. With a horrible roar, this astonishing wind grabbed the tarp from the kiva, jerked out every stay, and ripped grommets wide open. The tarp launched as if it were wrapped around a comet. Just as suddenly, the wind subsided. The tarp fell to the ground out in the desert, crumpled like a wad of newspaper.

I imagined the looks on the workers' faces, the stillness as they stood in the silent heat of their excavation. I could feel the pressure increasing in the air over my head. It seemed as if the wind might suddenly pop the cork on this ceremonial room, sucking up the tarp, the woman, these bones, and me, hurling us into the sky. I moved by quarter inches, making a meditation out of this unhurried and tedious work, not wanting to wake the ghost of these bones, if there was such a thing.

Sleep, I thought. Do not wake. Keep dreaming your dreams of

the underworld, of plant roots grinding through the earth. We will be done in no time, gone before you know it, and you will be buried once again.

The scattering of these bones had been the last thing to happen here. They were right on the floor. The possible stories this skeleton held were endless: a murder in a deserted house; a body thrown into an abandoned room; an old man taking shelter in the skittering snow of winter and dying alone in the years after his pueblo was abandoned, no one left to bury him.

Based on Hopi stories and archaeological finds, it is believed that Homol'ovi was abandoned after a series of devastating floods. Cropland was destroyed by the rampaging Little Colorado River late in the fourteenth century. Pools of stagnant water would have gathered behind logjams and in flood-scoured holes. There would have been an infestation of waterborne insects, black waves of mosquitoes and deerflies in the desert. I thought of this person dying in the grip of chills, a once beautifully woven blanket pulled up to his trembling lips.

. . .

The woman from Mexico sat facing me. Our tools rested on the ground while the tarp rumbled overhead. There was no need to talk. The wind outside held our full awareness, as if we were waiting for a tornado to snatch us up. There was nowhere else to go from here. This room was dead, bones everywhere.

The flap opened above us, letting in a spray of sand. The man with the clipboard climbed down the ladder and squatted among the bones. He glanced around and saw that our further digging had only confirmed his fears. The skeleton was completely scattered, no way around it.

"We're going to close off this room," he said. "We'll start backfilling it tomorrow."

All this work, I thought. So much desire. Digging sixteen feet straight down by one-eighth-inch increments, only to reach the floor and have to cover it back up without answering the many questions of archaeology.

I picked up my tools and climbed back into the wind, struck suddenly by the hot, open sky of Homol'ovi. Survey markers whipped furiously like prayer flags. I walked the black metal dustpan back to the two women huddling on the ground like desert scavengers. They had most of the yellow bowl exposed and had started on a gray hulk of a corrugated jar nearby. I set down the pan, then followed a path of survey flags down off the hill, looking for solitude, ten or fifteen minutes away. Digging in graveyards is exhausting, the atmosphere at the excavation an unsettling combination of obsession and restraint, as we all picked and scratched ever so gently into the ground.

Eventually, I came to a thicket of coyote willows. Inside I pushed through tamarisk trees, their exotic, feathery branches draping across my shoulders. The air was still inside these desert trees. I reached a lagoon of slow, clear water. A few bubbling islands of green-velvet algae drifted out in the middle. This was why the pueblo had been built in this location. It was an oasis, a fitting place for the water-god katsinas to have come dancing.

I knelt at the water's edge and cupped my hands beneath the surface. The water was tepid and smelled like fish and cow piss. Still, it was good water, moving gently toward the red-stained bed of the Little Colorado. Water trickled out of my hands, sounding jubilant and silver-toned. I rubbed my knuckles clean and rinsed my forearms, scraping with fingernails to get off the embedded sweat and wind-dust of Homol'ovi. The dust dripped back into the water, blood-colored beads turning to threads beneath the surface and disappearing.

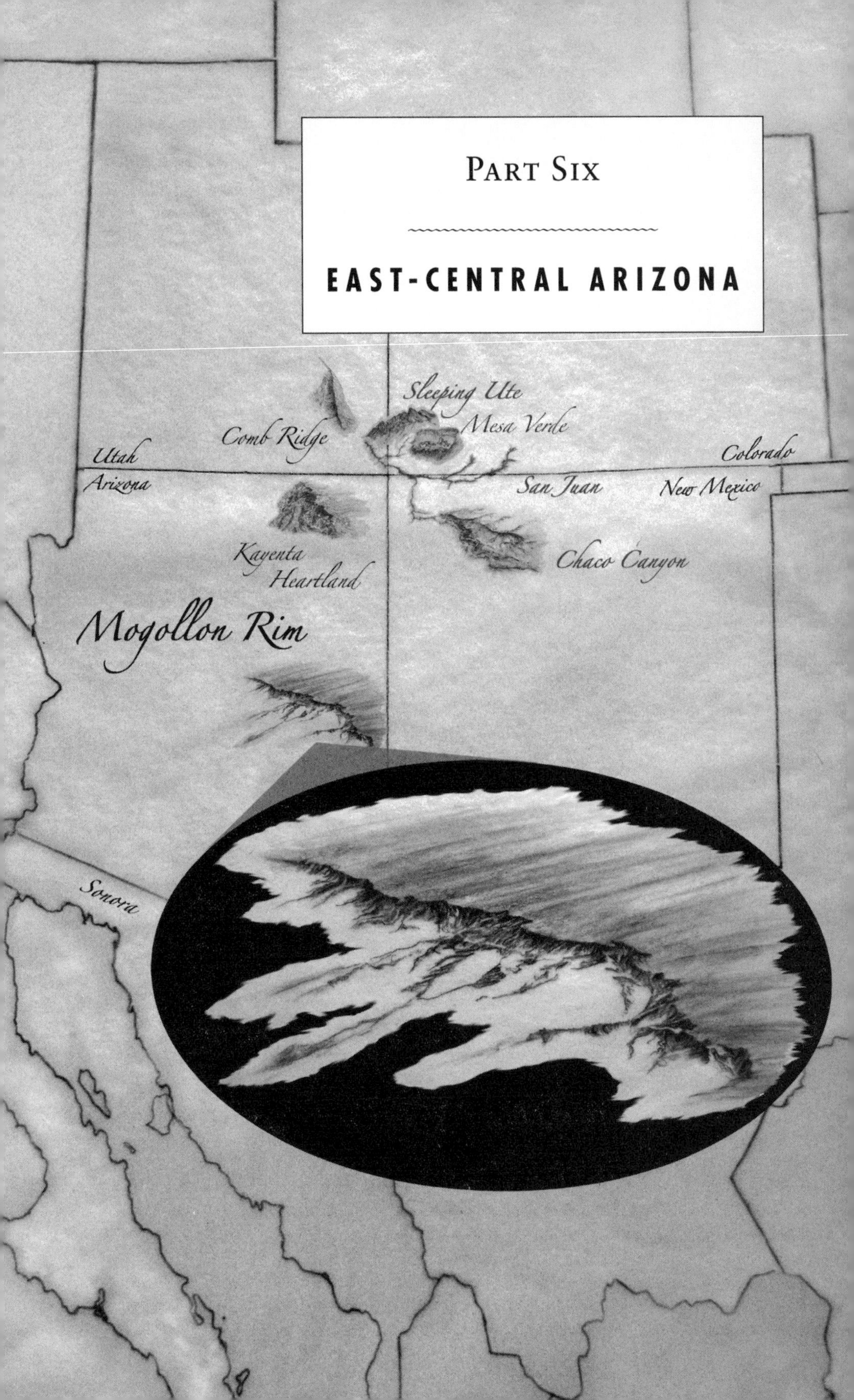
Part Six
EAST-CENTRAL ARIZONA
Sleeping Ute
Mesa Verde
Comb Ridge
Utah
Arizona
Colorado
San Juan
New Mexico
Kayenta
Heartland
Chaco Canyon
Mogollon Rim
Sonora

The Clock

AT THE EDGE OF THE FOREST

I heard voices, and I woke. It was just before dawn. An inkling of light touched the sky outside the tent. The wind was fierce, belting through a copse of juniper trees and piñon pines. I could barely hear them, the men talking, coming closer.

Regan and I were camped with Jasper, who slept between us, covers pulled to his chin. We had come to the ruins of a fourteenth-century pueblo positioned on an ecological boundary south of Homol'ovi. The dry lands end here, and a dense pine forest begins, one that goes on to blanket an eighth of the state of Arizona. Beyond Homol'ovi and the Little Colorado River, the land becomes a single bare platform of slowly lifting desert. Over twenty miles the elevation increases enough that juniper trees begin to appear. Ten miles after that the first piñons darken the horizon, and in another ten miles a wall of heavy ponderosa pines overcomes the landscape. The desert ends, and right at the edge of these big pines are the ruins of this pueblo.

No one but us should have been here this morning, miles from the nearest paved road.

"Did you hear that?" Regan whispered.

"Yeah," I whispered back. "Someone's here."

"Three of them," Regan said.

I immediately slipped into my clothes; pulled on my socks, then my boots. Warm hat. Gloves. We were nearly at 7,000 feet in elevation, the morning brisk. The voices were starting to fade, heading off the other way. I laced my boots faster.

"Archaeoastronomers," I whispered to Regan. It was the only thing I could imagine. I knew of a few rock art panels in the direction the men were heading. Maybe they were coming up to check the sunrise, to see how its first light interacted with the rock art figures. Why else would someone be here before dawn?

"I'll follow them," I whispered again, zipping open the tent door. "I'll be back."

"Or they're pothunters," Regan warned.

"Yeah, I thought about that."

True, they might have come with shovels and screens, maybe guns—diggers looking for artifacts to sell on the black market. But it seemed somehow more likely that they were archaeoastronomers, judging by the hour of their arrival.

"I'll just see what they're up to," I said, and I zipped the door closed behind me.

The three voices had gotten well ahead of me in the chill wind. The men knew exactly where they were going, no pausing or looking for directions. They had been here before. I took off after them.

In the first light, pieces of pottery began appearing up the slope I was following—black-on-white, black-on-red, yellow ware. Back in the fourteenth century, people had been living in settlements all around the central pueblo, now little hills and collapsed walls. When I neared the top of the mesa, I stopped in shadows, where I could see two of the three men above me. One carried camera equipment. They moved informally, unaware that I had followed them, that anyone else was out here at all. Their shoulders were jacked up against the wind, their heads down as they moved. They unloaded their gear in an upheaval of large basalt boulders covered with rock art.

I looked for shovels, screens, perhaps a weapon that might identify them as pothunters. Nothing of the sort. They had a sole purpose. They had come for the sunrise. The two men sank down in front of a tall block of a boulder black as charcoal, taking shelter, their gloved hands tucked into their coats. I approached through the trees, slowly, my hands at my sides.

As I walked into the open, a forest became visible. It swept the countryside south of here, a dark green sea unlike anything one encounters on the Colorado Plateau.

The man with the camera saw me first, a clean-shaven face caught suddenly at the sight of a stranger coming out of the woods. The slightly older man, with a trim gray beard, saw me next. Both their faces went half-blank with confusion. I could see in their eyes that this site was not public knowledge.

I opened a hand, unarmed, friendly. I had to shout over the wind, asking if they were here for an alignment. The photographer did not move. The bearded man stood up. He seemed to be thinking, There are enough oddities and coincidences in the world, why not a man appearing from the woods who knows these ancient maps?

The photographer rose behind him. We peeled off gloves to shake hands. They introduced themselves, both from the Museum of Northern Arizona in Flagstaff, a photo archivist and an archaeologist. They were here for the sunrise. And the third man? I asked.

The photographer said, "He's the steward for this site, working with the Forest Service, and he's kind of old, so it's taking him a while to get up here."

"And you've come for an alignment?" I asked again.

The archaeologist, Jerry Snow, told me that the rock art panels seemed to be a kind of calendar. He had been coming for years, charting different sunrises, documenting the way first light strikes various images carved in the rock.

I explained that my wife, son, and I were camped down below, that we had heard them come through, figured it could mean only one thing. They laughed. Snow said that there weren't many of us in the world. I nodded even though I was not one of them, not an archaeoastronomer. I was at least in on the secret, peeping into this subculture of people documenting prehistoric astronomy, inscrutable alignments once established with the turning sky.

The third man approached with some difficulty, planting a thick walking stick ahead of him. He came out from around the black boulders, his peaked hood protecting his ears from the wind. When he approached me and stopped, his body was like a truck lurching to a halt. I could not read the age of his face back under his hood—seventy years old, maybe eighty—but his expression was serene, not at all surprised to see me here this morning. He introduced himself as Joe, the steward for the place, assigned by the U.S. Forest Service.

With a handshake I felt his large hands, a working man. He overlapped his hands on the knob of his wooden staff.

I thought there had probably been stewards here for generations, for centuries, wizards and eccentrics, dawdling rubes waving their sticks in the air, plodding up here to make sure the light was still coming on schedule. Joe smiled under the shadow of his hood, his shoulders heavy over the walking stick.

Snow, the archaeoastronomer, pointed out various facets of the rock art panel, touring me through tightly scrolled spirals and distinct but hardly identifiable symbols.

"Most of the activity seems to be based around this central spiral," he said, pointing at it on an east-facing plane of basalt with numerous figures carved into it. He explained how just before the summer solstice, a perfect sliver of light comes across the large spiral in the middle, and its tip touches the very center, like the tip of a knife.*

This morning he did not know what the sun would do. We were halfway between the spring equinox and the summer solstice. Snow was documenting every increment of seasons he could think of.

"Of course you're welcome to be here and watch the event," he said.

"Thank you," I replied, mulling his words. *The event.* He did not know exactly what would happen, but he knew that the sun would rise and illuminate this rock art. Event enough.

. . .

Not three minutes later, the sun lifted in the east, a luminous orange turtle. The photographer swung out his tripod, although it would still take some time for the light to thread through these boulders and touch the appropriate spiral.

Snow asked, "What time you got?"

---

*The same kind of spiral is found on Fajada Butte in Chaco Canyon, arranged like a clockface so that daggers of light form intentional patterns at the winter and summer solstices and the spring and autumnal equinoxes. The same spiral-and-dagger arrangement can be found at numerous places across the Colorado Plateau. Other renditions have also been documented in Texas.

The photographer pushed back the sleeve of his coat and said 5:53.

The sun lifted through a haze of dust that was being blown some sixty miles away in the Painted Desert. There was enough dust in the air between the sun and us that I could look straight at it for a second or two at a time. I was amazed at the sun's roundness, the perfect globe it formed above the horizon.

I now saw why people had carved their images in this location. The full distance of light was visible from this knuckle of a mesa, no rooftops or heads of trees to block the view. Sunlight came directly from the other side of the planet, striking a gallery of symbols positioned on the line where the desert to the north gives way to the forest in the south.

What time you got?

6:03.

The sun began beating back the dust storm, its light becoming too brilliant to face. We shielded our eyes and turned away, feeling warmth soak into our bodies.

What time you got?

6:04.

Shadows cataracted across the rocks, lining up with various etchings. Ducking my head, moving lower, I made sure my body did not block any of these images. Keys were turning all around me, locks opening as the light passed over lesser spirals and figures of animals. Snow lifted his hand and watched the shadows of his fingers, playing with the light, seeing how many seconds remained before it reached the central spiral. He pulled out his tape measure and took quick measurements. Joe stood back, watching, a gnome with a peaked hood and broad shoulders.

What time?

6:10.

The light rolled quickly down the spiral, and within a minute it severed the image exactly in half, one side in light, the other in shadow. The photographer moved from place to place, crawling over the rock, taking pictures from different angles as the clockface revealed itself. The straightedge formed between light and shadow cantilevered across the boulder, one by one touching other images carved in the rock. As each figure came into alignment, it seemed to be a coordinate on a Cartesian chart—the abscissa of the shadow line, the ordinate of stone.

"This is what I was hoping to see," Snow said, and he began describing each figure, telling me how the figures fit in certain houses of the sun, how they are addressed by the light in orderly, annual sequences. Basically, Snow was describing a form of astrology, perhaps used in its oldest and most original sense: a study of celestial motion.

The light show ended when all the carved figures were fully illuminated. We moved down off the boulders into a bit of shelter below, where we sat shoulder to shoulder as if we had known one another for years. Joe kneaded the handle of his walking stick. The light kept coming, falling across pine forests the color of mint, showing the way to the Mogollon Rim.

WATCHTOWER

MOGOLLON RIM

There is a line that splits the Southwest in half, a clean, undeniable boundary. The Mogollon Rim (the Spanish double *l* pronounced as a *y*) is as abrupt as a deep-sea trench dropping thousands of feet into cliffs and sheer ravines. This geographic line cuts across Arizona's midriff, a split that extends from the Nevada border in the west, where the Grand Canyon ends, to New Mexico in the east, along the upper San Francisco River. North of this split lies the high, arid landscape of the Colorado Plateau, an evenly laid country of buttes, mesas, isolated mountains, and gulfs of desert. To the south the terrain wrinkles and folds into green mountains and dark, water-fed canyons. It is as if along this rim the world divides.

A chain of towers stands on the brink of this division, modern signal stations erected in a row, sentinels keeping watch for fires. On a summer day I stood in the observation room of one of these towers, a wood-frame box teetering 120 feet off the ground on a lattice of metal legs. A set of winding, open-air stairs ascends the tower, accessing this room through a hatch in the floor. A circular fire-spotting map takes up most of the space inside, leaving a small margin around it, where I stood nearly up against the glass looking across the very curve of the earth. Hundreds of miles spread around me, nothing but forest to be seen in all directions, a verdant topography of pine, spruce, fir, and oak patched with radiant, grass-colored aspen groves.

I stepped from one window to the next. Wires and cables howled manically in the wind as I stared into the abyss below. Although I had lived and traveled in the country surrounding the Mogollon Rim, never had I climbed one of these towers, never seen how truly immense this forest is.

David Wilcox, a researcher out of the Museum of Northern Arizona, once told me that the Mogollon Rim is where the Pueblo world divides, as if snapped like a ruler across a knee. Wilcox had opened a map and chopped his hand along the rim, showing how the cultural Southwest was split.

"This was the true division," he said. "When you look at how the Southwest shaped up, you see that people eventually fell away from the Mogollon Rim to the north and centered on Hopi, Zuni, Acoma, and along the pueblos of the Rio Grande. Meanwhile, another segment of the population fell to the south."

That was where my eyes lingered, to the south. The people I was following had gone that way. I stood for a long time at the southern window, hands clasped behind my back as I looked off the edge of the rim into vast, intersecting canyons tucked below. The first Spanish explorers in the sixteenth century called this region *despoblado*, having a very difficult time crossing it with their horses and ranks of soldiers and missionaries, finding it a dark and forbidding land.

"Fire's picking up." The voice came from behind me.

A spotter stood on the other side of the small room. He was aiming a pair of sturdy binoculars over my shoulder at a wildfire running about twenty miles to the southwest, out in the Hellsgate Wilderness. I could see it clearly even without binoculars. Black fists of smoke wrenched up from orange fronts of flame, white plumes shooting into the air bright as bone, entire stands of trees hastening to explode. The spotter was looking for finer details than I could see, judging the wind speed between here and there, calculating how many acres were igniting every minute, how quickly this fire might reach the rim.

Other wildfires burned in the distance, columns of smoke fifty, one hundred miles away, each angled uniformly to the northeast by prevailing winds. The spotter kept his binoculars trained on only the closest fire. The others were in jurisdictions of different towers.

Every summer is like this in the forests of east-central Arizona, wildfires coming like weather, triggered by dry lightning storms or runaway campfires. They all head north toward the wall of the Mogollon Rim. The spotter lowered his binoculars and sat back on a stool, the same stool he had been using for years, every day of the summer from light until dark sitting in a glass observatory.

"Still just a small fire," he said. "We'll see what it does."

The spotter told me he had seen a wildfire last year jump from ten acres to twenty-seven thousand in one day. Smoke plumes had risen a hundred thousand feet into the air, their black bellies filled with lightning. "It was like the whole world was on fire," he said.

Today was mild, fires moving at an even pace, waiting for a stronger wind so they might have a chance at fame and burn a quarter of the state of Arizona in one fell swoop.

A sudden gust of wind kicked up, and the tower bucked like a frightened animal. I spread my feet a little wider apart and leaned against one of the windowsills for support. I mean, hell, we were just in a little wood-and-glass matchbox on metal stilts tethered to the ground with four cables. The spotter chuckled as he checked the needle on his wind speed indicator.

"It's just sixty miles an hour," he said. "Ain't nothing. You should be up here at a hundred."

I smiled at him.

. . .

Clans that traveled south and met this rim must have been dazzled by the possibilities presented below. When they came—at first a trickle in the eleventh century, then a deluge three hundred years later—they would have looked over the Mogollon Rim into forested canyons running with water, where they would be able to grow corn fatter than anything eaten in years. In this country before them, drinking water could be used for cleaning hands and washing bowls, not just hoarded in ceramic ollas out in the desert. They would have a new life.

Excavations along the Mogollon Rim have turned up hills full of ruins, and inside of them are ample remains of migrants from the

Colorado Plateau. The clans of Pueblo ancestors brought their entire, mobile civilization with them, their baggage packed full with pots of seed corn and woven rugs. They caravanned across the desert with their projectile points, balls of precious quarried clay for ceramics, and jeweled bone hairpins. Gathering at the Mogollon Rim, these travelers stayed long enough to assemble alliances. They mixed art styles with locals and with other migrants coming from other, distant places. The Mogollon Rim was a cultural threshold, a place to stop for a generation or two and take stock.

For the most part, Pueblo people were foreigners here, refugees from wars and drought in the north. Coming from the Painted Desert, the unforgiving country around Monument Valley, the waterless reaches of Canyonlands, and the wasteland of northwest New Mexico, they must have stopped speechless over this alien, green expanse. Some no doubt sharpened their blades, eyes narrow, looking for enemies in the obscuring terrain and forests below, watching for both hunter-gatherers and rival bloodlines that also had traveled down from the north.

Traveling south from the Mogollon Rim, one is faced with many options, as routes diverge quickly. The Mogollon Rim is a watershed, its drainages fanning out to the horizons. A route south along Tonto Creek leads to the lower Salt River, where in the fourteenth century the widespread, sedentary towns of the Hohokam had been established for nearly a thousand years. The Hohokam had a healthy population growing corn and cotton along more than six hundred miles of irrigation canals, and they may not have been entirely welcoming of expatriates from the north. A southeast route would have led these migrants down into cold, muscular rivers and creeks where the Mogollon culture—deer hunters and opportunistic farmers who had lived in the forest for some thousand years—held sway. The migrants must have looked across these rich, southern lands wondering what treaties could be struck with the people living out there, what battles must be fought.

These northerners stopped to take a breath before diving into the south, sending scouts ahead and marrying into other groups to establish stronger alliances and associations. Pottery was traded along the Mogollon Rim like calling cards as these travelers teetered on the edge, gazing over the swift drop before them—while everyone living in the south perhaps looked to the rim, where the desert wayfarers had massed, preparing for them as if for a coming fire.

. . .

When I called Jeff Clark, a researcher specializing in Southwest migrations, I was surprised to discover that he already knew I would be coming to see him. It was a cold call, no references, but he told me he had gotten word that a writer was traveling south, working site by site from the eleventh to the fourteenth century toward the Mogollon Rim. I asked who had told him.

"The archaeology grapevine," he explained simply. "There's a long chain of researchers looking at prehistoric migration. We keep in touch."

Clark invited me to his office at a research center in Tucson, and when I arrived, I found his walls covered with maps. One entire wall was papered with topographic maps, all lined up so that a whole landscape ran seamlessly from floor to ceiling, from one corner to the next. I looked curiously behind his door, swinging it out slightly, and saw that he had kept going, continuing maps off the wall and onto the back side of the door, stopping only for the doorknob. These he dotted with stickers of different colors and sizes, indicators of migrant settlements, incoming pueblos from the Colorado Plateau. Clark had rebuilt a landscape of geography and migration inside his office.

Sitting behind a computer, tapping at the keyboard to find the right file, Clark beckoned me over. He said he had found something crucial he wanted to show me. He explained that from data gathered by many archaeologists over the past century, he had been able to decipher a pattern of movement off the Mogollon Rim, an early-eleventh-century blueprint that established the course for the fourteenth-century migrations.

"Here," he said, and pushed his chair slightly out of the way so that I could see.

The image he had pulled up on his screen looked like a weather map—barometric pressure gradients lined out like a storm cell hovering over central and southern Arizona, fingers of cold northern air pushing into warmer southern reaches. It was a map of people, though, not weather. Clark explained that he had been looking at the distribution of household vessels in the archaeological record—corrugated pottery used for cooking, a staple of ancient Pueblo people. This kind of pottery had first appeared on the Colorado Plateau in the early centuries A.D. Around the eleventh century, it started showing up along the Mogollon Rim and in the country to the south. Clark had produced the map we were looking at by plotting the spread of this pottery style. He drew the butt of his pen across the computer screen, pointing out paths of ceramic distribution, the discrete corridors people and information must have taken down off the rim—some heading for the Tonto Basin of central Arizona, others working their way farther south toward the town of Safford and all the way to Tucson. This all happened in the days of Chaco, an early southward advance off the Colorado Plateau. These were exactly the same lanes of travel followed in the fourteenth century as whole pueblos and villages came over the rim.

One of Clark's colleagues, a man named Patrick Lyons, had put together a similar map marking the thirteenth- and fourteenth-century appearance of ceramic plates with perforated edges, a style that originated in the cliff dwellings and pueblos of Kayenta, in northeast Arizona. The function of such plates is unknown, but a Hopi story tells of traveling clans carrying a small perforated vessel with which they could create springs as needed. Whatever they were, they stand out now as cultural markers of people moving off the Colorado Plateau. Lyons found that these curious plates began appearing in the south at the same time northern landscapes were being depopulated. He took this as proof that migrants were infiltrating sites hundreds of miles away from where they began.

When Lyons's dots were connected, they matched the routes laid out by Clark's study of corrugated pottery from a couple of hundred years earlier. These layers of maps show the exact routes taken by people walking hundreds of miles time and time again.

These were not lost and wandering tribes. People from the ancestral homeland on the Colorado Plateau knew exactly where they were going on their way south, their movements soundly articulated along established tracks of communication and trade. Migrants had safe and specific passages to follow, associations leading into the occupied lands below the Mogollon Rim.

"Seldom would they have entered unknown territory," Clark told me. "They traveled to where they had ties, following lines set by other migrants who'd come through long before them."

. . .

While the wind shuddered and howled around the fire tower, I swiveled a set of brass sights into place, lining up the spotting table—a circular map representing every piece of ground that could be seen from the tower. I wanted to set visual lines across the landscape, get a clear sense of wide-scale geography while I had the opportunity. By looking through a paper-thin gap in a brass plate, I aligned a taut, vertical thread on the other side of the map with the tip of the Sierra Ancha thirty-five miles to the south. I could see the nick of another tower out there. This was a line I had traveled extensively back in my twenties. During those months of hard foot travel, I had come upon many tall, narrow dwellings stuck high up in cliff cracks, blueprints of pueblos barely ascending from pine needle floors.

I rotated the brass sight along a ring around the map until I was lined up with a fire tower above Hog Spring Canyon east of here. Behind it lay Forestdale Valley, one of the richest archaeological regions in the rim area, its slopes heavily adorned with fallen fourteenth-century pueblos and kivas. Beyond that, directly on the other side of Baldy Peak in the east, I remember the sound of windshield wipers in a heavy rain. When I was very young, during a lashing summer storm, my mother had hitched a ride for us in a mail truck. I can still hear the driver singing in Spanish.

I had my own chronicles of migration across these vistas, personal corridors crossing those of ancient bloodlines. This whole place is a spiderweb of histories, threads of signals and recollections connecting numerous points on the horizon. I aligned the spotter down the throat of Canyon Creek, slightly to the southeast, where my father and I once found pottery broken in a creek bed, potsherds glistening under clear running water. And then I moved it to where my mother and I used to pick wild raspberries by the buckets and then went home to a cabin near the Blue River and boiled pots of jam.

The fire tower radio crackled, a message coming in from one of the other towers. A voice said, "Red flag day. Hold your post till nineteen hours. Pass it on to Deer Springs. Over."

The lookout got off his stool and picked up the handset. He pushed the microphone against the corner of his mouth. His tone was direct and official, alert to the graveness of his job, as if he were standing guard between two warring nations, the Mogollon Highlands to the south, the Colorado Plateau to the north.

"I'll keep my post here," he said. Then he switched channels and called ahead, "Red flag day. Hold your post till nineteen hours. Pass it on to Gentry Tower. Over."

The wind was increasing, the forest as parched as kiln-dried lumber, and small fires were finding footholds all across the horizon. Red flag day.

Another crackling voice came back, driven through a repeater antenna, Deer Springs responding to the call and moving the message ahead to the next tower. I rotated the sight on the spotting table until it aimed east along the Mogollon Rim to where the spotter had sent his message. Looking at the back of someone's head, I thought. And that person looking at the back of someone else's head ten miles away. I was impressed with the work here, this line of signal stations shuddering in the wind, this landscape covered with processions of memories.

. . .

That evening I walked along the edge of the Mogollon Rim, where a breeze rose cool across my face. The wind had died down since the afternoon. Through the soft hum of the breeze I could hear cicadas clicking in steep gullies of trees below me, a sound like castanets in the dark. Crickets also were singing, thousands of tiny bowstrings sawing back and forth to a single rhythm.

Dusk's phosphorescent sheet faded from the western horizon.

Night settled in. The crickets quieted as the temperature dropped, although it was still warm enough for just a light jacket. I scanned the distance for any sign of light—a ranch, a gleaming town. There was nothing down there, so few people living in this region these days that they evade the eye. All I saw were stars and the pulse of a wildfire in the blackness. The nearby fire the spotter and I had been watching looked as if it were floating in space, a glittering and unaccountable nebula. Softly volcanic light appeared through folds of smoke, while bright knife blades darted in my direction fifteen miles away. There came a sudden flare, a wind kicking up. I watched acres of trees ignite at once, columns of flames leaping a hundred feet into the air. The blaze would not reach the rim tonight, I figured. I could sleep soundly knowing that. Still, I watched the flames with caution as they hopscotched ahead. Soon they were blotted out by their own smoke, and all I could see was a muffled, glowing core.

Building Large

ALONG THE MOGOLLON RIM

A burned forest lay gripped in death. Black bones of trees stood naked across the land, eyes smoldered back into their sockets, arms crucified in the heat. They went on for miles, their shadows severe, their numbers teeming. A wildfire had breached the rim. It was two fires actually, both converging into a blaze of historic proportions, overtaking a number of Forest Service fire towers and reducing a good amount of east-central Arizona to ash and charcoal. The fire finally petered out as it made a run for the Colorado Plateau, where the desert spreads like a flat hand.

I walked through the remains of this fire, ground cool now, a forest of dead trees creaking around me like old men. I was walking a circle, tracing a ruin that stood from ash and charred, fallen branches. It was a great kiva, one of the largest ever built. All the grass had been incinerated, duff and pine needles turned to dust, so it was easy to see the outline of this twelfth-century settlement. It was positioned along an eastern reach of the Mogollon Rim toward the town of Show Low. Five archaeologists were digging in rooms adjoining the kiva. The fire had driven them off the land the season before, and now they had returned, digging deeper, pulling up ceramic vessels and fragile ceiling beams. When the settlement was established nine hundred years ago, the Mogollon Rim was a secluded frontier far from Chaco, Mesa Verde, and Kayenta.

With my hands clasped behind my back, I stepped over helter-skelter stones, kiva walls collapsed into a circle. I counted my paces until I made it all the way around, calculating a circumference of about 230 feet, putting the great kiva at nearly 70 feet across, bigger even than Chaco Canyon's great kivas.

Fourteen great kivas like this one are positioned along the Mogollon Rim, creating a veritable island of ceremonial rooms built on northerly floor plans all alone in the forest. In the twelfth century, these were the first lifeboats to appear from the slowly sinking ship of the Colorado Plateau.

Sarah Herr, who has excavated a number of these remote ceremonial sites, believes that they were constructed by Chacoan exiles. "You can see in the way they built their kivas," Herr told me, "they were not aware of certain ceremonial traits that were core to Chaco. They were not from the center. But in many ways, they are Chaco kivas, and they are very much out of place."

Herr explained that these kivas lack the massive roofs customary in the north. They were probably equipped with a perimeter of timbered ramadas that would have turned them into open stadiums, precursors of the dance plazas that came later. Such an architectural change would have remarkably altered the feel of these structures and the ceremonies held there. Instead of being held down in the dim underground, ceremonies on the Mogollon Rim were plein air, full of light and sky.

Herr sees these large, open kivas as signs of migrants who were looking for a way to connect with one another along the margin of the Mogollon Rim. They were using the kivas to welcome others of their kind, gathering into congregations in a region where it would have been easy to drift apart into social oblivion.

"I think that these people were passing beyond their cultural threshold," Herr said. "They were becoming a different culture here. Having to craft your life far from your home population changes you. Usually in the archaeological record in the Southwest, you get a sense of defined social structures, gender and age divisions. But my work here pretty much shows these divisions all breaking down. Everybody's got to join in to make things work. Life is a little riskier out on the edge. Men have to start taking care of the children, doing more of the cooking. It must have been an amazing and frightening time."

Maybe these people were castaways looking for a better life in a far country, a religious sect fleeing the decline of Chaco, or the fortunate few who anticipated the social breakdown and drought of the thirteenth century and were getting ahead of the game by migrating south. Herr sees them coming to a plentiful land where other inhabitants were few, at a time of booming populations and declining agricultural returns back on the Colorado Plateau.

. . .

The day after touring the burned-out great kiva, I went into a place where the fire had not reached, Forestdale Valley, which lies immediately below the Mogollon Rim south of the Lake of the Woods—an idyllic landscape of pines and springs. Its brook and many green-bladed cattails had been spared the blackness of the burn, leaving stands of pines and healthy cottonwood groves.

In Forestdale Valley, Barbara Mills was heading up the University of Arizona's Archaeological Field School. She strode straight across a dish of ground that had once been a great kiva. Under the shade of full, green ponderosas, Mills's steps were lively, stretched out like those of a parading soldier. She counted every step across the kiva. When she reached the other side, she looked at me with resolve.

"About twenty-four meters," she said.

Nearly eighty feet across.

I nodded my head, impressed. The dish Mills had crossed was what remained of the largest great kiva I had ever seen, a circle even wider than the one I had paced in the burn.

Mills is a frank and tidy woman, her voice calm with certrainty. Although she has a rigid appearance—her body slender and strictly vertical—she has an elegant femininity about her. When she speaks, her hands sometimes move as if fitting on a necklace. Mills wanted me to understand the significance of this kiva—not merely that it was just about the largest structure of its kind in the pre-Columbian Southwest, but that right next to it a sizable pueblo had been built two hundred years later by busy northern migrants. The great kiva was contemporaneous with late Chaco, a twelfth-century relic. The neighboring pueblo and its wide-open dance plazas were associated with the later rise of Antelope Mesa and Homol'ovi in the thirteenth and fourteenth centuries, when the Mogollon Rim turned from a quiet frontier into an occupied boardwalk.

"This became a popular place," Mills said, giving me a brief and reflective smile.

Mills walked me from the great kiva a few hundred feet over to the ruins of the fourteenth-century pueblo next door, where college students and graduate supervisors were working with surveying equipment, cameras, and notebooks, swarming like bees on their flowers. They were piecing together a path of Pueblo migrants who had come through and left numerous settlements with large rooms and brawny masonry. At their peak the fourteenth-century Mogollon Rim pueblos were very different from what Chacoans had left behind two hundred years earlier. The newer kivas were rectangular instead of circular, and they were relatively small, some only the size of a modest bedroom. In place of the larger kivas came great plazas.

Mills and I walked into the middle of one such plaza, the pattern of a broad, open square outlined around us within the remains of exterior walls. This was one of the largest plazas in the Southwest. Mills, a ceramics specialist, kept bowing to pick up potsherds from the ground. She oriented each piece in the air for me, grasping it lightly between her thumb and forefinger and angling it in just the right way to show how it would have fit into a vessel's original shape. She knew the ceramics in this area well enough to distinguish families of different brush techniques in the painted designs, to tell the work of a left-handed potter from a right-handed one.

The pieces she picked up were colorful, a style of decoration known as *polychrome.* This new style marked a dramatic change across the Southwest. Black-on-white vessels, which had been a staple for seven hundred years, were hardly made after the thirteenth century. White wares suddenly came to a halt and were rapidly replaced by colorful new styles. In some vessels the black-on-white essence was preserved when bowl interiors were painted with black designs on white backgrounds, and bowl exteriors were completely washed in red paint. Designs became more brazen than their predecessors, employing

Fourteenth-century Tonto Polychrome bowl with black-on-white imagery on the inside and solid red paint on the outside. Prepared for cataloging at the Arizona State Museum in Tucson. CRAIG CHILDS

new off-symmetries and large iconic images. Such a swift and thorough change strikes Mills as a cultural revolution.*

"This was about migration," Mills said. "It has to do with people moving, new social institutions being formed, new technologies coming up. The designs on these vessels were being used to broadcast regional identities, social identities. You can see individual potters in their work, and those potters were making a decision to be part of a larger cultural entity, reinforcing a new homogeneity in designs, participating in some broad, new cultural context."

Mills noted that fourteenth-century polychrome serving bowls are physically larger and more boldly decorated, especially on their exterior surfaces, than those of the black-on-white tradition that preceded them. She picked up a red rim, the broken lip of a vessel, and filled in the rest with her imagination, using her hand to form a

*Design motifs appearing on many polychromes of this era and region are directly related to images seen on preceding Tsegi Orange Ware from the Kayenta region. In turn orange ware images date back to much earlier red ware ceramics from southeast Utah, indicating clear relationships through geography and time from north to south.

broad, orbital rim in the air. She told me that the kinds of serving bowls found at this pueblo are some of the largest known. Since this site also has the largest plaza around, the size of the bowls is not surprising.

All across this region Mills has found that serving vessels correlate in size with the plazas where they are discovered. Pueblos with exceptionally large plazas have exceptionally large bowls with well-defined exterior designs. Those with smaller plazas have smaller bowls with less daring designs. She sees this as a function of visibility, that the vessels were broadcasting messages that needed to fit the spaces around them. In a large plaza one would have constructed a big enough vessel to serve many people and would have decorated it with imagery that could be read from clear across the grounds.

"There is no doubt these bowls were made to be seen," Mills explained. "First you have the white wares, which are bright. They did well for hundreds of years. Then they start using red. It's a psychological effect. Fire trucks are red. Stop signs are red. It is a strong, innately meaningful color. Then they burnish the reds to make them shinier. Then they start painting black designs on the outsides of red vessels, and then they outline their designs with white paint, and all the while the bowls keep getting larger. It's a continuum toward greater visibility."

It is a continuum, I thought, of plateau people, Pueblo ancestors expanding their reach. These migrants liked things big and flashy, building high on the land, moving easily into showy polychrome pottery. They were full of change and influence wherever they went.

I once spoke to a colleague of Mills's, a ceramics specialist named Patty Crown, who had exhaustively studied thousands of fourteenth-century polychrome wares. Crown concluded that their designs contain an artful language in themselves, a detailed expression of an ideology that once spread rapidly and completely across the Southwest.

In her analysis Crown noted an abundance of flowers, birds, stars, clouds, and butterflies painted on vessels—images never seen here before. The hard geometry of an earlier era of black-on-white styles softened into spiraling imagery, still orderly and mathematical in its approach, but given over to more playful asymmetrical scrolls and serifs. Crown concluded that this shift in imagery signaled the rise of the Flower World, what the Hopi call *siitálpu,* a belief in a beautiful and chromatic spiritual dimension that parallels this physical one. It is an ideology that perhaps arose when desert dwellers moved from the austere country of drought into the mountains, with their silver flashes of creeks and springs. The stiff sunlight of the Southwest becomes mollified through pine boughs. Less infernal than the desert, less bitter, this is a region where moss grows and damp fields of ferns spread around springs. A different mind-set is created in a place like this. The cultural transformation that came to these people might have resulted as much from a change in scenery as from the consequential mechanisms of mass migration.

Crown noted that these new designs and their accompanying pottery swept like wildfire through the Southwest, arriving faster than any change she has ever seen in the archaeological record. It was like a sign from a prehistoric gospel, preachers from the north gathering their flocks in these southern lands. Everyone was beginning to communicate in a mutually agreed upon language of pottery as polychromes spread down off the Mogollon Rim into the cultures already living below.

As Mills walked me through these ceramic gardens of color, I told her that this transition zone between the Colorado Plateau and the Mogollon Highlands seems like an important cultural juncture. I had noticed in my travels that people always returned to the same places to do basically the same things. People appeared to be pausing at the most remarkable geographic transition in the Southwest, where the Mogollon Rim splits the north from the south, where they left oversize kivas, huge plazas, and the largest, most ornately colored vessels ever seen.

"Something about the land changes people, molding them into repeating patterns," I said. "Maybe it's just the changed sense of light here, the altered presence of water, a different way of moving."

Mills did not wholeheartedly agree with me: too speculative, too many circumstantial details of cultural histories to pin everything on the kind of environment the people were living in. Considering my opinion, though, she said there was a place that I must see.

. . .

Mills and I packed our lunches, and she led me through the forest. Her pace was quicker than the one I usually have in the woods, and I had to increase my gait to match hers. Her movements were quick and willowy, like a deer's. After half an hour of winding up a slope of pine shade, our steps sparkling in dry beds of needles, Mills and I reached the top of a bluff, where the ground slumped into weathered pits as big as houses. These depressions were old, well carpeted in pine needles. Thorned locust trees grew up through them, and many bulky pines. Among the pits were tall mounds, like pyramids clothed in soil and forest duff. We were in an ancient village of some sort. We stopped before one of the pits and peered down its deep and shaded slope. This was what Mills wanted me to see.

"This is one of the first great kivas ever built," Mills said.

"How old?" I asked.

"Fourth century A.D.," she said.

Surprised to hear this, I let the time and the place sit in my mind for a moment. I usually associate great kivas with the desert of the Colorado Plateau, where massive public architecture appeared at least in the eleventh century A.D., perhaps as early as the sixth century. I did not know that great kivas had been built this far south and so long ago, back in the beginning of time, when large-scale agriculture was just starting to take hold in the Southwest.

"I had no idea they were making great kivas back then," I said.

"They weren't making many," Mills replied. "This is an isolated site."

Mills and I walked around the deep pit, skirting its rim. Mounds surrounding it marked the spots where nearly seventeen hundred years ago, wood and earthen buildings stood, structures that would have been truly colossal in their day. Something about this location invited a vast scale, I thought. Perhaps it was because this is the highest, most continuous region of green in the desert Southwest, a truly immense peak on the land. Perhaps it was wholly circumstantial, the nature of people on the move settling in a water-rich locale on the verge between north and south.

We found a clearing at the edge of the bluff for lunch and opened our packs on the crisply needled ground. We sat beside each other. I peeled an orange. Mills ate her sandwich.

"Curious that you get these remarkable sites in the fourth century, in the eleventh, and then in the fourteenth century all in about the same place," I said. "Is there a connection between them?"

"No," Mills answered. "There's too much time between each site. After these earliest sites people went on, and no one lived here for quite a while after that."

"It seems odd, though," I said. "All this happening right here."

Mills merely shook her head. She was a scientist, a woman working with only the cleanest and most robust evidence she could find. Uncanny connections had their place, but not in her research.

I felt that these old kivas must have been part of a rhythm drilled into the people who traveled through this forested country. Their feet beat the ground like drums.

"No connection at all?" I asked once more.

Mills stared off the edge of the bluff.

"This place was unoccupied for long periods, enough to break the continuity between the people up on this bluff and those who lived later down in the valley," she said. "As an archaeologist, I don't see a relationship."

"And not as an archaeologist?" I ventured.

Mills ate her sandwich and looked down through the trees, where ruins of pueblos lay along the green floor. Then she smiled, almost mischievously, as if to tell me what she could not say as a respected archaeologist: that the earth has lines, patterns to be followed, where people are pushed along by the very form of the land.

"It is a beautiful valley," she said.

Salado

BELOW THE MOGOLLON RIM

Slants of sunlight lead down into bracken ferns and the murmuring heads of Indian paintbrush. A cow elk moves under the applause of aspen leaves.

Beneath the Mogollon Rim water pours from springs, whole creeks ushering from great open mouths in the rock. Climbing down edge by edge into heavy shadows, you might slip on the slick, dry pine needles and tumble a hundred feet before catching the anchor of a stump above layers of inner cliffs laced with lichen. Down there green squids of bear grass grow alongside agaves with daggers drawn. Fingerling ledges peep around corners into plunge holes of wind. Coming down, grabbing whatever root or trunk or shoulder of rock is available, you might feel like a metal lure thrown over the side of a boat, shining and spinning as you descend, growing darker through cobwebby oak trees and underbrush lapping arm over arm. Wild grapes shrivel into puckered raisins. Thorn-studded raspberry bushes crawl all over wracked boulders. Steep corridors of light and shadow level off into cluttered maple trees, their autumn leaves turned to fine red parchment. Freshly fallen trees lie in their own splinters and shafts of light. Yellow columbine flowers with ornate, stellar interiors have turned to seed. By January the hummingbirds have long fled south. In cataclysmic canyons the occasional winter rains turn to snow—but rarely more than an inch or two at a time. A hearty dollop of bear scat rests beneath its halo of morning steam. Cliffs lean into cliffs. A canyon floor is stricken with fallen timber, cockeyed bridges of old-growth spruce and Douglas fir toppled long ago and locked between the walls over a thunderous creek. Sycamore trees burst into maniacal white branches crawling all over the sky. The echoing laughter of water rises through alleyways of stone.

As I gathered water from a creek along one of these canyon floors, the metal clank of my pot sent up an echo. Walking a full pan to my camp, I could hear every ripple and fall of water around me. Sleeping bag laid out, small stove set up, I had my life arranged. I sat on the cold bedrock floor. I poured fuel into my stove, then set flame to it with a lighter. A small torch ignited, brightening a sphere around me.

To get here I had spent days pinching along ledges, grasping handholds above pools of gaping, dark water. It is rigorous work traveling in this country below the Mogollon Rim. The sandstone boneyard of the Colorado Plateau is gone. In the north a canyon like this would be brightly colored in reds and oranges, sandstone swept back like a woman's long hair. Here the rock is dark, igneous in nature, broken into blocks and square towers.

This is where cliff dwellings return to the archaeological record. I had seen them up in the crags as I was passing through, masonry houses slowly crumbling from their perches. Their ceiling beams were lashed together with bear-grass cordage. These were the first cliff dwellings I had seen since Kayenta, as if the terrain between here and there would not permit them. In this next region south, geology gathers into deep mazes, into shelves and alcoves where cliff dwellers preferred to live.

Many cliff dwellings below the Mogollon Rim are truly staggering, built flush into harrowing precipices, their rockwork precariously but somehow firmly balanced upon the thinnest of ledges or tucked into cracks thousands of feet up remote canyons. A great deal of labor was invested in these sites, yet many were occupied for no more than a single generation.

Who were these fourteenth-century cliff dwellers? Often they are referred to as the Salado culture. Like *Anasazi,* the term *Salado* applies to a set of archaeological traits, to a period of time, to a region, but not to a single group of people speaking the same language or

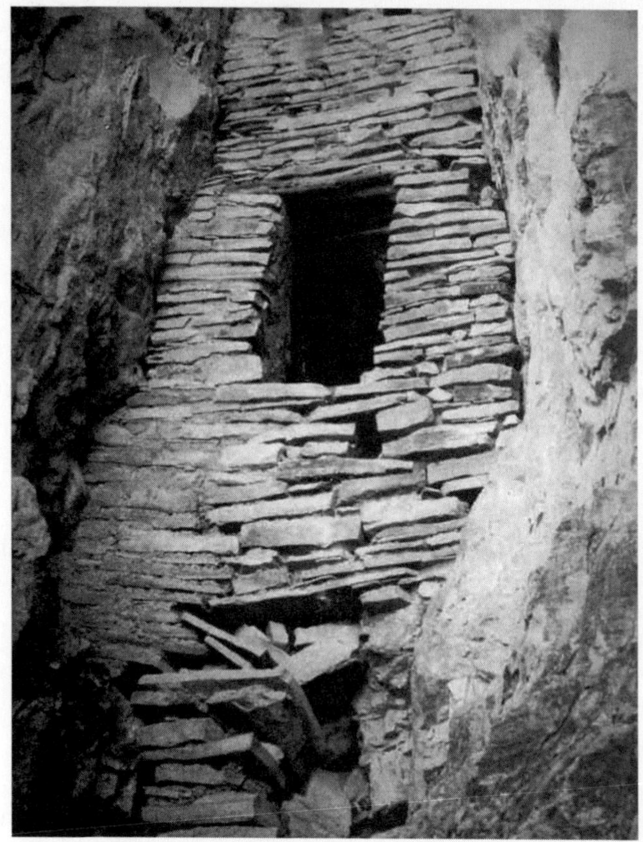

Salado cliff dwelling in the highlands south of the Mogollon Rim. CRAIG CHILDS

calling themselves by one name. Salado is a massive cultural convergence based in east-central Arizona, where migrants collided with numerous indigenous heritages that had been in place for centuries. The upheaval that ensued—a cultural florescence of new pottery and architecture, religion and trade routes—is known as Salado.

In the fourteenth century, large pueblos appeared on higher ground with the Mogollon Rim at their backs and with flanks of smaller pueblos guarding them out front. Farther to the south are columns of cliff dwellings like armor taking the brunt of a southward advance, as if cultural movement down from the Colorado Plateau was accomplished by strategic, broadly orchestrated tactics.

Migrants had paused on the Mogollon Rim long enough to assemble themselves and create a solid cultural front before moving south again, pushing into the highlands.

Thirteen major cliff dwellings stand in this canyon where I traveled, their arrangement forming an arc that seems to have protected a central pueblo about ten miles back. Just above my camp, atop spindles of rock, are masonry turrets, twenty outposts peering down into the canyon. All of these were short-lived sites, occupied for thirty or forty years at the most. It is difficult to say whether residents walked freely out of these cliff dwellings or whether their heads were impaled on their own wooden vigas by local hunter-gatherers who may have had no love for pushy northerners on their land, resisting the onslaught of this new Salado culture.

Nobody is here now. Deep in the Apache reservation, one must follow game trails or paths of tumbled boulders to get around. Sitting alone in a dark canyon with a pot of dinner before me, I felt emptiness where alliances and wars once took place, dark eyes of ruins standing high above me in the night.

. . .

One side canyon was clogged with catclaw bushes. I shoved through them in the morning, the backs of my forearms marked with dots of blood as I pushed ahead. The catclaws gave way to a small brook and badges of shade beneath oaks and the stiff netted leaves of hackberry trees. As I headed upstream, my boots became soaked as they crushed through dead thatches of riparian grass. I was traveling up a steep tributary in search of a cliff dwelling I had heard of, the largest in all the Mogollon Highlands, now guarded by the wilderness of the Apache reservation.

Terraced pools of water led the way, gentle sounds, falls and burbles. I followed these to a rock outcrop, a short cliff, and in its face was a cave. Spring water spilled from the cave's mouth. I dropped my pack at the entrance and stepped inside, the ground and the walls gnarled with gypsum, calcium, and ivory-smooth travertine. Water dripped from the ceiling, filling the cave with innumerable small sounds and leaving everything thoroughly coated in white as it dried. Star-pointed sycamore leaves that had blown into the cave were turned to sculptures all over the floor. I moved cautiously, careful not to snap any of these fragile stone leaves with my boots.

A narrow thread of a stalactite, thin as a pencil, descended fifteen feet through the dim, nearly touching the floor. I reached out and lightly touched its cold form with a finger, realizing it was a plant root dangling down from a crack, flash-fossilized by calcium in the water. The cave was like a house of wax, everything captured in place. Rivulets of water trickled down the walls. The water seemed like a blessing: so much prosperity.

I knelt at a clear pool in the quarter-light, took water in my palms, and washed it across my forearms. The cuts from the catclaw bushes came to life as soon as I bathed them, tracks of blood skittering across my skin. I cupped a mouthful of water and drank. It tasted like good, earthen water, like rusty pipes.

I left the cave and carried my pack farther up the canyon to where a community of cliff dwellings began to show under rock overhangs. It looked as if an entire town had been built along the south face of the canyon, masonry structures in various states of disrepair, the ground below them dressed in shattered polychrome vessels. I passed over potsherds that were red as watermelon and embellished with black and white paint.

This cluster of sites, some 175 rooms in all, was first documented in the 1930s by the esteemed archaeologist Emil Haury, then a young, pipe-smoking man with a tattered hat and a notebook in hand. Haury was one of the earliest Southwest archaeologists to notice signs of prehistoric migration, and this canyon produced his first strong pieces of evidence. He dug up skeletons and artifacts that looked to him like those of northern Peublo people, those he called Anasazi—skulls permanently flattened on their back sides from the use of cradle-boards in infancy (an attribute customary among Colorado Plateau people), tools and weaving styles reminiscent of those seen in north-east Arizona. But Haury saw far more than migrants. He excavated ample signs of local groups that had been living in the area for many generations, people he called Mogollon. The cliff dwelling appears to have been constructed by both natives and migrants, a mixed house, the essence of Salado.

Haury dug up finely woven cloth and cotton-spinning tools here, suggesting textile manufacture among the residents. He found numerous ceramic vessels and baskets, an arsenal of hunting and fighting weapons, and a ceremonial room with objects still neatly placed on an altar. This had been a complicated settlement with many family names and occupations, their customs drawn from distant places.

Haury's black-and-white photographs from the 1930s look exactly like what I saw as I ascended this canyon: ledgy rock formations, isolated blocks of cliffs, and prehistoric structures both large and small bound into south-facing exposures. I passed beneath a diamond-bladed sun painted on a rock face, its red and white rays alternating inward along rings of concentric circles. As I began to count the rings, I noticed another painting just beyond. It was a mural, a pictograph of what looked like a woven blanket, rectangular and four feet across, something hung on the wall at the back of a room. It was neatly packed with geometric designs—red alligator teeth, oval tick marks, red squares with turquoise interiors and within them yet smaller red circles like inlays of jewels. Thirty-three squares in four rows. Eighty-one red teeth along the upper and lower selvages. A left-to-right symmetry cut in half by turquoise lines meeting in a split globe at the top. No space on the rock remained unpainted. Even the background was washed with a flat, white clay.

I had never seen such a mural anywhere in the Southwest. Even Hopi kiva murals do not have such sharpness. I realized I was walking into a vital settlement that had been arranged so that a person must enter through painted walls, colorful standards.

I continued up the canyon's slope into the marmalade light of late afternoon and reached a massive core of residences. I had been searching for this enclave, knowing of its existence from Haury's reports, and still I was stopped short by the sight of it, suddenly faced with three-story walls, square buildings butted into each other, wooden vigas protruding from stone-and-mortar facades twenty feet tall.

Some walls were as clean as canvases, plaster the color of caramel dried and crackled from age. Where the plaster had deteriorated, I could see methodical stonework beneath—thin, banded rocks with only a skim of mortar between. The masonry looked almost Chacoan, so finely done, although this nucleus of buildings appeared nearly two centuries after Chaco's decline, most of the construction occurring around A.D. 1320.

As I began walking along these buildings, window-shopping, I saw the labor of many different hands, sundry architects and stonemasons. Front walls made mostly of adobe—thick, bread-loaf walls with very little stone inside—stood flush against almost pure rockwork. The adobe reminded me of southern techniques, more like those of low-desert Hohokam than high-desert Pueblo folk. Meanwhile, adjacent masonry looked as if it had come straight down off the Colorado Plateau. I was seeing a collision of large cultural groups, a much greater melting pot than I had witnessed in the north, understanding now why archaeologists had invented the term *Salado*. A name was needed to describe what happened at this time in this place. In the fourteenth century, the Mogollon Highlands were a key political, cultural, and probably religious boundary. The entire Southwest from Mexico to the Four Corners was fusing along a rugged, shared margin of forests and mountainous canyons. This cliff dwelling stands at the crux.

This is also where strict archaeological definitions and labels lose their potency. Things were never as simple as Salado or Anasazi. Where or when did one end and the other begin? In the thirteenth century, during a time of increasing cultural movement and unrest on the Colorado Plateau, Mesa Verde and Kayenta rose to power with their massive cliff dwellings. Shortly after their fall, fourteenth-century Salado cliff dwellings appeared just to the south beneath the Mogollon Rim. These events are not isolated from each other, but are strung together like a row of falling dominoes, Anasazi turning into Salado. An exodus was under way, gathering new members and probably losing old ones; expanding, contracting, and pushing ahead with shields, pueblos, polychrome pottery, and cliff dwellings. A vigorous cultural force was dropping through the Southwest, following the rains.

. . .

I entered a front door, ducking into shafts of eclipsed light beneath a splintered ceiling, stepping lightly on a floor of dust, rubble, corncobs, and broken pottery. I could tell that the site had been excavated, the floors not as heaped and disorderly as untouched sites. Haury had been here.

One room led to the next. A hatchway in a floor dropped to a lower level, which turned through another doorway, and another. I passed interior walls painted with faded designs—a spiral, a geometric stairstep, a human figure with a hand upraised. In one room I found a shield figure done in bold white paint, the circular shield itself fringed with a sophisticated design.

It had been a long time since I had seen a shield figure, the last one being in the mesas of Kayenta—a big white circle on a wall above a cliff dwelling. There are others in southeast Utah west of Comb Ridge, a plethora of them painted and pecked into the cliffs around Canyonlands, and a small number roughly cut into the wall plaster of Cliff Palace at Mesa Verde (there are also many later shield figures near the Rio Grande in northern New Mexico). I laid out a map in my mind, locating every shield figure I had ever seen, defining a geographic pattern, the realm of northern Pueblo ancestry linked directly to that of Salado. Nearly every shield figure I knew of was associated with a nearby cliff dwelling, and they all seem to represent conflict, people moving into the land with shields raised or backing against cliffs, fighting for ground.

I moved beyond this shield figure and into a room deep within the dwelling, where I swept a colorful piece of pottery out of the dust, another bit of artwork. It was a small part of a broken bowl, only a thumbnail, its exterior painted with a series of white forks and simple bands. I flipped it over to see what had once been painted inside the bowl, like turning a playing card to find its rank and suit. The inside looked very different from the outside, an elaborate play of colors and designs typical of a style known as Fourmile Polychrome. If the shield figure represents conflict, this style of ceramic speaks of alliance.

Fourmile Polychrome appeared in the Mogollon Rim country early in the fourteenth century as migrants entered the region. Its bowls are known for their complex interior designs, no two the same, as if they were private art meant to be seen solely by small audiences, by the people looking into them. Meanwhile, the exteriors are consistently simple, conveying a message of uniformity. This inside-and-out code seems to say, *We are all the same people on a larger scale, while in our confidential, personal places we are very different.*

This ceramic style is a fusion of patterns from the Four Corners and from the classic Mimbres icons farther south, hatchwork and white outlines known from Kayenta. The actual technique of making these bowls was shared only among small groups, specialized families or clans. Poorly executed replicas of Fourmile Polychrome have been found, where potters attempted to duplicate what they had seen at a glance, finding the finely tuned Fourmile composition difficult to match. One misplaced line would throw off the poise of the entire design. Many such imitations were probably discarded even before they were fired, the potters stymied.

I envisioned the whole of this vessel made in a quiet room, woven drapes drawn across the door. I saw a woman painting its surface with a brush made of elk hair, paint permitted in the smallest doses, mind steady and not the slightest tremble in her hand, maybe a quiet song guiding her through the design. The paint used was mineral based, sharper in appearance than the more common organic paints of the day. Bowls were fired at a high and steady temperature, giving them a solid feel, a ring to the tap much like that of the coal-fired yellow wares from the north.

The sherd in my hand gave me a glimpse of what had once been a gorgeous bowl filled with colors and geometry. It was like holding a piece of a code, a single word of an ancient language.

. . .

A curator at the Arizona State Museum in Tucson, where I was working in a basement full of shelved artifacts, came to me near the end of the day and said there was one last thing I should see. He had already brought at least fifty pots down from storage, and I had spent hours sketching them and rubbing the exhaustion out of my eyes. It was not that the work was dull. Every pot that came to me elicited a burst of anticipation, the art of yet another highly skilled pre-Columbian potter revealed. But my eyes were tired.

I could not say no to the curator, of course. This vessel he wanted to show me had come from one of the canyons below the Mogollon Rim, and as far as he was concerned, it was the finest artifact in the collection. I stood from my worktable and followed him.

The curator, wearing sneakers and suspenders, led me through corridors of basement shelves overburdened with artifacts, bowls stacked inside bowls. Almost everything we passed had come from excavations in central Arizona, rows of colored pottery. In a back corner the curator unlocked a vault and swung its heavy door open with the full weight of his body.

In the vault, he passed over a vessel shaped like a duck and a bowl painted with an expansive black bat inside it, the bat's body and wings filled with spirals and crosshatches. He reached to a shelf nearly over his head and slid out a large, saffron-colored bowl. When he turned the inside of it toward me, I was immediately transfixed. I saw many things in its design, patterns within patterns. It was a Fourmile Polychrome.

Black and white paint nearly filled the inside of the richly colored bowl. Spars and slender lines crossed each other around an ecstatic arch decorated with black lattices and crosshatches. The painstaking symmetry that I knew from the Colorado Plateau had been taken to a new level, the image within the bowl made asymmetrical but ultimately well proportioned, an extraordinary level of creativity. The inside of this bowl was a place of secrets, designed to be seen only by people close enough to be served from it—family and guests.

I felt as though I were prying, staring blatantly into this confidential vessel. I did not look away, though. The designs were too magnetic. What intimate proclamations were they making? Filled with food, the bowl might have been presented in a ritualistic fashion, as in a Japanese tea ceremony. As each morsel was taken, a communiqué would have begun to appear in the bottom of the bowl. Nothing needed to be spoken, the images arranged in a certain manner perhaps to deliver a message: *We know the Snake Dance. We claim lineage to the dry red river. We will overrun the land.*

. . .

I remained at the cliff dwelling into the night, staying awake and listening to springs drip in the dark canyon below. I did not build a fire or light my stove. I simply sat outside the ruin and watched constellations wheel around the canyon. I kept my body tight against the air, which lingered around freezing, my arms together across my chest, my hands clasped below my chin to keep the cold off my throat.

Sometime in the night I stood. My clothes were loud as they rustled for the first time in hours. Stretching out my legs, I entered the dwelling through one of its many doorways. Cold air drifted from room to room. I felt my way with a hand in front of me and with careful, shuffling steps. I hunkered down in the middle of the room. Stars appeared through decayed places in the roof. I pulled a lighter from my coat pocket and flicked on a single small flame. It was enough to cast a dome of light. I lifted the lighter overhead.

Most of the room's ceiling had caved in centuries ago. The ceiling of the next story also had fallen through in places. I let my eyes trail across interior details: splintered ends of timbers, a small grotto built into the corner like a shrine, and vertical posts standing in the rubble. I followed the lighter from room to room, crawling from door to door under fallen roof timbers. The small flame illuminated a tunnel in the back of the dwelling, a hidden corridor standing nearly two stories tall. It ran about fifteen feet before closing into a small closet of a room with a short doorway for an entrance. I crept along the narrow passage and entered the back room, finding a low ceiling not much higher than the doorway.

When I entered the chamber, a chill ran up my spine and into my shoulders. I had brought secret little fears with me into the room—fear of the dark, fear of the unknown, fear of ghosts, fear of what happens in the murky hours long before dawn in a coffin of a ruin. I let each fear pass over me until it subsided.

This concealed room and its passage seemed too clandestine for merely a household storage area. I imagined that it was a place to hide the children and the precious seed corn. I thought of fire drills I had learned in school, and bomb drills, dropping to the floor, hiding under a desk. Had the people here, living along a contested frontier, done the same? Middle of the night, torches lit, children all running for this hidden passage? I heard the soft padding of bare feet as they filed into this chamber, where they fell silent until someone told them they could come out. Were they given piki bread made of corn and fire ash as a treat for a job well done, for being prepared in case an enemy attack should happen some night?

I brought the lighter down to see the floor, then turned it back upright so that the flame would not dip too near my thumb. Corncobs were everywhere, each chewed clean of its kernels by rodents.

These people had been seeds, I thought. A cultural bank for the future planted among the cliffs. They had brought everything with them, an ancestry of genetically specialized cotton and corn, languages and dialects preserved from the old country, and family histories kept like a map of trails through hazardous topography. They had come to conceal themselves, to hide among springs and cliffs, all the while dragging with them an entire civilization. A people of giant stone pueblos was not far behind.

The Highland Pueblos

KINISHBA AND GRASSHOPPER

My walking changed entirely when I realized someone else was here. As far as I knew, no roads or trails were nearby, yet I found on the ground the fresh prints of someone wearing tennis shoes, someone no more than half an hour ahead of me. Traveling across the White Mountain Apache reservation, I was in a pine forest at dawn, walking now in the opposite direction from the shoe prints to try to get away. I had been moving freely, perhaps not as aware as I should have been, but now that I knew another person was nearby, I walked as if through a city at night, eyes training on every shadow. I ducked into a space between trees, and a twig caught on my shoulder. The twig bent. I flashed out a hand and grabbed it before it snapped.

I did not want to make any unnecessary sound, having been alone and wishing to stay that way. I moved along deer trails and across fallen logs, obscuring my route. The trees lifted around me, heavy trunks and limbs. They were not humped into canopies like cottonwoods or alders, but were instead dark pillars, each making a line for the sky. They grew very close together in places, dog-hair forests of young pines and thickets of manzanita bushes.

I looked for this person in tennis shoes as I moved, maybe an Apache hunter out to see the sunrise or someone keeping track of strangers. I ducked under a tree that had fallen into the arms of another, figuring no one else would choose this particular course. I crouched as I went, turning my shoulders through the gnarled branches, left hand touching the ground to keep my balance. I turned left where my senses told me to turn right, skirting through lichen-covered boulders and hulks of manzanita. I thought, This should dust my trail, going against the grain. We should be free from each other now.

But the prints were there again. One tennis shoe track, then another. Surprised, I studied them, thinking, Male. He was not carrying a heavy load, not in a hurry, but moving easily.

My eyes strained into the trees. Sunrise was falling through holes in the forest, long dashes of light touching the ground. There was no one. I looked behind. No one there either. But he had to be nearby.

I returned my attention to the tracks, moving around them like a crab, careful not to scuff even a fleck of soil. I had never felt especially at ease on the reservation. A rock was always falling somewhere in the distance, a twig snapping. When I was a child, my father used to bring me onto the reservation with permission from the tribe, and we fished small creeks and built campfires at night. He told me stories about what he had seen deeper in the reservation, coming upon a lone saddle horse hobbled in the forest, no rider anywhere in sight. He told me he had seen young Apache men go by, walking along a creek, and they said not a word to him.

Later, when I was older and traveling on my own in this high country, I waved to an Apache man standing maybe an eighth of a mile away below a block of cliffs. The man lifted a rifle, sighted it over my head, and popped off a couple of .22 bullets. He was just shooting across my bow, but it was enough to get me moving. I had the necessary permits, blessings of the tribal government, but there is no central authority to call upon deep in the forest.

The first set of tracks I had seen this morning had been going with me, eastbound. This time they were turned around and heading west. It seemed like a strange way of walking, the same way I would walk if I were not trying to get anywhere, taking one path through the trees and then another. It was coincidence that we had run across each other this way, only coincidence. I rose and moved off at a sharp angle from the tracks, taking yet another unlikely passage down a steep slope of pines.

Bits and patches of the forest revealed and withdrew themselves as I moved. My eyes fell on a conspicuous shape ahead, and I paused before placing my next step. It was the black hull of a trunk left from a forest fire long ago, not, I realized, a hooded man in a dark cloak. I had spent too many years in the desert, wearing tan-colored clothing in a tan-colored land, where no one could see me and I could see anyone; clear and open sky; escape hatches of canyons falling into the earth all around me. Now, in this green country, someone was tapping on my shoulder, whispering my name from behind. I kept turning my head but saw no one.

I moved ahead but then stopped again. There was another track, wavy prints of the same tennis shoes. It was someone traveling alone. At least I imagined this to be true. The idea of coincidence drained away. But what else could it be? I was not being followed. In fact, I was the one following. But when you start tracking this closely to someone, the loop begins to close, and you start chasing each other's tails. I turned and fled across a gully, keeping my steps light.

Again the tracks were there, across dry pine needles, leading into a gap of crackled gravel. I felt as if time had doubled back on itself, a piece of paper folded so that we were walking on top of each other. I dropped to the tracks, outlining one with my finger, making a circle around it. *Who are you?* There must be a thousand different paths to take, I thought. You could walk in any direction, yet you are here again and again.

Then I thought, Maybe there are not a thousand paths. Maybe there are only a few. Maybe only one. The earth contains inevitable confluences. We come back again and again no matter who we are or when we come. I thought of my stepfather taking gravity measurements of the earth's surface, finding some places heavier than others, some more physically luring. Was this such a place? Had we been drawn into this forest, the two of us?

I crouched over the tennis shoe prints, looking through a sunrise slant for a stranger among the pines. I noticed a fleck of white on the ground and moved toward it, digging up a potsherd with my fingertips. It was from a black-on-white jar, fine and stark paintings on the outside curve suggesting a specific cultural heritage: people from the north, perhaps a leftover from the twelfth century, when Chaco migrants came through. As I examined this sherd, time seemed even leaner. I could put my hand through it. The half hour or less between the tennis shoe person and me felt hardly longer than the centuries stacked between this pottery and me. Who was following whom?

I looked around for a good climbing tree, a juniper with stout branches. It was time to get my bearings, to find my way out of this forest. An abandoned pueblo lay somewhere nearby. It was my destination this morning. If I could get high enough, I would be able to see it and make a quicker escape down to a free base, a pile of ruins that would be my safety.

I let my pack down and climbed the branches of a stocky tree, going up to the light fist by fist. At the top I found myself on the side of a mountain looking down into a bald spot, a place where pine trees gave way to junipers that opened into a dry pastureland. There a partly ruined pueblo stood in the first long bolts of the sun. This was Kinishba, one of the great fourteenth-century pueblos of the Mogollon Highlands. Two stories tall, Kinishba's shadow ran long through sage exactly on the margin where the juniper trees ended, as if the pueblo had been intentionally positioned in an environmental surf.

It was miles away. With legs tucked under a heavy branch and my back against the scaly juniper trunk, I relaxed. It was good to be in the open. I was a desert animal in need of the sky. My senses unpacked their bags, put things back where they belonged, and took stock of the geography. I was surrounded by low hunches of mountains, the solid green of ponderosa pines. In just about the center, in waves of sage, the pueblo grew brighter beneath the rising sun, shifting from black-and-white to color as I watched.

I climbed out of the tree, boots descending one branch to the next. I jumped the last eight feet, landing in a crackling sponge of pine needles. With my weight hunched to the ground, I stopped and listened. I had clattered the twigs coming down. Anyone within fifty feet would have heard me. I peeled my eyes through the pines and the alligator-skinned juniper trees. No one.

. . .

It used to be only hunter-gatherers lived here. The northern migrants who showed up in the fourteenth century were out of place. They were master farmers from the desert, people of wide-scale social organization, pueblo builders. By contrast, the Mogollon culture that had occupied this region for centuries, if not millennia, was one based on an older, more rural lifeway. When foreigners arrived looking for water, for good places to grow crops, expansive pueblos suddenly appeared at crucial intersections of travel. Hunting rose to a feverish pitch. The deer bones found in these pueblos show certain butchering marks, signs that the game animals were quartered in the field, then brought to local pueblos for processing. The hunter-gatherers were probably feeding meat to the pueblos, and in return they may have received ceramic vessels, imported stone tools, and loom-woven textiles. Maybe they earned sleeping quarters, fine rooms. Eventually, the hunting grounds went vacant. Deer were hunted clean off the land, and within ten years natives living in the highlands were forced from mobile hunting and gathering to a life dedicated almost exclusively to farming.

Some must have remained in the backcountry, though. They would have shrunk back and camouflaged themselves, eating what they could, and occasionally taking down a traveler for his goods. Only the wildest people would have stayed in the forest as these masonry capitals grew all around them with high walls and restricted interior plazas.

Crouched at the base of this tree where I had landed, I looked out through the shadows, thinking, Who is this person walking in tennis shoes? Hunter-gatherer? I was coming out of one of the dark places on the map, unoccupied territory, which is becoming scarcer year by year. Who still lives out here?

I pulled over my pack, unzipped a pouch, and took out a sack of almonds. I gathered a handful and placed them in my breast pocket. I put the bag away, shrugged on my pack, and started moving again.

. . .

I once spent a summer evening out here with several archaeologists sitting in the dark, the air cool. Fire bans were in effect then, the tinder dry. We sat around a cold ring of stones where a campfire would otherwise have been started. The starry sky was broken by black jags of pine trees.

Jeff Reid was doing the talking. With the bold presence of an orator, his southern accent theatrical, Reid commanded the night.

"The original Mogollon people were people of diverse resources, not like those northern folk coming in on them," Reid said. "They preferred deer and rabbits in their stew rather than corn, corn, corn, corn, like the Anasazi did. They added some cactus, some mesquite beans, because within a short linear distance you could get a lot of different cuisines in the mountains. You could be down low in desert vegetation and desert resources in no time. It was good country for moving around, for getting places."

None of the other archaeologists sitting around the cold fire ring had Reid's seniority or stature. Any comments they offered were brief, questions of only four or five words. They listened quietly to Reid, an icon among them. He had come to visit an archaeological field camp. Everyone else had been toiling all day, sorting potsherds or walking survey lines under the afternoon sun, while Reid had driven from his home in Tucson in an air-conditioned car.

Reid had done his time in the field. Most of his career had been dedicated to a single pueblo, nearly a thousand rooms of masonry known as Grasshopper Pueblo, a highland sister to Kinishba. Like so many sites from previous centuries on the Colorado Plateau, Reid found unequivocal evidence of multiple ethnic groups living together at Grasshopper. Migrants and locals had come together to set up one of the largest pueblos in the Mogollon Highlands.

Reid called the locals he uncovered at Grasshopper "the home team." A second group that he was able to decipher he called "Anasaz-ized Mogollon," then offered "Mogollon-ized Anasazi" as an alternative: people who at some point left the highlands for the Colorado Plateau, where they picked up pottery, habits, and probably northern bloodlines through marriage and then brought everything back here. A third group Reid recognized as a pure strain of northerners, those he explicitly called Anasazi.

"I believe in a high degree of mobility," Reid said. "During the seventies, when archaeologists were into the concept of trade, we started playing around with the movement of people—not simply migration as a one-way event, but chronic movement: joint use of regions, a lot of residential mobility and temporary occupation of sites. Even these large pueblos were fairly short-lived."

Against a background of evening crickets, Reid sounded like half poet and half sports commentator. His pauses were expertly paced, some words clipped, some drawn out.

"Now, almost all Pueblo archaeologists believe in movement," Reid continued. "You can get out of the woods just like that. I'm a firm believer that you'll freeze your ass up here. Gotta be cutting firewood all the time. It's much easier to go up over the rim back toward the Little Colorado when it's cold, up to Winslow and you're back in the desert. Or go south or east or west. Any direction. You can go to Sedona—*very chic for an Indian*—you can move back and forth and take advantage of resources that are fairly close together. This was a key location, the center of everything you'd ever need. I actually don't think the ponderosa pine forest itself provides a lot of resources for a long-term occupation."

One of Reid's colleagues working at Grasshopper, a researcher named Joseph Ezzo, had uncovered fine-grained details of these migrations. The same way ceramicists look at atomic structure to determine where a pot was made, Ezzo analyzed bone chemistry and tooth enamel from burials to determine where exactly people were born. A chemical signature of local soils passes through nutrients in food and is imprinted into certain molars, forming an indelible birth certificate. By contrast, the cells of skeletal bones are completely replaced every decade. Ezzo examined isotopes from burials and from the soil samples and was then able to tell where a person was born and where that person spent the final decade of his or her life. In people's teeth and bones Ezzo discovered an itemized map of migration.

A certain block of rooms at Grasshopper Pueblo was found to contain the burials of people who had traveled from the Colorado Plateau where they were born, then settled in east-central Arizona long enough to acquire a new isotope signature in their bones. They were interred near a second neighborhood whose residents had all been born locally. Beside this neighborhood was a third compound belonging to people who were born here but whose artifacts and architecture are strikingly reminiscent of northern traditions. These were the same three groups Reid believed he had uncovered in his years of research, proof of an ethnic convergence in the highlands—and proof that different people were strictly keeping to their own precincts within the larger pueblo, much like what had been done in Chaco Canyon three hundred years earlier. Only here the genetic origins of these people were from a much larger realm than just the Colorado Plateau. All of the Southwest was drawn together.

Ezzo took his findings a step further and identified marriages between these different groups. Women with northern isotopes in their molars were showing up buried in neighborhoods belonging to people with local isotopes. Curiously, these women seem not to have given up their northern heritage. They were all found buried with a similar suite of artifacts, pottery that stands out among all the other graves: large vessels and styles that clearly descended from the Colorado Plateau. Women from the north were marrying into local families, moving into in-law residences, and at the same time maintaining their own imported traditions.

This is why the supposed "disappearance of the Anasazi" is so easily revealed as a misreading of the past. Pueblo people from the Colorado Plateau kept their identities and carried them into the distance, easy to pick out among the smaller rooms and the generally less elaborate pottery of southern people. The rooms belonging to these northern migrants are built with more stonework, less mud, and larger floor plans. The clay used for their pottery was frequently imported from more than a hundred miles to the north, and even some of their pigments were brought specifically from homeland sources on the plateau itself. The kinds of wood they preferred for their fires were different even when they all lived in the same environment.

Sitting in the dark, surrounded by cricket song, Reid said that his excavations brought to light a whole new way of seeing migration in the Southwest. His crews had found northerly, T-shaped doorways leading into rooms where migrants were living, signs coming directly from Kayenta or Mesa Verde or even Chaco. Reid waved his hand in the air, explaining how people had gone this way and that, surges of humanity abandoning one place, building another. And always they kept their identities, easily visible centuries later. He thought the people from the north must have seemed pushy with their big architecture and big pots, probably religious zealots of some sort. The local hunter-gatherers were no match for these invaders, these travelers. Northerners were marrying their way in, inundating local traditions with their own, changing the whole show.

. . .

I walked down out of the forest, leaving the tennis shoe prints behind. Pines thinned into junipers. I came across shattered red pottery, pausing to nudge out a few of the larger pieces with a finger, turning them over to see their painted sides. Like putting them back to sleep, I turned each sherd back to the position in which I had found it. Several feet down the slope a rodent had discarded from its burrow an apron of plain colored sherds, unearthing prehistory as steadily as it would any stone or root.

These signs of habitation increased as I descended into a sunlit basin filled with squat juniper trees. Small mounds of former buildings appeared among the trees, outpost sites with pottery scattered all around their flanks. These had probably been satellite houses, what today would be specks of night lights out past some rural town, farmhouses and isolated ranches. I noticed a wide variety of ceramic styles at these outlying sites, some of the sherds black-on-white, leftovers from an earlier time; some brownish corrugated vessels that were in vogue for centuries; and some decorated wares in scores of fourteenth-century designs and colors, each style evidencing the changing fancy of the day.

The ground bared its chest to the sky, open for all to see. Canes of high-elevation cacti grew all around, along with slender knives of narrowleaf yuccas. I was passing from the terrain of hunter-gatherers into an agrarian landscape on my way to the crowded municipal center of Kinishba—a massive inward-facing pueblo that once had at least eight hundred rooms and stood three stories tall.

The walk I was taking must have occurred thousands of times, tens of thousands of times, in the past. People traveled from neighboring pueblos, down from the rim, and up from southern deserts.

I noticed a few sandy-colored potsherds as I walked, evidence of northward travels from the low deserts nearer to Mexico. People had come from all over to trade at this highland pueblo, to participate in dances, to ask if they could live on nearby property.

I dug several nuts out of my shirt pocket and walked on, chewing as lines began to appear around me, boxes of many former rooms pushing up through sage and yucca. I was now walking through the drafting-table design of an expansive compound, Kinishba's ruined rooms. I sensed manners and social regimentation in the way the site was laid out. It was not the monastic atmosphere I had once imagined in the halls of Chaco, but a busy, orderly setting, an urban trade center. Everyone had a place, some families having doorways that opened prominently onto plazas, others living in smoky, poorly lit rooms deep in the pueblo's interior.

I approached the still-standing hulk of Kinishba. Two stories of reddish brown stonework remained around an open plaza, the walls thrown open to erosion, construction timbers sagging into their rooms. An archaeologist named Byron Cummings had built this place, not, as one might imagine, the prehistoric cultures that were here originally. Cummings actually restored this portion of the ancient pueblo in the 1930s, constructing a new Kinishba atop the old one, much the way Earl Morris had rebuilt the great kiva at Aztec. He followed the older building's footprint and salvaged its stones straight out of the ground. His re-creation was now falling apart, returning to the state Cummings had found when he had first arrived. No one was here to maintain it.

I entered this new Kinishba through heavy blocks of building stones. Many were still carefully masoned into place, and just as many were prostrate on the ground. Cummings had done shrewd work, tapping small chinking stones into place and mixing red mortar out of local soils to match the pueblo that had once stood in this basin. He had built these long, elegant walls along the tracks of the older walls below and had cut fresh timbers to support the roofs above. I passed through interior rooms where ceilings had fallen in, allowing light to enter from second-story passageways. Sunlight pierced splintered beams, illuminating masses of stone rubble on the ground.

The ruined, rebuilt, and again ruined fourteenth-century pueblo of Kinishba. REGAN CHOI

Cummings had intended for this to be a national park. It was to be a living museum, a monument to prehistoric Kinishba. But visitors never came. Cummings had erected a caretaker's house, and it too was abandoned. With no one to patch the occasional leaks and structural failures, many of the roofs caved in, and the walls began to fall. This ghost that had been conjured back to life began sinking once again into the earth, physically neglected like everything before it. It is the rule of this land, of its many meeting places. We keep coming, yet we do not stay. We keep building, and we leave ruins behind.

As I walked through the masonry wreckage, I thought that Cummings had truly succeeded in building a monument to Kinishba. This has become a memorial to migration, a testimony of movement. Both arrival and desertion are honored.

Doorways opened around me onto floors marked with drip lines from leaking roofs, tar paper rotten and hanging where repairs had been attempted. In the corner of one room was the black charcoal scar of a campfire, remnants of a recent squatter who had lived here for some time. The name Duane and the date, 82, were carved into the wall.

I stepped out through a collapsed doorway onto the rectangular arena of a plaza. The space was as sweeping as a ball field, its grounds studded with translucent stalks of grass dead from the winter. Fresh tufts of green were already popping up. From the middle of the plaza I glanced at the surrounding forests, wondering if the man with the tennis shoes was watching me. I felt safe now, standing within a crumbling pueblo. I thought people must have felt something like this in the fourteenth century, guarded from the dark and unknown forests by a stonework castle.

Land's End

POINT OF PINES

A fire tower stands at land's end. It is a spoke of steel around which the weather flows, the plate glass windows of its observation room looking north at the green rug of the Mogollon Highlands and south over a sharp rim down into the desert of southeast Arizona. The tower is a sentinel, part of a chain that once relayed messages of oncoming wildfires across the country. Now it is a broken link, abandoned. The temperature gauge, wind speed indicator, and radio have all been yanked from the walls, leaving a tangle of wires hanging out. The fire-spotting table is gone, and the stool for the spotter was taken away long ago.

If the door had not been locked, I would have stepped inside to get out of the freezing wind. Instead I huddled on the south side as a storm came down from the north, blasting wind through the fire tower's metal shafts and cables. Wildly driven snowflakes raced past me at 7,550 feet, my hands stuffed into my coat. The observation room jerked fiercely in the wind, and I with it. I felt as if I were standing atop a lighthouse shoved out into thundering surf, storm waves driving against it, the foundations shuddering. The trees below faded behind a gauze of blowing snow in a late-spring storm, a freak blizzard.

This is where the chief pueblo of the highlands was built, a place now called Point of Pines. In the fourteenth century, it held the largest, most centralized population in the area, nearly two thousand rooms sprawling from a core pueblo into nearby satellites. Archaeologists working here in the 1950s discovered the remains of an enclave of migrants out of the Kayenta region. When these migrants arrived from the collapsing settlements of the Colorado Plateau at the very end of the thirteenth century, there was already a thriving pueblo here, local highlanders living in a group of modest one-story structures. Sixty or seventy families from Kayenta showed up and built a number of pit-houses around the most central pueblo at Point of Pines. After establishing this base, they quickly got about building their own multistory compound, sticking it like a gaudy church right in the middle of this preexisting community.

Culturally, the people already living at Point of Pines were about as far from the Colorado Plateau as one could get, with virtually no northern pottery or northern architectural traits. If anything, they had closer relations with people in the south, possessing some sandy-colored pottery that had originated along the Gila River down in the lower desert. These locals were entirely different from the Pueblo migrants, who came in with large, brightly colored vessels and architecture that towered stories above the natives' one-story buildings.

The stonework employed by the migrants was neatly banded, not in the least resembling local building techniques. It looked as if a Kayenta edifice had been picked up from the Colorado Plateau and was then wedged into this settlement like a trophy home. Built right into the original pueblo, its rooms averaged six feet wider than those in the local dwellings, and its numerous doorways and windows mostly faced inward, blocking access from the surrounding community. This was hardly an ethnic neighborhood; it was an encroachment.

At about the same time, an underground kiva was constructed a short distance away. It was D-shaped, a half-moon, unlike any other kiva known in the highlands. It was identical to kivas from Antelope Mesa and regions well up into Cedar Mesa in Utah, and similar to D-shaped buildings in Colorado, such as those of Sand Canyon Pueblo. Notably, its floor plan looked like a miniature version of Pueblo Bonito in Chaco Canyon. These migrants had brought all of their cultural baggage down to Point of Pines and set up shop in a clearing immediately north of where the fire tower now stood, just a five-minute walk away.

I perched on the tower's trembling deck, looking across the world, fully aware of why these northerners had come to Point of Pines, why they had erected their palatial compound here. They were tower builders. People from the Colorado Plateau were accustomed to elevating themselves, dating back to the high, eleventh-century great houses they had built around Chaco Canyon and even the sixth-century kiva they had built there five hundred years earlier. This jut of land was perfect for them, an ideal place for a pure Pueblo establishment. It was classic Anasazi.

If one were to extend archaeologist Nieves Zedeño's cultural line south from Chinle Wash, it would pass through the great kivas at the Mogollon Rim and continue straight to Point of Pines. This was a clear destination, a place written in the earth like prophecy. Southwest geography is riddled with meridians, lines to follow, and archaeological evidence merely highlights what is already there.

These northerners came directly down this line off the edge of the Mogollon Rim. They brought with them strains of corn, beans, and squash that were previously unknown here, products of the Colorado Plateau, and they did not share. None of these strains have been found in any of the surrounding sites.

They did not share their pottery either. Excavators at Point of Pines were first clued in on the presence of outsiders when they found stores of colorful vessels that looked utterly out of place among the simpler, monochromatic wares abundant in the area. They dubbed this new pottery style X Polychrome, now known as Maverick Mountain Polychrome, a derivation of earlier pottery made in the Kayenta region of northeast Arizona in the thirteenth century. Even though these northerners lived at Point of Pines for thirty years, their native pottery was not incorporated into surrounding households. In such close quarters this degree of isolation had to have been forced. A feeling of strangeness must have hovered in the air every day, a sense of life in this pueblo being out of balance.

This life continued for thirty years, long enough for people to get comfortable, for children to grow up and have children of their own. After thirty years, however, occupation by the northerners came to a sudden and fiery end. I once saw the remains of that end in a series of bins in an archaeological collection. The bins were filled with

Fourteenth-century Show Low Polychrome vessel near Point of Pines. IRVIN FERNANDEZ

masses of burned corn excavated from Point of Pines, the kernels turned molten and fused together. Each room belonging to migrants was burned early in the fourteenth century, many of the chambers loaded with freshly harvested corn. Excavators found bodies in the burned wreckage, in one room a man, a woman, and two children sprawled on the floor. A skull was unearthed, its shell blackened and popped open, revealing a powdery gray lump inside. The lump was a carbonized brain, evidence that these people had still had their soft parts intact near the time of the fire. It seems that they had been burned alive or shortly after their death. Curiously, none of the surrounding rooms lived in by locals had been damaged by the fire. Only the proud migrant enclave had been burned.

When I went through the museum collection of charred corn—shapes made grotesque by the extreme heat—I could not help recalling children burned alive in the Four Corners and a history of sites across the Colorado Plateau that had been torched in autumn or early winter after the corn harvest was in. Corn burns much hotter than wood, a high enough temperature to shatter rock and melt adobe walls. The great house of Chimney Rock had been burned full of corn, as had the largest pueblo on Antelope Mesa and myriad others.

Fire followed these people down from the north. On the Colorado Plateau fire had been used as a ritual, people igniting their kivas before leaving. Fire also had been used as an act of war. At Point of Pines it is not clear what this conflagration meant, but it was no accident. The blaze had gone from one ceiling to the next. Lex Lindsay, an excavator who had dug these rooms in the 1950s, told me that the fire had to have been intentional, that the ceiling timbers had not burned all the way through before the next rooms had ignited, as if arsonists had been running ahead through interlocking doorways, plunging torches into caches of corn, smearing wooden posts and beams with pitch and lighting them. As the upper stories collapsed into flames, the imperious enclave crumbled, and the reign of the Kayenta migrants came to an end at Point of Pines.

It has been assumed that the highland locals were the culprits, able no longer to put up with these migrants who had overstayed their welcome, but there is nothing but circumstantial evidence for this. Lindsay told me he wished he had brought in an arson specialist, but the site is buried again, the whodunit mystery left unsolved. Looking into the remaining bins of black corn, I wondered who else the guilty party might have been. Maybe it was another group of outsiders, people bent on vengeance for some past transgression that had occurred on the Colorado Plateau.

The migrants who built this place had shown up a short time after the height of the massacres in the north, coming here quickly, making a straight push more than three hundred miles south from their homeland, and finally taking refuge in another culture's pueblo as if hiding out. If this was the case, these migrants may have set up their first pit-houses at Point of Pines as a probationary settlement, demonstrating their worth to the locals, perhaps as masons, potters, weavers, or the keepers of particularly useful ceremonies. Once they were allowed into the pueblo itself and began construction of their own site, they might have maintained their distinctiveness in order to keep their value in the community, refusing to water down the very traits that made them valuable to begin with. Meanwhile, an enemy group from the north may have tracked them here, taking thirty years to reach Point of Pines on their own path of migration and revenge.

One theory I have not heard about the catastrophe at Point of Pines is that the fire might have been started by the northern residents themselves, that internal factions may have clashed after being cooped up together for three decades. Maybe it often happened this way among Pueblo people, disagreements flaring up within these inward-facing rooms until a decision was made, the whole place set on fire, people killed, and then it was time to move on. Restless and bickering, these northerners may have been ready at any moment to burn their homes and move away.

Shortly after this conflagration the rooms were rifled for any remaining tools or vessels—perhaps survivors digging through cooling ash for whatever they could find of their previous lives, or locals coming in to see what goods might be left. A few shanties were set up in the rubble, cramped quarters occupied for less than a year, and then the ruins were entirely abandoned.

After that a wall was built. It surrounded the remaining pueblo, the most substantial perimeter wall known in the fourteenth century. It remained in place for well over a hundred years while the locals went about their lives. Perhaps the wall was erected to discourage reprisals for the burning. Or it was a message: Point of Pines will take no more of these northern people, these people of fire.

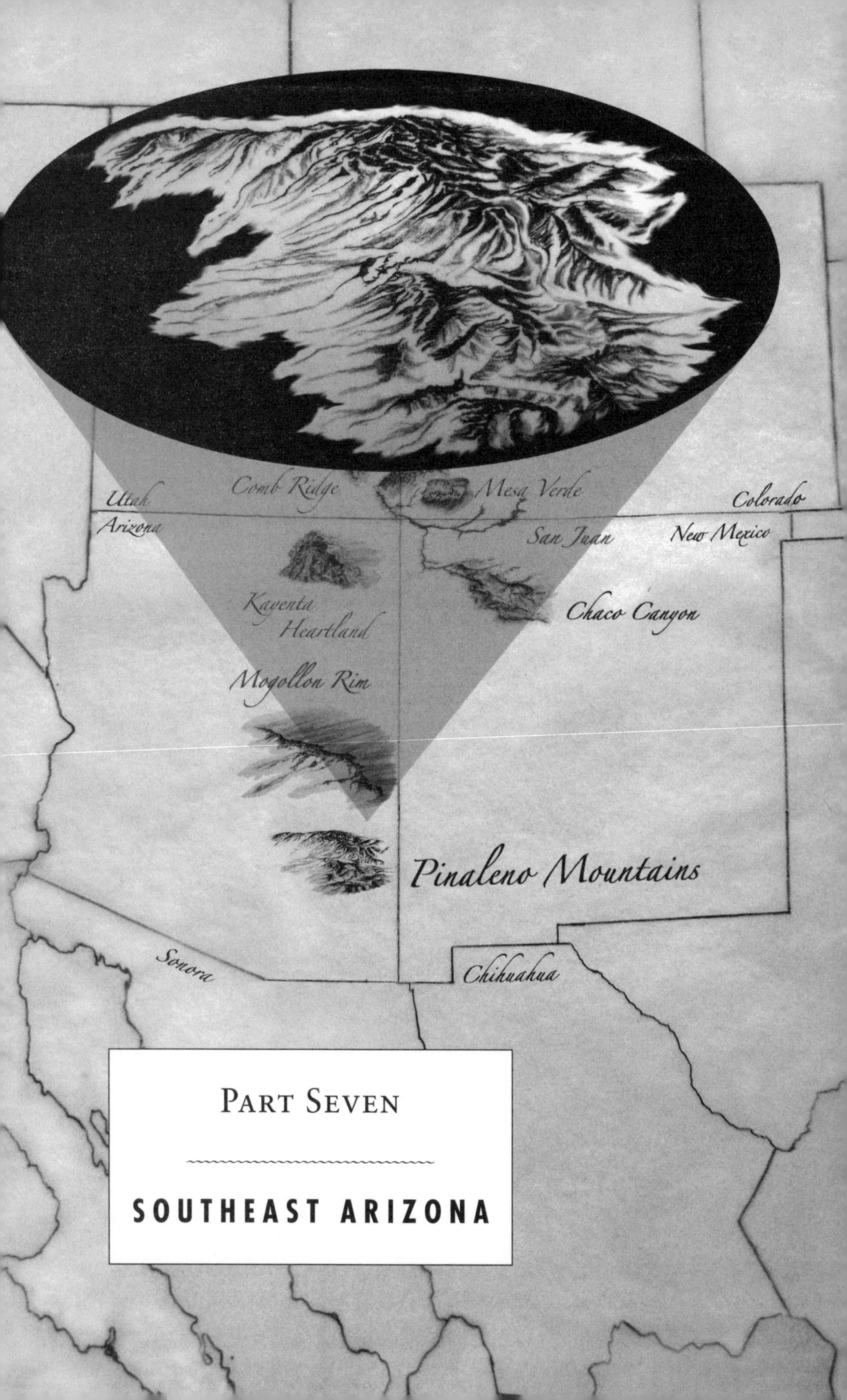

Part Seven

SOUTHEAST ARIZONA

Flowers Along the Way

BONITA CREEK

The storm did not let up. Below the snow line it turned into a lazy rain, showers passing quickly between beams of sunlight. The canyons trickled steadily day and night, threads of fresh water spilling toward the desert to the south. The back roads were terrible. I drove with my family across the southern end of the San Carlos Apache reservation, clods of mud kicking up into the truck's undercarriage, the backs of the side-view mirrors plastered with reddish brown mire. My feet danced between clutch, accelerator, and brake, as I spun the steering wheel back and forth. The rocking motion put Jasper to sleep. Two stuffed animals were pushed in around his head in the car seat to keep him from jiggling awake.

Regan is better at this kind of driving than I am, but she seemed content to lean against her window and watch the slow progress of canyon heads coming up around us. Lackluster volcanic walls lifted, and the road cut back into them, where decades ago it had been blown out with dynamite and bulldozed. I downshifted the truck through a creek at the bottom, parting water around the headlights, steam huffing up from under the engine as we climbed the bank on the other side. A switchback carried us up to a place where Regan took her socked feet off the dashboard and asked me to stop. I did, and she pulled out a small pair of field glasses to scan up higher along a crest of cliffs. Watching through the windshield for dwellings, she had spotted a row of alcoves, on which she was now focused. Tattered bolts of clouds tore around the cliffs.

"Anything?" I asked.

She put the binoculars away and said that it was hard to tell, probably better if we kept going and found a place for the night. It was getting late.

As we came down into the next drainage, the truck slid on a steep, slick track. Regan sat up into her seat belt. I kept nudging the wheel, tapping the brakes, gritting my teeth. Canyons opened around us as the road teetered between them, hollow banks of cliff trilling with rainwater streams. My hands buzzed nervously, gripping the steering wheel too tightly. The truck angled off of center and slid down heedless of brakes. I tugged the steering wheel to keep us barely in control.

"I think this is our place for the night," I muttered.

Regan reached down to the floor and got out her boots. "Sounds like a good plan," she said.

It was about as far as we had intended to go. At least we were in the right drainage, heading for a deep, midnight canyon that led to where a prehistoric shrine of ceremonial objects had once been found.

The windshield slashed with rain, wipers throwing water back and forth. As soon as we came to a terrace, the first flat place to camp, I plowed to a halt. No need to get off the road—no one else would be coming through. Even if we wanted to, we were not going to be able to drive out for at least two days.

I shut off the engine, and Regan laced up her boots. The rain played a snare drum on the roof. After sitting for a while, waiting for the rain to slow, I smudged a view hole out of the fog on my window. Outside were groves of prickly pear cactus, their pads big as dinner plates. Mesquites with bony limbs stood around them, half shrub, half tree. We were nearly down out of the highlands and into the desert of southeast Arizona, a much warmer place than the highlands or even the Colorado Plateau.

The rain turned into a light sprinkle, and Jasper woke in the quiet. The stuffed animals fell from around his head as he let out a frustrated moan, trying to lean forward but finding himself restrained. He let out an angry shriek.

"All right," I said and opened the door.

I stepped out into a squish of road mud, then immediately onto a firm, gravelly surface, a rocky transition soil between desert and mountain. The air smelled of damp mesquite, a touch of cold. I needed to set up our tent and the stove, fill the water bottles for the night. I headed for the back of the truck.

The rain remained soft throughout the night. It pattered on the tent like a small animal coming and going, a gentle rhythm that rocked us to sleep. In the morning the rain had pretty much stopped. We got moving early, loading Jasper into a framed pack on my back. We set out for the day through shafts of fog and splintering gates of gray-black stone. The praying leaves of jojoba bushes surrounded us, and we tried not to touch them, endeavoring to stay as dry as possible.

A procession of boulders led down to where the valley pinches into a canyon. Below us, the canyon looked like a dark well, the entirety of the valley taken in by a sliver in the earth. We followed. It was a sluice, a hallway tightly wound into volcanic rock of many colors. Jasper rode silently behind me, the motion quieting him as we skittered down the rock. Walls rose high over our heads, quickly sinking us into a geologic gut.

I was surprised to see a canyon this narrow and deep around here. Its shape reminded me of certain places on the Colorado Plateau, features of geography that some call slot canyons. You do not see many such canyons in this part of the Southwest; the geology usually will not allow it. But here the rock had the right consistency, resisting and yielding in the right proportions, enough to mirror the path of running water. Colored in earthen pastels, this rock was once the molten interior of the planet, boulders of the inner earth ripped from their foundations and carried upward in a boiling froth of gas and magma. We walked among many shades of a volcano's basement: waves of red tuff, gunmetal basalt, and smooth, black rock shot with white crystals. The black rock was still wet from the rain, and I reached out to touch it as I passed. It felt as slick as a frog's belly.

The canyon had a liquid flow, squeezing down into a thin, turning corridor. A boulder nearly a full story tall had fallen into the canyon and was wedged over our heads, an iceberg of volcanic rock. Even Jasper craned his neck to see what we were staring at. The dark hulk hung over us, thousands of tons suspended in perfect tranquillity.

Two flycatchers dove out from beneath this pendulous chunk of earth. Their wings and their startling chits sliced the air around us. They had built an April nest. I could see a small lip of grass and bovine hair pouting from under the wedge high above. The birds had tucked their fragile eggs under the boulder, a cunning place to hide their beloved future. We moved on, letting the birds go back to their nest.

I kept seeing Regan ahead fading in and out, turning corners, swallowed by this place as Jasper pointed ahead each time, exclaiming, "Mama!" Along the floor red penstemons grew from wet gravel, their leaves beaded with rainwater. I stopped at one of the flowers, knelt, and took a red trumpet between two fingers, where it rested like powdered velvet. As I lifted it slightly, a pearl of water came loose, rolling down the crease of my fingers into my palm.

. . .

Much older flowers had once been found here. They were discovered in a ceremonial cache, a treasure of small artifacts stored in a polychrome jar. Forty-one finely articulated wooden flowers, divided into three separate clusters, had been kept in this jar. One cluster had been painted a rich sky blue, another a pale turquoise; the remaining three had been left the natural dun color of their wood. At the museum that now houses this cache, I had touched one of these ancient flowers in the same way that I touched the penstemon in the canyon, two fingers in a cotton glove slipped under a petal, lifting a paper-thin scale of colored wood to feel its give.

The curator had immediately stepped forward, lifting his hand to stop me.

"No, no," he said. "If you want them moved, I can do it."

I withdrew my fingers and looked at him. He was poised as if I were touching the rarest da Vinci. He had allowed me to handle many artifacts, trusting me with bowls and baskets and fine wooden tools, but not these. I apologized.

He took a half step back.

The flowers were out on an examination table, lying on a thin white cushion. Their petals were made from thinly cut wedges of wood, each sewn to the next with a fine-spun cotton thread. Among such finds in the Southwest, it was the most intact, so delicate and undamaged.

Originally, the flowers had been stored inside a large tomato-colored vessel—a wide-mouthed jar, its body plump and painted with geometric details. An inverted bowl had been placed over it to protect the treasure within. The jar, now kept like an estranged parent in the ceramics room, was of the style once called X Polychrome, which belonged specifically to migrants who had moved into Point of Pines in the fourteenth century. This cache had belonged to people who had come from Kayenta. They had hidden it in a cave above Bonita Creek in southeast Arizona, perhaps a crucial store of artifacts spirited away just before the burning at Point of Pines.*

Along with the flowers, the jar also contained sixty-five miniature baskets, each hardly larger than a silver dollar. These baskets were arranged on the examination table beside the flowers. A dark, pitch-painted brown, they were nested into each other and sewn one to the next through their middles.

Next to the baskets on the table were other contents of the cache: wooden buttons painted green and black; eight wooden cones; a bird-shaped pendant; three terraced headdresses made of painted wood.

I felt as if a holy ark had been opened, a precious cache of religious objects. I was not sure if it was sacrilege to look so blatantly at

*Such protective behavior is also known from Antelope Mesa, in northeast Arizona, where the most sacred of a pueblo's ceremonial paraphernalia was removed from a kiva and hidden in a nearby canyon in the fall of 1700, just before the pueblo was sacked and burned by opposing Hopi forces.

these relics, or if we were being appropriately solemn, the curator ready to stay my hand at the slightest transgression.

Only three caches of this nature have been found in the Southwest. One was discovered in a cave just east of Comb Ridge in Utah: a prehistoric jar hidden in a high sandstone escarpment that required a rope to reach it. Within the jar were fifty halves of small, round gourds strung together much the way these flowers and the miniature baskets were bound. There were also four wooden birds and various wooden fetishes tied together.

A second ceremonial cache came out of the Kayenta homeland, found buried in a cave up in the red cliffs of northeast Arizona: a large corrugated jar containing twenty-six painted wooden sunflowers of excellent craftsmanship. The cache also contained a set of handsomely carved wooden birds and a number of wooden cones almost identical to those found along Bonita Creek, three hundred miles south of Kayenta.

The similarity of these three discreet caches found in southern Utah, northeast Arizona, and southeast Arizona is significant. They form a path from north to south, from the Colorado Plateau down to a gateway canyon beyond Point of Pines.

The cluster of turquoise-colored flowers had in their center a bundle of wooden buttons painted a luminescent silvery blue, the color of a night moth. These little nubs of painted wood were positioned to represent the flowers' reproductive organs, their seat of nectar. I smelled them, just in passing, and they smelled of dust.

. . .

I let the penstemon slip off my fingers and hurried ahead to find Regan. She came into view where the canyon spread wide open, a private passage revealed wholly to the sky. Stone turrets stood hundreds of feet above us.

Birdcalls emitted from ahead in a lavish corridor of trees lining Bonita Creek. Over it a black hawk cried from up in the white limbs of a sycamore. There were slender willow switches and sprays of yellow flowers along the creek. Nearer to the water I lowered my pack to the ground, soft and russet-colored from autumn leaves that had fallen five months earlier. The sun was just starting to come out. Regan and I pulled Jasper free and put him down. His little boots sank into the leaves. His hands plunged immediately into wet sticks and grass, his eyes two strokes of lightning contacting the earth. No stone or leaf escaped his fascination as he plowed through the underbrush.

I followed him with my warnings, my hand clearing his path through the wet grass. At every other step, I peered up through the smooth, bone-white sycamore branches, their mad weavings holding up the sky. Gazing through them, I noticed the tight cluster of a small cliff dwelling in a high cave above the creek. The structure was difficult to make out, blending perfectly with the cobbled rock face, shrunken back into the shadow of an overhang. Its chambers were smoothly plastered, making them appear like rounded bread loaves—no longer the banded masonry one sees in the north.

Migrants entered southeast Arizona from the Colorado Plateau in the fourteenth century, pushed by fires burning behind them, by a search for water and good growing conditions, or merely by a need to keep moving. As they journeyed through a landscape of intermarriages, conflicts, and alliances, they changed, picking up new traits and genes. What remains of what was once called Anasazi is difficult to know, turned into Salado, introduced to a new world. The presence of painted wooden flowers hidden in a jar and buildings suspended in the cliffs suggests strong, direct ties between the Colorado Plateau and southeast Arizona. In one form or another, the legacy of Pueblo ancestry was still alive this far south.

Jasper teetered through the plants. He led me to the creek, where a lush arbor closed in above us and water shot due south, murky with rain and runoff. Rainwater, dabbed off the grass, appeared on Jasper's face and shirt. He snatched a stick off the ground and chucked it into the creek. It landed along a slow edge of the water, where it turned like a compass needle waiting for a direction. Then it touched the current and sped downstream.

"There it goes," I said, dropping around Jasper's body, containing him in my arms.

I cocked his shoulders so that he could see where I was pointing.

The stick swept down a tunnel of alders and sycamores. It clipped through stripes of sunlight on its way to the desert, the Gila River, the land beyond.

"Bye-bye," I said. "Tell it bye-bye. There it goes."

Jasper flexed his hand in the air, waving goodbye to the stick.

Crossroads

SAFFORD

In a sheeting rain I stood illuminated by my truck's headlights. Water drained off the hood of my poncho. I held in my hands a pair of tent poles, nearly wishing for this rain to end but thinking better of it. It would end soon enough, and a featureless Southwest drought would return.

All the way from Bonita Creek, gunning the truck out of slick canyon roads, I was ready for dry ground. The driving became easier as we dropped into the desert—no more mud, just crushed rock for soil. We stopped ten miles outside the town of Safford in southeast Arizona to set up camp.

Now I was putting tent poles together in the white flare of headlights and erecting our small, waist-high tent on the gravelly earth, my hands coming up caked with wet grains of rock. When I pulled the sleeping bags and pads out of the back of the truck, I walked them over to the tent with only cursory cover under my poncho. Everything was damp already from days of travel and storms. Besides, tomorrow we would be in the town of Safford and would find a Laundromat. We planned to throw everything we had into the dryers, boots and all.

I made the bed inside the tent, a cozy little space, sleeping bags laid out like blankets, a bottle of drinking water at each of our heads. The one thing we had kept dry was the bundle of baby things. I pulled out a toy animal and inserted it into one of the tent pockets. As I carefully unfolded a little striped sleeping shirt and a wool cap inside the tent, my hood pulled back to keep it from dripping, I thought of early photographers on global expeditions hiding their precious glass plates from the weather, of botanists pressing plants in the wild jungle and sacrificing everything to keep their samples safe. In this case baby gear stood above all else in importance.

I backed out of the rain fly and zipped the tent closed behind me. I crouched for a moment in the glare of the headlights, looking into sharp, twisted shadows of intermittent creosote bushes that perfumed the air with a familiar sweet and bitter scent, the smell of rain in the southern desert. We had passed completely out of the highlands into a new territory.

I walked to the truck and cracked open the driver's door just enough to reach in and shut off the headlights. Darkness returned to the outside world. Regan and Jasper peered up from reading a book beneath the dome light. It was Regan's birthday. I had told her I'd set up the tent tonight.

Regan smiled, pleased to be dry with her son. Ducking down through waterfalls and cliff dwellings below Point of Pines and following the sopping path of Bonita Creek for a day, we had not been dry for some time.

"Tent's ready," I said. "Happy birthday."

While Regan managed the impressively mechanical chore of getting a one-year-old situated in a two-person tent, I went to check on another truck parked near us. A bumper sticker read TREE HUGGING DIRT WORSHIPPER. I pulled my arm out from under my poncho and knocked on the camper shell.

"Come in," a man called from inside.

I opened the door and found Colin, the traveling companion who had moved through the Kayenta region with me. He had come to meet us and help with the management of a small child in the backcountry. A tall, lean man, he reclined in the cramped camper reading a book by headlamp. He lay in a nest of climbing rope. Wadded up behind him was a thin, greasy sleeping bag. In his twenties, he worked as an itinerant climbing instructor for Outward Bound. He spent his off-seasons in the wilderness and was just now returning from a few weeks of highland travel. No baths or showers in that time but for creeks and rain. He smelled like a wet dog.

Colin put down his book.

"Rain," he said.

"Bunches," I replied. "All cozy in here?"

Colin looked around, giving his camper shell an honest assessment.

"All's good," he said.

He was just a few inches too tall to stretch out completely in his truck bed, so he lay with his body crimped at the knees.

"How's the leg?" I asked.

"It's got screws in it," he said in a matter-of-fact tone.

He had taken a fall in the wilderness—broke his femur and had to crawl out on his hands and one knee. That was eight months ago. Scrambling around the backcountry for the past few weeks, he'd managed to break off one of the screws holding his leg together.

"I'm mobile enough, though," he added. "The leg feels okay."

I rested my arms on the rim of his tailgate for a moment. The roof of his shell hissed as if sand were being poured over it, the rain keeping up a strong pace.

"Into Safford tomorrow," I said. "Let's get some food. And find a Laundromat, get all our things dried out."

"Good plan," Colin said. "Carne asada burritos on the east end of town."

Colin needed a new tire on his truck, the one on the rear driver's side thin to the metal. A trip into Safford was a necessity. And we all needed to load up on supplies before making the next push into the backcountry. Safford assured us we would get what we wished for: hot food, tire shop, pay phones, library, Laundromat.

. . .

The Laundromat in Safford was humid. It smelled of powdered detergent, cigarette smoke, and hot dryer lint. We waited for our gear to dry, boots clomping around and around in the dryer. We were travelers and we looked it, completely out of place. Colin was wearing camouflage pants and had a big knife on his hip. His cowboy hat was limp from use. He walked through the Laundromat with the supple grace of a rock climber, a mere trace of a limp in his left leg. Regan looked even more peculiar, the only Asian in the Laundromat, perhaps in all of Safford. She had an air of purpose as she toted Jasper on her hip, our son gleeful in his overalls, gripping a headlamp in his fist, his favorite toy. I looked like a grizzled bear, standing at the front window, watching the rain, pondering the world buried beneath this building as if I were devising a crime.

The main street had recently been widened, and an archaeological recovery crew had been brought in to deal with whatever artifacts were unearthed. One of the archaeologists who had worked on the project told me that they had found prehistoric settlements everywhere they had dug, the place just filthy with signs of occupation, communities dating from the twelfth to the fourteenth centuries. Every few feet a new prehistoric find had been unearthed in the expansion work. Excavators had come upon a small pueblo built by locals in a thirteenth-century style common in southern Arizona, where adobe walls were erected atop cobble footers. Encircling this site were numerous fourteenth-century pit-houses of northern design—migrants positioned on the edges of a local pueblo. These migrants had installed a number of open-fire ceramic kilns, and, curiously, the nearby pueblo had been full of what appeared to be migrant ceramics. The style of pottery brought by these travelers from the north is known as Salado Polychrome—big, colorful pots that were well received.

Safford lies along the Gila River, a major east-west corridor that was fully occupied long before those migrants arrived early in the fourteenth century. The Hohokam irrigation empire west of here, in the Phoenix and Tucson areas, had a strong influence on the Safford region, and there is ample pottery from the Mimbres region in southwest New Mexico. Pueblo people out of the north, carriers of Anasazi ancestry, walked into a heavily occupied valley, its slopes terraced with hundreds of small farming communities. Field houses and single-story adobe settlements were all over the place. This was already one of the busiest crossroads in the entire Southwest, and when these migrants arrived, everything changed; it became Salado.

Scholars in the mid-1900s thought the Salado had been an invading army, a prehistoric group that appeared from the north and decisively conquered southern lands like Huns. In this vision the Salado overpowered local social regimes and replaced them with heavily consolidated settlements awash in multicolored pottery. As the whims of archaeology changed, however, this theory was abandoned, and the very idea of a Salado culture began to fade. The concept of migration was replaced by notions of in situ development, each group staying put and working through its own local process. The thought of conquering Salado forces plunging across the land was simply too Hollywood for archaeologists of the time, who explained the rise of polychrome pottery as a matter of trade, not migration or invasion.

But more recent investigations have revealed that people were indeed in motion across long distances in the fourteenth century and that colorful pottery was traveling with them. Salado has come back into favor, but it is no longer just an invading force. Now it appears to be a cultural revolution, less an actual people than a spread of ideas and artifacts across the Southwest as migrants established new trade routes between distant communities, opening lanes of commerce and communication. Salado was the new world order as the old-guard cultures of Hohokam, Mimbres, Mogollon, and Anasazi were swept up into a cohesive assembly.

If you come down off the Mogollon Rim, major drainages will lead you to certain places, such as the Salt River, the Tonto Basin, the middle Gila River. In the fourteenth century, these were gathering places that became Salado strongholds, defined by how people once moved across the land. Safford was one such center, the southern end of Nieves Zedeño's line, a bastion of Salado pottery, of innovative architecture and increasing populations.

As I watched the rain from the Laundromat window, an old man sat beside me on an orange plastic chair at the front door. He was smoking incessantly, a gatekeeper whiling away his time to the sound of dryers tumbling clothes. With hardly a shine of recognition, he kept track of everyone coming and going. A Mexican woman was folding shirts on a table as if kneading bread dough, and across from her an Anglo man was trying to match his socks. Several Apaches draped bedsheets over their arms, smoothed out pants on hangers, and leaned against the machines as their clothes dried. Their children drove wobbling laundry carts like race cars between lanes of washing machines. The younger kids just stared at each other from behind their mother's legs. The place seemed like a migrant camp, people from all the local ethnicities rubbing shoulders to do their laundry.

The old man at the door stubbed out one cigarette and tapped another into his hand. He kept glancing at me and Regan and Colin. Not staring, just keeping track of us. We were rabble from the wilderness, flushed out by the rain and seeking shelter in town. He regarded us with a hint of distrust.

I wanted to ask him if he had ever seen anything of archaeological significance around Safford. Usually old men in small towns love to talk about the mummies they've seen or the arrowheads they keep in a drawer at home. But this man did not seem to be in a mood for talking. I left him alone.

I imagined an old man much like this seven hundred years ago. He would have been leaning against an adobe wall or sitting with legs folded beneath the shade of a ramada made from spindles of ocotillo wood. From there he would have seen the first incoming migrants. With the even expression of an oracle, he would have studied them walking down out of the highlands, seen them mingling in the markets. Their eyes would have been different, their clothing, the way they carried themselves, the weapons slung over their shoulders. They were people on a mission. Maybe their scouts came first, stopping to ask about living conditions, whether there was anywhere left to grow a little corn. *And here, have a look at this pottery we've brought. Maybe we can trade it for venison or beans.*

The old man would have watched as his countrymen gathered to see cleverly colored globes of Salado Polychrome being unwrapped from traveling burdens. Everything changed at that moment. Everyone wanted one of those pots. They were the most radiant vessels ever seen.

Handily, Salado Polychromes were easy to make. Their dramatic, painted designs required organic paints that could be gathered just about anywhere, while firing utilized low temperatures that allowed for mass production without a heavy impact on local fuel-wood supplies. These newcomers could outfit a whole valley with new multicolored pottery in nothing flat.

Large Salado Polychrome bowl – the size of a large mixing bowl— a black-on-white-on-red form known as Gila Polychrome, excavated from near Safford. In storage at the University of Colorado Museum in Boulder. CRAIG CHILDS

These were not the sturdiest pots being traded. In fact, they were not always constructed from the best clays. What they lacked in quality manufacture, however, they made up for in color, size, and elaboration. Painted on the outside so they could be seen from afar, large jar designs leaped out as if dipped in neon. Sharply interwoven figures played around the exterior of pots and bowls, seamless balances of positive and negative space creating a geometry much like what was once seen on the Colorado Plateau. These designs looked like old northern ones, pumped with electricity, circles and spirals sprung wide open, stars and waves rippling. Encased within the larger images were intricate cameos of lesser spirals and squads of triangles on pots big enough to wrap your arms around.

Affordably and rapidly made, these new pots swamped local ceramic traditions. They were soon being used in every known social context, appearing in equal abundance in burials, kitchens, living rooms, and ceremonial chambers. At a site in northern Mexico, sixty of them were found lined up along a wall like trophies. Their distribution was not restricted to the graves of males or females, to young or old, to poor or rich. Everyone had access. It was a revolution, and it soon stretched from Phoenix to El Paso, making its way to northern New Mexico and to Sonora, Mexico. One major production center appears to have been right here around Safford, the seat of Salado.

The old man who at the time sat and watched this cultural incursion would have known where it was all going. The pottery was greasing the way for many more migrants. Sitting in his shade, he would have watched the newcomers erect their own audacious masonry settlements, completely unlike any of the cobbled, mud-wall villages that were here to begin with.

These newcomers built a crowning pueblo atop a butte just outside Safford. This compound would have looked like a foreign castle peering down at the local farming peasantry below. The old man would have watched it go up, not surprised to see such a dominating monstrosity coming from these Pueblo people who brought with them stories of war and butchery, hardened travelers with exotic customs. For instance, whereas the locals still cremated their dead, these travelers brought full-body burial rites with them from the north. Everything about these migrants was different.

The high pueblo they built just outside town is today called Goat Hill. When it was partially excavated, archaeologists found the remains of people who had come from three hundred miles away. In the open center of this circular pueblo, they uncovered a half-moon-shaped kiva that is similar to the Kayenta kiva at Point of Pines and to other kivas all the way up into southeast Utah. Like most Colorado Plateau kivas, this one had a bench along its curved interior wall, a ritual sipapu in the floor, a deflector and a shafted ventilation system, and what appear to be foot drums styled after those of Mesa Verde and Chaco. Also like other northern kivas, anchors were found in the floor where looms had been fastened. These asylum seekers were making ceremonial art, pottery, and textiles that they spread liberally among the locals.

The fourteenth-century migrants came not all at once, but in orderly waves, as if their movement had been carefully orchestrated. A group from the Kayenta heartland was the first to arrive at Goat Hill, building an arc of rooms on the high western margin of the butte. Shortly after that, a second arc of rooms, built along the eastern side by a different group of migrants, completed the circle. This second group came with their own distinct architectural signatures tracing back to Antelope Mesa. Even though the two groups arrived at slightly different times, both came from northeast Arizona, albeit from different parts. Together they built one visibly cohesive core, the two sides of the circle meshing perfectly. Joined in the center by a D-shaped kiva, this pueblo seems to have been a planned reunion, something broken and then put back together in another place. It looks like a prophecy coming to pass.

The migrants reconstructed their whole cultural world, not only around Safford but also along every primary waterway in southeast Arizona. The next river west of Safford is the San Pedro, flowing north out of Mexico to a place where excavations and surface surveys have revealed clusters of pueblos that look as if they were lifted off the Colorado Plateau and laid down here, nearly four hundred miles to the south. Their blocks of rooms are positioned in a way that suggests a sophisticated political and cultural order previously unknown in this southern region—the same order you see far to the north, where matrilineal arrangements of clans and societies are reflected in the floor plans of pueblos. These people were rebuilding their civilization down to every social detail, and they were doing it within earshot of many local communities. The Anasazi, thought to have vanished, were here in force, this time in the guise of Salado. Their uncounted Pueblo settlements sprang up in every valley of southeast Arizona. A Spanish expedition that came through in the 1540s encountered one of these pueblos after it had been recently abandoned, reporting that the "strongly fortified dwelling" looked out of place, more like ruins and occupied pueblos that the expedition had seen in the north on the Colorado Plateau. A journal from the expedition noted that this settlement, made of bright red earth, must have been built by "civilized and warlike foreigners [who] had come from far away."

Migrant enclaves from the Colorado Plateau stretched as far west as Tucson, almost a hundred miles from Safford. An excavation that took place a short distance from downtown Tucson unearthed what looks on the surface to be a Hohokam-style site. But inside they found many signs of migrants, such as slab-lined fireboxes and mealing bins that carry a strong Kayenta influence. People also kept birds in these rooms—hawks, falcons, eagles, domestic turkeys, and imported macaws—in numbers rarely seen among lowland Hohokam people. The place is inundated with hefty, colorful pottery and various subtle ceramic markers of travelers from the Colorado Plateau, such as perforated dishes known from Kayenta cliff dwellings and pueblos. It is also marked by northern-style burials juxtaposed with southern-style cremations. When tree-ring dates were analyzed from this site, they confirmed migration theorists' suspicions: the trees had been felled for construction in A.D. 1320, the peak of migration in the Southwest.

Many Hohokam scholars have preferred the notion that this seething rabble of migrants played only a minor role. They have viewed the Hohokam as a stable stay-at-home culture able to resist anything a migration-plagued people could throw at them. Their argument is steadily weakening, however. In the fourteenth century, northern pottery swept through even Phoenix, the Hohokam core, like a flood. The last known Hohokam sites are literally swamped with it. The presence of colorful Salado Polychrome at these sites has often been dismissed as having been acquired through trade from far away. But recent analysis shows that it is made of local clays, fired right on the premises.

The long-enjoyed tradition of Hohokam ball courts—public grounds where games were played and ceremonies may have been held—came to an abrupt halt around the time the outsiders showed up. At that point Hohokam labor was redirected from building ball courts to building imposing mounds on which walled compounds were established.

Were these new platform-mound structures defensive responses to invaders, or were they incorporations of a bold northern ideology? The Tohono O'odham, who now live in southern Arizona, call the people who ruled these Hohokam platform mounds *siwañ,* a word that is phonetically out of place in the O'odham's Pima language. When spoken out loud, *siwañ* is nearly identical to *shiwanni,* a word from the Colorado Plateau and a Zuni term for their rain priests. *Siwañ* and *shiwanni* are similar enough in two completely different languages that they suggest a connection, a word left in the southern lands by northern travelers. The name of rain priests from the north was planted like a flag in the mighty Hohokam platform mounds of southern Arizona.

With so many people coming and going, new trade routes were opening all over, moving raw goods and pieces of art to new places. More settlements than ever before were right next door to each other, ethnicities and cultures and languages heaped together and connected by traders and migrants. Everybody now had the same painted icons on the same colorful pots in their living rooms, a revolution of style regardless of what language they spoke or what ethnicity they belonged to.

This was not, however, a docile revolution. All across the lower Southwest, settlements from this time period have a defensive appearance, and excavators have dug mangled human skeletons from the ground. Many communities established by migrants look like fortresses, placed in impregnable locations and built with defensible gated entries and perimeter walls. Wherever this new Salado culture appeared, migrants were there, a movable civilization with a smoldering history of burned-down pueblos trailing for centuries behind them.

The old man I imagined in Safford would have recognized the first of these people to arrive, identifying them merely by the way they walked, by the gazes they carried. He would have seen their pottery and nodded slowly to himself, knowing that the world was about to change.

. . .

At the Laundromat door the old man stubbed out yet another cigarette and started the next one. Smoke passed in and out of him until it seemed that he must consist more of smoke than of flesh. Every time the door opened with a new customer hauling in a bin of laundry, I was relieved for the fresh scent of rain from outside. The old man just watched, taking silent note of who was coming, who was going.

When we had everything bagged up and dry, I made several trips to and from the truck, Jasper hoisted in one arm, laundry in the other. Outside the air was rich with moisture, tires hissing as traffic passed along the highway through the middle of town. Clouds were skidding around a massive, singular mountain rising over Safford to the south. Waterfalls were coming off this mountain, thin white streaks barely visible through the rush of storms. Just shy of 11,000 feet in elevation, the highest pinnacle of the Pinaleno Mountains stood over my head, 8,000 vertical feet off the desert floor, the second-highest mountain in Arizona. It looked like a thunderous god. I loaded warm stacks of folded bedclothes into our truck beneath it.

I went back in for the last load, and as I backed out the door, I said goodbye to the old man, the first direct exchange we had had the whole time. He nodded slightly.

Mountain of Shrines

THE PINALENOS

I woke from a bed of ice in the upper reaches of the Pinaleno Mountains. Powder frost slid from my bag as I sat up and looked into the blue hole of dawn. Heavy trunks of Douglas firs stood all about, dark against the brightening snow. I was surprised how late it was. I had slept in, and a sound had woken me. I turned and looked across the ice-crusted snow. My traveling companion was already up, his sleeping bag empty. The sound had been the scratch of his boots on hard snow. I looked around. He was gone, having slipped into the woods.

The sky was visible all around, broken by ascending shafts of spruce and fir trees. I felt as if I had woken at the very tip of the earth. My companion was a man named Walt, a researcher studying the ecological history of isolated mountain ranges in southeast Arizona, ranges known as the Sky Islands. Walt was interested in how plants, animals, and insects use these mountains as migratory steppingstones between the tropical south and the montane north. For certain species, for jaguars and butterflies, this is the only way to bridge the Americas, leapfrogging over the desert from the Sierra Madre toward the Rocky Mountains.

Walt's and my studies in migration overlapped like the weave of a loom, mine following an ancient passage of people and his tracing species of moths, birds, mammals, and reptiles. Knowing Walt, he was probably off listening for the first spring birdcalls this morning, walking across snow with a notepad open in his hands.

I dressed inside my bag, a Houdini act with pants and shirt, my shoulders punching at the tight nylon enclosure. I had slept with all my clothes bundled around my feet. My boots were outside, turned upside down so frost would not collect in them. I unzipped and emerged into the forest on a snowy pillar of earth. My boots were stiff as wood. I laced them and moved away from my bag to the base of a tree, where I steamed the snow with morning urine. Heads of dead grass bent over, their seed husks encased in hoarfrost. I moved off through the trees, looking for the first place sunlight would clear off some of the cold.

Slabs of light began falling between the trees. The sun was rising. I walked into bright hallways, moving from one to the next, glimpsing through the trees the open veil of sky around me. In winter, subzero winds throw volleys of ice off this mountain into the desert below. In summer, the wind coils around this peak into fifty-thousand-foot swells of thunderheads. I have seen this mountain swallowed by its own weather, volcanic bolts of lightning flashing from under its hooded clouds. This mountain held the final shreds of winter in April, these banks of snow being the last of their kind so far south on the continent.

When I reached a perch of snow and rock, the sky opened wide. I could see the full arc of the planet. Beneath me was a clear view for more than a mile down to the solid ground of the desert. Other Sky Island mountain ranges were scattered about, but none as tall as the Pinalenos. These others looked like buffalo shrugging their way across the land, hirsute peaks tethered to the desert by sinuous paths of greenery. They looked like veined organs, living things. Even from many miles away I could see where their pines fell into oak brush, narrowing down to luminescent green threads of cottonwood trees, then a haze of creosote bushes and the blank stare of dry, saline earth at the bottom.

Towering above southern Arizona, this mountain must have been powerful in the minds of the people who once lived and traveled below it in pre-Columbian times. Its slopes are jeweled with ancient shrines, its summits made like altars, with potsherds shaved into the shapes of coins and left as offerings. Caves throughout the Sky Islands are stashed with wooden katsinas and painted offerings.

Hanks of human hair are hung in natural subterranean passages, and precious stones are positioned around springs.

It is said among indigenous cultures as far south as Mexico, Central America, and South America that within lone mountains like this lives Tlaloc, the oldest deity on these continents, the pan-American rain god. For the Olmec people the god was Epcoatl, the seashell serpent, and for the Maya Chaac, a deity living at the bottom of a spring-fed well. Among the Aztecs, Tlaloc wore a net of clouds and a crown of heron feathers.

Offerings for Tlaloc are still left in the mountains of Central America. At high, prominent springs or caves in Guatemala or the Yucatán, one is likely to find the head of a decapitated rooster (replacing the turkey, which was commonly used in the past) along with pools of melted wax from votive candles. Mountains and their springs have always been sacred throughout the Americas. Even today among the modern pueblos of the Southwest, elements of the katsina religion mirror these Tlaloc cults.

In the Pinalenos a ceremonial cache of painted bowls, baskets, and fat ceramic jars was found when a Boy Scout dropped his flashlight into a crack in the side of a mountain. The flashlight tumbled into the darkness. Someone going in to retrieve it found that it had landed near a collection of bulky, sealed jars. When the seals were broken and the bowls that capped the jars were removed, raw prehistoric cotton was found inside. The entire collection was soon crated up and helicoptered out, eventually taken to a museum. Radiocarbon dating of the stored cotton revealed that it came from the sixth century to the fourteenth century A.D. Cotton had been added to the jars from the time the first great kiva was built at Chaco up through the Salado era. Eight hundred years of pilgrims had carried loads of white, farm-grown cotton up this mountain and stuffed them into big globes of jars. Eight hundred years is a long time to be carrying anything into a not-especially-prominent cave high on a very tall mountain. This suggests a continuum, people walking on each other's heels over the centuries to take offerings to the same place. Similarly, mountainside caves throughout Mesoamerica are known to contain ancient water shrines. Many of these shrines involve large ritual storage jars stocked with seeds and agricultural produce that are considered symbolic forms of water. For the Aztec, these jars were overseen by the rain god Tlaloc, who stored in them various manifestations of rain—beneficial rain, flood, dew, ice, mildew, and drought. The modern Tlaxcalan people of southern Mexico say that 14,000-foot Mount Malinche is home to a water goddess who lives in a cave among hundreds of great ceramic ollas. Under her command, spirits are said to leave the cave in the form of hailstones and return with various seeds, fruits, and grains that they place inside the ollas. Similar stories stretch from southern Mexico northward, from the Zapotec culture in Oaxaca to the Huichol, who now live in the Sierra Madre Occidental. Perhaps eight hundred years of cotton offerings found in ceramic ollas in the Pinaleno Mountains of Arizona belong to this meridian of traditions, indications of water stockpiled inside a rain deity's house.

Walt was looking for fauna as evidence of species passing through. I was looking for shrines that tell of people passing through carrying their cosmology with them, a religion founded on water, clouds, caves, and mountains. I knew of cracks and caves where ancient people had reached underground water, where they left beads and painted arrows as offerings. They had carved stairways in the rock to reach springs that they decorated with turquoise and miniature ceramic vessels.

A group of Hopi men had recently traveled to this mountain. Knowing of it from old stories, they went to a dome of rock where offerings had been left in prehistoric times, and there these tribal representatives placed their own contributions. The Pinalenos were a momentous landmark along a complicated migration route that is remembered to this day.

. . .

Some people turned back from southeast Arizona late in the fourteenth century. This mountain was a boundary where far-reaching Pueblo clans stopped and returned to the Colorado Plateau, leaving much of southeast Arizona abandoned in the fifteenth century. Migrants had shown up and revolutionized the place, only to have it fall out from under them, seemingly as a result of overcrowding and social collapse. But it was not just migrants who left. Nearly everyone living in this part of the Southwest walked away.

The pressure of so many outsiders, and the accompanying shock of dramatic social upheavals, was simply too much to endure. The whole of the Southwest had united into something that looks like a single cultural body, where many different groups joined together under a rising ideology called Salado. But the integration did not last. The end result was that the entire Southwest was destabilized. Communities began falling apart. A century of woodcutting, hunting, and intensive farming had decimated the land during a time of unprecedented growth. Pueblos began competing for resources. This competition shattered critical trade networks, severing the cultural fabric that held these regions together. The sharing of resources, ideas, and artifacts in the area ceased. People began to scatter once again, heading for distant sanctuaries. Birthrates declined. People died younger as malnutrition coursed through their remaining settlements.

The great pueblos of Grasshopper, Kinishba, and Point of Pines fell empty. Even Homol'ovi, far to the north along the Little Colorado River, was abandoned. Smaller, one-story pueblos in the highlands and in the southern desert were erected as a last stand, returning to an earlier form of settlement, but even those lasted no more than a couple of decades before this territory was vacated entirely. It is telling that most of these sites in the last years of occupation were blanketed with colorful pottery, stars fallen to the ground. Local settlements that had been inhabited for seven hundred years came to hasty ends, the final layers of their archaeological records heavily dosed with circus-colored Salado Polychrome.

Much of the proud irrigation domain of the Hohokam fell apart in these years, a collapse even more remarkable than the fall of Chaco and the subsequent abandonment of the Four Corners. If ever there was a deathly wind to sweep away the lives of many people, it happened in the fifteenth century, and not during the so-called disappearance of the Anasazi almost two hundred years earlier. Often this final collapse is blamed on environmental catastrophe and overuse of the land, but the culprit was far more likely social upheaval.

Can the caving in of Southwest cultures, the scattering of the ancient Hohokam in the desert and the Mogollon in the highlands, be blamed on the Pueblo diaspora down from the Colorado Plateau? Did the raving, polychrome ideologies of these northerners strike at the foundations of everything, their inherent restlessness and the Chacoan blaze in their eyes upset whatever balance might have existed in the Southwest? I believe this was the case.

So much of the territory surrounding this mountain is marked by foreigners in the fourteenth century, prior to the evacuation of nearly every settlement: bird trade; multicolored pottery; big, high citadels peering across the land, kivas packed inside. The Salado reformation that encompassed the Southwest was the last thing to happen before everything fell apart. I am inclined to believe that the impetus for this change came from the north. The rising drought of the twelfth and thirteenth centuries had been a stone dropped in the cultural pool of the Southwest, sending people rippling southward in search of better climates and viable population centers in the fourteenth century. The ripples magnified into waves as other cultures were encountered, absorbed, and overtaken. Black-on-white pottery no longer adequately expressed what people needed to say, and they turned to color and consecutively larger vessels, as new pueblos appeared all over the land and new kivas erupted across central and southeast Arizona. This all rose to a peak like a fire, and when the very last point had burned, these places lay vacant in the fifteenth century, pueblos charred in rituals of abandonment.

The northerners were too much. Perhaps they were too busy with religion, clogging springs and caves with shrines so that Tlaloc could hardly breathe, praying nonstop for the rains to come back. Or they were too loud, too quick to draw weapons. They needed too many timbers with which to erect great ceilings, too much water for mortar and cotton and corn. All of this ended with a final form of pottery, a late version of Salado Polychrome recently identified as Cliff Polychrome, with painstakingly intricate bands painted around exterior bowl rims and jar necks, as if people were frantically squeezing their signatures onto what little unpainted space remained, making their last desperate claims in a time of social collapse.

Many people from across southern and central Arizona, both migrants and locals such as the Hohokam, turned to the refuge of the Colorado Plateau at this point. They walked to the Hopi mesas, where they returned to an old way of life, growing corn in fields of sand under a barren sky, pleading their ancestry so that they could establish a good place to live among ancient northern pueblos such as those of Antelope Mesa. The arduous journeys these people took to get out of southern and central Arizona to reach the Colorado Plateau became the sacrosanct tales of their place in the world—stories of pueblos destroyed behind them, teaching lessons of mobility, perseverance, humility, and temperance.

Not everyone returned to tell their stories, however. Some went in a different direction when central and southern Arizona emptied. These people continued moving south. They had left the Colorado Plateau and were not going back.

. . .

Later in the morning Walt and I found each other near one of the Pinaleno summits, where we walked together among brows of snow. As the sun lifted, the mountain seemed to be coming apart, its ice cap creaking open. April meltwater began to flow, snow-filled meadows flooding. Rivulets gathered into streams between dark trunks of spruce and fir trees. With no creek beds to follow, no ravines, water simply ran everywhere atop this mountain, overflowing their banks of snow. Faces of ice gaped skyward from beneath the clear sheen of flowing water, their frozen mouths and eyes wilting open, giving way to spring.

We walked up a dirt road that led toward the top. It had become a gully of mud-water running in braids and meanders. The water quickly accommodated our passage, filling the holes of our prints. The forest around us roared with morning wind, trees bustling together, then springing apart. The skies were clear, wind sharp and cool. The sun burned into the snow, melting long rays out of the ice. What at dawn had been silent and unwilling was now leaping to attention, all eyes open and awake, rushing to the thousand tasks of April.

Water flowing up here would never reach the desert far below. Whole rivers were disappearing into the mountain this morning, sinking into vaults and aquifers within. A number of years back, I studied the hydrology of the Galiuro Mountains—the range immediately west of the Pinalenos—where radiocarbon dating had shown that much of the flowing water was fifteen thousand years old. This is fossil water, leaking out from the mountains' cavernous underworld; water stored since the last ice age and doled out in measured quantities.

Each of these Sky Island ranges is like an iceberg floating on the desert—great caches of water encased in a skin of rough stone and pine needles. Water eventually relaxes off this busy surface into networks of unlit fissures, filling small spaces between grains of solid rock. The mountains become subterranean lakes. The interior stone becomes an invisible river. This, I believe, is the reason for shrines on the mountains of southeast Arizona: there is water inside them.

Walt and I walked up the road of mud and snow, winding higher toward the peak. Above us the mountain lifted to a fine top, where a Forest Service fire tower stood in the wind. Built in 1933 to watch for fires in all the surrounding world, the tower is a steel lattice ninety-nine feet nine inches tall, capping the mountain with one last upward reach. The wind screamed through its crossbars and cables as we approached its stairs. Walt unhooked the feeble sign that read DO NOT ENTER.

Narrow wooden steps made tight turns up through the tower's insides. Our red-knuckled hands gripped the rails as the wind loomed across our bodies. I thought that the tower might snap into a thousand pieces, an antique hurtling off the top of the mountain as if made of balsa.

There was so much wind that the air was filled with alarm, yet the skies surrounding us were clear. This was the wind du jour coming south-by-southwest, the same wind that sails across these mountains day after day, year after year. For decades it has been shrieking with hardly a pause across this high spoke of a tower. For thousands of years it has been bending these slopes of sea green trees.

Climbing the stairs, I noted the manufacturer's name stenciled onto the tower's steel: AERMOTOR. Longtime manufacturer of windmills. Tower builder. The modern Southwest is covered with the company's rickety metal temples: fans plunging metal rods into the earth in search of water, and high fire lookouts lined up perfectly from one viewpoint to the next, something future archaeologists could easily take to be a sign of a religion, a mass ideology. Shrines, if they didn't know better.

We plodded slowly up the steps, wind catching us off guard, tripping us as we caught railings and pulled ourselves ahead. My sense of height and depth increased with every narrow wooden step. The final turn of the stairwell ended at a shut door. The observation room was closed, secured with an old padlock.

Walt and I stood together in this high cage of steel looking over the ring of the earth. We saw secluded mountains littered across the desert. Mexico loomed in the south, its rising mass of mountains dark where they led toward the Sierra Madre Occidental. Distances fell into gray shapes cluttering every horizon: New Mexico, Arizona, Mexico. We were both still, transfixed. Every wire and bolt head sounded with a tremolo whistle. I could hardly speak a word, braced next to Walt, shoulder against the tower's metal frame for support.

Lines of involuntary tears salted my face, and I could feel them tightening my skin as they dried. I squinted through the wind at the foothills of the Sierra Madre, far off in Mexico.

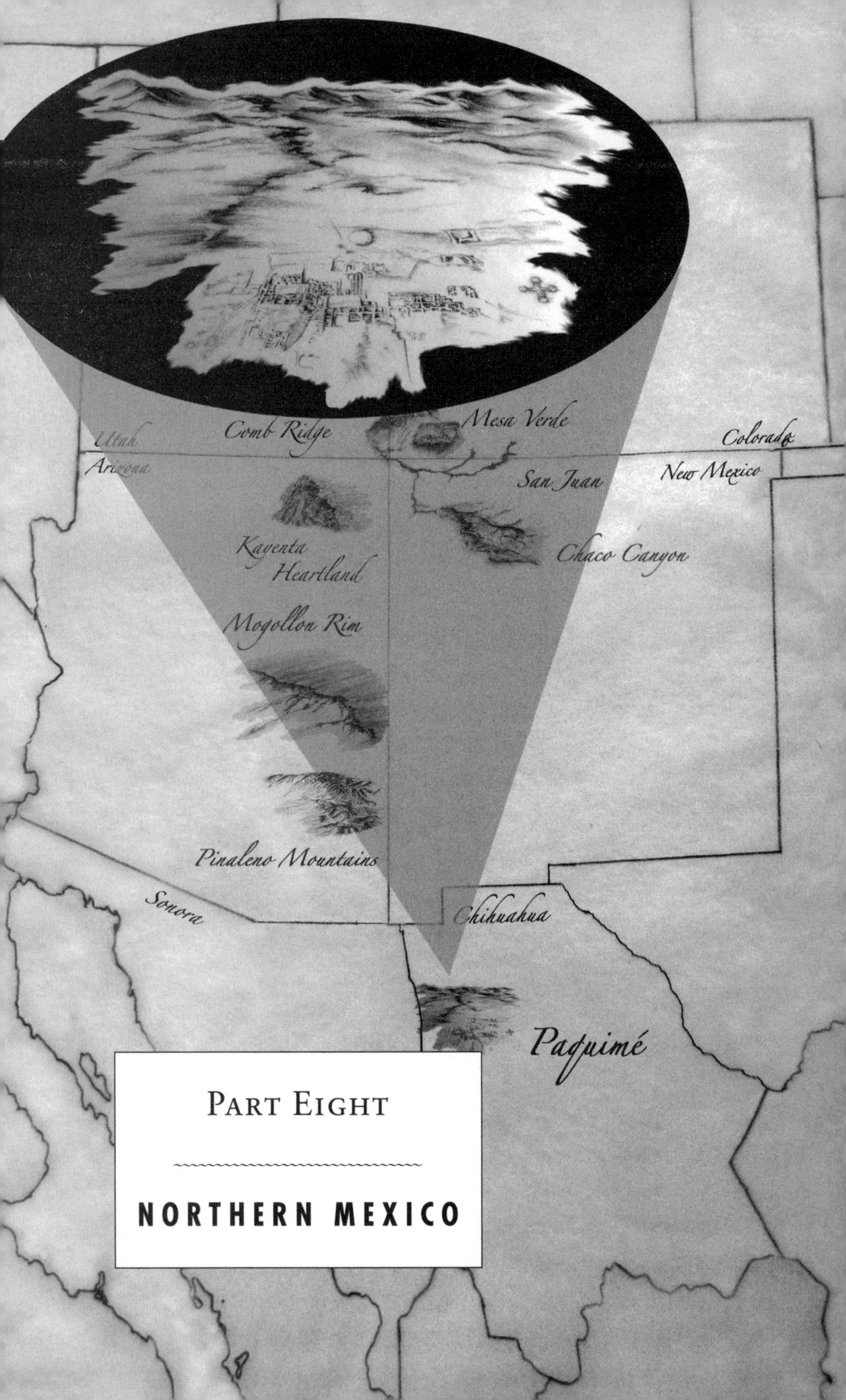

Part Eight

NORTHERN MEXICO

The Far Side of Mesoamerica

SIERRA SAN LUÍS

There is said to have been a road through the Sierra San Luís, a prominent thoroughfare that existed until as recently as fifty years ago. Even buses supposedly took this road, rattling Mexican school buses transporting chickens and people between Sonora and Chihuahua.

How quickly the land takes itself back.

We could not see a road anywhere. Four of us had come in a caravan of two trucks, crossing washed-out rockslides in the bottom of a canyon where creek water parted around our grille plates. It felt safer to have two trucks driving so far into the Mexican outback: we could pull each other out of a quagmire with chains and tow straps. We drove a hundred feet apart, losing sight of each other around tight bends.

There was no road at all, not even a hint of one. Maybe our map was wrong, it being an outdated map. We had seen old tire ruts about half a mile back, a heartening sign as we tried to drive as deep into this canyon as possible. When we could drive no farther, we would load gear into our packs, leave our trucks, and continue on foot. We pulled in the side-view mirrors so we could fit through narrowing canyon passages. Regan worked the steering wheel with jarring motions, and it seemed as if we would run out of passage at any moment—nowhere to turn around, radio antennas bowing back and snapping against overhanging branches.

We stopped and got out in calf-deep water, walked a short distance ahead to judge the terrain. Two college students, both studying Southwest archaeology, had joined Regan and me. One was a stocky, darkly bearded man named Eugene, the other a leaner man with a van Gogh beard named Darin. Regan and I were working as their mentors, our official job being to teach a month of archaeological fieldwork, coming to northern Mexico in search of undocumented sites. The four of us stood on the canyon floor seeing nowhere to turn around. We talked about trying to back out but were fairly certain one or both of the trucks would become mired. We needed forward momentum and the grind of our lowest gear.

Eugene, a man of grim, bearlike countenance, strongly objected to our using this creek as a highway. He was angry about it, saying he would not drive it another foot. "I'm walking from here," he announced. "I'll catch up with you up canyon somewhere."

"We've got to get these trucks out of here," I said.

"Let a flood take them; I don't give a shit," Eugene said. I enjoyed the almost brutal forwardness of his company, never a word minced.

Neither truck was his, of course, so he was free to say whatever he wished. I thought of taking his advice, if you could call it that, and leaving our trucks on the canyon floor. The one Regan and I drove was fairly old, its engine and suspension making many unwanted sounds. Not a good highway vehicle, but the only one Regan and I owned. The truck behind us was much newer, not entirely scratched and dented like ours. It belonged to Darin, who did not like the idea of a flood washing his truck away. This whole business of driving in these conditions made him nervous, the undercarriage of his truck scraped raw on rocks. He looked upstream, contemplating the so-called road, hands on his hips.

"I don't like this either, but I'm not leaving my truck in the bottom of this canyon," he said over his shoulder, aiming the arrow of his voice straight at Eugene.

Eugene did not care what we did. He said so. He dragged his pack out of the back of Darin's truck, and when we got back in and drove ahead, he followed us on foot, like a straggling camp dog. Eugene and Darin had already been out for months taking notes on archaeological sites across the Southwest. The two worked surprisingly well together, having formed a relationship that was both efficient and biting. Meanwhile, Regan and I were coming up from the south, where we had been trekking through jungle ball courts and temples of the pre-Columbian Maya. We had spent time in Guatemala and Honduras, where, dazzled by the archaeology of southern empires, we had found ancient plazas as big as football fields and had strolled among pyramids where broad ceremonial roads had once been cut through the bush.

Now we were in northwest Mexico based on rumors. Asking around, we had heard from a Mexican rancher that he had found a cave up in this canyon. Inside this cave, half-buried in dust, he had found a pouch of beans. In isolated, homegrown Spanish this rancher had described a small, finely woven sack tied closed, beans hard as pebbles inside. The pouch was faded, but he could see that it was decorated, probably woven on a loom with dyed strands of cotton. I had handed the man a pen and my open journal, where he had drawn what he remembered of the design, geometry similar to images I had seen on ceramic vessels and carved into rock in the prehistoric Southwest. This was the same kind of image I had once seen woven into the soles of an exquisite pair of white sandals on the Colorado Plateau and cut into a threshold stone in Spruce Tree House at Mesa Verde.

We had not asked the rancher where exactly this cave was; he had given us enough information. We had simply followed the nearest road marked on a map, an eastbound line through the Sierra San Luís, looking for whatever else these ancient weavers might have left behind. Having tracked the movement of prehistoric populations, I believed that evidence of their passage should appear just south of the border in places where water runs.

This area has long been considered a pre-Columbian no-man's-land. Archaeologists in the United States have largely ignored northwest Mexico. Yes, there are a handful of impressive sites in the area, but overall the Mexican border is believed to have been a sort of cultural void between the Southwest proper and Mesoamerica. This bias has lived on even as research has begun to uncover signs of substantial civilization along key waterways coming off the Sierra

Madre just south of the United States. We were here to see for ourselves, following a hunch into the Sierra San Luís, which I believed was a stepping-stone between the Sierra Madre and the Sky Island mountains of southern Arizona, a route that eventually led over the Pinaleno Mountains, up Bonita Creek, into the highlands, and onto the distant deck of the Colorado Plateau.

At half a mile an hour we drove along the tapering bottom of the deep canyon. Stones clattered under our trucks. Just ahead the mass of a flood-driven tree blocked the creek; burled roots hung in the air. We got out and considered our options, standing mid-calf in cool water. Desert vegetation grew above us. Fierce rays of agaves protruded from ledges. It was a long way to the pines, up into the heart of the mountains where we were heading. The fallen tree needed to go.

I could see a few bends ahead, groves of cottonwoods, alders, and walnut trees crowding along the creek. I reached my cupped hands into the water and washed my face as if trying to cleanse myself of these metal containers we had driven so far into the wilderness.

Eugene came marching up on foot, the slab of a backpack hanging from his shoulders. When he saw our predicament, he stopped and scowled at us from a distance. He knew what we were going to have to do. We got out a tow strap and tied one end around the tree, knotting it into a Medusa's head of a root burl. I hooked the other end onto the front of my truck and tried rocking the obstacle free. Regan directed outside, keeping me from lurching back into a hole, while I bucked back and forth, moving between the accelerator and the clutch. All I did was muddy the water and fill the air with the acrid smell of a burning clutch. The tree would not budge.

I looked out the window, back downstream. Along the inside bend of the canyon was a minor high spot we had passed, a logjammed sandbar. Maybe we could make a ten-point turn there—hoping not to get stuck sideways.

"Let's get this tow strap off," I said. "We'll get the trucks turned around back there. We can leave them stashed. I don't think a flood's coming anytime soon."

Darin took a deep breath, and I saw his body letting go of his attachment to his vehicle. He knew as well as I that one cannot predict floods with much accuracy. We backed down the creek, tailpipes gasping steam. Eugene stood in the creek and watched.

Crunching up onto hulls of bone-dry driftwood, we managed to get both trucks turned around. I pulled the emergency brake and shut off the engine under the narrow shade of alder trees, their trunks lavished with flood debris.

We took what we needed—several days' worth of gear and food stuffed into backpacks—and left the trucks there. Eugene led the way. Where the canyon widened, our sandals slapped wet across floors of curled, crackling leaves, half cups of native walnut shells littered about. Floods had not cleaned this place out since at least five months earlier. We let go of our trucks for now and slipped up through the canyon.

. . .

We set our first camp in the timber kill of an old flood, big trunks of cottonwoods held in each other's arms. We slept without tents, smoothing beds of leaves and sand beside the water.

The next morning we moved on, dropping our packs every half hour, every ten minutes, to scramble up and explore high caves, their deeply sheltered floors dusty and covered with broken rock. Bighorn sheep had been wintering in them, leaving behind gray clods of droppings and scuffed sleeping beds. None of these caves showed any signs of human occupation. We found not even a scrap of pottery or a sliver of glassy jasper or chalcedony brought in to make tools.

In the pleasant heat of the afternoon we came upon a deep pool along the creek, sunlight sinking into its bottle-glass depths. We stripped off our clothes and dove in, stung by the cold of the water below. I swam across and climbed out, dripping on the warm cliff stones, then continued hand over foot up to a craggy ledge, where I sat. My three companions glided underwater, rising for breaths in flurries of bubbles, laughter, and splashes, hair thrown back. There was no way we would have gotten the trucks this far, and I was relieved by this fact: no sign of a road, no way a machine could reach into this canyon.

I looked high, seeing caves arcing up the walls and black crevices that I thought might hold cliff dwellings. But I could see no dwellings, no ruined footers.

The next day was the same, and the day after that, the canyon branching into long, slender arms of tributaries. As we traveled, I began to wonder whether I had been mistaken believing I would find archaeological remains here. I thought this place would be rife with signs of prehistoric culture, at least a bit of black soot on the cave ceilings, flecks of charcoal on the floor. But I was going on just a tad of evidence, a bag of beans in a cave, an insignia woven into the bag's fabric.

A library of study materials had come along in our packs, and we sat in the evening reading, our camp nested into gray boulders toppled one upon the next. The boulders were round and smooth, polished by water into glossy eggs. We had a fire down between them, flickering light sending monstrous shadows up the canyon walls. We read by this shifting light, each of us reclining on a boulder, packs used to soften our backs. This was an after-dinner ritual, taking an hour or two to flip silently through diagrams and pages printed darkly with words. A human skeleton has been documented at a burial site south of here, nearly all of its bones, including the face of the skull, painted red. Not far from these human remains, ancient water diversions have been recorded along mountainsides, holding back soil for farming plots. Explorers who came through in the nineteenth century told of spectacular ruins in remote canyons, sites that have been all but forgotten.

Overall, little data was available on northwest Mexico. We had a few reports with us that dated back to the 1800s and some from the 1950s. More recent work from the '80s, '90s, and 2000s came from the archaeologists María Elisa Villalpando and Beatriz Braniff, who consider this region not so much part of the American Southwest, but the northwesternmost reaches of Mesoamerica. They both refer to this part of the world as the Northwest rather than the Southwest. It is telling that neither of these researchers lives in the United States, their frame of geography coming from the south rather than the north.

Over the years research in Mexico has steadily extended Mesoamerican civilization northward, from the Toltec and Aztec regions up toward the northwest Mexican states of Jalisco, Nayarit, Durango, and Sinaloa. Places once seen as cultural gaps are now recognized as centers of highly complex prehistoric societies rich with their own vastly engineered settlements. Hillsides in these northern states have been found leveled off and topped with houses, ball courts, and even minor pyramids.

Meanwhile, archaeologists in the United States have been bearing southward, dissolving previous cultural boundaries as they discover chains of continuity between once distant geographic realms. Pueblo sites have been discovered outside Safford and along the San Pedro River in southeast Arizona, looking as though they were taken directly off the Colorado Plateau. Mesoamerica and the Southwest are being brought ever closer together, and we had come to the Sierra San Luís to see if they actually might touch.

The word *Anasazi* had grown fainter with every mile I had traveled south, silenced under the Hopis' *Hisatsinom* and *Ancestral Puebloan,* muffled through the thick pines of the Mogollon Highlands, taken in by *Salado*. It was lost to prehistoric marriage among the many different peoples inhabiting southeast Arizona, but still it existed, visible in pottery designs, in kivas, in mobile pueblos.

Pages were turned slowly around the fire, notes scribbled in the margins. Our light dimmed until we were reading near the tips of our noses. Someone got up and broke some driftwood, stirred up sparks, and gave us another ten minutes of good light.

When the fire again dwindled, I set down the paper I'd been reading and leaned back onto the boulder. A path of stars swayed over the canyon. Our fire fell to coals. No one got up for more wood.

. . .

Following the creek together in the middle of the day, we found a place for lunch under a stone ledge overhang. Darin hunted into the shade and found a hole hand-ground out of the bedrock. It was a smooth cylinder worn straight down like a posthole, used to crush grains and seeds. Nearby was another and another. We gathered around with serious grins of discovery. We had been looking for

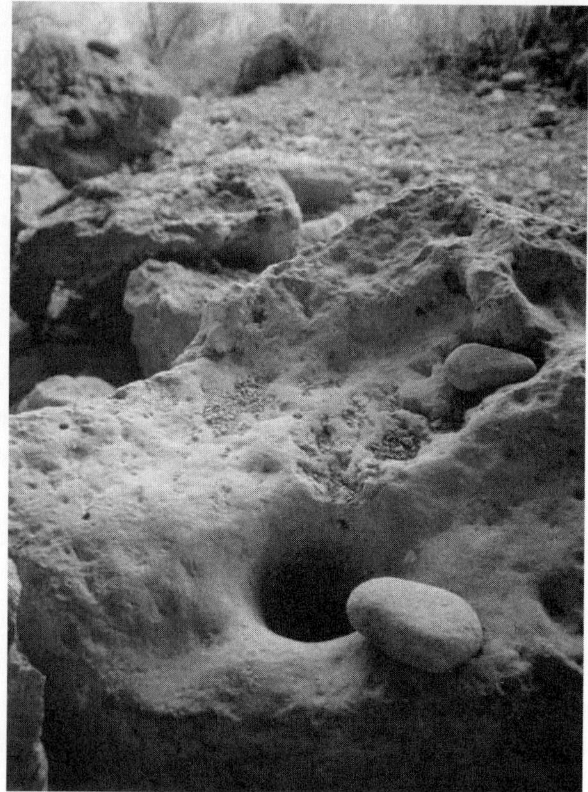

Grinding hole and grinding stone found in the Sierra San Luís protected by an overhanging cliff wall. REGAN CHOI

anything, a simple sign of humans. This was our first find. We abandoned lunch and began creeping through this shelter eroded from the canyon wall, scrabbling our fingers in fallen bedrock and black wood rat droppings. We came up with numerous thumbs of corncobs and several knots and loops made of plant fibers.

Curved flakes of gourd skins appeared from the dust, and several wooden topknots from squash. Each item was announced, and we gathered around it, passing a flake of worked stone from one set of hands to the next, turning seed husks and corncobs in our fingers. The amount of corn was impressive. We counted the rows on each cob we found, coming up with different numbers, inferring that each was its own genetic strain. I knew of a site not far south of here where pre-Columbian corn had been analyzed, revealing its age to be around four thousand years old, some of the first domesticated corn to come up from the south.

Corn—the rudiment of Southwest culture—was first cultivated in the Tehuacán Valley of Mexico about five thousand years ago. Derived from a tropical grass that still grows in Central America and southern Mexico, the domestic version known as *Zea mays* reached the Southwest around the fourth millennium B.C. (although the date keeps getting pushed back by new discoveries). It followed a route up from the Sierra Madre across the stepping-stones of the Sky Islands. A corn sample thirty-seven hundred years old was found at the head of Bonita Creek between the town of Safford and Point of Pines. Farther north along this passage of corn is a stash on the Colorado Plateau, immediately north of Antelope Mesa, dating to nearly four thousand years old, defining a clear walkway of ancient agricultural motion.

Most early crops of corn, beans, and squash came into these northern regions from southern Mexico, appearing in a slow fashion that suggests seeds were being passed along by groups of mobile hunter-gatherers rather than by any concerted cultural effort. Then, around A.D. 400, there came a sudden rush of new crops into the Southwest. Cotton, jack beans, green-striped cushaw squash, and warty squash appeared in one fell swoop as if an arrow had shot up from the south, a firm route established between Mesoamerica and the Southwest. Along with this push came kiva-style pit-houses on the Colorado Plateau and the first noteworthy gatherings of people and architecture at Chaco Canyon. People who had been relatively isolated in the Southwest were suddenly connected with a much larger civilization far to the south.

Just as suddenly and at the same time, amaranth, a grain native to the Southwest, first appeared in the Tehuacán Valley of southern Mexico. Turquoise mined in New Mexico showed up in Guatemala. A reciprocal flow had begun.

We noticed that this cave had no potsherds whatsoever. Ceramics did not show up in this region until the earliest centuries A.D. I wondered if this was one of the old sites, a stopover for corn four thousand years ago. Even without cliff dwellings or kivas, we knew we were on a route of some sort, perhaps the very bridge between Mesoamerica and the Southwest we had been searching for. Instead of finding a sign of northern people on their way south, we seem to have found southern corn on its way north. Turning corncobs in my fingers, I sensed lines of travel pushing and pulling across the Americas.

After an hour of animated searching—crawling on the ground, laying aside spiderwebs with our fingers—we returned to our lunches. Dusting off our hands on our pants, we sat in the shade and the dirt. Regan pulled a knife from her pack and slivered open an apple, cut it into fourths, and distributed the pieces. I broke a hard block of sweaty cheese and shared it. A can of tuna fish was passed around, the tuna scraped out with a hunting knife, with an index finger, with a stick.

I balanced a cracker loaded with tuna on my knee and leaned back against a rock that had fallen from the shelter's ceiling. There was no sign of architecture, and nothing leading me to believe that anyone had poked into this cave more recently than a few thousand years ago. This cave was meager compared to the others we had seen, just an arc of shade in the rock, a place for simple convenience rather than a place to live for a long time. But it had been used.

"We should go south," I said, looking out where the creek ran thin over white cobbles. "Get deeper into the mountains. What do you think?"

Eugene said, "We'll get lazy, all this water. I'm up for going deeper."

Regan looked at the wink of sky visible through the canyon outside the cave. She was heartened to be here, to find this site of corncobs, this place of seclusion and running water. She would have been content exploring the Sierra San Luís for another couple of weeks. But she, too, was thinking about the south.

Darin concurred.

Beautiful as this place was, we needed to get back to our trucks and keep moving.

The City

PAQUIMÉ

There are not many lights between far mountain ranges in the lower Chihuahuan Desert. *Llanterías,* tar-paper tire vendors with no electricity, sit like washed-up bones along the side of the highway at night. On this arid, subtropical plain flanking the Sierra Madre in northwest Mexico, the highway is mostly empty, oncoming headlights rare. AM radio stations fade in and out, picking up in sequence a symphony from Tucson, an avid polka from somewhere in Mexico, and then a theatrical preacher broadcasting out of El Paso through a bath of static.

The passing desert is nothing but darkness. If you are familiar with the land, you know that out there stands a conspicuous hill. The hill is old, its top built up many centuries ago. It is a high lookout with a gently graded ramp spiraling up to its peak, a ceremonial procession worn now into ruins. Atop this hill is a stack of rubble left from a round tower that once had four symmetrical rooms built within. In daylight, standing upon this load of fallen stones, you can see roads in the surrounding country—not just Mexican two-tracks but ancient roads as broad and faded as those of Chaco. Not much relation to Chaco, some scholars will quickly suggest, as if the Colorado Plateau and northern Mexico should not be discussed in the same sentence.

From atop this impressive hill in northwest Mexico, you can also see numerous high points in the distance, and from each of these you can see many more. Within the local area, about fifty miles in all directions, twenty-four specific mounds are in direct view of one another. If you were to walk to the tops of these mounds, you would find human-made platforms, small pyramids, or stone circles, the stones having been split by intense heat. Fires were once lit on these points, lights that would have been visible like sudden starbursts from miles away, messages crossing great distances in a flicker. At the hub of this faraway signal network is this single, round tower.

In turn, this masonry tower can be seen by a crucial site, a prehistoric city larger and more tightly packed than anything preceding it in the Southwest. It is the fallen center of Paquimé, and among its eroded quarters stands a high room with a narrow window conspicuously installed in its corner. If you were to look through this window from a seat worn by centuries of sitting, you would see the tower in the dry distance. Certainly, the landscape around Paquimé was orchestrated so that the tower could be seen, the hub of a signal relay.

Back in the 1970s an American researcher named Charles Di Peso ambitiously excavated 317 of Paquimé's 2,000 central rooms, and one night he lit on fire a dead-dry yucca to see how far its light might carry. Word came back that it could be seen clearly across twenty-five miles, and Di Peso figured that if it had been more than just a yucca, it would have been visible from much farther away. He believed, like researchers who came after him, that these high points represent a complex signaling system, an assertion borne out by more recent satellite-based geographic analysis. Line-of-sight connections around Paquimé appear to have been intentionally arranged with repeating patterns so that if one relay went down, a message could still be transmitted by others. Whatever message this might have been, these researchers say, whether military or ceremonial or both, it must have been very important.

An identical signal network was defined around Chaco, but many archaeologists are careful not to draw parallels. Mexico is Mexico, the United States the United States. Among many it is one of the deadly sins of Southwest archaeology to say that Paquimé and Chaco, hundreds of years apart and four hundred miles away, had much to do with each other.

A paved highway runs northwest to southeast across northern Chihuahua, and at night the only significant lights along it begin to appear around the town of Nuevo Casas Grandes. First small houses are lit up, followed by gas stations and tiendas, and then you are in the middle of a well-lit town.

We parked our two trucks on a street and stepped out into the buoyant marketplace atmosphere typical of so many Mexican towns. Families were strolling this evening, and Mexican men were drinking, already laughing loudly. Teenagers carried themselves in a way that spoke of sex, young bodies pressing against each other, flirting, kissing. We walked through the many scenes of Nuevo Casas Grandes as if through a carnival, fresh from the wilderness, our clothes smelling of sweat and wood smoke.

We bought tacos, many of them, and ate with drips of amber cow grease running down our hands. After the tacos we sat in a dark movie house with a dusty shaft of projector light flickering over our heads. It was some love story/western. I practiced my Spanish for a little while, trying to figure out what the dubbed voices were saying, but it was a Hollywood movie, dialogue unrealistic. Translating became a chore, and I eventually gave up and just sat in the dark, inhaling the profundity of civilization. When you come from the outback, it is enough to sit through a movie and not necessarily watch it. The smell alone was plenty for my senses, perfume and the disintegrating plush of seat cushions.

I thought of the land around Nuevo Casas Grandes, places we had driven through to get here. For miles encircling this movie theater was darkness, nothing but scrubland and scattered *ejidos* (government-owned tracts) where Mexican farmers were now asleep.

There is a reason this bright town is here, seemingly in the middle of nowhere. Nuevo Casas Grandes sits beside the great ruins of Paquimé, both the modern and ancient settlements built on a piece of land where the water table is high. In the middle of prehistoric Paquimé, Di Peso's crews unearthed a well. In its day this well would have been accessed through a warren of hallways leading to an interior room with a hatchway that in turn led forty feet straight down to water dug out by the residents. They had built an ample staircase spiraling into the ground beneath the city to this subterranean pool. These stairs looked like altars when Di Peso's crews uncovered them, jewelry and shells found littered down the winding steps, along with ceramic vessels, carved stone, and many precious artifacts. This well was not merely a place to collect water, but a ritual space leading to what must have been a serenely calm and dark body of water far below ground.

This is why Nuevo Casas Grandes exists, and the prehistoric city of Paquimé before it: water exists in an otherwise empty land. Water brings admirers, commerce, movies, and taco stands. It brings outsiders and highways, a magnet in the desert.

When the movie was finished, we walked almost dazed into this place of water, streetlights, and stolen cars. A well-dressed couple of youths, about sixteen years old, engaged in a feral kissing match against a lamppost, and we had to skirt around them. We grinned at all that we saw, astonished by the humming, electrical ambiance of civilization.

We drove our trucks a short distance and set a quick camp just outside town along the shallow and warm-smelling Rio Casas Grandes. We sat on our tailgates facing away from the town lights toward the dark ruins of Paquimé, as vacant tonight as a cemetery.

. . .

Settlements were established at Paquimé in the early centuries A.D., but not until the thirteenth century did the site become a crucial and heavily populated axis, rising in concert with cultures that were dropping out of the north. Paquimé reached its height in the fifteenth century, next in line for the southward cultural expansions, only this was larger than anything preceding it and had to do with far more than northern travelers. Even Chaco pales in comparison, in size, wealth, and complexity. This was now the paramount settlement in all of the Southwest, the biggest thing ever to happen.

If you look down at the fifteenth-century remains of Paquimé from a low-flying plane, they seem unnecessarily complex, with walls zigzagging in and out of one another and rooms ranging in size from thirty square feet to more than a thousand. The floor plan appears to be a work of art in itself.

What little was excavated by Di Peso and his crews reveale quimé to have been a revolution in art on many levels. Coppe being forged, made into bells and ornately detailed lost-wax dants. Ceramic vessels were formed in the shape of women's b their ceramic skin covered with multicolored, geometric image clining figures complete with nipples and vulvas: one would drunk from their heads. Similar vessels of men were made in rel squatting positions, one hand almost absentmindedly hooked c penis, the other smoking a pre-Columbian cigarette. Like the wc these men are painted head to toe with rich geometric forms sp to the sphere of Paquimé.

The city had low-ceilinged sweatshops built for the mass pr tion of goods, cramped workspaces where slaves or servants o cialists made shell jewelry. Meanwhile, whole houses nearby occupied by prosperous artisans and the political elite who a ently ruled the city. There was a bold hierarchy, a vast differen tween those who had and those who did not. Clear evidence for divisions was found in the 317 rooms Di Peso excavated.

My wife, our two companions, and I traveled through wh Peso and his crews had unearthed, separating from one anothe in the morning, slowly perusing Paquimé's raised floor plan ir vate. I passed through broken-down hallways, some of the rer ing walls knee-high and others up to my chest. A steady, dry blew in from the Sierra Madre in the distance, gusts of air da through narrow passages, threading into ventilator shafts and merous T-shaped doorways—more T shapes than I knew Chaco or Mesa Verde. Just the presence of these shaped portals gested a connection between northern Pueblo people and here, kind of cultural, architectural thread. The wind sent yellowish swirling around my feet, adobe crushed into dry meal.

Di Peso had put together a comprehensive, eight-volume re on his excavations. As I walked, I thumbed through his pages ir head, rebuilding parts of this site: here a rash of human sacri buried neatly beneath a plaza; over there a space that had once an indoor ball court; farther off rooms strung with stone gongs we ing a few hundred pounds each. The numbers of artifacts Di found verge on the obscene, ancient storerooms packed to

ceilings. Nearly four million shell artifacts were excavated, most found in storerooms and work spaces as if ready for distribution.

I moved from room to room heading for a central, open area in what was called the House of the Macaws, one of the many precincts within Paquimé: House of the Dead, House of the Well, House of the Serpents, and so on, inventive names given by Di Peso himself. Just when I turned a corner to enter a plaza, I came upon a little red sign blocking the ruined doorway ahead. The sign lay in the dust, a piece of wood with the word ALTO painted on it.

I stopped. The sign clearly meant "this place is not a playground." The voice of Mexican authority. I looked at the sign for a moment, still carrying in my body the memory of wilderness, not accustomed to messages of this nature. I changed my posture, stiffened a little, and looked into the plaza beyond, not taking a step forward.

The plaza was outlined with compact adobe boxes with perfectly circular openings in their faces and polished, cigar-shaped rocks that would have been slid into place to seal these openings closed. The plaza looked as though it were surrounded by an elaborate series of

Fifteenth-century macaw pens missing their roofs in a plaza at Paquimé. REGAN CHOI

locks and channels. These were pens where tropical macaws had been bred and raised, captive birds brought up from jungles far to the south. The birds would have poked their red-feathered heads through these circular portals to see daylight outside. This style of pen kept their bones from becoming malformed by sunlight deficiency, unlike the much poorer attempt at aviculture that occurred centuries earlier at Chaco, where only crippled birds were produced. At Paquimé the raising of birds was elevated to an art form practiced by specialized groups, the macaw pens humidified to replicate their home environment in Central America. The breeding of these birds was done on an industrial scale at Paquimé, thousands of macaws hatched for their bright green, red, and blue feathers. Four hundred forty-nine macaws and three hundred domestic turkeys have been found interred in centrally located burial pits throughout the city—probably a small number considering that most of Paquimé is still unexcavated. Many of these birds appear to have been ritually sacrificed, an indication that Paquimé may have been a ceremonial center where a great deal of artifact production went toward ritual events, burials, and sacrifices. The fact that Paquimé was a desert breeding center for tropical birds makes me think of the story told to me by T. J. Ferguson about the migration of the Lost Others. Ferguson had said that in Zuni oral tradition a large number of people once followed a parrot far to the south, away from their homeland on the Colorado Plateau. Did that parrot lead them to Paquimé, to a place that was no doubt a commercial source of tropical birds and feathers for the rest of the Southwest? The story may very well be an account of Pueblo people coming here to engage in aviculture and bird trade.

I did not go beyond the sign imploring me to stop, but stood at attention before it, the plaza in front of me a reservoir of bright April sunlight. The cool morning was starting to wear off.

What a spectacle in the open desert, I thought. Rising five stories, Paquimé had been a grand cultural soapbox of the times. There are many theories as to what exactly this place was—an expensive, later knockoff of Chaco, or a creation all its own on the Mesoamerican fringe? A kingdom ruling the land, or a local bastion minding its own business?

. . .

I drank beer with archaeologist Steve Lekson as we sat in folding chairs under the awning of a trailer. We were attending a symposium on Southwest archaeology and were relaxing between sessions in a dirt parking lot. The beer was cold, fresh out of an ice chest. Lekson, a highly respected archaeological scholar from the University of Colorado, was touting an idea he had conjured and was making famous around the Southwest. He called it the Chaco Meridian. He explained that if you drew a line north out of Chaco, you would hit Aztec, New Mexico, home of Chaco's immediate architectural progeny back in the twelfth century. If you took that same line four hundred miles due south, you would end up smack in the middle of Paquimé in the thirteenth and fourteenth centuries. This four-hundred-mile line is so accurate that even modern surveyors would be hard-pressed to repeat it.

"Coincidence?" Lekson asked. "I don't think so."

Lekson's voice is bookmarked with notes of irony and sarcasm. In his version of Southwest prehistory, a convoy of Chacoan elite left for Aztec, fifty-five miles due north of their original site, in the twelfth century. When they were done with Aztec, they turned around and followed the same line due south four hundred miles across rugged terrain, never once losing their bearings. Chacoans had already proven themselves capable of such navigational feats, having engineered roads across the desert as if charting courses at sea. When the Chacoans reached this part of what is now northern Chihuahua in Mexico, Lekson believes they found loose villages lying about, people growing plots of corn and making easy pottery. Newly arrived migrants from the Colorado Plateau whipped everyone into shape, shouting orders this way and that, and pretty soon had a new ceremonial city built for themselves at the foot of the Sierra Madre. Here they indulged in heavily ritualized habits of human sacrifice as they had at Chaco, wearing necklaces made of human bones and dressing in feathers of turkeys and exotic jungle birds as they presided over colorful rituals.

"Everything starts with Chaco," Lekson reiterated. "That place is the strongest and earliest stable pattern you get in the Southwest. Pueblo Bonito shows up, and then you get Aztec. All sorts of big things happen, and boom—Paquimé shows up right on schedule, third in line."

Lekson sat with his beer, posture perfectly controlled but relaxed, peering out at a hot New Mexico day beyond the awning.

The academic papers Lekson has written are touched with relieving humor, something rarely seen in scientific journals. He has called this Chaco-Aztec-Paquimé union a ménage à trois, writing that "Chaco and Paquimé have been the subject of sordid, tittering speculation for some years."

He wrote, "Chaco was too old, Paquimé too young. We looked at their ages, we looked at the maps, and we knew it would never work. However, something cartographic caught my eye. Chaco and Paquimé were on the same meridian. That is, they were exactly north-south of each other. Chaco-Paquimé might be May-December, but, positionally, they made a striking pair."

I once looked Lekson straight in the eye, the two of us alone, and asked if he still believed his meridian theory after nearly every other archaeologist in the Southwest had choked when she or he had heard it. To have carried the religious, political core of a civilization hundreds of miles exactly along a longitude of 107°57'25", following a line set up between the key north-south great houses of Pueblo Alto and Tsin Kletsin back at Chaco, did seem a bit specific. Lekson looked right back at me and said yes, he still believed in his meridian.

Everyone in Southwest archaeology has something to say about Lekson. He has stirred up academic dissent and discussion as far away as Central America, where archaeologists previously paid very little attention to what was happening in the American Southwest, a far and dusty corner of the world. Suddenly, it was sounding as though we might have a full-blown civilization on our hands, pre-Columbian people who were capable of making complex and long-distance decisions moving en masse along ceremonial corridors spanning countless horizons.

Lekson wanted to test his theory. He halfheartedly wanted to be proven wrong, just to get more conversations going, to give Southwest archaeology a jump start. At the trailer Lekson and his colleagues had set up a table on which they had placed many potsherds unearthed at a crucial archaeological site between Chaco and Paquimé. They believed that they had found a missing link in the desert near the New Mexico town of Truth or Consequences, and the sherds partly proved their point. The sherds had the look of Mesa Verde pottery but had been made much later, coming from far south of Mesa Verde. Lekson was certain that these were signs of migrants who had walked down from the north across New Mexico.

Lekson had invited naysayers to have a look at the potsherds for themselves. A troop of four researchers descended on us from across the parking lot, where a hundred cars were parked for the symposium. I lowered my beer to my lap as they approached through stiff summer sunlight. Laughter sparked by Lekson's many joking comments faded as his colleagues straightened their faces to watch these gentlemen step into their camp.

"Come in, come in," Lekson said, beckoning them into his fortress of ice chests and shade.

No one got up or offered a seat. Three of the gentlemen walked right past the potsherds that had been set out, but a particularly keen ceramicist from the Museum of New Mexico veered off to methodically study them.

The first gentleman to approach greeted Lekson, old friends long parted. There was no need to shake hands. The debate took only four or five words to begin.

"It is irrational to assume this is all about migration, that it isn't simply a matter of trade, which as you know has been soundly documented," the man said.

There was not a second of silence before Lekson jumped in. "It's irrational to assume it's not about migration," he retorted. "This is more than pottery moving around. We're looking at large groups of people making great distances."

"You have nothing to back you up."

"I have everything to back me up."

I left the beer in my lap, captivated by this escalating argument. I thought this is how it must have happened centuries ago in the

Pueblo world, factions splitting under the summer sun, accusations thrown by gentlemen until camps divided.

After carefully examining each of the potsherds, the ceramicist from the museum finally entered the circle. He carried one of the sherds in his hand, and he dropped to one knee in the dust in front of Lekson. The ceramicist spoke with a nearly continuous stutter that made it impossible not to pay very close attention to his every word. He was Lekson's match, his intellectual equal. He began describing what he saw in these supposed Mesa Verde–like potsherds, explaining that Lekson may have been premature in his assessment.

Lekson sat back in his chair and listened. The ceramicist talked with excruciatingly halting words, saying he did not deny the similarities between Mesa Verde pottery and these sherds, but this did not constitute a migration.

Yes, something was migrating, the ceramicist continued. There is no question about that. But was it people or ideas or just vessels going from hand to hand and altering the iconic designs in places where they arrived? These questions were not answered by a mere collection of potsherds.

Lekson knew this, and he accepted the ceramicist's argument with ample quiet and consideration. Still, Lekson had been on the land, traveling between critical archaeological sites, and was sure in his gut that the connections went far beyond trade. Traits of Chaco are all over Paquimé: T-shaped doors at every turn, dramatic hilltop architecture, an overwhelming collection of never-before-seen artifacts, and the abundant use of birds. Great kivas around Chaco and Aztec, built in the eleventh and twelfth centuries, had huge stone disks stacked beneath their massive ceiling timbers, and these buried disks were found peppered with offerings. The same sorts of heavy disks had been stacked in a ritualistic fashion beneath timber posts in fourteenth- and fifteenth-century Paquimé. There are bird feathers galore, fire signals, and pre-Columbian roads at both Chaco and Paquimé. For Lekson, Paquimé was the new Chaco.

Some time ago I learned to use Lekson's name with care when speaking among archaeologists. For the most part others squirm at his theories. Why, exactly, I have trouble seeing. I do not wholly agree with Lekson, but his ideas seem to be pointing in the right direction. It is true, Paquimé and Chaco are a spectacular two-of-a-kind among the thousands of lesser archaeological sites identified across the Southwest. They certainly have their differences, with their own regional influences and varied scales of production. The mention of their similarities, however, causes many archaeologists to squirm. There is somehow a need for Chaco to be its own isolated entity in the southwest United States and for Paquimé to be its own entity in northwest Mexico. The Chaco Meridian threatens that need, challenging something at the core of Southwest archaeology.

On the surface Lekson's theory of the Chaco Meridian is not mild-mannered enough for traditional Southwest archaeology. This has long been a gentlemen's science. The late and eminently respected Emil Haury, who worked some hellishly hot digs in Arizona, was said never to have cursed, even after taking strong plugs of whiskey at the end of a field season. The Chaco Meridian is too boisterous for this institution, leaping onto the stage without remorse or apology, claiming a much more spectacular and calculating civilization in the American Southwest than most had imagined.

If, indeed, an organized group of Chacoans walked a straight line for four hundred miles carrying their whole civilization to Mexico without missing a beat, then erected an incomparable urban monument once they got there, these ancient people were not the small-town folk—the rural weavers and potters—they are so often portrayed to be. Reframing them as a vastly complex amalgam of cultures that had the sky and earth accurately mapped, moving political forces across great distances, changes the whole picture.

What I hear in the most guttural responses from Lekson's opponents is a defensive fear that goes beyond mere archaeology. I believe that his theory threatens our very identity as a modern civilization. We are accustomed to thinking of these ancient people as *different,* as *old,* while we are *new, improved.* We have forms of mobility and wide-scale cultural sophistication truly unique in history, right? This is why the period in the Americas before 1492 is generally called prehistory, a time before time, before history began. Stone Age people were nothing like what we are today in our global village. Right?

The ceramicist balanced on one knee in the dust was being cautious, wishing to move ahead in measured, quantifiable steps. He thought Lekson's flight of archaeological fancy a fine enough idea, but Lekson should be careful flaunting it as a sound academic theory.

The naysaying gentlemen and the ceramicist eventually walked back across the parking lot, and we sat alone. Left in their own company, Lekson and his colleagues sat looking into the heat outside their awning.

"Got out of that relatively unscathed," Lekson said with a smile, sweat beading on his forehead.

. . .

I walked away from Paquimé's ruins into a field beyond the cap of a flat-topped earthen pyramid, beyond the edges of Di Peso's excavation, where a dry breeze skimmed across hard-packed dirt. I stopped and looked back at a roofless, manicured city where people, including children, had once been buried seated upright; where an effigy mound had been constructed in the shape of a horned serpent, its eye marked with a white stone engraved with the serpent's likeness. If this site had been in Arizona or Utah, anywhere in the United States, it would have been an archaeological trophy far greater than Chaco, and legions of researchers would be poring over it. Instead, it has taken a cultural backseat to the likes of the Anasazi because it is in Mexico. Indeed, the prehistoric Four Corners may have been only the northern periphery of the cultural Southwest, while Paquimé, which reached its peak between the thirteenth and fifteenth centuries, acted more as a true geographic, political center.

Smaller settlements existed in this location long before Paquimé itself. Excavations from eleventh-century villages buried under Paquimé have unearthed pottery imported from the Little Colorado River region of northeast Arizona, nearly four hundred miles away. Researchers found wares from both the Four Corners area and from the west coast of Mexico. From the beginning, this place was a cultural repository for a much more extensive region, connected to far provinces like the Colorado Plateau well before Lekson's Chaco Meridian came into play. The common archaeological view of Paquimé as existing on the periphery is false. This ancient city, or the communities surrounding it, may have been where many migrants from the north were heading. It is probably no coincidence that Paquimé rose to power while Chaco was disbanding, and reached its apex in the time that nearly all of the Southwest was in motion. Lekson may be right: all roads that once led to Chaco now lead straight to Paquimé.

But Paquimé is not Chaco. I spoke with archaeologists Chris and Todd VanPool, who were excavating a settlement just south of here. Chris told me she believed that this region was much more politically and religiously tied to Mesoamerica than to the Puebloan Southwest. She recognized combined elements, similar motifs between north and south, but overall Paquimé, with its giant ball courts, highly centralized power structure, and plethora of horned-serpent imagery, clearly reminded her of Mesoamerica. Her husband, Todd, listed a litany of artistic, iconographic, architectural, and ceramic boundaries that were never crossed between Salado and Paquimé. He named numerous small but obvious differences in the way people from Salado and Paquimé painted the same icons, differences that told him there may have been a schism between north and south. In a gentle, articulate voice, Todd explained, "The Paquimé region's horned serpents are either painted white, filled with negative space, or they're filled in with red. They're never black."

Chris echoed, "Never."

Todd continued, "The Salado region, despite the fact that they have white paint and red paint, always paint theirs black."

Chris said, "The symmetry of these painted serpents in these two cultural regions is very different; everything is a hundred and eighty degrees apart." Without pause, Todd added, "In every way that they could differ, they did."

The VanPools were saying Lekson was incorrect, that the Puebloan north did not move down and erect Paquimé, that in fact substantial differences existed between the north and the south. I mentioned that regardless of coloration or symmetry, the same horned-serpent icon was being used in the two places, making them culturally similar.

Chris replied, "I would argue that a really powerful deity bridges two worlds, and that's what makes it powerful."

In southeast Arizona and the boot heel of New Mexico, not far north of Paquimé, purely Salado communities existed contemporaneously within a few miles of solely Paquimé-related communities, and there is little sign of integration between the two. Salado sites have pottery from the north. Paquimé sites have pottery from the south.

Only a few settlements include large amounts of both kinds of pottery, and in these cases northern and southern styles are segregated within the communities. Different kinds of pottery had very specific connotations and uses. For example, Salado wares were used for daily living, and around ball courts only pottery from Paquimé is found—spectacularly decorated Ramos Polychrome with red, black, and even yellow designs on a white background. Salado wares were not to be used at ball courts, which were in themselves features of a more southerly culture.

"These are different intellectual traditions, different religious traditions," Todd explained. "Both these groups have horned-serpent concepts, but they work hard to maintain their distinctiveness."

Chris said, "It may be like some Christians making a cross one way and others making it another way: you're very similar, you have basic tenets, but you keep separate. Like Eastern Orthodox versus Roman Catholic. I believe the Americas share many central religious tenets. The horned-serpent images that are pan-American all have to do with sky and underworld, water and earth. They're prevalent in every single group, and in many groups they are paramount. We see it with the Aztecs and Olmecs. We see it in the eastern woodlands of North America, where there are feathered-rattlesnake images. We see it at Paquimé. There are horned, feathered serpents at Chaco in petroglyphs. These are icons tied to traditions that had to do with the propagation of rain and water, traditions that lie at the root of these cultures."

For its distinctive forged metals and Mesoamerican-style ball courts, Paquimé was still a fundamental part of the rest of the Southwest, a key to this complex, prehistoric lock. Mixed in with unique Mexican images on Paquimé pottery are the same designs I saw etched into a floor stone at Mesa Verde in Colorado, the same geometric icons painted on cliffs around Hovenweep in Utah, and inscribed into the caprock of Antelope Mesa in northern Arizona. The Southwest, including northern Mexico, appears to have once contained a single cultural identity marked with regional variations that were in turn connected to Mesoamerica along the chain of the Sierra Madre. There was a continuous line of people whose most powerful gods dwelled in springs, clouds, and water-filled mountains.

If Pueblo migrants were here, signs of them are hidden by the intense hierarchy and wealth of Paquimé. No doubt, they are somewhere in these ruins. If bright lights and big city drew migrants from the Four Corners to the Little Colorado River and the Mogollon Highlands, certainly the glare of Paquimé must have had a tremendous grip on them. Not far from Paquimé are the ruins of a ninety-room masonry pueblo built in a northern style that actually outlived Paquimé, signs of northerners in Mexico.

In the end Paquimé was destroyed, its ruins strewn with unburied corpses. You would expect such a thing in the Southwest; it had happened before. Parts of Chaco were marked the same way, as well as many settlements around the base of Mesa Verde and Sleeping Ute Mountain in southwest Colorado, and on down through the Mogollon Highlands. It looks like full-scale warfare hit Paquimé sometime around A.D. 1450, when each house was strategically sacked. For months afterward the area must have reeked of death, corpses blackening in the sun. Who knows the reason for this destruction: failed alliances, internal disputes, or merely time to move on?

The fall of Paquimé occurred just as major settlements were abandoned across most of the Southwest and the intricate cultural systems of Salado and Hohokam fell apart. This did not happen all at once. Migrants traveling south in the thirteenth and fourteenth centuries had brought a boom to the lower Southwest. Too many people moved too quickly into what was once a landscape of dispersed settlements, turning them into urban centers as people massed around pueblos and large villages wherever there was water. Then came a century of complex demographic upheaval between 1350 and 1450. Resources diminished, and the health of the people deteriorated. Populations declined and retreated to a few core areas, and soon many of those areas were empty. At least forty thousand people living in parts of southern New Mexico and southern Arizona simply vanished from the archaeological record.

Paquimé, a bastion of growth and art at its height, died in the face of this dramatically unsettled environment. It was the last great collapse in the prehistoric Southwest. After many centuries of occupation, the city was soon buried by wind and dust. Only a small portion of its fifteenth-century climax was now exposed, beige geometric walls crossing in and out of one another in warm spring sunlight. I looked across the ruins toward the Sierra Madre in the distance, thinking, When the cities burn, you go to the mountains. You climb back into the earth, into places dark with water.

Coming into the Mountains

SLOPE OF THE SIERRA MADRE

The bar had a single, clear lightbulb suspended over its door. It hung by a kinked pair of wires. A red, hand-painted advertisement for Tecate beer was peeling off the outside wall. The bar was small and smelled of cigarette smoke. A few men played a slow pool game in the back. They weren't comfortable with Regan being here, a woman sitting in a men's bar. They might have thought she was a whore, even in this little logging town, but they said nothing to us. They just watched her subtly as they moved around their pool table.

I heard the grumbling downshift of a logging truck outside. The trucks were coming every ten, fifteen minutes on this night, hauling huge rounds of trees out of the Sierra Madre, the Mother Mountains, and parading them like chained beasts along the main street.

We had driven out of the desert and up the pine-bristled slope of the sierra. The bartender standing across the bar from us was gregarious, sixty or so years old, his thinning black-and-gray hair slicked back, barbershop clean. He didn't care if a woman was in here or not. We had been talking with him for half an hour, drinking beer and exchanging news. We told him where we had been, a couple of weeks in the mountains camping out beyond the roads and some time at Paquimé.

With both hands spread on the bar, Gilberto the bartender asked what we were looking for out there in the barrancas.

I told him we were travelers interested in the wilderness.

"La tierra salvaje," I said. The wildland.

Gilberto tilted his head when I said this, unsure what I meant.

My Spanish was not the finest. How to explain? *El campo* might have served me better, but that is a place for vacations, a bucolic countryside of picnic blankets and Sunday fishing. We were looking for the fray in the land, some hidden, interior place, wild country. I told him we walk in the deep land, *en tierra adentro.* In Spanish there is no word for the wilderness I was trying to describe. There is not one in English either.

Gilberto nodded and asked if we were looking for treasure, for Sierra Madre gold.

We all laughed, a little uneasy.

Darin, sitting on the stool to my left, put a cigarette in his mouth and leaned forward to meet Gilberto's outstretched lighter.

Darin said, "Estamos buscando a muertos."

"¿Los muertos?" Gilberto asked, his face suddenly reserved.

"Estamos interesados en ruinas, la prehistoria," Darin said, taking an appreciative drag off his cigarette. "Somos estudiantes de la arqueología."

Gilberto studied us for a moment. He seemed unsure of us all of a sudden, knowing that we were students of archaeology, that we were looking for the dead. He slipped the lighter back under the bar. He had a large brass belt buckle emblazoned with a leaping buck. He was a hunter. He would have known about the countryside, the farther places.

"La gente se ponen nerviosa cuando se trata de arqueólogos," Gilberto said. "Piensan que el gobierno podriá confiscar su tierra."

People are nervous about archaeology here, fearing the government might confiscate their land for its pre-Columbian value.

I nodded. Land ownership can be tenuous in Mexico.

Eugene, brooding to my right, laughed darkly as he swiveled his beer bottle between his fingers.

"No somos arqueólogos," Eugene said. We are not archaeologists.

Eugene looked down the line of us and asked, "How do you say in Spanish that we're just glorified vagabonds?"

Regan explained that these two were students and she and I were their instructors for a semester of field studies. But more so we were friends, traveling companions.

"Somos personas cuidadosas," Regan said, telling Gilberto that we were careful people. Her voice was calm, a tone asking him please not to judge us for our boldness, or for the broken, inarticulate nature of our Spanish.

She said, "Entendemos que estos lugares son muy delicados, muy personales. Cómo se dice, sensitive?"

She was telling him we understand the fragility of these archaeological sites, that we are as careful as we can be.

Gilberto nodded slowly. "Frágil," he said.

"Sí, frágil," Regan said.

The bar was quiet for a moment.

Gilberto smiled and said, "La gente de aquí los llama Anasazi."

I sat forward over my beer. "Anasazi?" I asked. People here call them Anasazi?

Gilberto laughed. "La palabra es incorrecta, por supuesto. La gente aquí es ignorante de arqueología."

I was impressed that he knew enough about archaeology to know that *Anasazi* is a displaced word down here—as he said, used out of ignorance. I figured the locals must have picked up the word from the north, maybe from other travelers looking for cliff dwellings. All the same, it startled me to hear *Anasazi* used this far south.

Gilberto explained that someone in town kept a so-called Anasazi mummy in a glass case and other artifacts from the mountains, ceramic vessels and woven textiles. He tipped his head in the direction, down the road. He said the idea offended him, stealing this mummy from the mountains and then charging people to see it.

"Disgustante," he said. "Pero usted puede pagar para verlos."

Regan told Gilberto that we might be interested in seeing these remains, just for a sense of what had been found in the area, but that we were mainly interested in sites farther back in the sierra.

Regan spoke with certainty and with delicate words, no bragging or exaggeration. She told Gilberto that we had no illusions about our travels. We were setting a path into delicate places, leaving boot prints. But we were careful, our camps subtle.

"Nos movemos con cuidado," she allowed. We move with care.

Gilberto considered us for a moment and then said he wanted to show us something. He excused himself and slipped out from behind the bar. He called back to one of the men at the pool table. Gilberto's nephew-in-law came to take over bar duty while Gilberto left through the front door.

"Maybe we shouldn't have told him all that," Eugene said down into his beer. "Now we're going to have Federales in here asking for papers."

"I think he has something to show us," Regan said optimistically.

The nephew-in-law stood back from the bar. He had heard everything that was said.

Ten minutes later Gilberto returned. He carried a worn manila envelope. He lit a cigarette, then pulled out a stack of photographs and laid them in front of us. The photo on top, the size of an index card, was of Gilberto with a dead white-tailed deer. It was a buck, three points to each antler, and in the photo Gilberto held the head upright, the animal's eyes glazed without focus. We all nodded approvingly. A good kill.

"Le di en el corazón," he said, pointing his cigarette at the deer, telling us it was a shot to the heart.

Gilberto slipped this photograph off the top and revealed another of the same deer.

He drew a breath off his cigarette and explained that he had gone hunting in the barrancas. The deer were in canyons, barrancas, that run through the Sierra Madre. He had traveled a long way on foot, following deer tracks into difficult places. The hunting is good back where people never go, he said. Soon he had found himself in a huge canyon. He had hunted through fallen trees and boulders big as...what? Bigger than this bar certainly.

Gilberto turned to the next black-and-white photograph. It was of a cliff dwelling, a bank of walls and dark roof beams tucked back into a cave. I had not seen anything of such stature since just below the Mogollon Rim in east-central Arizona. There was no need for reserve between us now. We leaned in from our bar stools as if Gilberto had just opened a treasure chest.

The site he had photographed had thirty rooms, maybe more. It was three stories tall at the back, where adobe walls snuggled against a soot-blackened cave ceiling. T-shaped doors were strung across the buildings like flags.

The next photograph showed globes of buildings bulging outward. This was a different site from the first he had shown us.

How many cliff dwellings are there? I asked.

Gilberto said they are everywhere.

We spread the photographs across the bar, each of us falling into details of wall construction, ceilings and doors and windows. The round olla-like buildings were like nothing else in the Southwest, some of their fat bellies nearly two stories tall, huge mushrooms.

Gilberto arranged five shot glasses along the bar. He pulled out a bottle of sotol he said was bootleg and poured each of us a drink. *Gratis.*

I looked at Gilberto, who was smiling. I lifted the shot glass to him and then touched it to my lips.

The sotol tasted smoky and as hard as gasoline. It had been distilled in the radiator of a junked car. Gilberto said it was the drink of the mountains. Down in the desert they drink tequila from the heart of the agave plant. In the highlands the traditional drink is sotol, distilled from the heart of the sotol plant, a saw-bladed yucca.

Gilberto was proud of his land. He had spent his life on the slope of the sierra. But never before had he seen such a thing as these cliff dwellings. If we wanted to know, he said, he would tell us where they were.

Yes, we wanted to know. He explained that a maze of dirt roads leads into the sierra, until finally there is only one road, and only a strong vehicle will be able to drive it. There are washouts, rockslides. In places it is hardly a road. There is a rancher named José who lives there and comes out on occasion for supplies on a mule, or sometimes in a vehicle lent by in-laws. José is a lonely, strange man, but very hospitable. In the barrancas beyond where José runs cattle are the cliff dwellings.

Gilberto placed his fist against his heart.

"Es un lugar importante en mi vida," he said.

I told him we would be careful, that we understood this was an important place to him. He poured another round.

We left the bar that night and stepped into the cool night exhilarated. The air smelled of freshly cut pine and diesel smoke. Laughing at our luck, having encountered Gilberto on a whim, we walked down the street of squat stores and houses. We had received the key to the Sierra Madre, and we teetered with a little drunkenness, amazed at our good fortune. A car rolled by packed with teenage boys.

One leaned out the window and shouted in painfully enunciated English, "How are you doing?"

"Bueno, graciás!" I shouted back.

The car erupted with laughter.

After them a flatbed came down out of the mountains. A single tree was secured to it, a massive trunk of a Mexican pine held down with chains. I was surprised to see a tree of such size, old growth still coming out of the Sierra Madre. The four of us stopped to watch it pass.

We got into our two trucks and drove into the forest outside town, where we slept beneath the pines.

. . .

Blades of firelight slipped through gaps in the rancher's woodstove. It was the next night, and we sat in the brass glow of a single oil lamp. Shadows of table legs and chairs flickered around us like busy cats. We had driven to José's home earlier that day, hours of dust and sickening bangs of rock on the undercarriages of our trucks, low gear most of the way at one or two miles per hour. As Gilberto had warned, in places it was hardly a road. We had driven until our nerves were wired into tight bundles of concentration. Now we unwound in the evening, invited into José's small house. Outside, the wind lapped and murmured at the stovepipe.

José stood and walked to the woodstove to take the kettle off. He poured hot water into five metal cups and slid a clean spoon with a jar of instant coffee across his faded, pink-flowered tablecloth.

Mes tras mes, he said. Month after month he is alone with no woman.

He complained that he had to make his own tortillas, wash his own clothes, kill and cook his own food. A wild turkey hung from a wooden peg behind us, freshly taken with a shotgun. It looked like a dark headdress on the wall.

Three hundred cattle, José said, on half a million acres, and no one else but him, a mule, and a couple of dogs.

"Muy solo," José said.

José looked to be about sixty years old, but he could have been much younger, his face worn beyond his years, his gray hair combed back. He wore a clean T-shirt under a button-down shirt. He sat on a stool made out of a tree stump, his hands laid flat on the knees of his faded jeans, his leather cowboy boots planted firmly on the floor. He had given us the only four chairs he had, three made of rickety wood and one an aluminum beach chair.

For guests, he said.

His Spanish was quick and blurred. We picked our way through his words, while he listened in turn to our slow hunt for adequate grammar. We had gotten the message across that we had been directed by Gilberto the bartender, that we were looking for cliff dwellings. José considered Gilberto to be overly sentimental.

"No es como él dice," José said. It is not as Gilberto says.

José told us that the canyons below here were *feo,* ugly. They were all cliffs and caves and forests too thick and steep for cattle. Terrible country. Shaking his head, leaning toward the table and then back away from it, José sputtered at us with a long description of why he did not like the cliff dwellings, speaking a language I barely recognized, the rapid dialect of a hermit. Cliff dwellings made him uneasy, houses of the dead, human bones eroding from the ground. He had no idea the age of the dwellings. A hundred years, a thousand years, what is the difference? He tried to stay away from such places, passing down there only to track lost cows. He had not so much fear as contempt for these places.

Bárbaros, he called these people, whoever they were. Barbarians. *Gente salvaje.* Wild people in the cliffs. Proper people live in houses. Why were they hiding?

"Y su cerámica," José said with disgust, stumbling out his words as if in disbelief. "To'o esta roto, nada entero!" All their pots were broken, nothing left intact!

He took this to mean their ceramics were cheaply made, the work of primitives. He had no idea how old these places and their artifacts were. When I told him the pots were probably five, six hundred years old and that they were broken from age, and not from poor manufacture, he said it hardly mattered. Ancient, new, what is the difference? They are dead.

"Es un malo lugar," José said. "Esta lleno de fantasmas." It is a bad place full of ghosts.

I quickly said, "Estamos interesados en el pasado."

José stopped and licked his lips. *El pasado,* the past, who has time for the past? He said he was lonely living with ghosts.

Then he smiled.

"Ahora, ustedes deben comer," he said, relaxing his shoulders, gesturing to the food he had set on the table, tortillas made with his own hands and yellow, rancid margarine.

We were hungry. We did not want to eat all of his food, though. We had brought plenty of our own. But we had already shown him our cans of beans, our bags of rice, and he had looked at them as if they were from another planet. He insisted that we eat his food, beans and tortillas, his ingredients hauled in a mule's saddlebags.

We smiled, thanked him for his hospitality, and reached out to tear off pieces of the tortillas. They tasted fresh, made today, powdered with burns and wood smoke. We ate quietly, with approving smiles and nods. The wind hemmed among the pines outside, and José paused, hearing it. The flame in the oil lamp shifted just slightly with the change in pressure. Shadows ducked through the room.

The Eye of Tlaloc

SIERRA MADRE OCCIDENTAL

I had been in jungle before, and this northern reach of the Sierra Madre was not jungle. The terrain we traveled through with a couple of weeks of supplies on our backs was mountainous, broken apart by fathomless barrancas, no trails except those left by animals. Brushy forests of Mexican pines, walnut trees, and big-toothed maples grew along the drainages where we set camp amid fallen boulders and hoops of wild grape. It was not jungle, but it was also not the Southwest that I knew—far too overgrown and pitched with shade. Unfamiliar birdcalls spilled from the canopy like silver coins. We were walking the far end of a mountain chain that starts near Mexico City almost nine hundred miles away and reaches nearly to the Arizona border, an unbroken line from tropics to desert. The heart of Mesoamerica lay to the southeast, and to the north was the Pueblo core of the Southwest. I felt as if I were on a bridge balanced between geographies and cultures.

Just as Gilberto had said, cliff dwellings were everywhere in this reach of barrancas. Even his photographs had not prepared me for the number of ancient settlements packed into nearly every cave we spotted—biscuit-colored adobe walls notched with black windows and conspicuous T-shaped doorways. The number of T shapes was startling, crowds of them of many sizes and a variety of dedicated forms, some nearly trapezoidal at their tops, some keyhole-shaped, and some perfectly square. We found broad T shapes through which two people could pass at once, and others as small as dollhouse doors, little niches barely large enough to fit a hand into.

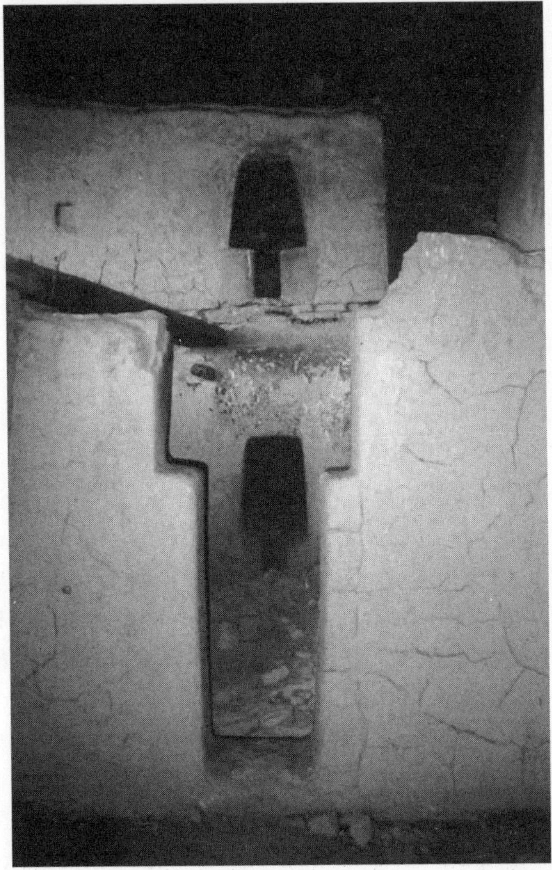

Successive T-shaped doorways inside a Sierra Madre cliff dwelling (the ceiling has collapsed between the first and second stories). REGAN CHOI

We climbed to these towering cliff dwellings and walked awestruck through their rooms and hallways. Some buildings were three stories tall, cave ceilings black with wood smoke. With frayed parts of baskets on the floors and painted bits of murals peeling off the walls, they appeared not to have been touched for centuries. We felt as if we had walked into a lost Mesa Verde. Not for an instant were we unaware of the antiquity surrounding us. As we climbed through thickets of poison ivy, as we cooked meals night after night, as we gathered water from springs, there was a constant sense that we were in someone else's house. Even when we got drunk one night on a bottle of Gilberto's bootleg sotol we had packed, two of us took off in the dark and found a ruin. Walking shoulder to shoulder through its rooms in the beam of a single headlamp, we were suddenly sober, hearing nothing but our own breath in these gaunt quarters.

After only eight days of moving through the barrancas, we counted forty-four cliff dwellings—enough rooms to have housed a few thousand people, a small city of interconnected sites. The broken pottery we picked off the dusty, cobwebby floors seemed to date to late in the fourteenth century, perhaps into the fifteenth, making these sites contemporary with Pueblo migrants swelling south from Arizona, those who did not return to the Colorado Plateau.

. . .

One morning I wandered up a canyon slope and found a cave set back in the face of a cliff. There, as expected, was yet another cliff dwelling. We were finding them everywhere like hornets' nests, compact and elaborate villages set high in the barrancas. Third-story chambers receded into the cave's frail dungeon light. My hands were dark with soil from climbing up through the forest. I looked as if I had been grubbing for potatoes. I did not wipe my hands on my pants when I reached the front of this dwelling. I walked slowly into it, stepping around broken pottery, pieces of Babicora Polychrome with red and black designs on a cream-colored background, and sherds of Ramos Black pottery as glossy as opals—both styles present during the height of Paquimé. There were also countless corncobs on the floor, evidence of massive agriculture. Polished tubs of grinding stones were set out, each filled with dry, blown leaves. Among these metates I saw the fragile shoulder of a discarded basket. People here had been proficient weavers, that was for sure. Almost every cliff dwelling we had seen had mats with diamond-twilled weaves or pieces of cotton fabric made on an anchored loom. In one place sixteen feet of finely braided rope was coiled in a corner. These residents were highly skilled craftspeople. Everything they did seemed touched with excess consideration. Even the larger timbers used for posts and beams had been planed flat and smooth with stone tools, as if taken from a modern lumberyard.

Out front, at the overlooking balcony of the cave, stood a row of bulbous chambers, adobe moons floating at the edge of the dwelling. These I had seen in Gilberto's photographs, plump chambers I imagined were used for storing grain, access allowed from above through circular door stones inserted into conical roofs. Their insides were as smooth as porcelain, brushed with a fine clay plaster.

There was no sound other than my light footfalls and birds squabbling in the forest below as I passed through these unusual structures. An adobe stairway led to a second story, and I followed it, stepping past tusks of fallen ceiling timbers. I hardly wanted to breathe, not wishing to break the stillness. T-shaped portals surrounded me as I ascended the stairs, showing the way into a lair of farther rooms beneath rafts of roof beams. When I reached the top of the stairs, I saw on the floor shreds of woven textiles and small wooden tools wrapped in dried animal sinew. It looked as though a closet had been turned upside down. A third-story room had caved in, its contents strewn across this second-story floor. Never had I seen so many pieces of artifacts. Indeed, it seemed that the people had stepped out one day and simply not returned, their belongings decaying over time. As I continued, it sounded as if I was walking on gravel and broken glass even though I took slow, gingerly steps around the plentiful corncobs and shattered pottery.

In front of me was a room with a circular floor. There was not much left of it besides the floor plan itself, its walls mostly fallen over. What walls remained were made of jacal, a lattice of adobe and wood unlike anything we had seen among these cliff dwellings, more like structures I knew from Kayenta, in northeast Arizona. I walked inside this open, round room. It was the first circular structure I had encountered in the barrancas (different from the grain storage rooms, which were mushroom-shaped and stood on round pedestals). The room reminded me of a kiva, or at least some architectural memory of one.

If it was a kiva, I thought, there would be a sipapu. Just off the circle's centerpoint I knelt and swept away wood slivers and mortar crumbs. There I found a small adobe pit no larger than a breakfast bowl, exactly where you would see a sipapu.

These were the people I had been following, I thought, a projection of Anasazi, the next step south of Salado. Something started at Chaco might have reached the Sierra Madre—the Lost Others of the Zuni, Hopi exiles, ancestors of the Pueblo. Kiva builders. People of the T. I seem to have found a kiva, a blueprint of a ceremonial structure carried down from the Colorado Plateau. I brushed debris back over the dish—this possible sipapu—stood up, and moved on.

. . .

I took my time in this ruin. Walls were painted with designs. Geometric images were etched into the plaster. I passed into one of the second-story rooms, where I walked across an expanse of corncobs and snippets of threadbare basketry. Against the back wall I found a shaft aiming straight down, its walls made with a sandpaper plaster different from that of any other room. I peered into the hatchway leading down this shaft and saw it was much deeper than I expected. I pulled out my headlamp and shined a light inside, maybe five, six feet down. At the bottom, faded under centuries of dust, was a collection of bones. The bones were still in place, articulated, outlining a body.

It was a bird, a fairly large one, with its clavicle hitched up against its breastbone. The pronged feet were barely visible, relatively flat, not sharp or curved as one would expect from a raptor or an owl that might have become lost in these rooms. I passed my faint beam from one bone to the next, deciding this had to be the remains of a turkey.

It must have fallen in, I thought. Domestic turkeys had no doubt been kept in this cliff dwelling once upon a time. Turkeys had been raised at nearly every major pre-Columbian settlement across the Southwest. Aviculturists at Paquimé had raised thousands of these plump ground birds, rearing them for their feathers, some for their meat, and many for what appears to have been sacrificial burials. These burials are curious, most of them consisting of decapitated birds. Hundreds of headless turkeys were found interred along with ceramic hand drums beneath a single plaza in Paquimé's House of the Dead. There is little doubt that these headless turkeys were part of some important and widespread ritual. It has been imagined that at Paquimé turkeys were decapitated for Tlaloc, a deity presiding over rain and drought. The hand drums may have been pounded to imitate the sound of thunder, a reminder of precipitation.

Headless turkeys have been found at sites all along the north-south route I was tracing from the Colorado Plateau to Mexico. They have been excavated from kivas at Chaco Canyon—very specifically placed between the ventilator shafts and the deflector stones, where human bodies were sometimes interred. Archaeologist Susan Ryan had uncovered turkeys without heads in her Colorado excavation on the Great Sage Plain.

The bird I saw inside this chamber had arrived long after the place was abandoned, though. It was not a cultural artifact. It couldn't be, the dust too thin on its bones. I thought it to be a dervish, a wild bird that had become disoriented inside the dwelling decades or centuries ago.

I sent my light along the train of its vertebrae, where the neck came to a sudden end. Its head was missing.

"That's strange," I said, almost a whisper.

I ran my light around the inside of the adobe hollow, thinking I would find a bird skull tumbled off to the side, but it was not there. I felt suddenly cold, aware that the head of this turkey had been intentionally removed.

Farther south a piece of Mayan artwork depicts a man playing a hand drum, which looks like those found buried with decapitated turkeys at Paquimé. The man seems to be presiding over a human sacrifice, in front of him a bowl containing the head of a turkey.

Among indigenous Mesoamerican cultures still active today, turkey heads are severed and offered to deities who control the waters within the earth. Among the modern Maya and the more northerly Nahua, the turkey represents Tlaloc, living in what is called the House of Rain, an underground realm full of water. The Mixe continue to sacrifice turkeys to mountain spirits, decapitating the birds at hidden springs, in caves, and on mountaintops. The Zapotec behead turkeys with stone knives, and numerous cultures sprinkle the blood of decapitated turkeys on their croplands to invite water. In the Southwest among the modern Pueblo people, turkey feathers represent rain. For the Hopi these elaborately colored and banded feathers are suggestive of the underworld, and the Zuni still place them in the fields where corn is planted. But there was no one currently living in the northern Sierra Madre to leave a decapitated turkey in this ruin. Was there?

This cliff dwelling had obviously been abandoned since at least the fifteenth century. I thought, Someone must have come back. A ritual was held by people who remembered old rites. A turkey was brought to this room and decapitated, a call to Tlaloc, a plea to an ancient water god.

I lifted my head from the chamber and turned off my light. For as long as I could, I stood without breathing, mouth barely open, eyes tracing across each shocking, remarkable shape.

Is that you? I asked silently. Are you the ones I have been tracking all this way?

. . .

There is a lonely history of explorers who have come into the north end of the Sierra Madre looking for cliff dwellings. Carl Lumholtz arrived in 1890 and reported on mysterious adobe villages deep in the wilderness of northern Mexico. Later, in the 1950s, Robert Lister came from the University of Colorado and dug out a number of cliff dwellings, proclaiming that the people who had lived here were part of a cultural complex that extended clear up to the Mogollon Rim. The next in this succession of archaeologists is Beth Bagwell, from the University of New Mexico, an unassuming woman who moves comfortably through the outback of rural Mexico.

Bagwell once showed me photographs taken during her doctoral field research in the Sierra Madre, shots of her truck mired midstream on a valley floor, muddy water up to the doors, and of multistory cliff dwellings snug inside their caves nearby. She wanted me to understand the physical sense of isolation she enjoyed, as well as the geographic rigor of sites she mapped and excavated with a small crew of Mexican assistants. Though the cliff dwellings Bagwell documented lie in another part of the Sierra Madre, a few hundred miles from the ones I was visiting, they were nearly identical.

balance returned, and I came into the next room, where I crouched in the center. Daylight tapered into a thin gloom.

I noticed that time had changed. It felt slower, my every motion given weight. Perhaps the shape of the doorways had done this, the first one forcing me to pause, the second damming my movement into a deliberate pace. The T required a changed stride, like the bow made before stepping onto the mat of a martial arts dojo.

I pulled a small red lamp from the pocket of my cargo pants and turned it on, sending a faint beam across the ground. Red was a good color for a place like this, allowing my natural vision to see beyond the burning circle that would be left by a white light. Part of a basketry dish lay like a dirty moon on the floor, its decayed edges revealing stranded lines of warp and weft. I did not touch it.

The next door slowed my movements even further, and I passed through feeling as if I were no longer touching the ground. I trained my light around me, finding the positions of ceiling beams and crumbled matter on the floor, bones and pottery and corncobs. At the back of the room the wooden ceiling ended, giving way to the cave's dark bedrock eaves. I kept walking to where I saw no more corncobs on the floor, no scraps of artifacts, only a fine, dry dust dimpled with mouse prints. The cave in the back of the dwelling had been left absolutely empty.

We had noticed this same phenomenon at a number of other cliff dwellings in the barrancas. In fact, Spruce Tree House up in Colorado had the same feature, an area nearly the size of a dance floor in the back of a Mesa Verde cave, accessed through a succession of T-shaped entries. It, too, had been found empty.

This stone vault funneled down until my head was cramped into my shoulders. I came to a shuffling crouch and shined the light up at a low, raw ceiling, where I saw daddy longlegs hanging by the hundreds, black masses of them, their legs spindling in every direction. They were vibrating all across the ceiling, rising and falling in a syncopated mass, troubled perhaps by the presence of my breath. I ducked my head beneath them, an inch of clearance all that remained. I set my hand down for balance and my open palm printed itself into dust as fine as bone powder. I thought my tracks might remain in this dry dust for the next thousand years, like the strange boot prints of men on the moon.

Then I heard something unexpected. A drop of water struck a pool ahead of me. I lifted my head and peered into the darkness.

. . .

I once spoke with a Hopi man who told me that the T-shaped portals I had been tracking represented underground mountains filled with water. I was sitting at the breakfast table in his home, his shelves decorated with old wooden katsinas: small effigies of dancers set on shelves like votive candles. They were representations of rain gods, painted and feathered spirits born from out of the clouds. Katsinas are very similar to Mesoamerican Tlaloques, which are the rain god Tlaloc's children and family: feathered, long-haired spirits said to brew rain, to pound on drums and create thunder. Among Mesoamerican tribes Tlaloques are often associated with certain mountain ranges, much like the Pueblo katsinas of the Southwest, who dwell in the clouds that gather around isolated mountains.

I was drinking tea, the Hopi man coffee. "You're interested in the T shape," he said.

I said yes and then lifted my tea and blew across it.

"I believe the T shape is a mountain underground," he said, and then was quiet, his face relaxed but thoughtful.

I did not want to ask an inappropriate question and halt the conversation, so I took a sip of my tea and set it back on the table. We both peered out the window, watching ripples of people moving outside. Children were on their way to school.

"How so?" I asked.

"I think it symbolizes an inverted mountain, a mirror of what is aboveground," he continued. "The mountain aboveground gathers clouds and rain. The mountain below draws rainfall into an underground lake."

The process he described sounded familiar. I had spent time studying the actions of rain and water in the Southwest, documenting stream flows and rates of groundwater recharge, patterns of rainfall and snowmelt. Mountains are where storms collect, where they unload the bulk of their moisture. That moisture then enters the ground and fills water tables and aquifers. The clockwork mechanisms of this cycle are made especially clear in an arid region like the Southwest, where every nod and turn of climate broadcasts itself through the ground, and through years, even generations. There are metaphorical mountains underground that mirror the tangible ones aboveground, bodies of water within the earth fed by precipitation on peaks scattered across the Southwest.

"It's the hydrological cycle," I said with a tone of realization. "A mountain aboveground sending water into a mountain below-ground."

The Hopi man nodded slightly.

Of course, I thought, pre-Columbian people knew the hydrological cycle, the way in which water transfers from the atmosphere to the ground and back. Living in the Southwest for thousands of years, people would have been keenly aware of the rhythmic relationship between precipitation and spring flows. They would have known how many years of good rain it would take to fill an underground lake, an aquifer, able to predict chances of survival and calculate how soon a migration might need to begin.

The Hopi man said, "The shape of the T is a mountain upside down. Its stem leads into the underworld where there is water."

Mythology and science tell the same story. Caves lead toward mysterious pools from which people are said to have emerged: the Tewas' *p'okwi koji,* the Hopi's sipapu. A religion is centered on the mechanics of water. Even modern hydrologists cannot adequately explain the direct correlation between climate shifts and water table fluctuations. Sitting at the man's wooden table, I thought, Perhaps they cannot explain it because they have not had to live and die by it for thousands of years. They are unaware that Tlaloc is breathing.

. . .

In this cave hidden behind the cliff dwelling, I remained absolutely still, listening again for the sound of water. It came, a second tone popping out of the dark, a pearl of water striking a pool.

As I listened longer, I heard two different drips falling from about the same height, landing in different depths of water, their tones barely off from each other. I moved ahead, and at the farthest corner of the cave my red light fell onto a dish of crystalline water. I crawled the last couple of feet to the edge of the basin. Constructed by hand, it was a bowl made of adobe sunken into the ground. Every ten seconds or so a new drop fell into the pool, followed shortly by the next. With each drip, fans of shadows arced and dissipated under my red light.

A spring was coming out of the rock. Two points of water budded from the ceiling, letting their drops go at a measured pace. I looked into the water. Small, clean stones rested inside. This was much like a cave in one of the Sky Island mountains in southeast Arizona, where in total darkness, through stalactites and swollen, lustrous walls, there is a natural dish of limestone standing like a baptismal font. All around it were once placed ancient beads, precious stones, coins of broken pottery, and seashells. All over the Southwest, caves are loaded with such offerings, springs decorated with feathers and prayer sticks. These places where water emerges from stone, dark holes into the underworld, are profoundly sacred.

As far as I could see, no one had left offerings at this water hole within the cliff dwelling, the entire back of a cave cleared out to present only a bowl filled with spring water. My breath trembled in the small space. I could hardly move, one knee on the ground, one palm flat and holding me still. I had passed through the smaller and smaller eyes of Tlaloc into a mythical lake inside the mountain.

Falling on each other's heels, these drips made a persistent rhythm. It was the cadence of cultural history in the Southwest, the ceaseless fluctuations of underground water slowly responding to precipitation. Drips patter quickly during wet years and shrink back to a bored tapping in times of drought. This is the timepiece that told people when they could stay and when it was time to leave, ticking through the centuries in the back of this cave.

Tlaloc is hydrology, I thought. The deity is a metaphor for the full hydrological cycle of moisture, ice, rain, snow, dew, and fog; pooling, draining, and evaporating. It is the movement of water, the lifeblood of the Southwest, a meter that any civilization here must obey.

I turned off my light in the back of the cave. I closed my eyes. It felt as if all these centuries, these thousands of years, were contained here, their processions playing out again and again as drips strummed the pool beside me. The same routes are traveled repeatedly, the same meridians followed across horizons, over hundreds of years. Anasazi, I thought, was never a people. It was a rhythm, a form of motion stirred up from the land. People merely fell into step.

Putting Back the Bones

FARTHER INTO THE SIERRA MADRE

Eugene was somewhere behind me. We had become separated while moving through steep sluices of scrub oak and poison ivy. I listened for him, for cracking branches and sought footholds. He was not there.

I climbed down wedges of boulders, looking off my shoulder a thousand feet into the forest floor below. I was climbing down into a canyon. Steeples rose all around me, trunks of toast-colored stone tapering into the sky.

With every handhold swept clean, tested with a knock of my fist and then weighted with my body, I dropped notch by notch. Tree branches poked me in the back, some so stiff they would not budge, and I had to wrap myself around them in order to pass by. I was looking for cliff dwellings, seeing what people had tucked into recesses. If I fell, I would crash through these nets of oak brush and would probably be caught, snagged by roots and tree limbs. If I was not caught, I would fall a good few hundred feet. I paid close attention, hot breath burrowing into my outstretched arm as I lowered myself.

I kicked at a toehold, checking to see if it was solid. It was not. A rock fell through oak branches. Dry leaves, shocked loose, showered down the corridor. I waited for the rock to finish as it thumped off ledges. It dragged my mind hundreds of feet down as the sound dwindled into the distance.

When I heard nothing else, I kicked again and found the next good hold. Oak branches made steady ladder rungs. My body stretched and contracted, fitting into whatever space was given. Aware of the length of my bones and muscles, I spidered down this passage, picking up a rhythm. I poured through holes in the brush and rock, nearly falling but with a touch of restraint, weighted, sliding down a pole of gravity.

The slope let me off on a ledge, and the ledge led me to another canyon, this one more gentle than the last. I followed it, not knowing whether Eugene was close behind or had taken another route, in which case we would not see each other until nightfall back at camp. I walked on dry leaves until I reached a concealed cave. Inside was a cliff dwelling. I walked into the cave, where I passed from a wash of daylight into shadow, entering a field of adobe rooms rambling off into the dark, one-story blocks arranged facing each other. It was a husky village with a low bedrock ceiling.

One of the large, round storage chambers I had come to know among these cliff dwellings had toppled on its side. It looked as if it had been pushed over, broken open like a ceramic piggy bank. Many of the olla-like chambers we had seen were damaged, usually by a single hole punched through the side, where it appears people broke into them long ago. I walked into the chamber's debris, then dropped to my haunches, finding a small shaft of wood in the dust. I picked it up.

Two circles were burned into the shaft, each tapped by a notch. A third circle was broken off at the tip. This was a fireboard. A wood drill had been spun against it, twirled back and forth until the wood grew hot enough to sprout an ember. The artifact was hardly longer than my index finger. I turned it slowly, feeling with a fingertip down into the smooth drill holes. It was a very human artifact, capable of starting a fire with nearly the efficiency of a match.

Would I have been surprised if I had walked into this cave and seen a man crouched over a hand drill, his back curved toward me as he worked swiftly down the wooden shaft? I would have stepped quietly through the half-light, he so intent that he did not notice as I came around and crouched nearby, smelling the soft burn in the air as he produced an ember. Once his fire began, snapping up through

A Sierra Madre cliff dwelling with a round, olla-like room in the foreground, probably a grain storage chamber. CRAIG CHILDS

dry twigs, I would have waited for him to look up, for our eyes to meet, centuries passing easily between us.

I set the fireboard back into the dust, placing it on edge the way I had found it. It seemed important not to alter the lay of objects in these dwellings. Everything had its place, as if each artifact were a dial tuned precisely by hundreds of years. I made my steps as slow and methodical as possible, boot soles planted on the dimly illuminated floor among broken pottery and a litter of corncobs.

A woven mat lay on the ground, rumpled as though someone had set it aside that morning, leaving behind an unmade bed. Partially unrolled in the dust, it was about four feet long, some of its edges chewed by decay. Its diamond twill weave was greasy and russet-colored. I crouched beside it and almost touched it with my fingers, but then thought, Burial blanket.

I looked through the vaporous light of the cave and saw a long bolt of a human leg bone nearby, a femur. It lay haphazardly like a discarded piece of firewood. Not far from it was a second femur, its ball standing out like a small white globe. A pothunter had found this place before me. He had dug up a burial and shaken a skeleton out of its woven mat right here. Perhaps he was the one who had pushed over the big olla to get inside.

I backed off from the mat and stood, turning slowly. Now that my eyes had adjusted to the light, I saw part of an arm and then the vacant mask of a pelvis. Narrow at the sockets, the pelvis belonged to a man. I realized that the reddish color in the mat's weave was flesh and organs turned to oily dust.

I took another step, feeling the softness of the ground. No one had been here since the robbery, maybe as long as a hundred years ago, judging by the accumulation of dust. Human bones stuck up from the ground like the ribs of a shipwreck dissolving at the bottom of the sea. Little clubs of hand and toe bones were almost out of sight.

The femurs, I noticed, were as long as my own, belonging to someone who may have stood a few inches short of six feet tall. That was unusually lofty for people of the prehistoric Southwest, who tended to stand at less than five feet. I recalled a tomb unearthed at Chaco where a perceptibly taller group of people than most was discovered. Those Chacoan burials have implied a specific ethnicity to some researchers, a genetically distinct family or group living among many others at the time. Perhaps the bones scattered around me also belonged to a certain people, a clan of significant stature in fifteenth-century northwest Mexico. If I could see the bones of more people from here, I could compare them and move toward an academic conclusion, but I wished to see no more bones.

I walked on into rooms where bats stirred through the dim, gray light. Brief whisks of sound and wings circled and darted around me, quickly escaping through doors and windows into other rooms. I continued along adobe alleyways until they opened into a vacant space in the back of the cave. There was no water in this spacious chamber, just a white stain of evaporated minerals where water had once dripped out of the ceiling, a memory of wetter years. I stopped and waited for my eyes to accommodate the withered light. The floor was smooth with chalky dust, no sign of artifacts anywhere. A hole had been dug, a crypt the size of an adult curled into a fetal position.

I stepped to its edge and looked in. The hole was empty, its sides slumped. The pothunter had known exactly where to go, digging for grave goods.

So they buried their dead back here, I thought. This space was a graveyard. It made sense. The home of Tlaloc, a place known as Tlalocan, House of Rain, is where the dead go, a watery paradise within a mountain. Maybe that is what such open chambers behind the cliff dwellings symbolized, the legendary place of the dead.

I studied the way the pothunter had dug, the slice of his shovel still visible. He had taken everything of value, leaving a scattered skeleton and its burial mat. A hollow feeling entered my body, standing at the site of a grave robbery.

I walked back out through the pallor, passing rooms and returning to the litter of human bones. Another of the man's arms was visible, and near that the fan of his shoulder blade. His skeleton had been dragged in a burial mat from a grave out to near the cave entrance. The light had been better here to sort the goods. Had this body been finely dressed? I wondered. Was he wearing jewelry, in his hair a bone pin inlaid with turquoise? Had the pothunter found vessels, clay figurines, copper pendants? There was no telling. All that remained were bones and the burial mat.

I walked slowly around what remained of the man, a step for every two breaths. I kept my mind as still as I could, although a ravenous hunger boiled beneath my skin. I had starving eyes, having come here to find a lost world, a sunken civilization. As I cleared my head in the muted light, the hunger faded, revealing itself as a simple question. *Who were you?* I looked around at the castaway bones, recognizing them as similar to my own, a man who had once lived, full of emotion and thought. A father, perhaps, a man who hunted or farmed, a weaver of baskets. A man who bent over with hurt upon the death of a family member or close friend. It was not so long ago that this man had been here spinning fires to life on a fireboard. We have hardly changed in this short time. Tools of stone have been replaced by plastic and metal, but our capacity for imagination, for sensation, has not altered.

I walked more slowly across the gravity of all these bones, taking three breaths for every step, and then five. Then I was still.

I heard a sound beyond the cave. Eugene was crashing through the brush. I listened to his labored approach. In this knotted topography he had somehow come to the same geographic conclusion as I had, exploring up the same cleft in the rock. I was not surprised. He and I were looking for the same thing, hunting for ruins. I turned and walked toward the entrance, where I came almost into the sunlight.

Eugene appeared from stacks of boulders wrapped in vines and thorned plants. He was dragging his fingers through his hair, pulling out twigs and crushed bits of leaves. He let out an animal sound, half frustration and half relief. Just as he got to the mouth of the cave, I said, "Hold on. There are human remains in here."

I knew Eugene did not like places with human remains exposed, where they could be seen. They filled him with dread. He was not entirely comfortable with this business of archaeology.

He stopped the moment I said something, one step into the cave's shadow. He saw the dim shape of my body. He took a half step backward. For a moment he did not move, his eyes tracking the ground until he saw the familiar billiard ball knob at the end of one of the femurs.

Standing not far from him, I said, "Pothunted."

Eugene looked at me and backed farther away, reaching the sun, his body stiff, draped in light. We faced each other like night and day. He swallowed.

"What are you going to do with it?" he asked, peering past me into the cave, where he could see hulks of old adobe quarters.

"With what?" I asked.

"With the skeleton."

I was confused by his question. But then I realized what Eugene meant. I had stumbled onto something. A robbery in progress. With the thinness of time here, it did not matter when the skeleton had been dug up. He wanted to know what kind of gesture I was going to make, because to him it mattered. These things have weight, they stack up.

Eugene stayed safely outside, as close as he wanted to get. Too close even.

"I don't know," I said, dumbfounded, looking at the ground, at the dusty bones scattered about.

I glanced back up at him and asked, "What would you do?"

Eugene shook his head and took another step back. He was regarding me as if I had fallen into a trap.

"I don't know," he said. He turned and walked away from the cave, saying, "I'll see you ahead somewhere. Good luck."

I stayed for some time at this edge of light and dark. The story needed to be put back in the earth, I thought, returned to its lightless depths, to the nameless well that lies beneath the sipapu. There would be, no doubt, orders of violation in my touching these bones. I was a person uninitiated in the meticulous lines of kinship that must have run through the people who lived here. Beyond that, though, a greater tribe exists, a landscape of humanity unbound by time. I owed this one deed to whoever this man had been.

I turned back into the cave. I reached down and picked up one femur from its dust bed, then the other, cradling them in my arms like wooden staffs. They clattered as I went, gathering more bones and carrying them back to the looter's hole. I poured them in. I returned for more—the pelvis, knobs of vertebrae. I picked up fingers and a kneecap, little knuckles in my palm, a shoulder blade carried like a dish upon my fingertips. I did not put flesh back on these bones in my imagination. My thoughts remained as still and delicate as everything else in this cave.

The last item I fetched was the woven mat, about the size of a bath towel. Its weave was ruddy from the body it once held. I carried it in both of my arms through doorways leading to the back of the cave, where I knelt at the looter's hole and tucked the mat around the bones, covering what remained of a prehistoric man.

With the blade of my boot, I shoveled dirt into the hole. I circled, pushing in twigs and wood rat droppings from every side. A choking dust lifted all around me, swirls and arms climbing, weaving up and over my shoulders. When the hole was full, I reached down with a hand and scuffed out my prints.

The Story the Conquistadors Told

AT THE WESTERN FOOT OF THE SIERRA MADRE

It was the fifth of May in a small Mexican town on the desert plain. A marching band of schoolchildren paraded down a dusty street. People in clean shirts and combed hair milled in front of the colorfully decorated tiendas, laughing and clapping as the band marched through: a wheezing pair of clarinets, a trombone blatting into the air, and the rest of the musical assembly one would expect. It was on this day, in 1862, that Mexican troops defeated French forces, sent to take over Mexico, at the Battle of Puebla: Cinco de Mayo.

The four of us had come down from the mountains on a long and broken road, arriving in town unaware of the day or even the month. We would have bathed in stream water had we known a celebration was going on. We would have washed our clothes, then wrung them out and hung them to dry among the maples and pines. We would have taken off our hats and combed our hair. But we showed up like dirty animals walking into a party, startled to be here after weeks of living among ghosts. The air around us flashed with life. A pair of barefoot children ran after a bicycle that was far too large for the little boy pumping its pedals.

A column of young girls marched past in their proper school dresses, a drumbeat leading them along. They were the pride of the town. Some teachers marched alongside, keeping their students in line with stern snaps of their voices. Other teachers smiled and laughed, carried away by the morning's festivities. Then the boys arrived in jeans and button-down shirts, spit-polished shoes scuffing along the street in formation.

We must have looked like strange creatures, the four of us standing close together and alert to every motion around us. We were still of a wilderness mind, trained for the single leaf falling, the bone on the ground. This town was uproarious in our eyes. I saw many faces, the coffee-colored skin of mestizos and the chocolate and burgundy complexions of natives. Three Opata-speaking women wearing bright shawls huddled together, little stumps of people compared to the taller Hispanics.

The high school girls came next in the parade. They were all seriousness and laughter, watching each other, forgetting the steps of the march. I noticed the way the Opata women looked upon these Hispanic girls with cool, reserved eyes.

A hundred years before the *Mayflower* reached the eastern seaboard of North America, the Spanish were here. They arrived in waves of military expeditions and marched across Mexico, a force never imagined in this land. Their horses wore steel chamfrons over their faces with protruding steel spikes as protection in battle. Never before had the natives seen such an animal, much less one bound by armor and ridden by a man with a glimmering shield on his arm, his body layered in breastplates and impenetrable leggings, his fingers like steel claws, his helmet like a scythe. Platoons of foot soldiers followed these horses, carrying wooden matchlock muskets and lances fifteen feet long, their polished steel points the length of a man's forearm. They must have been an awesome and terrifying sight as they crossed northern Mexico.

On their journeys Spanish scribes and generals reported endless indigenous settlements in northern Mexico, adobe pueblos and houses terraced all across the landscape. They wrote of encountering native communities with well-planned streets running between buildings, an attention to detail that impressed even these foreigners who had already waged war in the great southern city-states of the Aztecs and the Maya.

The Spanish conquistadors found elaborate markets in northwest Mexico—slaves being bought and sold, exotic goods arriving from extensive trade networks. In the late sixteenth century, the Spanish explorer Baltazar de Obregón mentioned traveling from "town to town and from province to province," telling of large cultural centers surrounded by satellite villages laid out with surprising and strategic regularity across the country. One expedition moved for eight months through this region and every two or three days came upon yet another central town that had never before witnessed a European face. This land appeared to be widely populated with a highly ordered civilization.

Early journals of Spanish travelers in northern Mexico relate their discovery of indigenous priesthoods and ceremonies of a celestial religion. There were native leaders with great wealth and power, their arms and chests draped with turquoise, their palanquins hoisted on the bare shoulders of young men. Of course, conflict started quickly between natives and the Spanish. Upon key hills and peaks fire signals were said to have erupted, sending word of war for hundreds of miles in all directions. In the battles that ensued, the Spanish were met with standing armies. Thousands of fighters—perhaps as many as ten thousand in one reported confrontation—gathered against them to the pounding of drums, the ringing calls of shell trumpets.

The musket ball was fired in return, singing swiftly through the air, naming the end of an era.

This story of cities and bejeweled leaders in northern Mexico spread far and wide. Returning conquistadors made this region sound like an undiscovered Arabia, where they had taken rest in adobe rooms decorated with fine textiles and turquoise, the women shy and beautiful. Anxious for countless Christian converts, Jesuit missionaries headed in this direction in the seventeenth century, a hundred years after the conquistadors, but they found neither great towns nor beautiful women. The few natives they encountered in this far region seemed sickly and pitiable, their faces weathered, their clothes threadbare if they had any at all. Barbarians, the missionaries called them. There were no standing armies, no pueblos to the horizons, and no fire signals on key hills. Believing that they had been lied to, the Jesuits indefinitely postponed any bid to construct missions in Sonora. The conquistadors' fantastic stories were utterly discredited. It was all, apparently, a farce.

Even twentieth-century archaeologists who briefly surveyed the flanks of the Sierra Madre in northern Mexico concluded that the first Spanish had probably met with only small, scattered populations, feeble resistance to thundering columns of conquistadors clad in leather and steel. Now when archaeologists draw maps of how populations ultimately fared in the prehistoric Southwest, they show a final massing around Hopi in northern Arizona and around Zuni, Acoma, and the upper Rio Grande in northern New Mexico. The Salado and Hohokam regions of central and southern Arizona are left blank, as is southern New Mexico and northern Mexico. But this map appears to be only partly correct. A small number of archaeologists have been looking closer at Sonora, Mexico, and have found surprising signs of late occupation. The tide is beginning to turn away from the Jesuits' story back to what the conquistadors said.

A team of archaeologists in the 1980s went in, using more refined techniques than earlier surveys had employed. This more recent work consisted of grids laid across the central part of the Valley of Sonora on the west side of the Sierra Madre, where the remains of hundreds upon hundreds of previously missed settlements were recorded. This survey team found large towns that had been occupied around the time of the first Spanish contact, and surrounding them were numerous satellite villages. Excavations revealed the foundations of sturdy-walled pueblos, pit-houses, and courtyards. Within a relatively short distance the team recorded the foundations of well over a thousand individual structures at more than two hundred different settlements.

When the survey was complete, William Doolittle, a principal investigator, wrote, "Although the Spaniards on occasion did stretch the truth for various reasons, they appear to have been quite accurate in their reports on conditions in eastern Sonora. The [previous] archaeologists, on the other hand, simply used a survey technique that resulted in their overlooking much important evidence."

This new survey estimated that ninety thousand people were

vel rapidly along trade routes, where it landed in bustling mar-aces. A host of European diseases moved faster than the Span-emselves, spreading to places the Spanish had not even reached. ; been estimated that up to 80 percent, and in some places 90 nt, of local populations perished. Even in Europe the plagues ıot been so devastating. American natives had no immunity to iseases, and towns of a thousand people were reduced to a hun- In a village of one hundred, ten may have lived, and those who ved were branded with images of horror, having witnessed un-inable deaths by bleeding from the skin, coal black corpses left ried all around them. Diseases moved up trade and travel routes ; the Rio Grande and entered the last northern pueblos. Between and 1641, the remaining Pueblo culture in Arizona and New co lost about 70 percent of its population and abandoned half settlements.

ıch devastation would have easily broken the back of this civi-on, leaving exactly what the Jesuit missionaries encountered e seventeenth century when they reached northern Mexico: a ıed people clutching to the land with their last breaths. Towns villages in Sonora had fallen into disrepair and within half a ıry became ruins. After a few hundred years little if anything left on the surface, the wind having sewn the earth back to-ɪr, closing over the wound of humanity.

he way was effectively cleared for Spanish colonization. Even-y, fair-skinned Spanish mixed with what remained of dark and ɪnt races, giving birth to the mestizo culture, to this town of pol-l faces, each a different shade of red, brown, or tan. The old zation has been mostly forgotten now, still widely and wrongly ght to have been nothing but a lie.

. . .

ve watched the morning parade, a man came up to us and intro-d himself as José Tena, a professor at a local agricultural college. nanner was cordial as he shook our hands, speaking Spanish ly for our benefit, asking if we were from the United States.

Sí. Arizona y Colorado," Regan said.

living below the west slope of the northern S the Spanish arrived. High signal stations had in on strategic hilltops, just as the Spanish had re cavations of these signal platforms revealed lay and heat-shattered stones beneath the surface, ev been lit on these highly visible points connecting di is ample evidence of temples and ball courts, as w ing heavily in brightly colored birds, textiles, sh colorful ceramics made around Paquimé and Southwest. Indeed, the maps of the last populatic historic Southwest should now include a huge a foot of the northern Sierra Madre. When peo fifteenth century—when Salado, Hohokam, a fell—this was one of the strongholds that surviv

Highly structured warfare had probably been gion. The first Spanish stepped into a hornet's rived, showing up during a period of massive cu and conflict much like what had been seen earli the Southwest. A temporary settlement the Spa lished in northwest Mexico is said to have been flict with local groups, and the Spanish fell b Madre for protection. The fact that heavily ar who had battled their way north through Mexi into the mountains pursued by a mostly Stone A ment to the military prowess of these natives.

When the explorer Obregón passed through nous Sonoran towns in the late sixteenth centur ies strung up in the streets. Heads, arms, legs, taken in battle between warring indigenous stat like banners from houses and terraces. These w trifle with.

How did the sixteenth-century Spanish find a tegic warfare and highly organized societies ar century Jesuits witness only a ruined people? The a catastrophic in its scope. European plagues that f were terrifyingly efficient. Smallpox was carried

He smiled, nodding, pleased to see us here. He was curious what had brought us. "No vemos muchos Americanos en este pueblo," Professor Tena explained. They did not see many Americans in this town.

Regan said that we had archaeological inquiries in this region. Hearing this, Professor Tena lit up with a broad smile and explained that we would of course be very interested in certain things that he knew.

"Aquí mismo, en este pueblo. Tenemos nuestra propia arqueología," he said, explaining that there was archaeology right here, in this town.

Professor Tena quickly looked around. The parade was about over, the marching band disassembling down the street.

"Tienen que venir conmigo," he said, beckoning us to come with him.

He was almost laughing at his good fortune of meeting people who shared his own zeal for *el pasado*. His hospitality was infectious. We followed him and talked as he walked swiftly. He asked where we were parked and said someone should ride with him. I offered, and he said, "Sí, sí, aquí."

I stepped up into his big Ford pickup and slid onto the clean bench seat. Professor Tena hung an arm over the steering wheel and started the engine. We turned down one dirt street and then another as I pointed to where my truck was parked. He honked and waved at Regan in the driver's seat to follow. As we continued through town, Professor Tena told me of a mammoth skeleton eroding out of a wash not far away, which he would also show me if I wished. I had no reason to doubt him about this. Folsom hunting points from the last ice age had been found north of here. But I was interested in the archaeology of Professor Tena's town, asking him about the site he had mentioned.

Professor Tena flashed his hand in the air over the top of the steering wheel, saying, "Usted verá muy pronto pero todavía falta." I would see very soon, but not yet.

We passed by old houses, buff-colored adobe worn and cracked, brightly painted window frames encasing rippled panes of glass. Some of the houses stood empty, roofs buckled, walls in ruins. Ancient knots of bougainvillea climbed some of the remaining walls, rushes of pink flowers.

We drove out to the edge of town to where fields were freshly plowed, and we pulled over beside a barbed wire fence. Pigs called gruffly from a wooden pen nearby. I could see the full spread of the land from our position, the dark foothills of the Sierra Madre swollen by mirages in the distance, and between here and there a gently knolled terrain faded into blond horizons. Regan drove up behind us and parked.

Professor Tena let down the fence and looked around to see who might be watching. He told us it was not his land, so we should not spend too much time here.

"Miren alrededor," he said, gesturing with his hand for us to have a look around.

I stepped over the dropped lengths of barbed wire and walked into soft soil recently plowed by a horse-drawn blade. I immediately saw potsherds roiled up from below. I dropped to a knee. I lifted one piece and then another, a broken piece of Babicora Polychrome with spools of painted designs just beneath the lip, and then a Madera Black-on-Red sherd with hard geometric figures. Another after that, and another. I shoveled my hand into the soil and came up with sherds slipping between my fingers. There was no need to put them back exactly as I had found them. They had no future but to be continually broken down by plows until they became the very beans and corn being grown here.

We all four had dropped to the ground within feet of the fence. We looked up at Professor Tena, astonished at this overabundance of pottery. He smiled and assured us, waving his hand, "Vayan, mas adalante." Go out there; look around.

We went, but slowly, eyes gripped by every inch of ground. An immense amount of numerous kinds of pottery was turned up, dazzling points of color and pasty, reddish gray sherds incised with complex, textured hatching. Most pieces were the size of silver dollars, evenly broken by years of plowing. I was dumbfounded and stood with my hands cupped together, holding bits of pottery I had gathered, intricate white, black, and red designs that might have been Villa Ahumada Polychrome or Ramos Polychrome, ceramics of the later periods. This had not been some modest village. It had been a center, a meeting place of trade and production. I looked across at Regan about twenty yards away. She also held her hands cupped before her. She looked toward me at the same moment, and our eyes could say nothing more to each other.

Like crows in a recently sown field, we kept dipping to the ground. I gathered what I thought were the finest pieces, dumped them, and then filled my hands again. I did this walking out to one of the adobe ruins, a place probably built in the 1800s. I stepped up to its one remaining wall and let spill whatever I was carrying. I reached out and touched the grainy, wind-hounded face, startled to see pieces of pottery sticking out of its surface like teeth. The adobe had been made of local soil rich with potsherds. My eyes ran up the one-story wall, seeing little disks and dishes, as if the remains of this past civilization could not be kept in the ground. They swept skyward, building a new culture.

As we toured the field, we passed by one another, stopping occasionally to look at the finds we held in our hands. Such wealth should have been no surprise, the Jesuits having been soundly discredited in their assessment of northwest Mexico. But it was impossible not to be awed. We were standing on a ruined trade center from the fifteenth and sixteenth centuries. This was the time that Paquimé fell, only decades before the Spanish arrived, the threshold between prehistory and history.

. . .

Following the drift of cliff dwellings southward from the Colorado Plateau, through the central highlands of Arizona, and down into the northern Sierra Madre, one would come next to Barranca del Cobre. In a landscape of enormous canyons in northern Mexico live a people known as the Tarahumara, or more locally the Raramuri. Some still live in caves, their complex kinship structure based on a lifeway that is part agricultural, part hunter-gatherer. It is an adaptive strategy that suits this sort of complex environment well, the same strategy that seems to have been employed by ancient people all across the Southwest.

These people's name, Raramuri, translates as "those who walk well." A reserved people, they are in fact famous for their ability to run great distances. Wearing only thin sandals, some Raramuri are known to cross 100 to 200 miles in only a few days. They have carried on kickball races for 450 miles, running day and night in difficult terrain. Runners from these southern barrancas recently came to Colorado to participate in a 100-mile ultramarathon on rough trails over timberline mountains. When they arrived, they made sandals by stripping old car tires and nailing treads together with metal pegs. They won the race hands down.

The sense of distance many archaeologists have concerning the Southwest is cast into question by the Raramuri. They could have closed the gap between northwest Mexico and Chaco in a week at even a casual pace. Whether they actually traveled to the north is unclear, but at least there is incontestable evidence that they or people like them could have traveled to the Colorado Plateau and back in short order. For them the whole Southwest would have been a close neighborhood.

Among the mountain shrines that have been documented between the Colorado Plateau and Mexico is one cave containing more than four hundred woven sandals. Most of these sandals are small, circular waffles that would have protected only the ball of the foot: runners' sandals. It is tempting to see this as a sign of the ancient Raramuri, "those who walk well," a shrine left in a land their ancestors once crossed with astonishing ease. Perhaps these are the Lost Others about whom the Zuni speak, a relic population of what was once called Anasazi now living in northern Mexico.

. . .

The modern Raramuri lay just beyond the reach of our journey, past the whistling arc of the first Spanish musket ball. This field of horse-plowed artifacts below the slope of the Sierra Madre, Professor Tena standing at the fence, was far enough. After this, prehistory ended and history began. The pre-Columbian era was done.

Regan and I moved on to join the others. With hands filled, we showed one another what we had found: pottery, beads, and small stone tools. Eugene picked up two conus shells, a kind imported from the Sea of Cortés, used as little tinkler bells with the ends sawed off and polished, the spires cleanly removed. Holes were drilled through them so that they could be attached to the fringes of dancers' skirts, around wrists and ankles, where they would have rasped to the beat of a dance. Eugene handed them to me, and I rolled them in my hand.

Professor Tena looked approvingly at what we had found. He then said that this was nothing. It was just one place among many. He swept his arm at the horizon where there were small mounds everywhere in the distance. They were all over the horizon, parts of a buried civilization extending as far as I could see.

"Ven, estan en todas partes," he said. Everywhere.

As we walked back to the trucks together, the pieces of artifacts we had found fell out of our hands, dropping one by one into the plowed field. By the time we reached the barbed wire, all I had left

Plow-broken potsherds and conus shells found in a field at the foot of the Sierra Madre. REGAN CHOI

were the two white shells. I turned and looked across the low desert hills, the unnamed city. The Sierra Madre, the Mother Mountains, lay farther, spreading across the horizon like a ravishing god. I rolled the shells between my fingers, feeling their polished smoothness, the wear of centuries. I reared back and tossed them. They sailed across the field and landed in fresh dirt, where they would be plowed under yet again.

Afterword

Early-winter sunlight passed between adobe buildings the color of spent straw. Shafts of light and shadow crossed narrow dirt avenues, landing on faded wooden windowsills, their paint flecking in a cold breeze. An old white pickup took a left turn and then a right as if navigating a maze, hardly room to drive between these closely packed residences. Sitting in the pickup's corrugated metal bed, I looked into passing alleyways, streets with no signs. I was in a Hopi pueblo in the dry plateau country of northern Arizona. Some of the buildings had sixteenth-century stonework showing through fading, unkempt adobe walls. Others were made partly of cinder blocks, an architectural technique picked up in the past century.

I had my son in my lap, his tiny hands mittened, cap pulled snug against the morning breeze. We were riding with a pickup load of surplus produce sent down from fields in Colorado, apples and onions mostly, sacks jostling and shifting around us, lumpy against my back. I felt like a thief of sorts, smuggled into this pueblo in a bed of winter foodstuffs. I thought about pulling out my journal and writing every salient detail I could see in the architecture, in the way these narrow streets ran. But someone might spot me. In the Hopi pueblos it is illegal for outsiders to take notes, pictures, sound recordings, anything. I simply kept to myself, watching adobe structures go by at two miles per hour. The closer we came to the center of the pueblo, the more adobe I saw and the fewer cinder blocks. One thing I did not see anywhere was a T shape. As an overall architectural feature, the T shape seems to have gone south and stayed there, having for the most part disappeared into Mexico. The shape is perhaps a marker of a more restless people, exiles maybe, or travelers who followed an ancient edict into the south and never returned: Anasazi. The Hisatsinom, by contrast, stayed on the Colorado Plateau, forebears of the Hopi.

In the older, inner reaches of the pueblo, we began stopping at certain doors. With Jasper on my hip, I hauled out bags and set them in the dust. I was directed by the eighty-year-old man who was driving the pickup, his rickety finger pointing this way and that, telling me the names of families we were delivering to—long, difficult names in a language far different from my own. Wearing gloves with the fingers cut off, I rapped on each door where I set the produce. Some doors were sealed tightly, others just slabs of wood barely keeping out the wind. No one answered.

It was not that they were hiding. Everyone was gone today, attending an important dance at Bacavi on Third Mesa, leaving this pueblo empty. It felt like a ghost town. On other days I knew Hopi pueblos to have kids in jeans running from door to door, old men sitting in the warming light, and decrepit Dodges and Pintos rolling by every half hour or so. Today it felt as if I were moving through an abandoned settlement, its residents swept away by an unexpected wind. In a few hours they would be back.

I set down another bag of apples and onions and knocked on a door. I stood for a moment, listening, hearing only a withering, dry breeze running through the pueblo's causeways. I returned to the pickup bed and snuggled Jasper into my lap as the engine groaned into first gear. We lurched ahead.

Papery onion skins blew around us as we rode through the pueblo's center and took a turn around a kiva. I sat up immediately for a better look at the building, setting Jasper's diaper-padded rear onto the cold truck bed. I got a knee up on a bag of onions as I watched the kiva go by. It was a simple aboveground structure standing alone, square-shaped, with tar paper showing from recent reconstruction work. An oily black stovepipe aimed straight out of the roof next to the leaning tips of a wooden ladder. The ladder led down through a ceiling hatch into the dark kiva below. I knew the ladder stopped in front of a depression in the kiva's floor, the sipapu, the fabled passageway from the underworld to the world of the living, a place that is both a threshold and a center point. Inside this sipapu, below the surface of the earth, is a legendary watery realm left only to spirits and gods, a place of katsinas.

I had heard many rumors about what happens in the sacred enclosure of a Hopi kiva. It was none of my business, really, the private rites of another civilization. But I could not help staring at the kiva, imagining inside a colorfully painted jar holding a clutch of wooden flowers dating back eight hundred years, a thousand maybe. I envisioned blankets threaded with claret-colored feathers. In the past few decades, several million macaw feathers have been recorded entering various pueblos for ceremonial use, and at least twice as many turkey tail feathers, along with those of eagles, hawks, and tropical birds imported from as far away as Africa. I imagined relics brought down the ladder for the shalako ceremony, or for the winter solstice: chest pieces of falcon wings, hairpins tipped with feathers from parrots and woodpeckers. This is where an ancient civilization keeps itself, a stronghold of remembered ceremonies.

These were someone else's secrets, not mine. I felt awkward staring at the kiva with such eager eyes, wanting to climb down its ladder and see what was hidden inside. I sat back down in the pickup bed, not wishing to be seen gawking in this tightly knit neighborhood, even if no one was watching. I picked Jasper up and put him in my lap as the pueblo and its bands of sunlight passed around us. The settlement seemed patient this morning, as if willing to wait centuries for its residents to return from the dance. Its earthern buildings would fall to ruins, leaving a dusty hill like a beacon atop this mesa. It will happen again. It always has. The rain will depart and the people will follow, walking a spiral that goes on without end.

TERMINOLOGY

ABANDON Archaeologists use the term to describe a place that has been left behind, but not necessarily for good. Abandonment occurs on different scales, including departing from a room, a building, or an entire geographic province. Places might be occupied by the same culture numerous times for thousands of years, experiencing periods of abandonment between periods of occupation.

A.D. *Anno Domini,* abbreviated as A.D. and Latin for "in the year of the Lord," is commonly used as a dating reference in archaeology. It defines an epoch that begins in the year A.D. 1 upon the apparent birth of Christ in the Middle East. Occasionally, A.D. is replaced with C.E., for Common Era or Christian Era. Far less known but gaining popularity in small circles is E.V., for era vulgaris (literally, common era).

ANASAZI A corruption of a Navajo word, *Anasazi* describes the early Pueblo culture that existed in the high and arid plateau country of the Southwest generally from 1000 B.C. (when corn agriculture was first established in the Four Corners) to A.D. 1300. Anasazi is not an ethnicity as much as it is a way of life—dryland farmers, hunters, and wild-plant gatherers living in complex kinship groups. It is defined by a collection of archaeological traits, such as black-on-white pottery, gray ware and red ware pottery, masonry architecture in later years, and the wide-scale importation of birds for ceremonial use, also in later years. There is much debate over whether this name is useful any longer, being too narrow to contain the ethnic complexity of this culture.

ANCESTRAL PUEBLOAN Ancestral Puebloans are ancestors of modern Pueblo people, and the term is steadily replacing *Anasazi.* It better encompasses an unbroken lineage of indigenous farmers from three thousand years ago to today. Whereas *Anasazi* refers to an archaeologically defined group existing solely on the Colorado Plateau, *Ancestral Puebloan* is much more geographically expansive and nonspecific, depicting the entire Pueblo ancestry, whether from the Southwest or from southern Mexico.

BASKETMAKER CULTURE The Basketmaker culture represents a transition on the Colorado Plateau when nomads who farmed only occasionally became residents living in sedentary communities where dependence on farming increased dramatically between the third century B.C. and the third century A.D. The period encompassing the Basketmaker culture ended in the eighth century A.D. as people added on to their pit-houses with aboveground structures and dependence on corn increased, at which point they are better known as Pueblo people.

B.C. This abbreviation for Before Christ is sometimes replaced with B.C.E., for Before the Common Era or Christian Era. In this system of marking time, years are counted in regression starting at 1 B.C., the year before the birth of Christ.

BLACK-ON-WHITE POTTERY Black-on-white was the most widespread decorative style seen among white ware ceramics in the Southwest prior to the fourteenth century A.D. Its black pigments came from mineral sources such as highly oxidized hematite or from boiled plant matter such as bee weed or tansy mustard.

CANYONLANDS This is a region of massive sandstone canyons in the high, sparsely vegetated desert of southeast Utah. It is centered on an iconic, geographic V formed by the confluence of the Green and Colorado rivers. Its northern third is known as Island in the Sky, where cliffs of Wingate sandstone form a series of enormous red buttes. The southwest third is a confounding region of canyons known as the Maze, which is bounded by the high Orange Cliffs. To the southeast lies the highly articulated terrain of the Needles.

CIVILIZATION Civilization is a form of social organization in which multiple heritages or ethnic groups are bound to a single system incorporating uniform architecture, communication, religion, technology, and perhaps behavior. The first Latin use of the word *civis* appeared in the early centuries B.C. to point out the difference between civil societies and barbarians. Archaeologists often shy away from the word when speaking of the prehistoric Southwest, not wanting to compare it directly to larger civilizations, such as those of Mesoamerica, Greece, and Rome. However, as more fine-grained archaeological data is assembled, the word *civilization* is beginning to appear more frequently among researchers.

CLIFF DWELLING This is a general term for a structure of jacal, masonry, or adobe construction built within a natural, sheltering alcove. Cliff dwellings have appeared on nearly every continent, known most famously in

Turkey, North Africa, and the American Southwest. Some are not, in fact, built in cliffs, but are in caves. Some are not dwellings either, but storage facilities or ceremonial sites. The term *alcove structure* has been used among archaeologists as a more accurate, though perhaps less captivating, alternative.

COLORADO PLATEAU An arid uplift covering 150,000 square miles of the northern Southwest, the Colorado Plateau is centered on the Four Corners region, where Utah, Arizona, Colorado, and New Mexico meet. This geographic province is the second-largest plateau in the world, consisting of numerous smaller uplifts dissected into canyons, mesas, and basins. It is a geologically stable region, a slowly rising island surrounded by the fractured Basin and Range province of southwest Utah, Nevada, and western Arizona and by the Rocky Mountains of Colorado.

CORRUGATED POTTERY A highly textured ceramic style, corrugated pottery is a specific Southwest form made from clay coils pressed together, then pinched or notched to form a functional and decorative surface. Almost always used as cookware, corrugated pottery is more efficient than smooth pottery at transferring heat throughout the vessel and is less susceptible to breakage caused by frequent heating and cooling. It is a style indicative of early Pueblo people on the Colorado Plateau.

DROUGHT There are three kinds of drought. *Meteorological drought* is a prolonged period with less than average precipitation. *Agricultural drought* is simply a lack of ample moisture in the soil, which may arise from any number of circumstances, from rainfall to soil management. *Hydrologic drought* occurs when reserves such as underground aquifers, rivers, or lakes drop below the statistical average due to consumption, climatic conditions, or both.

DRYLAND FARMING In areas of little rainfall where surface water is rare, dryland farming is the customary technique. Basically, it is farming without irrigating, relying on precipitation stored in the soil. Dryland farming comes with its own suite of practices to capture whatever moisture is available, such as leaving crop stubble in the field to catch blowing snow or building low dams to hold surface runoff. It also requires specific strains of crops. Hopi blue corn, for instance, can be planted a foot deep, whereas most midwestern corn must be planted no more than two inches deep.

EAST-CENTRAL ARIZONA East-central Arizona is perhaps the most diverse region of the Southwest, beginning in the north around the Painted Desert and the Little Colorado River, then running south over the forested Mogollon Rim. It ends roughly along the Nantac Rim below Point of Pines, but it could easily extend to the Gila Mountains and the course of the Gila River in southeast Arizona. In the west it is bounded by the Tonto Basin and the rugged Mazatzal Mountains, in the east by the New Mexico border between the Blue and San Francisco rivers. Much of the region is now occupied by two Apache reservations.

FIREBOARD This is a flat piece of wood from a few inches to a foot long, often taken from an agave stalk, against which a wooden spindle is spun to create a hot ember. Upon the first curl of smoke to come off the fireboard, one would pass the hot ember into a bed of dry grass or some other flammable material. Lifting the glowing tinder to the mouth, one would blow a winnowing breath across it. A second breath would start a bright flurry of sparks. A third would produce a quick, small flame, which would be moved away from the face and settled out of the hands into a waiting cache of kindling. Having more small sticks already broken is important, so that they can be placed quickly on the rising flames. For a supple, practiced hand, this procedure should take no more than one minute. For the inexperienced, it could take days or weeks to get a fire going, if ever.

FOUR CORNERS This region is centered on the meeting of the states of Colorado, Utah, Arizona, and New Mexico. It is the only place in the United States where a person can stand in four states at the same time. Beyond state boundaries, the term describes a larger geographic province of arid canyons, buttes, basins, and a few scattered mountains that extend throughout the San Juan River Basin, as far north as Moab, as far south as the Chuska Mountains, as far west as Kayenta in Arizona, and as far east as the headwaters of the San Juan.

GREAT HOUSE In its broad definition, a great house is an expansive type of household that appeared in late Victorian times in Europe and continues today in the form of family mansions. In the Southwest, however, a great house is a large masonry building with a formalized floor plan, best known from the eleventh century A.D. It is often multistory, with high-ceilinged rooms and interior kivas. Often a great kiva is included. Based on archaeological findings, these structures appear to have been mostly ceremonial, with few residents, although at different times they also acted as dwellings. Great houses outside Chaco Canyon appear to have been more domestic than those in the canyon. The oldest great houses began in the eighth century, and at the time their plans resembled those of villages near the Dolores River in Colorado.

GREAT KIVA Examples of public ceremonial architecture, great kivas are semi-subterranean and usually circular. They range between thirty and eighty feet across and were used by large groups for ritual purposes.

HISATSINOM A Hopi word, Hisatsinom refers to the ancestors of the Hopi, who arrived at their current location in northern Arizona after centuries of migrations, with some clans starting as far away as southern Mexico and some as nearby as Kayenta and the Four Corners. The Hopi have several words that refer to ancestors, such as *motisinom* and *pavatsinom,* each having a relatively nuanced definition.

HOHOKAM While prehistoric groups were pursuing dryland farming on the Colorado Plateau, the Hohokam were practicing intensive irrigation agriculture along the Gila and Salt rivers in the Sonoran Desert of southern Arizona in the Phoenix basin, in the Tucson area, and in the desert beyond. They grew cotton, corn, agaves, and many other crops and are estimated to have built a thousand miles of irrigation canals across the desert. The Hohokam are well known for their ball courts and for handmade platform mounds on which community structures were built.

HOPI This Native American tribe lives on a 2,450-square-mile reservation in northeast Arizona. The reservation is located inside an 18,000-square-mile reservation belonging to the Navajo, a tribe not directly related to the Hopi. Every primary Hopi settlement, or pueblo, maintains its own autonomous government. At the turn of the twenty-first century, the Hopi reservation had a population of 6,946. In addition, 5,000 off-mesa Hopi also are enrolled in the tribe.

HYDROLOGICAL CYCLE Water on this planet moves continually between the biosphere, atmosphere, lithosphere, and hydrosphere. That is, water falling as rain or snow is naturally stored in aquifers, oceans, lakes, rivers, glaciers, snowfields, or topsoil. This water eventually evaporates off the surface or is transpired by plants. The vapor is stored in the atmosphere before it returns to earth in the form of precipitation. The cyclic flow of water is known as the hydrological cycle.

KATSINA (KACHINA) A modern Pueblo ceremonial repertoire, the katsina religion originated in the Southwest around the fourteenth century A.D., although earlier components have been noted. It is still a strong religion, mostly in the western pueblos of Laguna, Acoma, Zuni, Hano, and Hopi.

KAYENTA This region in northeast Arizona centers on Marsh Pass and the mesas surrounding Tsegi Canyon. It finds its western and southern limits in the Grand Canyon, its eastern limit along Chinle Wash, and its northern limit around the San Juan River. Prehistoric people living in Kayenta (often called the Kayenta Anasazi) appear to have kept their distance from ninth- to twelfth-century Chaco. They were a couple of hundred years behind Chaco in accepting the advent of the pueblo and large-scale architecture. In fact, Chaco-style great houses, which spread throughout the Four Corners region, were never built within the Kayenta sphere, implying that the people here may have intentionally kept pressure from Chaco at bay.

KIVA Kivas have been in use as ritual and community spaces among Pueblo people for the past fifteen hundred years. Ranging from the size of a small bedroom to eighty feet across, kivas are round, rectangular, or O-shaped and are generally built underground. Prehistoric kivas have formalized floor plans and orientations that suggest an architectural or religious code. Small kivas were both domestic and used for small, family-scale rituals. Great kivas were more specialized ritual structures used by larger groups.

LUNAR STANDSTILL Rarely will one find a reference to lunar standstills in standard astronomy texts, yet the standstill cycle is the subject of important alignments at ancient megalithic sites around the world. In short, the lunar standstill is a rhythm set up by the moon's off-centered orbit around the earth. A major lunar standstill occurs every 18.6 years. At the winter solstice during the standstill, the full moon reaches its highest possible position in the sky, and during the summer solstice it reaches its lowest possible position. Thus the moon during its standstill is not still at all but moves across most of the sky throughout the year, rising and setting at many different points on the horizon. A minor standstill fits between major standstills when the moon keeps to a very narrow path directly overhead. In other words, a major standstill is a wide pendulum swing of the moon, while a minor standstill is a more settled equilibrium. This lunar cycle of 18.6 years accurately defines long-term periods such as decades or centuries far better than the sun, which is restricted to annual and daily patterns.

MANO A mano, from the Spanish word for hand, is a hand tool made out of stone that is used with a metate to grind food, pigments, or medicines. Some manos are the size of a potato, to be used in one hand, while others are more like rolling pins, requiring two hands. During the Basketmaker era, as agriculture first became prevalent in the Southwest, most manos were of the one-handed variety. Not until later centuries, when corn became a more crucial staple, did two-handed manos become more common.

MASONRY Masonry, a method of building using stone and mortar, became common in the northern Southwest between the eleventh and thirteenth centuries A.D. Early homesites on the Colorado Plateau were originally made out of wood and mud. These were pit-houses with nearby farm plots. After about ten years, if not maintained regularly by permanent residents, a pit-house would have been an uninviting place to live. Insects would have infested the walls, while wood rats would have moved into the spaces between ceiling beams. Around the eleventh century, people started building houses out of stone. This new construction technique allowed buildings to stand for centuries, although most masonry unit pueblos were not occupied for that long. Masonry structures also were far easier to keep clean than pit-houses. The first masonry structures, called great houses, are thought to have been rarely lived in. Instead they were treated like shrines, decorated with garlands of turquoise and painted vessels, while people continued to occupy outlying homes made of wood and mud. From the twelfth century on, masonry was widely used (although older forms of architecture persisted where needed), and many families in the Southwest eventually had living quarters made of stone.

MESOAMERICA Mesoamerica reaches from central Mexico into Central America. It is a cultural landscape of celebrated pre-Columbian societies such as the Olmecs, Maya, Toltecs, and Aztecs. This region existed in a quickly accelerating Neolithic state that began with domestic food production about 6,300 years ago. In the eighth century A.D., the Maya built a 230-foot-tall temple at Tikal and numerous other temples of similar stature. Metallurgy was common. Combined armies of tens of thousands of warriors clashed in epic battles. A number of written languages were in use, now understood from a variety of sources: logs of shipments of cocoa and corn; legendary stories carved into rock pillars; and inscriptions on vessels and walls telling the exact year, month, and day when kings took power. The Aztec capital of Tenochtitlán, in southern Mexico, might be considered the height of Mesoamerican civilization. The city was built on a lake, so that it appeared to be floating, and was approached by long causeways set across the water. Hundreds of massive temples and pyramids stood over canals like those in Venice, and fresh water arrived through a network of aqueducts. At its height in the fourteenth century A.D., Tenochtitlán had at least 200,000 residents.

METATE A metate is a stone surface on which food, pigments, or medicines are ground. Metates range from deep, well-worn troughs to simple slabs that have been cursorily scratched to make them more abrasive.

MOGOLLON CULTURE Occupying a mountainous region of central Arizona and southwest New Mexico, Mogollon is, along with Hohokam and Anasazi, one of the core cultural groups that existed in the prehistoric Southwest. Although Mogollon people farmed, they relied more on wild plants and game than did neighboring Hohokam and Anasazi groups. They did not engage in trade as extensively as did other people of the time. The Mimbres people, a New Mexico branch of the Mogollon, stand out for their extensive trade and elaborately painted ceramics. Like other names used in Southwest archaeology, Mogollon refers to a cultural group identified by certain archaeological traits, not a single, easily defined people.

MOGOLLON RIM The Mogollon Rim is a geographic brink that drops off sharply along its southern edge. It stretches across 350 miles of Arizona, dividing the state in half from east to west and also dividing the whole geographic and ecological Southwest. The southern Colorado Plateau and its desert ends at the rim. Although the Mogollon Rim is most visually abrupt between Milk Ranch Point and Forestdale Valley in east-central Arizona, it is part of a much larger geographic trend of rough terrain that begins around the Mogollon and San Francisco mountains in New Mexico and continues west by northwest to the Grand Wash Cliffs and the end of the Grand Canyon near the Nevada border. To the north of the rim lies a gradual fifty-mile slope rising out of the desert, its rock surface incised as if by a laser into long and isolated canyons. All the water from that side feeds into the half-dry floor of the Little Colorado River. South of the rim the land falls steeply into forested chasms, where creeks run clear and cold, draining through deep and numerous canyons toward the Salt River. Water heading south eventually flows into the low Sonoran Desert, to the city of Phoenix and beyond.

NAVAJO The Navajo left their Athabascan homeland of southeast Alaska and British Columbia around the eighth century A.D. but probably did not arrive in the Southwest until around the fifteenth century, a couple of hundred years before the Spanish. An early tree-ring-dated Navajo site near La Plata, New Mexico, is from 1541. They now occupy one of the largest reservations in the United States and are one of the faster-growing ethnic populations in the Western Hemisphere.

NORTHEAST ARIZONA Ecologically and geologically diverse, northeast Arizona meets New Mexico along a linear series of 8,000- to 9,000-foot peaks on the Defiance Plateau. It also runs along the Utah border around Monument Valley and the convoluted stone landscape of the Rainbow Plateau. Its western boundary is formed by the Echo Cliffs and Marble Canyon at the upper reaches of the Grand Canyon. The southern delineation is the Little Colorado River from St. Johns through the Painted Desert.

NORTHWEST NEW MEXICO Northwest New Mexico, made up mostly of Tertiary shales and fluvial sandstones, is an easily defined basin that drains into the San Juan River. This basin is encircled by the Chuska Mountains and the Arizona border to the west, the Zuni Mountains and Mount Taylor to the south, the procession of the Sierra Nacimiento and Nacimiento Peak to the east, and the Colorado border, where elevation rises sharply, to the north. In the middle of this basin is Chaco, the wealthiest and most influential center ever built on the Colorado Plateau.

PAHANA This is a Hopi term for a white person or Anglo.

PIKI BREAD Best known among the Hopi, this corn-based bread consists mainly of cornmeal and wood ash. (If the ash is pure, it has a clean taste of grain and stone.) The bread is baked in thin sheets that resemble fine pastry.

PIT-HOUSE This type of structure was used for both dwellings and public spaces at different times throughout the settlement of the Southwest. Semi-subterranean pit-houses are round, square, or rectangular, with thatched, mud, or timbered roofs. Often the features inside, such as hearths, deflector stones, benches, and entryways, are arranged according to a strict plan. Oversize pit-houses from the early centuries A.D. are thought to be the precursors of ceremonial kivas.

POLYCHROME POTTERY Polychrome (multicolored) pottery first appeared in the Southwest in the form of black-and-white designs painted on a red or orange background, thus making three colors. Examples of this style include St. Johns Polychrome, Kayenta Polychrome, and Salado Polychrome. Farther south, in New Mexico, Texas, and Mexico, wares, such as Ramos Polychrome, were painted with red, black, and even yellow designs. Polychrome pottery came late to the Southwest, not making a strong appearance until the end of the thirteenth and beginning of the fourteenth centuries. Within a decade or less, this kind of pottery became the dominant decorated form in the Southwest, entirely replacing the seven-hundred-year-old tradition of black-on-white ceramics.

PRE-COLUMBIAN The cultural era of the Americas prior to 1492, and the arrival of Christopher Columbus under the flag of Castile, is considered pre-Columbian. A reliable alternative used in the Southwest is *pre-Hispanic. Precontact* has also been widely used, referring to contact between European and American civilizations, placing it prior to the very late fifteenth century.

PREHISTORY In the Americas, *prehistory* and *pre-Columbian* are generally synonymous, referring to the era before European contact. However, the division between history and prehistory is usually defined not by cultural contact, but by the advent of writing and the detailed recording of history. The Maya had a complete written language that has been exhaustively deciphered by modern researchers, putting into question the ubiquitous use of the word *prehistory* regarding the pre-Columbian Americas. In the Southwest, history was kept in a variety of ways besides written language. Highly complex oral traditions developed, and stories were printed in rock art or on decorated vessels. People had history even if they did not have writing.

PUBLIC ARCHITECTURE A piece of public architecture is a building or space constructed for use by groups larger than households. Their presence implies organized labor and perhaps some form of corporate governance. Archaeological remains of public architecture in the Southwest include great kivas, plazas, great houses, platform mounds, ball courts, and roads, which were used in public ceremonies, games, markets, meetings, festivals, and pilgrimages. Modern analogues are churches, concert halls, schools, government buildings, and sports arenas.

PUEBLO The Spanish word for town, *Pueblo* is used in capitalized form to describe a native people now centered in northern Arizona and northern New Mexico. You would say that a person is Pueblo or that he or she is from Cochiti Pueblo or Zuni Pueblo. Pueblo people derive mainly from a farming culture that has existed in the Southwest since at least the fourth century B.C. Corn domesticated in Mexico reached Arizona 4,500 years ago, then northern New Mexico 4,000 years ago, and became big in the Mesa Verde region of southwest Colorado in the fourth and fifth centuries B.C. Many Pueblo people have local roots going this far back. When not capitalized, *pueblo* refers to compact adobe and stonework towns in which Pueblo people have occasionally lived for the past thousand years.

RED WARE POTTERY This ceramic type was originally manufactured on the western half of the Colorado Plateau (in northern Arizona and southeast Utah) as far back as the eighth century A.D. Red ware vessels are made with iron-rich clay that is fired in an oxidizing kiln and often swabbed with a dark red slip for luster. True red ware will appear saturated all the way through with color when a potsherd is viewed edge-on. Imitation red ware, of which there were many types in the ancient Southwest, was merely painted with a red clay slip before firing, and its interior is gray or white.

ROCK ART In the Southwest rock art comes in two forms: petroglyphs and pictographs. Petroglyphs are cut, scratched, ground, or pecked into rock surfaces. Pictographs are painted, using rich pigments such as rust red hematite or bright ones such as kaolin clay or copper. Archaeological references to Southwest rock art often regard the work as either a suite of widely recognized symbols or simply ornamental, graffiti-like images. Some Pueblo people say that some rock art expresses in detail their ancestral clan symbols and ancient allegories.

SALADO Salado is what became of the old-guard cultural groups of Hohokam, Anasazi, and Mogollon when they were thrust together in the southern Southwest in the thirteenth and fourteenth centuries by mass migrations and escalating trade. It is a cultural phenomenon identified by Salado Polychrome pottery—namely, Gila Polychrome—and heavily aggregated settlements that in some cases lasted into the early sixteenth century.

SALADO POLYCHROME This style of pottery became fashionable throughout the Southwest in the fourteenth century A.D. It was made in low-heat kilns using whatever fuel was available, generally wood that burned to ash while the vessels were still being fired. Because of this economical manufacturing technique, Salado Polychrome could be made quickly and in great amounts. It represented a revolution in artistry, with its rich, painted symbology and huge urn shapes. Salado Polychrome was made by just about everybody in the Southwest during the fourteenth century. Far more widespread than any previous pottery, it was a traveling billboard, the iconic images painted on its surfaces seen from Arizona to Texas, from northern New Mexico to Chihuahua, Mexico. Because of its cheap manufacture, Salado Polychrome vessels were not the sturdiest or finest of the time. Their weaker construction can be strongly contrasted with yellow wares and White Mountain Red ware, both of which resulted from long, hot, well-timed firings. If you tap a piece of Salado Polychrome, it will make a heavy sound, but if you tap a piece of yellow ware or White Mountain Red ware, it will sound like a bell.

SHIELD FIGURE Appearing as both pictographs and petroglyphs, shield figures are circular rock art images that began appearing in the thirteenth century A.D., often representing a decorated round shield hiding a person who is sometimes holding a spear or bow. Most of these images have been found in the desert of southeast Utah, pecked into cliffs along the Green River and painted in caves in the Needles near the Colorado River, and many are to the east in the upper Rio Grande area. A chain of rock art shields continues south out of Canyonlands into Arizona and into the cliff dwellings of Kayenta. The last of these figures have been found at a few sites below the Mogollon Rim. It has long been thought that these images are indicative of violence and conflict. They appeared at the same time that the entire Southwest was embroiled in cultural and climatic instability.

SIITÁLPU This is a Hopi word referring to the Flower World, a luminously colored spirit realm that exists alongside this one. Symbology depicting such a world appeared most frequently in the fourteenth century as migration peaked in the Southwest. It was painted on clay vessels; carved or painted on stone, wood, or bone; and in one case made into an enormous earthen effigy. Some see the rise of siitálpu imagery as a sign that philosophies were changing. They believe that it represents a shift from stern ideologies harking back to Chaco, where ancestors were worshipped and territorial claims were secured. New siitálpu stars, clouds, animals, serpents, and faces lead some researchers to believe that a new ideology was loosening ties to the past and former lands. It allowed ancestors to move out of the ground in which they were buried and into clouds, flowers, and stars, where they were free to follow their children on long migrations.

SIPAPU A shallow dish or hole purposefully built into the floor of a kiva, the sipapu symbolizes a passage from one world to the next. Traveling through the sipapu into the present world—the Fourth World, at least by Hopi accounts—people were said to encounter Maa'saw, a terrifying human-like visage with gaping eyes and a burned, skeletal head. Maa'saw, wearing two burdensome necklaces of turquoise and bones, is Caretaker of the Place of the Dead and was the first to have control of fire. This figure was a dreaded and revered god who now rules the Hopi's current reality. There are many versions of this story, most of which are imperfectly written down, their meanings obscured as they were translated from varied and nuanced oral traditions into Anglo written traditions.

SOUTHEAST UTAH This region, often known as Canyon Country, is made mostly of massive, red Jurassic and Triassic sandstones exposed around the Green, Colorado, San Juan, and Dirty Devil rivers. It is bounded in the north by the Book Cliffs, in the west by the Aquarius Plateau (above the Waterpocket Fold and Capitol Reef), and in the east by the state of Colorado. The combination of deep, solid sandstone and four vital rivers has resulted in a convoluted realm of canyons that continues south about twenty miles into Arizona, around Glen Canyon.

SOUTHWEST The geographic extent of the Southwest has been defined in numerous different ways. Perhaps the clearest is that it runs north to south from Durango, Colorado, to Durango, Mexico, and east to west from Las Vegas, New Mexico, to Las Vegas, Nevada. This is only a gross designation, however, and does not take into account the Southwest's regional subtleties, such as Canyonlands and the Uncompahgre Plateau, or the long arc of the Sangre de Cristo Mountains. Dry but diverse country, the Southwest ranges from more than 14,000 feet in the San Juan Mountains to basins that lie below sea level near the Sea of Cortés in Mexico. It encompasses the high Great Basin desert of the Colorado Plateau; the low Sonoran Desert in southwest Arizona and northwest Mexico; the Mojave Desert in the west; and the mid-level Chihuahuan Desert, centered on the International Four Corners, where New Mexico, Arizona, and Sonora and Chihuahua, Mexico, more or less come together. Along with numerous isolated mountains, the Southwest includes three central alpine regions: the southern Rocky Mountains in the north, the Mogollon Highlands and Sky Islands in the middle, and the subtropical, northernmost Sierra Madre Occidental in the south. The Southwest's surface is crisscrossed with global geological trends: a narrow chain of mountains winding sinuously for five hundred miles from Colorado to Mexico and the Colorado River, cutting a flawless southwesterly course of gorges through the Rocky Mountains, across the Utah desert, and into Arizona, where it jostles through the Grand Canyon, then falls into a due north-south trend straight to the Sea of Cortés. Above that an exclamation mark runs along the Wasatch Plateau in Utah, leading into the crest of the Kaibab Plateau in northern Arizona and ending in a single, punctuated heap at the San Francisco Mountains outside Flagstaff. All of these large-scale features are formed by vast geological structures, massive faults and continental fractures in the earth's crust. This occurs within a space about a quarter the size of Australia, resulting in a compact puzzle of landforms and environments.

SOUTHWEST COLORADO A highland region generally above 5,000 to 6,000 feet in elevation, southwest Colorado is primarily gray Cretaceous shales and sandstone. It is bounded in the north by the Dolores River and the Uncompahgre Plateau, in the west and south by Utah and New Mexico, and in the east by the massive complex of the San Juan Mountains. The area is lifted like a podium over much of the upper Southwest. From here one can peer easily across distant regions—fifty miles into the basin of Chaco (in New Mexico) and eighty miles across the spangled horizon of Monument Valley (in Utah and Arizona).

T SHAPE Primarily found in the form of certain prehistoric Pueblo doorways, the T shape is also seen in stone carvings, wall niches, and designs in basketry, textiles, and painted pottery. It is painted on walls and is stamped into ceramic mug handles. It comes in a variety of forms from a keyhole shape to a truncated crucifix. The T shape appears sporadically outside the Southwest in other parts of the Americas such as Peru and southern Mexico, where it can be found in pre-Columbian architecture, art, and jewelry. In Mayan hieroglyphs it is *ik'*, which means breath, wind, and vital essence.

TLALOC Tlaloc imagery in Mexico dates back to 800 B.C., making it the oldest recognizable religious complex in the Americas. The deity Tlaloc encompasses a variety of related themes: mountains, clouds, mist, rain, drought, caves, springs, a watery underworld, crops, fertility, and renewal. In essense Tlaloc is a rain god and has long been the focus of mountaintop and cave offerings and sacrifices, including human sacrifices, especially that of children. Tlaloc iconography is abundant in Mesoamerica and is also prevalent in prehistoric rock art and pottery decoration in the southern Southwest, especially among the Mimbres and Jornada Mogollon (there are seventeen Tlaloc rock art figures at Hueco Tanks, in the desert near El Paso, Texas, a rock outcrop marked by caves, shaded alcoves, and natural depressions where rainwater gathers). Both the symbolic and the practical aspects of Tlaloc religion are very similar to those of the Pueblo katsina religion still practiced in the Southwest.

WHITE WARE POTTERY This type of pottery, best known from the Colorado Plateau, often is made from gray Cretaceous clay and the vessels are coated in slips of white kaolin clay, from which porcelain also is made. The clean white cast of these vessels is achieved by reducing the oxygen inside a kiln, which prevents the iron in the clay from oxidizing, or turning the vessel brown, gray, or even red.

ZUNI This Pueblo tribe has a reservation of just over 700 square miles in northern New Mexico and an isolated 12,000-acre reservation in northeast Arizona near the Little Colorado River. The Zuni language appears to be unrelated to any other language in the world, although one researcher has argued that its cognitive structure is similar to that of Japanese.

Bibliography

Adams, E. Charles. *Homol'ovi: An Ancient Hopi Settlement Cluster.* Tucson: University of Arizona Press, 2002.

Adams, E. Charles, and Andrew I. Duff, eds. *The Protohistoric Pueblo World, A.D. 1275–1600*. Tucson: University of Arizona Press, 2004.

Adams, E. Charles, and Kelley Ann Hays, eds. *Homol'ovi II: Archaeology of an Ancestral Hopi Village, Arizona*. Tucson: University of Arizona Press, 1991.

Adams, E. Charles, and Charla Hedberg. "Driftwood Use at Homol'ovi and Implications for Interpreting the Archaeological Record." *Kiva* 67, no. 4 (2002): 363–84.

Adams, E. Charles, Vincent M. LaMotta, and Kurt Dongoske. "Hopi Settlement Clusters Past and Present." In *The Protohistoric Pueblo World, A.D. 1275–1600*, edited by E. Charles Adams and Andrew I. Duff. Tucson: University of Arizona Press, 2004.

Akins, Nancy J. "Chaco Canyon Mortuary Practices: Archaeological Correlates of Complexity." In *Ancient Burial Practices in the American Southwest: Archaeology, Physical Anthropology, and Native American Perspectives,* edited by Douglas R. Mitchell and Judy L. Brunson-Hadley. Albuquerque: University of New Mexico Press, 2001.

Akins, Nancy J., and John D. Schelberg. "Evidence for Organizational Complexity as Seen from the Mortuary Practices at Chaco Canyon." In *Recent Research on Chaco Prehistory,* edited by W. J. Judge and J. D. Schelberg, 89–102. Reports of the Chaco Center 8. Albuquerque, NM: Division of Cultural Research, National Park Service, 1984.

Allison, James R. "Surface Archaeology of the Red Knobs Site, a Southeastern Utah Great House." *Kiva* 69, no. 4 (2004): 339–60.

Ambruster, Carol W., and Ray A. Williamson. "Sun and Sun Serpents: Continuing Observations in South-Eastern Utah." In *Archaeoastronomy in the 1990s,* edited by Clive L. N. Ruggles, 219–26. Loughborough, Eng.: Group D Publications, 1990.

Anyon, Roger. "Hopi Traditional Uses of and Cultural Ties to the Coronado National Forest." Paper prepared for Coronado National Forest, Heritage Resources Management Consultants, Tucson, AZ, 1999.

Bagwell, Elizabeth A. "Architectural Patterns Along the Rio Taraises, Northern Sierra Madre Occidental, Sonora." *The Journal of Southwestern Archaeology and History* 70, no. 1 (2004): 7–30.

Barrett, Elinore M. "The Geography of the Rio Grande Pueblos in the Seventeenth Century." *Ethnohistory* 49, no. 1 (2002): 123–69.

Benson, Larry, Linda Cordell, Kirk Vincent, Howard Taylor, John Stein, G. Lang Farmer, and Kiyoto Futa. "Ancient Maize from Chacoan Great Houses: Where Was It Grown?" *Proceedings of the National Academy of Sciences of the United States* 100, no. 22 (2003): 13111–15.

Bernardini, Wesley. "Conflict, Migration, and the Social Environment: Interpreting Architectural Change in Early and Late Pueblo IV Aggregations." In *Migration and Reorganization: The Pueblo IV Period in the American Southwest,* edited by Katherine A. Spielmann, 91–109. Anthropological Research Paper 51. Tempe: Arizona State University, 1998.

Billman, Brian R., Patricia M. Lambert, and Leonard L. Banks. "Cannibalism, Warfare, and Drought in the Mesa Verde Region During the Twelfth Century A.D." *American Antiquity* 65, no. 1 (2000): 145–90.

Blackiston, A. Hooton. "Casas Grandian Outposts." *Records of the Past* 5, no. 5 (1906): 142–47.

———. "Cliff Dwellings in Northern Mexico." *Records of the Past* 4, no. 2 (1905): 355–61.

———. "Cliff Ruins of Cave Valley, Northern Mexico." *Records of the Past* 5, no. 1 (1906): 5–11.

———. "Prehistoric Ruins of Northern Mexico." *American Antiquarian and Oriental Journal* 27 (1905): 65–69.

———. "Recently Discovered Cliff Dwellings of the Sierra Madres." *Records of the Past* 8, no. 1 (1909): 20–32.

Bowen, Thomas C. "A Survey of Archaeological Sites Near Guaymas, Sonora." *Kiva* 31, no. 1 (1965): 14–36.

Bradley, Ronna Jane. "Recent Advances in Chihuahuan Archaeology." In *Greater Mesoamerica: The Archaeology of West and Northwest Mexico,* edited by Michael S. Foster and Shirley Gorenstein, 221–39. Salt Lake City: University of Utah Press, 2000.

Brand, Donald D. "Aboriginal Trade Routes for Sea Shells in the Southwest." *Yearbook of the Association of Pacific Coast Geographers* 4 (1938): 3–9.

Brody, J. J. *Anasazi and Pueblo Painting.* Albuquerque: University of New Mexico Press, 1991.

Bullock, Peter Y. "Does the Reality of Anasazi Violence Prove the Myth of Anasazi Cannibalism?" In *Deciphering Anasazi Violence: With Regional Comparisons to Mesoamerican and Woodland Cultures,* edited by Peter Yashio Bullock, 35–44. Santa Fe, NM: HRM Books, 1998.

———. "A Multidimensional Appraisal of Anasazi Mortuary Practice." In *Deciphering Anasazi Violence: With Regional Comparisons to Mesoamerican and Woodland Cultures,* edited by Peter Yashio Bullock, 93–103. Santa Fe, NM: HRM Books, 1998.

Burton, Jeffery F. "Hunters and the Hunted: The Prehistoric Art of Tom Ketchum Cave." *Kiva* 53, no. 4 (1998): 335–56.

Cameron, Catherine M. "Migration and the Movement of Southwestern Peoples." *Journal of Anthropological Archaeology* 14 (1995): 104–24.

———. "Pink Cert, Projectile Points, and the Chacoan Regional System." *American Antiquity* 66, no. 1 (2001): 79–102.

Cameron, Catherine M., and H. Wolcott Toll. "Deciphering the Organization of Production in Chaco Canyon." *American Antiquity* 66, no. 1 (2001): 5–13.

Carpenter, John, and Guadalupe Sanchez, eds. *Prehistory of the Borderlands: Recent Research in the Archaeology of Northern Mexico and the Southern Southwest.* Tucson: Arizona State Museum, 1997.

Christman, Ernest H. *Casas Grandes Pre-Columbian Pottery Decoded: Of Gods and Myths.* Albuquerque, NM: Tutorial Press, 2002.

Clark, Darell F. "A Net from Chihuahua, Mexico." *Kiva* 32, no. 4 (1967): 121–27.

Clark, Jeffery J. *Tracking Prehistoric Migrations: Pueblo Settlers Among the Tonto Basin Hohokam.* Anthropological Paper 65. Tucson: University of Arizona Press, 2001.

Clune, Dorris. "Textiles and Matting from Waterfall Cave, Chihuahua." *American Antiquity* 26, no. 2 (1960): 274–77.

Cordell, Linda S. *Archaeology of the Southwest.* San Diego: Academic Press, 1997.

———. "Tracing Migration Pathways from the Receiving End." *Journal of Anthropological Archaeology* 14 (1995): 203–11.

Cordell, Linda S., and George J. Gumerman, eds. *Dynamics of Southwest Prehistory.* Washington, DC: Smithsonian Institution Press, 1989.

Courlander, Harold. *The Fourth World of the Hopis.* New York: Crown Publishers, 1971.

Crary, Joseph S., Stephen Germick, and David E. Doyel. "Exploring the Gila Horizon." *Kiva* 66, no. 4 (2001): 407–45.

Creel, Darrell, and Charmion McKusick. "Prehistoric Macaws and Parrots in the Mimbres Area, New Mexico." *American Antiquity* 59, no. 3 (1994): 510–25.

Crown, Patricia L. *Ceramics and Ideology: Salado Polychrome Pottery.* Albuquerque: University of New Mexico Press, 1994.

Crown, Patricia L., and W. James Judge, eds. *Chaco and Hohokam: Prehistoric Regional Systems in the American Southwest.* Santa Fe, NM: School of American Research Press, 1991.

Crown, Patricia L., and W. H. Wills. "Modifying Pottery and Kivas at Chaco: Pentimento, Restoration, or Renewal?" *American Antiquity* 68, no. 3 (2003): 511–32.

Danforth, Marie Elaine, Della Collins Cook, and Stanley G. Knick III. "The Human Remains from Carter Ranch Pueblo, Arizona: Health in Isolation." *American Antiquity* 59, no. 1 (1994): 88–102.

Dean, Jeffrey S. *Chronological Analysis of Tsegi Phase Sites in Northeastern Arizona.* Tucson: University of Arizona Press, 1969.

———. "Kayenta Anasazi Settlement Transformations in Northeastern Arizona, A.D. 1150–1350." In *The Prehistoric Pueblo World, A.D. 1150–1350,* edited by Michael A. Adler, 29–47. Tucson: University of Arizona Press, 1996.

———. "Prehistoric Settlement in Long House Valley, Northeastern Arizona." *Museum of Northern Arizona Bulletin* 50 (1973): 25–44.

Dean, Jeffrey S., and John C. Ravesloot. "The Chronology of Cultural Interaction in the Gran Chichimeca." In *Culture and Contact: Charles C. Di Pesos's Gran Chichimeca,* edited by Anne I. Woosley and John C. Ravesloot, 83–103. Dragoon, AZ: Amerind Foundation, 1993.

Diehl, Michael W. "Changes in Architecture and Land Use Strategies in the American Southwest: Upland Mogollon Pithouse Dwellers, A.D. 200–1000." *Journal of Field Archaeology* 24, no. 2 (1997): 179–95.

———. "The Intensity of Maize Processing and Production in Upland Mogollon Pithouse Villages, A.D. 200–1000." *American Antiquity* 61, no. 1 (1996): 102–15.

———. "The Interpretation of Archaeological Floor Assemblages: A Case Study from the American Southwest." *American Antiquity* 63 (1998): 617–35.

Di Peso, Charles. *The Reeve Ruin of Southeastern Arizona.* Dragoon, AZ: Amerind Foundation, 1958.

Di Peso, Charles C., John B. Rinaldo, and Gloria C. Fenner. *Casas Grandes: A Fallen Trading Center of the Gran Chichimeca.* Flagstaff, AZ: Northland Press, 1974.

Dongoske, Kurt E., Michael Yeatts, Roger Anyon, and T. J. Ferguson. "Archaeological Cultures and Cultural Affiliation: Hopi and Zuni Perspectives in the American Southwest." *American Antiquity* 62, no. 4 (1997): 600–608.

Douglas, John E. "Autonomy and Regional Systems in the Late Prehistoric Southern Southwest." *American Antiquity* 60, no. 2 (1995): 240–58.

———. "Distant Sources, Local Contexts: Interpreting Nonlocal Ceramics at Paquimé (Casas Grandes), Chihuahua." *Journal of Anthropological Research* 48, no. 1 (1992): 1–24.

Downum, Christian E. "Summary and Conclusions." In *Archaeology of the Pueblo Grande Platform Mound and Surrounding Features.* Vol. 4, *The Pueblo Grande Platform Mound Compound,* edited by Christian E. Downum, 221–80. Phoenix: City of Phoenix Parks, Recreation, and Library Department, 1998.

Doxtater, Dennis. "A Hypothetical Layout of Chaco Canyon Structures Via Large-Scale Alignments Between Significant Natural Features." *Kiva* 68, no. 1 (2002): 23–47.

Doyel, David E., ed. *Anasazi Regional Organization and the Chaco System.* Albuquerque, NM: Maxwell Museum of Anthropology, 2001.

Duff, Andrew I. "The Process of Migration in the Late Prehistoric Southwest." *Journal of Archaeological Science* 29 (2002): 31–52.

Dunn, Mary Eubanks. "Ceramic Depictions of Maize: A Basis for Classification of Prehistoric Races." *American Antiquity* 44, no. 4 (1979): 757–74.

Durand, Kathy Roler. "Function of Chaco-Era Great Houses." *Kiva* 69, no. 2 (2003): 141–69.

Earl, Timothy. "Economic Support of Chaco Canyon Society." *American Antiquity* 66, no. 1 (2001): 26–35.

Eck, David C. *Across the Colorado Plateau: Anthropological Studies for the Transwestern Pipeline Expansion Project.* Vol. 11, *The Anasazi of Wide Ruin Wash and the Hopi Buttes.* Albuquerque, NM: Office of Contract Archaeology and Maxwell Museum of Anthropology, 1994.

Ellis, Florence Hawley, and Laurens Hammack. "The Inner Sanctum of Feather Cave: A Mogollon Sun and Earth Shrine Linking Mexico and the Southwest." *American Antiquity* 33, no. 1 (1968): 25–44.

Elson, Mark D. *Expanding the View of Hohokam Platform Mounds: An Ethnographic Perspective.* Anthropological Paper 63. Tucson: University of Arizona Press, 1998.

Emory, W. H. *Military Reconnaissance of the Arkansas, Rio del Norte, and Rio Gila Under the Command of Gen. Stephen W. Kearny.* Washington, DC: C. B. Graham, 1847.

Ernandes, Michele, Rita Cedrini, Marco Giammanco, Maurzio La Guardia, and Andrea Milazzo. "Aztec Cannibalism and Maize Consumption: The Serotonin Deficiency Link." *Mankind Quarterly* 43, no. 1 (2002): 3–40.

Evans, John H., and Harry Hillman. "Documentation of Some Lunar and Solar Events at Casa Grande, Arizona." In *Archaeoastronomy in the*

Americas, edited by Ray A. Williamson, 133–35. Los Altos, CA: Ballena Press, 1981.

Ezzo, Joseph A., Clark M. Johnson, and T. Douglas Price. "Analytical Perspectives on Prehistoric Migration: A Case Study from East-Central Arizona." *Journal of Archaeological Science* 24 (1997): 447–66.

Ezzo, Joseph A., and T. Douglas Price. "Migration, Regional Reorganization, and Spatial Group Composition at Grasshopper Pueblo, Arizona." *Journal of Archaeological Science* 29 (2002): 499–520.

Fagan, Brian. *Chaco Canyon: Archaeologists Explore the Lives of an Ancient Society.* New York: Oxford University Press, 2005.

Fearn, Miriam L., and Kam-Bui Liu. "Maize Pollen of 3500 BP from Southern Alabama." *American Antiquity* 60, no. 1 (1995): 109–17.

Feinman, Gary M. "An Outside Perspective on Chaco Canyon." In *Anasazi Regional Organization and the Chaco System,* edited by David E. Doyel, 177–82. Albuquerque, NM: Maxwell Museum of Anthropology, 2001.

Ferg, Alan, and Jim I. Mead. *Red Cave: A Prehistoric Cave Shrine in Southeastern Arizona.* Arizona Archaeological Society, 1993.

Fiedel, Stuart J. *Prehistory of the Americas.* Cambridge: Cambridge University Press, 1992.

Finn, Christine. "Leaving More Than Footprints: Modern Votive Offerings at Chaco Canyon Prehistoric Site." *Antiquity* 71, no. 1 (1997): 169–78.

Fish, Suzanne K., and Paul R. Fish. "Prehistoric Desert Farmers of the Southwest." *Annual Review of Anthropology* 23 (1994): 83–108.

Foster, Michael S. "Intrusive Ceramics." In *The Pueblo Grande Project: Material Culture,* edited by Michael S. Foster, 119–65. Soil Systems Publications in Archaeology 20, vol. 4. Phoenix: 1994.

Fowler, Andrew P. "Brown Ware and Red Ware Pottery: An Anasazi Ceramic Tradition." *Kiva* 56, no. 2 (1991): 123–44.

Fowler, Andrew P., and John R. Stein. "The Anasazi Great House in Space, Time, and Paradigm." In *Anasazi Regional Organization and the Chaco System,* edited by David E. Doyel, 101–22. Albuquerque, NM: Maxwell Museum of Anthropology, 2001.

Gaede, Marc, and Marnie Gaede. "100 Years of Erosion at Poncho House." *Kiva* 43, no. 1 (1977): 37–48.

Gentry, Howard S. *Agaves of Continental North America.* Tucson: University of Arizona Press, 1982.

Gifford, James C. *Archaeological Explorations in Caves of the Point of Pines Region Arizona.* Tucson: University of Arizona Press, 1980.

Gilman, Patricia A., Veletta Canouts, and Ronal L. Bishop. "The Production and Distribution of Classic Mimbres Black-on-White Pottery." *American Antiquity* 59, no. 4 (1994): 695–710.

Gilpin, Dennis. "Chaco-Era Site Clustering and the Concept of Communities." *Kiva* 69, no. 2 (2003): 171–205.

Gosser, Dennis C., Michael A. Ohnersorgen, Arleyn W. Simon, and James W. Mayer. "PIXE Analysis of Salado Polychrome Ceramics of the American Southwest." *Nuclear Instruments and Methods in Physics Research* B 136–38 (1998): 880–87.

Guernsey, Samuel James. *Exploration in Northeastern Arizona: Report on the Archaeological Fieldwork of 1920–1923*. Papers of the Peabody Museum of American Archaeology and Ethnology. Cambridge: Harvard University, 1931.

Gumerman, George J., ed. *Themes in Southwest Prehistory.* Santa Fe, NM: School of American Research Press, 1994.

Hagstrum, Melissa. "Household Production in Chaco Canyon Society." *American Antiquity* 66, no. 1 (2001): 47–55.

Hard, Robert J., José E. Zapata, Bruce K. Moses, and John. R. Roney. "Terrace Construction in Northern Chihuahua, Mexico: 1150 B.C. and Modern Experiments." *Journal of Field Archaeology* 26, no. 2 (1999): 129–46.

Hartmann, William K., and Richard Flint. "Migrations in Late Anasazi Prehistory: 'Eyewitness' Testimony." *Kiva* 66, no. 3 (2001): 375–85.

Hartmann, William K., and Betty Graham Lee. "Chichilticale: A Survey of Candidate Ruins in Southeastern Arizona." In *The Coronado Expedition from the Distance of 460 Years,* edited by Richard Flint and Shirley Cushing, 81–108. Albuquerque: University of New Mexico Press, 2003.

Hassig, Ross. "Anasazi Violence: A View from Mesoamerica." In *Deciphering Anasazi Violence: With Regional Comparisons to Mesoamerican and Woodland Cultures,* edited by Peter Yashio Bullock, 53–62. Santa Fe, NM: HRM Books, 1998.

Haury, Emil W. "Evidence at Point of Pines for a Prehistoric Migration from Northern Arizona." In *Migrations in New World Culture History,* edited by Raymond H. Thompson, 1–8. Tucson: University of Arizona Press, 1958.

———. *Mogollon Culture in the Forestdale Valley, East-Central Arizona.* Tucson: University of Arizona Press, 1985.

———. *Point of Pines, Arizona: A History of the University of Arizona Archaeological Field School.* Tucson: University of Arizona Press, 1989.

Haury, Emil W., and Carl M. Conrad. "The Comparison of Fiber Properties of Arizona Cliff-Dweller and Hopi Cotton." *American Antiquity* 3, no. 3 (1938): 224–27.

Haury, Emil W., and Lisa W. Huckell, eds. "A Prehistoric Cotton Cache from the Pinaleño Mountains." *Kiva* 59, no. 2 (1993): 95–145.

Hays-Gilpin, Kelley A., Trixi Bubemyre, and Louise M. Senior. "The Rise and Demise of Winslow Orange Ware." In *Rivers of Change: Prehistory of the Middle Little Colorado River Valley, Arizona*, edited by E. Charles Adams, 53–74. Tucson: University of Arizona Press, 1996.

Hays-Gilpin, Kelley A., and Jane H. Hill. "The Flower World in Prehistoric Southwest Material Culture." In *The Archaeology of Regional Interaction: Religion, Warfare, and Exchange Across the American Southwest and Beyond*, edited by Michelle Hegmon, 411–28. Boulder: University Press of Colorado, 2000.

Hensler, Kathy Niles. "Social Boundaries Set in Clay: Trade Ware Patterning in the Tonto Basin of East-Central Arizona." *Journal of Anthropological Research* 54, no. 4 (1998): 477–96.

Herr, Sarah A. *Beyond Chaco: Great Kiva Communities on the Mogollon Rim Frontier.* Anthropological Paper 66. Tucson: University of Arizona Press, 2001.

Hibben, Frank C. *Kiva Art of the Anasazi.* Las Vegas, NV: KC Publications, 1975.

Hill, J. Brett, Jeffrey J. Clark, William H. Doelle, and Patrick D. Lyons. "Prehistoric Demography in the Southwest: Migration, Coalescence, and Hohokam Population Decline." *American Antiquity* 69, no. 4 (2004): 689–716.

Hough, Walter. *Antiquities of the Gila and Salt Valley in Arizona and New Mexico.* Bureau of American Ethnology Bulletin 35. Washington, DC: Government Printing Office, 1907.

———. *Culture of the Ancient Pueblos of the Upper Gila River Region, New Mexico and Arizona.* Bureau of American Ethnology Bulletin 87. Washington DC: Government Printing Office, 1914.

———. "Sacred Springs in the Southwest." *Records of the Past* 5, no. 6 (1906): 164–69.

Hovezak, Timothy D., and Leslie M. Sesler. *Cultural Resource Survey of the Chimney Rock Forest Health Initiative Project Area, San Juan National Forest, Pagosa Ranger District, Archuleta County, Colorado.* Dolores, CO: La Plata Archaeological Consultants, 2004.

Hrdlcka, Ales. "A Painted Skeleton from Northern Mexico with Notes on Bone Painting Among the American Aborigines." *American Anthropologist* 3, no. 4 (1901): 701–25.

Huckleberry, Gary A., and Brian R. Billman. "Floodwater Farming, Discontinuous Ephemeral Streams, and Puebloan Abandonment in Southwestern Colorado." *American Antiquity* 63, no. 4 (1998): 595–616.

Hurst, Winston B. "Chaco Outlier or Backwoods Pretender? A Provincial Great House at Edge of the Cedars Ruin, Utah." In *Great House Com-*

munities Across the Chacoan Landscape, edited by John Kantner and Nancy M. Mahoney, 63–78. Tucson: University of Arizona Press, 2000.

Hurst, Winston, and Jonathan D. Till. "Some Observations Regarding the 'Chaco Phenomenon' in the Northwestern San Juan Provinces." Paper presented at the 67th Annual Meeting of the Society for American Archaeology, Denver, CO, March 23, 2002.

Hurst, Winston, Jonathan Till, Nancy Shearin, and Dale Davidson. "A Network of Ancient Roads in Southeastern Utah." Paper from the Pecos Conference, Dolores, CO, 2000.

Jalbert, Joseph Peter, and Catherine Cameron. "Chacoan and Local Influences in Three Great House Communities in the Northern San Juan Region." In *Great House Communities Across the Chacoan Landscape,* edited by John Kantner and Nancy M. Mahoney, 79–90. Tucson: University of Arizona Press, 2000.

Jett, Stephen C., and Dave Bohn. *House of Three Turkeys: Anasazi Redoubt.* Santa Barbara, CA: Capra Press, 1977.

Johnson, C. David. "Mesa Verde Region Towers: A View from Above." *Kiva* 68, no. 4 (2003): 323–40.

Jones, Terry L., Gary M. Brown, L. Mark Raab, Janet L. McVickar, Geoffrey Spaulding, Andrew York Kennett, and Phillip L. Walker. "Environmental Imperatives Reconsidered: Demographic Crises in Western North America During the Medieval Climatic Anomaly." *Current Anthropology* 40, no. 2 (1999): 137–70.

Kaldahl, Eric J., Scott Van Keuren, and Barbara J. Mills. "Migration, Factionalism, and the Trajectories of Pueblo IV Period Clusters in the Mogollon Rim Region." In *The Protohistoric Pueblo World, A.D. 1275–1600,* edited by E. Charles Adams and Andrew I. Duff. Tucson: University of Arizona Press, 2004.

Kantner, John. "Political Competition Among the Chaco Anasazi of the American Southwest." *Journal of Anthropological Archaeology* 14 (1996): 41–105.

———. "Rethinking Chaco as a System." *Kiva* 69, no. 2 (2003): 207–27.

Kidder, Alfred Vincent. *An Introduction to the Study of Southwestern Archaeology: With a Preliminary Account of the Excavations at Pecos.* Department of Archaeology, Phillips Academy, Andover. New Haven: Yale University Press, 1924.

Kincaid, Chris, ed. *Chaco Roads Project Phase I: A Reappraisal of Prehistoric Roads in the San Juan Basin.* Albuquerque: Bureau of Land Management, New Mexico State Office, 1983.

Kintigh, Keith W. "Coming to Terms with the Chaco World." *Kiva* 69, no. 2 (2003): 93–116.

Kohler, Timothy A. "The Final 400 Years of Prehispanic Agricultural Society in the Mesa Verde Region." *Kiva* 66, no. 1 (2000): 191–204.

Kuckelman, Kristin A. "Thirteenth-Century Warfare in the Central Mesa Verde Region." In *Seeking the Center Place: Archaeology and Ancient Communities in the Mesa Verde Region,* edited by Mark D. Varien and Richard H. Wilshusen, 233–53. Salt Lake City: University of Utah Press, 2002.

Kuckelman, Kristin A., Ricky R. Lightfoot, and Debra L. Martin. "The Bioarchaeology and Taphonomy of Violence at Castle Rock and Sand Canyon Pueblos, Southwestern Colorado." *American Antiquity* 67, no. 3 (2002): 486–513.

———. "Changing Patterns of Violence in the Northern San Juan Region." *Kiva* 66, no. 1 (2000): 147–65.

Lambert, Marjorie F., and Richard J. Ambler. *A Survey and Excavation of Caves in Hidalgo County, New Mexico.* Monograph 25. Santa Fe, NM: School of American Research, 1965.

Lange, Richard C., Craig P. Howe, and Barbara A. Murphy. "A Study of Prehistoric Roofing Systems in Arizona Cliff Dwellings." *Journal of Field Archaeology* 20 (1993): 485–98.

Larralde, Signa. "The Context of Early Puebloan Violence." In *Deciphering Anasazi Violence: With Regional Comparisons to Mesoamerican and Woodland Cultures,* edited by Peter Yashio Bullock, 11–28. Santa Fe, NM: HRM Books, 1998.

Larson, Daniel O., Hector Neff, Donald A. Graybill, Joel Michaelsen, and Elizabeth Ambos. "Risk, Climatic Variability, and the Study of Southwestern Prehistory: An Evolutionary Perspective." *American Antiquity* 61, no. 2 (1996): 217–41.

LeBlanc, Steven A. *Prehistoric Warfare in the American Southwest.* Salt Lake City: University of Utah Press, 1999.

Lekson, Stephen H. *The Chaco Meridian: Centers of Political Power in the Ancient Southwest.* Walnut Creek, CA: AltaMira Press, 1999.

———. *Great Pueblo Architecture of Chaco Canyon, New Mexico.* Albuquerque: University of New Mexico Press, 1986.

———. "Rewriting Southwestern Prehistory: New Studies Suggest an Overarching Political System Dominated Much of the Southwest from A.D. 850 to 1500." *Archaeology* 50, no. 1 (1997): 32–55.

———. *Salado Archaeology of the Upper Gila, New Mexico.* Anthropological Paper 67. Tucson: University of Arizona Press, 2002.

———. "Unit Pueblos and the Mimbres Problem." In *La Frontera: Papers in Honor of Patrick H. Beckett,* 105–25. Albuquerque: Archaeological Society of New Mexico, 1999.

———. "Was Casas a Pueblo?" In *The Casas Grandes World,* edited by Curtis F. Schaafsma and Carroll L. Riley, 84–92. Salt Lake City: University of Utah Press, 1999.

Lekson, Stephen H., Michael Bletzer, and A. C. MacWilliams. "Pueblo IV in the Chihuahuan Desert." In *The Protohistoric Pueblo World, A.D. 1275–1600,* edited by E. Charles Adams and Andrew I. Duff. Tucson: University of Arizona Press, 2004.

Lekson, Stephen H., and Catherine M. Cameron. "The Abandonment of Chaco Canyon, the Mesa Verde Migrations, and the Reorganization of the Pueblo World." *Journal of Anthropological Archaeology* 14 (1995): 184–202.

Lekson, Stephen H., Curtis P. Nepstad-Thornberry, Brian E. Yunker, Toni S. Laumbach, David P. Cain, and Karl W. Laumbach. "Migrations in the Southwest: Pinnacle Ruin, Southwestern New Mexico." *Kiva* 68, no. 2 (2002): 74–101.

Lindsay, Alexander J., Jr. "Anasazi Population Movements to Southeastern Arizona." *American Archaeology* 6, no. 3 (1987): 190–98.

———. "Tucson Polychrome: History, Dating, Distribution and Design." In *Proceedings of the Second Salado Conference, Globe, AZ, 1992,* edited by Richard C. Lange and Stephen Germick, 230–37. Phoenix: Arizona Archaeological Society, 1992.

Lipe, William D. "The Depopulation of the Northern San Juan: Conditions in the Turbulent 1200s." *Journal of Anthropological Archaeology* 14 (1995): 143–69.

———. "Social Power in the Central Mesa Verde Region, A.D. 1150–1290." In *Seeking the Center Place: Archaeology and Ancient Communities in the Mesa Verde Region,* edited by Mark D. Varien and Richard H. Wilshusen, 203–32. Salt Lake City: University of Utah Press, 2002.

Lipe, William D., and Michelle Hegmon. *The Architecture of Social Integration in Prehistoric Pueblos.* Occasional Paper. Cortez, CO: Crow Canyon Archaeological Center, 1989.

Lister, Florence C. *Pot Luck: Adventures in Archaeology.* Albuquerque: University of New Mexico Press, 1997.

Lister, Florence C., and Robert H. Lister. *Earl Morris and Southwestern Archaeology.* Albuquerque: University of New Mexico Press, 1968.

Lister, Robert H. *Archaeological Excavations in the Northern Sierra Madre Occidental, Chihuahua and Sonora, Mexico.* Series in Anthropology 7. Boulder: University of Colorado, 1958.

———. "The Chihuahua Field Season." *El Palacio* 42, nos. 4–6 (1937): 31–32.

———. "Excavations in Cave Valley, Chihuahua, Mexico: A Preliminary Note." *American Antiquity* 19, no. 2 (1953): 166–69.

———. "History of Archaeological Field Work in Northwestern Mexico." *El Palacio* 67, no. 4 (1960): 118–24.

———. "Survey of Archaeological Remains in Northwestern Chihuahua." *Southwestern Journal of Anthropology* 2, no. 4 (1946): 433–54.

Lofton, Delsie. "An Archaeological Survey of the Middle Chinle Valley." Master's thesis, Arizona State University, May 1974.

Luebben, Ralph A., Jonathan G. Andelson, and Laurance C. Herold. "Elvino Whetten Pueblo and Its Relationship to Terraces and Nearby Small Structures, Chihuahua, Mexico." *Kiva* 51, no. 3 (1986): 165–87.

Lumholtz, Carl. "Explorations in Mexico." *Royal Geographic Society of London* 21 (1903): 126–42.

———. "Explorations in the Sierra Madre." *Scribner's Monthly Magazine,* November 1891, 532–48.

———. "Report of Explorations in Northern Mexico." *Bulletin of the American Geographical Society* 23, no. 3 (1891): 386–402.

Lyons, Patrick D. *Ancestral Hopi Migrations.* Anthropological Paper 68. Tucson: University of Arizona Press, 2003.

———. "Cliff Polychrome." *Kiva* 69, no. 4 (2004): 361–98.

Mahoney, Nancy M., Michael A. Adler, and James W. Kendrick. "The Changing Scale and Configuration of Mesa Verde Communities." *Kiva* 66, no. 1 (2000): 67–89.

Malotki, Ekkehart. *Hopi Tales of Destruction.* Lincoln: University of Nebraska Press, 2002.

Malville, J. McKim, Frank W. Eddy, and Carol Ambruster. "Lunar Standstills at Chimney Rock." *Archaeoastronomy* 16 (1991): 243–50.

Malville, J. McKim, and Nancy J. Malville. "Pilgrimage and Periodic Festivals as Processes of Social Integration in Chaco Canyon." *Kiva* 66, no. 3 (2001): 327–44.

Malville, J. McKim, and Claudia Putnam. *Prehistoric Astronomy in the Southwest.* Boulder, CO: Johnson Books, 1993.

Malville, Nancy J. "Long-Distance Transport of Bulk Goods in the Pre-Hispanic American Southwest." *Journal of Anthropological Archaeology* 20 (2001): 230–43.

Marshall, Michael P., John R. Stein, Richard W. Loose, and Judith E. Novotny. *Anasazi Communities of the San Juan Basin.* Albuquerque, NM: Albuquerque Photo Lab, 1979.

Martin, Paul Sidney. *Mogollon Cultural Continuity and Change: The Stratigraphic Analysis of Tularosa and Cordova Caves.* Chicago: Natural History Museum, 1952.

———. "The 1928 Archaeological Expedition of the State Historical Society of Colorado." *Colorado Magazine* 6, no. 1 (1929): 1–35.

Massam, J. A. *The Cliff Dwellers of Kenya: An Account of a People Driven by Raids, Famine and Drought to Take Refuge on the Inaccessible Ledges of Precipitous Mountains, with a Description of Their Ways of Living, Social System, Manners and Customs, Religion, Magic, and Superstition.* London: Cass, 1927.

Mathien, Frances Joan. "The Organization of Turquoise Production and Consumption by the Prehistoric Chacoans." *American Antiquity* 66, no. 1 (2001): 103–18.

———. "Political, Economic, and Demographic Implications of the Chaco Road Network." In *Ancient Road Networks and Settlement Hierarchies in the New World,* edited by Charles D. Trombold. Cambridge: Cambridge University Press, 1991.

Mathien, Frances Joan, and Randall H. McGuire, eds. *Ripples in the Chichimec Sea: New Considerations of Southwestern-Mesoamerican Interactions.* Carbondale: Southern Illinois University Press, 1986.

Mathien, Frances Joan, and Thomas C. Windes. *Investigations at the Pueblo Alto Complex, Chaco Canyon, New Mexico, 1975–1979.* Santa Fe, NM: National Park Service, 1987.

McCluskey, Stephen C. "Calendars and Symbolism: Functions of Observation in Hopi Astronomy." *Archaeoastronomy* 15 (1990): S1–S16.

———. "Lunar Astronomies of the Western Pueblos." In *World Archaeoastronomy: Selected Papers from the Second Oxford International Conference on Archaeoastronomy Held at Merida, Yucatan, Mexico, January 1986,* edited by A. F. Aveni, 355–64. Cambridge: Cambridge University Press, 1989.

McGuire, Randall H., and Dean J. Saitta. "Although They Have Petty Captains, They Obey Them Badly: The Dialectics of Prehispanic Western Pueblo Social Organization." *American Antiquity* 61, no. 2 (1996): 197–216.

McGuire, Randall H., and Michael B. Schiffer, eds. *Hohokam and Patayan Prehistory of Southwestern Arizona.* New York: Academic Press, 1982.

McKenna, Peter J., and H. Wolcott Toll. "Regional Patterns of Great House Development Among the Totah Anasazi, New Mexico. In *Anasazi Regional Organization and the Chaco System,* edited by David E. Doyel, 133–43. Albuquerque, NM: Maxwell Museum of Anthropology, 2001.

Mills, Barbara. "Recent Research on Chaco: Changing Views on Economy, Ritual, and Society." *Journal of Archaeological Research* 10, no. 1 (2002): 65–117.

Mills, Barbara J., and Patricia L. Crown, eds. *Ceramic Production in the American Southwest.* Tucson: University of Arizona Press, 1995.

Minnis, Paul E. "Four Examples of Specialized Production at Casas Grandes, Northwestern Chihuahua." *Kiva* 53, no. 2 (1988): 181–93.

———. *Social Adaptation to Food Stress: A Prehistoric Southwestern Example.* Chicago: University of Chicago Press, 1985.

Minnis, Paul, and Michael Whalen. "Casas Grandes: Archaeology in Northern Mexico." *Expedition* 35, no. 1 (1993): 34–43

Minnis, Paul E., Michael E. Whalen, Jane H. Kelley, and Joe D. Stewart. "Prehistoric Macaw Breeding in the North American Southwest." *American Antiquity* 58, no. 2 (1993): 270–77.

Morenon, Pierre Ernest. "Chacoan Roads and Adaptation: How a Prehistoric Population Can Define and Control Its Social and Natural Environment." Paper presented at the 40th Annual Meeting of the Society for American Archaeology, Dallas, 1975.

Murray, W. B. "Calendrical Petroglyphs of Northern New Mexico." In *Archaeoastronomy in the New World,* edited by A. F. Aveni, 195–203. Cambridge: Cambridge University Press, 1982.

Naranjo, Tessie. "Thoughts on Migration by Santa Clara Pueblo." *Journal of Anthropological Archaeology* 14 (1995): 247–50.

Neely, James A., and Alan P. Olson. *Archaeological Reconnaissance of Monument Valley in Northeastern Arizona.* Flagstaff: Museum of Northern Arizona, 1977.

Neitzel, Jill E., ed. *Great Towns and Regional Polities in the Prehistoric American Southwest and Southeast.* Albuquerque: University of New Mexico Press, 1999.

———, ed. *Pueblo Bonito: Center of the Chacoan World.* Washington DC: Smithsonian Books, 2003.

Nordenskiöld, G. *The Cliff Dwellers of the Mesa Verde, Their Pottery and Implements,* translated by D. Lloyd Morgan. Stockholm: P. A. Norstedt & Söner, 1893.

Novelli, Cona. "Two Polychrome Vessels Depicting the God Quetzalcoatl." *Artifact* 6, no. 3 (1968): 1–6.

Ortman, Scott G. "Conceptual Metaphor in the Archaeological Record: Methods and an Example from the American Southwest." *American Antiquity* 65, no. 4 (2000): 613–45.

Ortman, Scott G., and Bruce A. Bradley. "Sand Canyon Pueblo: The Container in the Center." In *Seeking the Center Place: Archaeology and Ancient Communities in the Mesa Verde Region,* edited by Mark D. Varien and Richard H. Wilshusen, 41–78. Salt Lake City: University of Utah Press, 2002.

Ortman, Scott G., Donna M. Glowacki, Melissa J. Churchill, and Kristin A. Kuckelman. "Pattern and Variation in Northern San Juan Village Histories." *Kiva* 66, no. 1 (2000): 123–46.

Pepper, George H. "Ceremonial Objects and Ornaments from Pueblo Bonito, New Mexico." *American Anthropologist* 7, no. 2 (1905): 183–97.

Peregrine, Peter N. "Matrilocality, Corporate Strategy, and the Organization of Production in the Chacoan World." *American Antiquity* 66, no. 1 (2001): 36–46.

Peterson, Ivars. "A Supernova Story in Clay." *Science News* 137, no. 25 (1990): 396–97.

Peterson, Jane D. "Salado Polychrome from Pueblo Grande: Indices of Ceramic Production Systems." In *The Pueblo Grande Project: Ceramics and the Production and Exchange of Pottery in the Central Phoenix Basin, Part One,* edited by David R. Abbott, 371–406. Soil Systems Publications in Archaeology 20, vol. 3. Phoenix: 1994.

Pierce, Christopher, Donna M. Glowacki, and Margaret M. Thurs. "Measuring Community Interaction: Pueblo III Pottery Production and Distribution in the Central Mesa Verde Region." In *Seeking the Center Place: Archaeology and Ancient Communities in the Mesa Verde Region,* edited by Mark D. Varien and Richard H. Wilshusen, 185–202. Salt Lake City: University of Utah Press, 2002.

Piperno, Dolores R. "On the Emergence of Agriculture in the New World." *Current Anthropology* 35, no. 5 (1994): 637–43.

Plog, Stephen. "Exploring the Ubiquitous Through the Unusual: Color Symbolism in Pueblo Black-on-White Pottery." *American Antiquity* 68, no. 4 (2003): 665–95.

Powers, Robert P., William B. Gillespie, and Stephen H. Lekson. *The Outlier Survey: A Regional View of Settlement in the San Juan Basin.* Albuquerque, NM: National Park Service, 1983.

Price, T. Douglas, Clark M. Johnson, Joseph A. Ezzo, Jonathan Ericson, and James H. Burton. "Residential Mobility in the Prehistoric Southwest United States: A Preliminary Study Using Strontium Isotope Analysis." *Journal of Archaeological Science* 21 (1994): 315–30.

Pringle, Heather. "North America's Wars: New Analyses Suggest That Prehistoric North America, Once Considered Peaceful, Was Instead a Bitter Battlefield Where Tribes Fought Over Land and Water." *Science* 279 (March 17, 1998): 2038–40.

Rakita, Gordon Forbes Martin. "Social Complexity, Religious Organization, and Mortuary Ritual in the Casas Grandes Region of Chihuahua, Mexico." Ph.D. diss., University of New Mexico, December 2001.

Rapoport, Amos. *House Form and Culture.* Englewood Cliffs, NJ: Prentice-Hall, 1969.

Reff, Daniel T. *Disease, Depopulation and Culture Change in Northwestern New Spain, 1518–1764.* Salt Lake City: University of Utah Press, 1991.

———. "The Location of Corazones and Señora: Archaeological Evidence from the Rio Sonora Valley, Mexico." In *The Protohistoric Period in the North American Southwest,* A.D. *1450–1750,* edited by David R. Wilcox and W. Bruce Masse. Anthropological Research Paper 24. Tempe: Arizona State University, 1981.

Reid, J. Jefferson, and David E. Doyel, eds. *Emil W. Haury's Prehistory of the Southwest.* Tucson: University of Arizona Press, 1986.

Reid, J. Jefferson, John R. Welch, Barbara K. Montgomery, and María Nieves Zedeño. "A Demographic Overview of the Late Pueblo III Period in the Mountains of East-Central Arizona." In *The Prehistoric Pueblo World, A.D. 1150–1350,* edited by Michael A. Adler, 73–85. Tucson: University of Arizona Press, 1996.

Reid, J. Jefferson, and Stephanie Whittlesey. *The Archaeology of Ancient Arizona.* Tucson: University of Arizona Press, 1997.

———. *Grasshopper Pueblo: A Story of Archaeology and Ancient Life.* Tucson: University of Arizona Press, 1999.

Renfrew, Colin. "Production and Consumption in a Sacred Economy: The Material Correlates of High Devotional Expression at Chaco Canyon." *American Antiquity* 66, no. 1 (2001): 14–25.

Reyman, Jonathan E. "Pata'tkwabi: Red Land of the South." In *The Gran Chichimeca: Essays on the Archaeology and Ethnohistory of Northern Mesoamerica,* edited by Jonathan E. Reyman, 320–35. Aldershot, Eng.: Avebury, 1995.

———. "Preserving Culture, Conserving Birds: The Feather Distribution Project." *Living Museum* 65, no. 4 (2003–2004): 3–7.

Riley, Carroll L. *The Frontier People: The Greater Southwest in the Protohistoric Period.* Albuquerque: University of New Mexico Press, 1987.

———. "The Sonoran Statelets and Casas Grandes." In *The Casas Grandes World,* edited by Curtis F. Schaafsma and Carroll L. Riley, 193–200. Salt Lake City: University of Utah Press, 1999.

Roberts, David. "Tracking a Vanished People Through the Sierra Madre." *Smithsonian* 27, no. 8 (1996): 60–73.

Rocek, Thomas R. "Sedentarization and Agricultural Dependence: Perspectives from the Pithouse-to-Pueblo Transition in the American Southwest." *American Antiquity* 60, no. 2 (1995): 218–39.

Roler, Kathy Lynne. "The Chaco Phenomenon: A Faunal Perspective from the Peripheries." Ph.D. diss., Arizona State University, May 1999.

Saitta, Dean J. "Power, Labor, and the Dynamics of Change in Chacoan Political Economy." *American Antiquity* 62, no. 1 (1997): 7–29.

Sánchez, Arturo Guevara. *Las Cuarenta Casas: Un Sitio Arqueológico del Estado de Chihuahua.* Col. Roma, Mex.: Instituto Nacional de Antropologia e Historia, 1984.

Sayles, Edwin B. *An Archaeological Survey of Chihuahua, Mexico.* Medallion Papers 22. Globe, AZ: 1936.

———. *Some Southwestern Pottery Types.* Medallion Papers 21. Globe, AZ: 1936.

Schaafsma, Polly. "Tlalocs, Kachinas, Sacred Bundles, and Related Symbolism in the Southwest and Mesoamerica." In *The Casas Grandes World,* edited by Curtis F. Schaafsma and Carroll L. Riley, 164–92. Salt Lake City: University of Utah Press, 1999.

———. *Warrior, Shield, and Star: Imagery and Ideology of Pueblo Warfare.* Santa Fe, NM: Western Edge Press, 2000.

Schaefer, Bradley E. "The Length of the Lunar Month." *Archaeoastronomy* 17 (1992): S32–S42.

Schillaci, Michael A. "The Development of Population Diversity at Chaco Canyon." *Kiva* 68, no. 3 (2003): 221–45.

Schillaci, Michael A., Erik G. Ozolins, and Thomas C. Windes. "Multivariate Assessment of Biological Relationships Among Prehistoric Southwest Amerindian Populations." In *Following Through: Papers in Honor of Phyllis S. Davis,* edited by Regge N. Wiseman, Thomas C. O'Laughlin, and Cordelia T. Snow, 133–49. Albuquerque: Archaeological Society of New Mexico, 2001.

Schmidt, Robert H., Jr., and Rex E. Gerald. "The Distribution of Conservation-Type Water-Control Systems in the Sierra Madre Occidental." *Kiva* 53, no. 2 (1988): 165–80.

Scott, Stuart D. *Dendrochronology in Mexico.* Papers of the Laboratory of Tree-Ring Research 2. Tucson: University of Arizona Press, 1966.

Shackley, M. Steven. "Sources of Archaeological Obsidian in the Greater American Southwest: An Update and Quantitative Analysis." *American Antiquity* 60, no. 3 (1995): 531–52.

Shaul, David Leedom, and Jane H. Hill. "Tepimans, Yumans, and Other Hohokam." *American Antiquity* 63, no. 3 (1998): 375–96.

Sherratt, Andrew. "Climatic Cycles and Behavioural Revolutions: The Emergence of Modern Humans and the Beginning of Farming." *Antiquity* 71, no. 272 (1997): 271–87.

Simon, Arleyn W., James H. Burton, and David R. Abbott. "Intraregional Connections in the Development and Distribution of Salado Polychromes in Central Arizona." *Journal of Anthropological Research* 54, no. 3 (1998): 519–47.

Simon, Arleyn W., and John C. Ravesloot. "Salado Ceramic Burial Offerings: A Consideration of Gender and Social Organization." *Journal of Anthropological Research* 51, no. 2 (1995): 103–24.

Smith, Watson. *Kiva Mural Decorations at Awatovi and Kawaika-a with a Survey of Other Wall Paintings in the Pueblo Southwest.* Reports of the Awatovi Expedition 5. Cambridge, MA: Papers of the Peabody Museum of American Archaeology and Ethnology, Harvard University, 1952.

Sofaer, Anna. "The Primary Architecture of the Chacoan Culture." In *Anasazi Architecture and American Design,* edited by Baker H. Morrow and V. B. Price. Albuquerque: University of New Mexico Press, 1997.

Sofaer, Anna, and Rolf M. Sinclair. "An Appraisal of Michael Zelik's 'A Reassessment of the Fajada Butte Solar Marker.' " *Archaeoastronomy* 10 (1986): S59–S66.

———. "Changes in Solstice Marking at the Three-Slab Site, New Mexico, USA." *Archaeoastronomy* 15 (1990): S59–S60.

Spence, Michael W. "From Tzintzuntzan to Paquimé: Peers of Peripheries in Greater Mesoamerica." In *Greater Mesoamerica: The Archaeology of West and Northwest Mexico,* edited by Michael S. Foster and Shirley Gorenstein, 255–61. Salt Lake City: University of Utah Press, 2000.

Speth, John D. "Do We Need Concepts Like 'Mogollon,' 'Anasazi,' and 'Hohokam' Today? A Cultural Anthropological Perspective." *Kiva* 53, no. 2 (1988): 201–9.

Spielmann, Katherine A. "Diet and Subsistence in the Classic Tonto Basin." In *Environment and Subsistence in the Classic Period Tonto Basin: The Roosevelt Archaeology Studies, 1989 to 1998,* edited by Katherine A. Spielmann, 183–93. Tempe: Arizona State University, 1998.

Stark, Miriam T. "Causes and Consequences of Migration in the 13th Century Tonto Basin." *Journal of Anthropological Archaeology* 14 (1995): 212–46.

Stein, John R., and Stephen H. Lekson. "Anasazi Ritual Landscape." In *Anasazi Regional Organization and the Chaco System,* edited by David E. Doyel, 87–100. Albuquerque, NM: Maxwell Museum of Anthropology, 2001.

Stein, John R., Judith E. Suiter, and Dabney Ford. "High Noon in Old Bonito: Sun, Shadow, and the Geometry of the Chaco Complex." In *Anasazi Architecture and American Design,* edited by Baker H. Morrow and V. B. Price. Albuquerque: University of New Mexico Press, 1997.

Stone, Tammy. "The Chaos of Collapse: Disintegration and Reintegration of Inter-Regional Systems." *Antiquity* 73, no. 270 (1999): 110–18.

———. "Kiva Diversity in the Point of Pines Region of Arizona." *Kiva* 67, no. 4 (2002): 386–411.

———. "Prehistoric Community Integration in the Point of Pines Region of Arizona." *Journal of Field Archaeology* 27 (2000): 197–208.

———. "Social Identity and Ethnic Interaction in the Western Pueblos of the American Southwest." *Journal of Archaeological Method and Theory* 10, no. 1 (2003): 31–67.

Sutherland, Kay. "Mesoamerican Ceremony Among the Prehistoric Jornada Mogollon." In *Rock Art of the Chihuahuan Desert Borderlands,* edited by Sheron Smith-Savage and Robert J. Mallouf, 61–87. Occasional Paper 3. Alpine, TX: Center for Big Bend Studies, 1998.

Swanson, Steve. "Documenting Prehistoric Communication Networks: A Case Study in the Paquimé Polity." *American Antiquity* 68, no. 3 (2003): 753–57.

Tagg, Martyn D. "Early Cultigens from Fresnal Shelter, Southeastern New Mexico." *American Antiquity* 61, no. 2 (1996): 311–24.

Till, Jonathan D. *Chacoan Roads and Road-Associated Sites in the Lower San Juan Region: Assessing the Role of Chacoan Influences in the Northwestern Periphery.* Unpublished Master's Thesis, Department of Anthropology, University of Colorado, Boulder, 2001.

Toll, H. Wolcott. "Making and Breaking Pots in the Chaco World." *American Antiquity* 66, no. 1 (2001): 56–78.

———. "A Reassessment of Chaco Cylinder Jars." In *Clues to the Past: Papers in Honor of William M. Sundt,* edited by Meliha S. Duran and David T. Kirkpatrick, 273–305. Albuquerque: Archaeological Society of New Mexico, 1990.

Toll, H. Wolcott, Eric Blinman, and C. Dean Wilson. "Chaco in the Context of Ceramic Regional Systems." In *Anasazi Regional Organization and the Chaco System,* edited by David E. Doyel, 147–58. Albuquerque, NM: Maxwell Museum of Anthropology, 2001.

Tower, Donald B. "The Use of Marine Mollusca and Their Value in Reconstructing Prehistoric Trade Routes in the American Southwest." *Papers of the Excavators' Club* 2, no. 3 (1945): 1–56.

Triadan, Daniela. *Ceramic Commodities and Common Containers: Production and Distribution of White Mountain Red Ware in the Grasshopper Region, Arizona.* Anthropological Paper 61. Tucson: University of Arizona Press, 1997.

Triadan, Daniela, and M. Nieves Zedeño. "The Political Geography and Territoriality of 14th-Century Settlement in the Mogollon Highlands of East-Central Arizona." In *The Protohistoric Pueblo World, A.D. 1275–1600,* edited by E. Charles Adams and Andrew I. Duff. Tucson: University of Arizona Press, 2004.

Trombold, Charles D. "Causeways in the Context of Strategic Planning in the La Quemada Region, Zacatecas, Mexico." In *Ancient Road Networks and Settlement Hierarchies in the New World,* edited by Charles D. Trombold. Cambridge: Cambridge University Press, 1991.

Turner, Christy G., II, and A. Jacqueline Turner. *Man Corn: Cannibalism and Violence in the Prehistoric American Southwest.* Salt Lake City: University of Utah Press, 1999.

Upham, Steadman. "Nomads of the Desert West: A Shifting Continuum in Prehistory." *Journal of World Prehistory* 8, no. 2 (1994): 113–67.

Van Dyke, Ruth M. "Bounding Chaco: Great House Architectural Variability Across Time and Space." *Kiva* 69, no. 2 (2003): 117–39.

———. "The Chacoan Great Kiva in Outlier Communities: Investigating Integrative Spaces Across the San Juan Basin." *Kiva* 67, no. 3 (2002): 231–48.

———. "Chacoan Ritual Landscapes: The View from Red Mesa Valley." In *Great House Communities Across the Chacoan Landscape,* edited by John Kantner and Nancy M. Mahoney, 91–100. Tucson: University of Arizona Press, 2000.

VanPool, Christine S. "The Shaman-Priests of the Casas Grandes Region, Chihuahua, Mexico." *American Antiquity* 68, no. 4 (2003): 696–717.

Van West, Carla R., and Jeffrey S. Dean. "Environmental Characteristics of the A.D. 900–1300 Period in the Central Mesa Verde Region." *Kiva* 66, no. 1 (2000): 19–43.

Varien, Mark D. "Persistent Communities and Mobile Households: Population Movement in the Central Mesa Verde Region, A.D. 950–1290." In *Seeking the Center Place: Archaeology and Ancient Communities in the Mesa Verde Region,* edited by Mark D. Varien and Richard H. Wilshusen, 163–84. Salt Lake City: University of Utah Press, 2002.

Varien, Mark, Carla R. Van West, and G. Stuart Patterson. "Competition, Cooperation, and Conflict: Agricultural Production and Community Catchments in the Central Mesa Verde Region." *Kiva* 66, no. 1 (2000): 44–65.

Villalpando, María Elisa. "The Archaeological Traditions of Sonora." In *Greater Mesoamerica: The Archaeology of West and Northwest Mexico,* edited by Michael S. Foster and Shirley Gorenstein, 241–53. Salt Lake City: University of Utah Press, 2000.

Vivian, R. Gwinn. "Chacoan Roads: Function." *Kiva* 63, no. 1 (1997): 35–67.

———. "Chacoan Roads: Morphology." *Kiva* 63, no. 1 (1997): 7–34.

Vivian, R. Gwinn, and Bruce Hilpert. *The Chaco Handbook: An Encyclopedic Guide.* Salt Lake City: University of Utah Press, 2002.

Walters, Harry, and Hugh C. Rogers. "Anasazi and *'Anaasází:* Two Words, Two Cultures." *Kiva* 66, no. 3 (2001): 317–25.

Wasley, William W. "A Ceremonial Cave on Bonita Creek, Arizona." *American Antiquity* 27, no. 3 (1962): 380–94.

Waters, Michael R. "Geoarchaeological Investigations in the Tonto Basin." In *Environment and Subsistence in the Classic Period Tonto Basin: The Roosevelt Archaeology Studies, 1989 to 1998,* edited by Katherine A. Spielmann, 7–47. Tempe: Arizona State University, 1998.

Whalen, Michael E. "Moving Out of the Archaic on the Edge of the Southwest." *American Antiquity* 59, no. 4 (1994): 622–39.

Whalen, Michael E., and Paul E. Minnis. "Architecture and Authority in the Casas Grandes Area, Chihuahua, Mexico." *American Antiquity* 66, no. 4 (2001): 651–68.

———. "Ball Courts and Political Centralization in the Casas Grandes Region." *American Antiquity* 61, no. 4 (1996): 732–46.

———. "The Local and the Distant in the Origin of Casas Grandes, Chihuahua, Mexico." *American Antiquity* 68, no. 2 (2003): 314–32.

Whiteley, Peter M. *Deliberate Acts: Changing Hopi Culture Through the Oraibi Split.* Tucson: University of Arizona Press, 1988.

———. "Re-imagining Awat'ovi." In *Archaeologies of the Pueblo Revolt,* edited by Robert W. Preucel, 247–65. Albuquerque: University of New Mexico Press, 2002.

Whittlesey, Stephanie M., ed. *Sixty Years of Mogollon Archaeology: Papers from the Ninth Mogollon Conference, Silver City, New Mexico, 1996.* Tucson: SRI Press, 1999.

Whittlesey, Stephanie, and J. Jefferson Reid. "Mortuary Ritual and Organizational Inferences at Grasshopper Pueblo, Arizona." In *Ancient Burial Practices in the American Southwest: Archaeology, Physical Anthropology, and Native American Perspectives,* edited by Douglas R. Mitchell and Judy L. Brunson-Hadley. Albuquerque: University of New Mexico Press, 2001.

Williamson, R. A. "Casa Rinconada: A Twelfth-Century Anasazi Kiva." In *Archaeoastronomy in the New World,* edited by A. F. Aveni, 205–19. Cambridge: Cambridge University Press, 1982.

Wills, W. H. "Ritual and Mound Formation During the Bonito Phase in Chaco Canyon." *American Antiquity* 66, no. 3 (2001): 433–51.

Wilshusen, Richard H. "Estimating Population in the Central Mesa Verde Region." In *Seeking the Center Place: Archaeology and Ancient Communities in the Mesa Verde Region,* edited by Mark D. Varien and Richard H. Wilshusen, 101–20. Salt Lake City: University of Utah Press, 2002.

Wilshusen, Richard H., and Scott G. Ortman. "Rethinking the Pueblo I Period in the San Juan Drainage: Aggregation, Migration, and Cultural Diversity." *Kiva* 64, no. 3 (1999): 369–99.

Windes, Thomas C. "The Prehistoric Road Network at Pueblo Alto, Chaco Canyon, New Mexico." In *Ancient Road Networks and Settlement Hierarchies in the New World,* edited by Charles D. Trombold. Cambridge: Cambridge University Press, 1991.

Windes, Thomas C., and Peter J. McKenna. "Going Against the Grain: Wood Production in Chacoan Society." *American Antiquity* 66, no. 1 (2001): 119–40.

Woodson, M. Kyle. "Migrations in Late Anasazi Prehistory: The Evidence from the Goat Hill Site." *Kiva* 65, no. 1 (1999): 63–85.

Woosley, Anne I., and John C. Ravesloot, eds. *Culture and Contact: Charles C. Di Pesos's Gran Chichimeca.* Dragoon, AZ: Amerind Foundation, 1993.

Young, Jon Nathan. "The Salado Culture in Southwestern Prehistory." Ph.D. diss., University of Arizona, 1967.

Young, M. Jane. "The Interrelationship of Rock Art and Astronomical Practice in the American Southwest." *Archaeoastronomy* 10 (1986): S42–S58.

Zedeño, M. Nieves. "Artifact Design, Composition, and Context: Updating the Analysis of Ceramic Circulation at Point of Pines, Arizona." In *Ceramic Production and Circulation in the Greater Southwest: Source Determination by INAA and Complementary Mineralogical Investigations,* edited by Donna M. Glowacki and Hector Neff, 74–84. Los Angeles: Costen Institute of Archaeology, University of California, 2002.

Zedeño, Nieves M., and Daniela Triadan. "Ceramic Evidence for Community Reorganization and Change in East-Central Arizona." *Kiva* 65, no. 3 (2000): 215–33.

For notes, additional photographs, and field illustrations, go to houseofrain.com.

Index

Italic page numbers refer to photographs.

About the Author

Craig Childs is a commentator for National Public Radio's *Morning Edition* and has written for the *Los Angeles Times, Outside, Audubon, Sierra, Orion,* and *Mountain Gazette.* He is a regular contributor to *High Country News* and *Arizona Highways.* His body of work has won the Spirit of the West Award, and he was also recipient of a Colorado Book Award. Childs has worked a wide variety of jobs, including jazz musician, journalist, gas station attendant, beer bottler, and river guide. He lives off the grid with his wife and two children at the foot of the West Elk Mountains in Colorado.